Gandhi's Australia
Australia's Gandhi

Gandhi's Australia
Australia's Gandhi

THOMAS WEBER

WITH A FOREWORD BY
RAJMOHAN GANDHI

All rights reserved. No part of this book may be modified, reproduced or utilised in any form, or by any means, electronic or mechanical, including photocopying, recording or by any information storage and retrieval system, in any form of binding or cover other than in which it is published, without permission in writing from the publisher.

GANDHI'S AUSTRALIA: AUSTRALIA'S GANDHI

ORIENT BLACKSWAN PRIVATE LIMITED

Registered Office
3-6-752 Himayatnagar, Hyderabad 500 029, Telangana, INDIA
e-mail: centraloffice@orientblackswan.com

Other Offices
Bengaluru, Chennai, Guwahati, Hyderabad, Kolkata, Mumbai, New Delhi, Noida, Patna

© Thomas Weber 2024
First published by Orient Blackswan Private Limited 2024
This paperback edition published by Orient BlackSwan in 2024

ISBN 978-93-5442-737-4

Typeset in
Adobe Jenson Pro 11.75/13.25
by Manmohan Kumar, Delhi

Printed in India at
Thomson Press, New Delhi

Published by
Orient Blackswan Private Limited
3-6-752, Himayatnagar Hyderabad 500 029, Telangana, INDIA
e-mail: info@orientblackswan.com

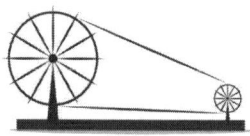

Contents

Abbreviations	ix
Foreword	xi
Rajmohan Gandhi	
Acknowledgements	xvii
A Personal Introduction	xix
1. Background: Gandhi and the World	**1**
Gandhi: A Brief Introduction	4
The Mahatma and the World	9
America's Gandhi	14
Britain's Gandhi	21
2. Gandhi's Australia	**28**
The Issue of Racism	30
Cow Slaughter	37
Other Issues	39
3. Gandhi and Australians	**43**
Some Little-Known Visitors	44
Harriet Winifred Ponder	48
Arthur H. Blacket	52
A. B. Piddington	56
Bertram Stevens and a Young War Correspondent	64

Contents

Alan Moorehead	71
R. G. Casey	73
Thomas Nesbitt's Letter to Gandhi	80
4. Australia's Gandhi: The Press Depictions	**82**
South Africa: The First Glimpses	83
Non-Cooperation and the 1920s	94
The Salt March and its Aftermath	103
Towards the End	123
Gandhi after Gandhi	144
Gandhi in the Australian Parliament	145
5. Australia's Gandhi: Organisations	**147**
Gandhi, Peace Movements, and Environmental Campaigns	147
Gandhi and the Quakers	157
Aid Organisations and Gandhi	161
6. Australia's Gandhi: People	**166**
Nonviolent Activism	167
The Australian Gandhian Movement	180
The International Centre of Nonviolence	186
Doing Gandhian Work in India	192
7. Australia's Gandhi: The Academy	**195**
Gandhi in the Academy	196
University Courses and Gandhi	198
Writings on Gandhi	207
Gandhi Orations	226

Contents

8. Australia's Gandhi: The Public — **232**
    Overseas Gandhian Visitors — 232
    Gandhi in the Movies — 257
    Gandhi Statues and Exhibitions — 260
    Gandhi and the Australian Indian Community — 268

Conclusion — **271**

Bibliography — 279
Index — 302

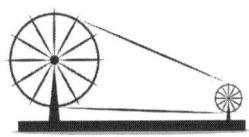

Abbreviations

ABC	Australian Broadcasting Corporation
ACT	Australian Capital Territory
ANU	Australian National University
CAA	Community Aid Abroad
CND	Campaign for Nuclear Disarmament
CWMG	*Collected Works of Mahatma Gandhi*
FFP	Food for Peace
GMA	Gandhian Movement of Australia
GPT	Gulf Peace Team
ICON	International Centre of Nonviolence
IGM	International Gandhian Movement
JP	Jayaprakash Narayan
MRAG	Melbourne Rainforest Action Group
NGO	non-government organisation
NSW	New South Wales
QCSS	Queensland Council of Social Service
SGI	Soka Gakkai International
UNIA	Universal Negro Improvement Association
UNSW	University of New South Wales
UQ	University of Queensland
WILPF	Women's International League for Peace and Freedom

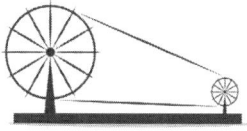

Foreword

In Delhi a long time ago, in March 1942, an Australian visitor complained to Gandhi: 'You have been to England and Europe, and stayed long in South Africa, but never been to Australia.' With a smile, Gandhi replied, 'It was no thanks to your government.' This of course was a dig at the White Australia policy that was being enforced in the visitor's country. The caller commented that Gandhi had made 'a very good reply'. Gandhi, it seems, agreed!

This is the sort of nugget that readers of Thomas Weber's latest Gandhi-related book, once more a product of relentless research, will receive.

The Australian visitor quoted by Weber was Sir Bertram Stevens, a former premier of New South Wales, who was in India in 1942 to measure the supplies the Allied powers then possessed in India for the war in progress against Japan. Gandhi, on his part, was in Delhi for the abortive negotiations that Stafford Cripps, member of Britain's war cabinet, was conducting with Indian leaders.

Stevens (we are informed by Weber) had no particular business matters to discuss with the Mahatma; he merely wished to make Gandhi's acquaintance. Gandhi made time for him during his early morning walk on the lawns of Birla House, where he was staying as the guest of his friend Ghanshyam Das Birla.

After making his sally, Gandhi pointed out to Stevens that Australia was large enough to 'absorb millions and millions of human beings'. Added Gandhi: 'I have followed the history of

Foreword

your country for over 35 years. White Australia is your policy, and *as a result you are without the wonderful accession of strength that would have been yours if you had followed the policy of brothering all'* (emphasis added).

Weber also informs us that the day before Stevens called on him in 1942, Gandhi had a twenty-minute conversation with a young unnamed Australian journalist. By way of parting, Gandhi told this 'Australian friend' that 'Yours is a wonderful nation.'

The world does not remain still. It changes. The White Australia policy was given up in 1973. Today, eighty-two years after the Gandhi–Stevens conversation that Weber reproduces, people of Indian origin make up more than 3 per cent of Australia's population of about 27 million. This percentage is likely to grow. Australia appears to want Indians, especially young Indians, and the latter seem more than willing to study, work, and live in Australia.

But this book by Weber is neither about an altering world nor about the new Australia, where many of the world's races have flocked, and where the vast country's indigenous population, also now around 3 per cent, seems finally to be coming into its own. What Gandhi thought about Australia plus what Australians thought and now think about Gandhi and his legacy is the book's agenda. Australia's importance to today's India adds to the book's value.

Starting with a comparison with the relationships that Britain and the US have had with Gandhi, Weber proceeds to give a remarkably detailed account of Gandhi's encounters with visiting Australians, of how Australia's individuals, media, and universities have perceived Gandhi over the decades, and of the present condition in Australia of Gandhi-connected activism for peace and nonviolence.

For more than thirty years, Weber, an Australian of Hungarian origin, has studied and presented numerous aspects of Gandhi's life and work. His considerable output includes a landmark (and meticulous) study of the Salt March, which turned out to be one

Foreword

of history's most unlikely and most effective forays for national independence.

This output also includes, among other works, *Gandhi at First Sight*, a compilation of reports by a host of interesting people of their first meetings with Gandhi; *Gandhi's Peace Army: The Shanti Sena and Unarmed Peacekeeping*; and *Beloved Bapu: The Gandhi-Mirabehn Correspondence*, which Weber co-edited with Tridip Suhrud.

Thanks to Gandhi's varied Australian interlocutors and observers, and thanks to Weber's formidable research about their interactions with Gandhi, some fascinating glimpses emerge from the author's latest book. Gandhi's personality comes alive, at times in fresh ways.

I may be allowed to add here a tiny Australia–Gandhi exchange that Weber seems to have left out. On 1 February 1947, when Gandhi was in the village of Amishapara in the course of his peace mission in riot-torn Noakhali, a group of British army men joined by an Australian soldier caught up with Gandhi. The Australian having introduced himself as a journalist, Gandhi laughingly said that journalists were 'dangerous' people, adding, 'I say so as a journalist myself,' which of course Gandhi was, right from 1903, when he brought out *Indian Opinion* in South Africa. Then, teasing the soldier-journalist about his country's White Australia policy, Gandhi humorously added, 'India is too hospitable.'[1]

A Foreword writer (let me add) may not agree with each and every one of the judgements offered in the book that he or she commends. I may also be allowed to point out something else. Weber's valuable study does not quite convey Gandhi's passion for equality and fraternity among divided communities, a passion that speaks directly to today's realities in India and the world.

[1] *Collected Works of Mahatma Gandhi*, Vol. 86, p. 418. The *Collected Works* item containing this account, taken from the *Hindustan Standard* (Kolkata) of 3 February 1947, does not name the Australian.

Foreword

This is hardly surprising. Proud of the empire that Gandhi sought to dismantle, most Australians who engaged with Gandhi during his lifetime were inevitably far more interested in the future of the British empire than in the future of an independent India. In fact, an independent India remained largely invisible to Australians until the final phase of World War II. During that War, moreover, when Japan seemed close to invading Australia, it was hard for Australians to see how the nonviolence advocated by Gandhi would protect their country.

It was not easy for Australians to notice that Gandhi, the foe of empire and champion of nonviolence, was also a lover of humanity—even though that last bit was suggested by the remark to Stevens, captured by Weber, about 'brothering' everyone. Even in 1947, when Gandhi strove to put out communal fires in different parts of the subcontinent, it was not easy for Australians to recognise that equality and solidarity among all Indians was Gandhi's dominant concern, or to notice that on 12 November 1947, which was Diwali day, he had asked the people of Delhi the following question:

'Can you, every one of you, lay your hand on your heart and say that every sufferer, whether Hindu, Sikh or Muslim, is your own brother or sister?'[2]

Ten weeks after posing this challenge, Gandhi was killed. Grasping the meaning of the killing, Martin Luther King, Jr. said this in Montgomery, Alabama, on 22 March 1959:

> They killed him, this man who had galvanized 400 million [Indians] for independence.... One of his own fellow Hindus felt that he was a little too favourable toward the Moslems.... Here was a man of love falling at the hands of a man with hate.... But the man who shot Gandhi only shot him into the hearts of humanity.[3]

[2] *Collected Works of Mahatma Gandhi*, Vol. 90, p. 18.
[3] *The Papers of Martin Luther King, Jr.*, Berkeley: University of California Press, 1992, Vol. 5, p. 156.

Foreword

A few of Weber's pages are about nonviolent activism in Australia, and he refers to a related 2011 book by another Australian, Sean Scalmer: *Gandhi in the West: The Mahatma and the Rise of Radical Protest*. How lovers of democracy can use nonviolent methods to confront a global current in favour of supremacy and authoritarianism may be one of today's most important questions.

Meanwhile Thomas Weber should be congratulated for producing yet another sturdy study connected to Gandhi. This latest one possesses the Weber hallmarks we are familiar with: thoroughness, the desire to give everyone their voice, and the inclusion of details that make the text more readable, not less.

Rajmohan Gandhi
Panchgani, Maharashtra
3 January 2024

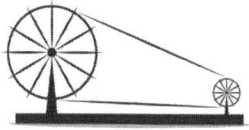

Acknowledgements

For helping to answer my queries, suggesting further avenues to explore, facilitating my research, and checking parts of earlier drafts of this work for inaccuracies and grammatical indelicacies, I would like to thank Niranjan Aggarwal, Dave Andrews, William Baskaran, Kinnari Bhatt, Jacques Boulet, Marty Branagan, Howard Brasted, Bob Brown, Robert Burrowes, Amit Dasgupta, Charles DiSalvo, Bevianne Fitch, Ela Gandhi, Rajmohan Gandhi, Don Gobbett, Michael Hamel-Green, Laurie Hastings, Margaret Hepworth, Geoff Heriot, Martha Ruth Hills, Dale Hess, Robin Jeffrey, Anthony Kelly, Santosh Kumar, Conny Lenneberg, David Lowe, Kama Maclean, Jarrod McKenna, Larry Marshall, Stephen Murphy, Vivian Papaleo, Dinesh Parekh, Narayana Rai, Carolyn Rasmussen, Stuart Rees, Malcolm Saunders, Sean Scalmer, Wendy Scarfe, Hilary Summy, Guy Tanter, Mark Thomson, Shabbir Wahid, Gambhir Watts, Linda Wilkinson, and Becky Wright.

I would like to especially thank those friends and colleagues who read the entire draft manuscript and made it much better than were my early attempts: Dennis Dalton, Graham Dunkley, Meg Gurry, and Brian Martin, and, as always, Marja Koskela. It is an honour to have Rajmohan Gandhi pen such a generous Foreword. My sincerest thanks. My gratitude also goes to Vidya Rao, Nilanjana Majumdar, and above all, to Proteeti Banerjee at Orient BlackSwan for shepherding the book through the publication

Acknowledgements

process. To those campaigners, activists, academics, and Indian community groups who have had strong Gandhi connections and that I overlooked, my sincere apologies. And it goes without saying that interpretations based on the information gathered is solely mine and only I should be blamed for any errors of fact.

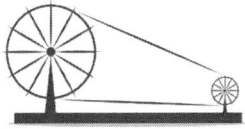

A Personal Introduction

After having read Sean Scalmer's book on the connection between Gandhi and the beginning of radical protest in the West (Scalmer 2011), and noting that for him 'the West' was limited to Britain and the United States of America, I started wondering about the Mahatma's connection with Australia—a part of the world not covered by the Australian Scalmer. As an Australian academic, I had taught subjects heavily featuring Gandhi, had written about him for around forty years, and had discussed him often with friends and colleagues. I knew that there were several books and lengthy articles on Gandhi and the West, on Gandhi and America, on Gandhi and Germany, and on Gandhi and Canada. This led me to wonder why I had not seen anything substantial on Gandhi's connections with Australia. Surely if America and Britain, and even Canada, could generate a literature on the connections between their societies and the Mahatma, Australia, being similar to them in so many ways, should have done likewise. However, it did not take long to realise that this literature was either missing from Australian bookshelves and journals, or was overlooked. And this of course raised the question of why this was the case. Intrigued, in 2017 I started to investigate the links, or the absence of them.

When I commenced work on this project, it had not occurred to me that I would have to write about myself. This may seem a little short-sighted, given that I have probably written more about Gandhi, and have possibly taught as many courses specifically

A Personal Introduction

based around Gandhi, than anyone else in this country. As a result, I have decided to include this personal introduction in order to deflect possible charges of unwarranted self-promotion in the section dealing with Gandhi and the academy, and to present my credentials for taking on this task.

While there was certainly no background that I could see as foreshadowing an interest in Gandhi during my childhood, for some reason I always knew that I would like to visit India. In my undergraduate years as a Law and Criminology student at the University of Melbourne, I occasionally joined in the evening India discussion group led by Sibnarayan Ray, Head of the Department of Indian Studies. I was studying Law, rather than Indian Studies and perhaps Comparative Religion, because to undertake a humanities major, one needed a final high school pass in a language or mathematics. I was no good at maths and had dropped it much earlier. Although I spoke fluent Hungarian (the language I spoke at home with my immigrant parents), it was not a recognised high school approved subject at the time, and I had flunked French. Law and Economics were all that were left and Economics sounded more boring than Law. So, in 1969, as an 18-year-old, still living at home with my parents, I became a Law/Criminology student.

This was at a time when Australia was still deeply involved in the Vietnam War; a war so unpopular that it forced the government to introduce a system of conscription to arrive at the numbers necessary for its commitment to the war effort. Twenty-year-old males, who did not even have the right to vote for another year, were entered into a ballot where the prize was a two-year stint in the army. I remember watching my fate being decided on television, the way many watch the tumbling of numbered lotto balls. The numbers were drawn from a barrel and all those with correspondingly dated birthdays had to report for 'National Service'. The process went on until the required numbers had been reached. Needless to say, it was the only lottery I ever won. After a brief period of mild panic, I thought that I should know more about

A Personal Introduction

this war I might have to take part in if my grades did not improve (they did!), or if the war was still ongoing when I graduated. I went on Moratorium marches, attended 'teach-ins', read extracts of the Pentagon Papers, and glanced into the works of Che Guevara. It also led to me reading the literature of civil disobedience and pacifism, which included an investigation of the life and thought of Mahatma Gandhi.

There was change in the air and the Labor Party won the 1972 federal election. Some of the first actions of the nascent government were to inform us not yet inducted draftees that our services would no longer be required, and to withdraw Australian troops from Vietnam. After graduation and a stint of factory work to build up some funds, in October of 1975, I headed to Indonesia, the first stop in a year-and-a-half on the road doing the fairly typical Australian backpacking journey to Europe, overlanding through Asia. The four months in South Asia included trekking in the Nepalese Himalaya, enjoying cultural programmes in Calcutta, observing Hindus in Varanasi, Haridwar, and Rishikesh, doing the tourist Delhi/Agra/Jaipur circuit, freezing on a houseboat in Srinagar, visiting the Golden Temple in Amritsar, and then crossing to Pakistan and travelling on to Afghanistan.

On this part of the trip, I read as much Indian history as I could. Gandhi, naturally, featured large. And, of course, if someone is in New Delhi, they have to pay respects to the Father of the Nation at the site of his cremation at Rajghat, and then visit the Gandhi Museum opposite. I did not know how much I was influenced by all this until half a year later, towards the end of 1976, when I visited Madame Tussauds wax museum in London. If my memory serves me right, somewhere in the room featuring leading political figures of the twentieth century, all unsmiling, straight of back, many with the left breasts of their grey suits or military uniforms heavily encrusted with medals, breaking the mould of sameness was a small man, stooping slightly, leaning on a stick. He was in (what appeared to be) an oversized nappy, with a shawl around his

A Personal Introduction

shoulders, wearing John Lennon round metal-rimmed glasses, with perhaps a hint of a smile on his lips. Mahatma Gandhi was visibly the odd man out in this distinguished, predominantly masculine assembly. Something about him touched me deeply and I resolved to find out more about this person.

When I returned to Melbourne in early 1977, I found work as a research assistant in Criminology at my old university, completing a book about police in Australia with one of my previous lecturers, and then at Melbourne's La Trobe University working on a book with others in the Legal Studies Department on Victoria's Magistrates' Court. And I started reading Gandhi in earnest. I read Louis Fischer's biography, Gandhi's own autobiography, and almost anything else about him that I could lay my hands on. By early 1979, I was ready to commit myself to some serious Gandhi study in India.

Universities are probably not the best places to learn about Gandhian philosophy, but I knew nothing about Gandhian ashrams and did not know any Gandhians. The then current edition of the *Commonwealth Universities Yearbook* informed me that there were four universities in India offering English language diplomas in Gandhian thought. On April Fool's Day, I flew to Madras (now Chennai). I contacted the relevant department at the leading university, only to be told that the head was on leave, so I made an appointment to talk to the next senior academic. The meeting was less than productive. I was invited to the home of the academic, who did not take me inside but sat me down on a chair outside and asked what present I had brought for his children. I did not know he had children and knew nothing of Indian culture. He took my pen, saying that would do, quizzed me about the other universities that I had discovered had Gandhi-related courses, and then dismissed me. Needless to say, I quickly crossed Madras off my list.

Next I journeyed to Mysore. The campus was pleasant enough and I liked Dr A. L. Shivarudrappa, the head of the Gandhi course.

A Personal Introduction

We talked for a long while and eventually he told me that I had too much knowledge to gain anything by attending his Gandhi classes. Quite candidly, he explained that the course was of a very low level, that it had been put on so that foreign students who had no Indian social network would have something to do in the evenings. He dissuaded me from enrolling, telling me that I should go home and somehow undertake a serious study of Gandhi. I never made it to the universities at Dharwad or Chandigarh and two months later, I was back in Melbourne.

Fortunately, I was immediately offered a job as a tutor in the Legal Studies Department of La Trobe University. It did not have a Law School at the time and Legal Studies was counted as a social science. As a staff member, I enrolled to undertake a Master of Arts degree by dissertation. If I had still been at the University of Melbourne, I would have been limited to doing an M.A. in Criminology or a Master of Laws, making any study of Gandhi rather difficult. Social Science is a very broad field and in 1981–1982, I received a La Trobe University Postgraduate Scholarship which enabled me to concentrate more or less full-time on researching and writing a dissertation titled 'Conflict and the Individual: A Gandhian Perspective'. With no background in Indian studies or conflict studies, I had become a Gandhi scholar. The dissertation ended up with various Gandhian publishers and in 1991, it was finally brought out by the Gandhi Peace Foundation in New Delhi as *Conflict Resolution and Gandhian Ethics*. That made me a published Gandhi scholar.

Sometime in 1982, Robin Jeffrey, a university colleague who was teaching a subject on Indian politics, asked me for some background material on Gandhi's 1930 Salt March to Dandi. Robin was a great teacher, always wanting to make lectures come alive for his students. He showed slides, conducted quizzes, and offered interesting personal insights into the key players. He requested information on the march itself, not on the leading figures or the politics surrounding the event, but about things

A Personal Introduction

such as the weather, the dust, the condition of the villages, how the marchers occupied their non-walking time, and the mood surrounding the event. I, rather foolishly, promised to peruse my ever growing Gandhi library and get back to him with the required information the following day. I should have known my Gandhi sources better. I searched in vain.

The relevant literature of the period generally talks at length about the growing unrest in India, about Indian National Congress' calls for independence, and the start of the anti-British agitation. There is also a detailed analysis of the aftermath of the Civil Disobedience campaign, but there is precious little describing the actual event itself. When I reported this to Robin the next day, he responded: 'I can't understand why someone hasn't re-walked the route. It would be a wonderful wee project.' I had been reading about Gandhi and his thought for years, but the time was coming when I felt that I really had to be on the ground in India specifically on a Gandhi quest, one that did not involve university courses. Re-walking the route of the Salt March seemed to fulfil my needs. In October 1982, having quit my university tutoring position, I headed back to India and spent some months in the National Archives and at the Nehru Memorial Museum and Library in New Delhi researching the Dandi March. I tracked down most of the still living ex-marchers, and headed to the Sabarmati Ashram in Ahmedabad, the commencement point of the political pilgrimage. In the early morning of 12 March the following year, I set off from the Ashram with some Gandhian friends towards the village of Aslali, the first lunch halt for the original marchers. I followed the timetable of the March, often staying in the same buildings Gandhi and the original marchers had stayed in, observed the route and recorded reminiscences, and, on the evening of 5 April, I arrived at the seaside village of Dandi where, fifty-three years ago, Gandhi had, on the following morning, picked up a handful of saline mud, breaking the iniquitous salt laws, and challenged the might of the British Empire.

A Personal Introduction

Following my walk, I met the Gandhian activist Sunderlal Bahuguna, one of the leading lights of the Himalayan tree-hugging, anti-logging Chipko movement. He had recently walked almost 5,000 kilometres along the length of the Himalaya, from Kashmir to Kohima in Assam. My 350 or so kilometre walk was nothing compared to his effort; nevertheless, he acknowledged me as a fellow traveller and through him I came into contact with the movement.

My luck held, and back in Melbourne I again managed to secure teaching positions at my old universities and started writing about the Salt March. Returning to India in 1985, I stayed and travelled with Bahuguna and read all I could about the Chipko movement. In 1987, I published *Hugging the Trees: The Story of the Chipko Movement*, my first Gandhi-related book, in New Delhi. The manuscript of the Salt March book went through several publishers, who promised much but delivered little. Eventually, ten years after I had completed the manuscript, Rajmohan Gandhi, one of the Mahatma's grandsons, read it and, thinking it worthwhile, instructed me to send it to his publisher and, in 1997, the 600-page *On the Salt March: The Historiography of Gandhi's March to Dandi* was published.

When I was in Delhi during my Salt March venture, I often visited A. K. Bose, the manager of the Gandhi Book House at Rajghat. He had supplied me with books on Gandhi for some years and had become a firm friend. When Bose was busy with customers in the public sales area, I often rummaged around in the relative chaos of the shop storeroom. During one of these times, I realised that there could be a possible important connection between two books that I had picked up. They were Charles Walker's *A World Peace Guard* (1981) and Vinoba Bhave's *Shanti Sena* (1963). Before then I had not known of Walker's work and was barely aware of the Sena. Following the publication of the Chipko book and the completion of the manuscript of the Salt March book, in 1987 I had the good fortune of securing scholarships that partially funded me for the next few years, as I researched

A Personal Introduction

and wrote a Ph.D. dissertation on 'Unarmed Peacekeeping and the Shanti Sena', about the post-Gandhi Gandhian peace army. From November 1988 until February 1989, I was back in India doing fieldwork, interviewing members of the Sena, which was at its peak under the leadership of Gandhi's chief disciples, Vinoba Bhave and Jayaprakash Narayan, between 1957 and 1975. Later, I had the good fortune to have the book, *Gandhi's Peace Army: The Shanti Sena and Unarmed Peacekeeping*, published in 1996, with a Foreword by the well-known peace activist and academic, Elise Boulding.

During the weeks that I spent working in the library of the Sabarmati Ashram looking at obscure Salt March-related sources and walking the ashram grounds daily, the question of how Gandhi could have left this utopia (or at least a place that must have been a rural utopia in 1930, instead of the small oasis surrounded by a very noisy and dirty urban sprawl that it had become by 1982), vowing not to return until India had achieved independence, bothered me. Visiting this ashram and Gandhi's next abode, Sevagram Ashram near Wardha, if one looks hard enough—even though the Gandhi literature makes little of it—it does not take long to realise that the institutions owe much to two of Gandhi's leading followers. While he is barely mentioned in the Gandhi canon, the ashram at Sabarmati would not have taken the shape it did and could not have functioned as smoothly as it was able to without the work of the Mahatma's 'nephew' (actually first cousin once removed) and then right-hand man, Maganlal Gandhi. The death of Maganlal left Gandhi 'widowed' and made his leaving of the Ashram more understandable. And while he is generally not mentioned at all in English-language Gandhi biographies, the Sevagram Ashram would not have existed without Gandhi's honorary 'fifth son' and wealthy benefactor, Jamnalal Bajaj. A similar close look at Gandhi's two ashrams in South Africa reveal something similar: Gandhi's Phoenix Settlement would probably not have come about without the influence of the journalist and

A Personal Introduction

lawyer, Gandhi's friend and collaborator, Henry Polak. And there would have been no Tolstoy Farm without the involvement of Gandhi's soul-mate, Hermann Kallenbach.

This led me to think about Gandhi in terms of influence—who had influenced him and who the Mahatma had in turn influenced—and here the major figures appeared to be founders of ways of thinking and acting rather than being involved with questions of real estate. I examined Gandhi's influence on the Norwegian philosopher and originator of the concept of 'deep ecology', Arne Næss; the founder of modern Peace Studies, Johan Galtung; E. F. Schumacher, who became well-known for 'small is beautiful' economics; and Gene Sharp, the doyen of nonviolent activism. These threads came together in my next book, *Gandhi as Disciple and Mentor* (2004).

In late 2004, along with my wife and daughter, I spent two weeks at the Gedong Gandhi Ashram at Candidasa in Bali. Although the founder, Ibu Gedong Bagoes Oka, was no longer alive, the institution still preserved the spirit of her strong Gandhian presence. As with the Gandhi Book House two decades before, fate intervened. While my family participated in yoga sessions, I went through the Gandhian literature in the Ashram's library. There, one day, I came across Mary Barr's collection of letters that the Mahatma had written to her. From this little book, I realised not only Barr's closeness to Gandhi, but also that she had vanished from the masculinised political Gandhi story as it is most often told. I quickly made a list of other Western women who should also have been remembered as part of that story, and about whom I should have known much more than I did. This led to another stay at Sabarmati Ashram, reading the letters these women exchanged with Gandhi, and any sources on them that I could find. This resulted, in 2011, in the publication of the book *Going Native: Gandhi's Relationship with Western Women*.

This research led to the reading of a cache of Mirabehn's letters to Gandhi. Madeleine Slade, to whom Gandhi gave the Indian

A Personal Introduction

name honouring the sixteenth-century mystic Rajasthani poet Mirabai, was his pre-eminent Western disciple. Most of Gandhi's letters to her (she mentions 650) are reproduced in Gandhi's *Collected Works*. However, her letters to him appeared to have all been lost. The Ashram archive staff, under the direction of Tridip Suhrud, turned up several dozen of her (often very lengthy) letters to Gandhi. We introduced and interleaved the letters, turning what was an instructive monologue into a far more valuable dialogue. The collection was published in 2014 under the title *Beloved Bapu: The Gandhi-Mirabehn Correspondence*.

In 2012, my publishers at Roli suggested that I might want to consider a book about first meetings with Gandhi to come out in time for the 100th anniversary of his return to India after the twenty-odd years he had spent in South Africa. The project was particularly interesting because it seemed like a fun undertaking that would teach me a great deal without an involvement in difficult theoretical issues. I managed to collect close to fifty autobiographical accounts of first meetings with Gandhi (some of which occurred on Mondays, his day of silence!). I introduced each one with a description of who the writer was—and they included friends, followers, religious figures, well-known writers, and celebrities—and followed each extract with a postscript containing further information, sometimes about the context in which the meeting occurred, or the significance of the meeting itself. The book, *Gandhi at First Sight*, came out in 2015.

Besides my writings on Gandhi, his followers, and guests, I also managed to introduce Gandhian elements into my teaching. In 1992, I inherited the core introductory subject 'Peace Studies' (later, 'Peace and Change') and became the co-ordinator of the Interdisciplinary Peace Studies Area at La Trobe University. I gave the subject a strong Gandhian base and continued to teach it until my retirement from active lecturing in 2011. In 1998, I introduced a more specific Gandhi-related subject, 'Politics of Nonviolent Activism'.

A Personal Introduction

During my years of thinking and writing about Gandhi, I have visited India at least a dozen times, totalling something like three years at Gandhian institutions, libraries with substantial Gandhian resources, and in the company of Gandhians. I keep close contact with many Gandhian scholars around the world, and hope that in my own small way I have done something to inform others of the best of Gandhian values.

1

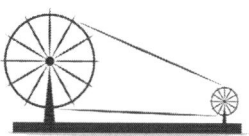

Background
Gandhi and the World

Mahatma Gandhi was not only the face of India's struggle for freedom from British rule, he was also an icon of the first half of the last century, and he remains one of the most recognisable figures in human history. Early on, his physical appearance and (un)dress were the most commonly reported on aspects of Gandhi in the British and American press and via the communications of those who had an audience with him. And that certainly seemed to be more important or understandable than what he stood for.[1] As Sean Scalmer, the author of a recent study of Gandhi's influence in the West, notes: 'To most Westerners the icon was more powerful and certainly more fascinating than the vicissitudes of an anti-colonial struggle.'[2] But that image changed over time and, after the Mahatma's death, his ideas became a common background for anti-bomb, anti-war, and social justice campaigns.

Much of what has been written on Gandhi's influence concerns Britain and the United States. My aim is to see how he was perceived in Australia, what his reception here was, and how

---

[1] For the fascination with Gandhi's appearance, see Sean Scalmer, *Gandhi in the West: The Mahatma and the Rise of Radical Protest*, Cambridge: Cambridge University Press, 2011, pp. 12–26.

[2] Scalmer, *Gandhi in the West*, p. 32.

he and his nonviolent praxis were utilised in various campaigns and academic settings. I aim to do this, first, by examining the other side of the coin: what Gandhi knew of, and thought about, Australia. Then I look at the stories of Australians who had direct interactions with Gandhi. The largest part of this investigation will focus on the reporting on Gandhi in the Australian press, there being very little other popular or influential analyses published in the country. Finally, I will investigate Gandhi's influence on the local peace, justice, and environmental movements, his affinity with religious groups, and his depiction in movies, books, exhibitions, and university courses, statues of him and orations given in his name, and festivals that honour him.

There are different ways of undertaking this task. Some studies have titles that seem to indicate that they are explicitly investigating the issues of perception and utilisation, for example Charles Chatfield's book on American perceptions of Gandhi,[3] C. Seshachari's intellectual history of and inquiry into Gandhi's connections with America,[4] Heimo Rau's book on Germans and Gandhi,[5] and Alex Damm's on Gandhi and Canada.[6] However, Chatfield's book is in large part a collection of documents published in America that featured Gandhi, Seshachari's work examines Gandhi in relation to major American thinkers and supporters, Rau's book is in reality a collection of scholarly articles by German academics about Gandhi, and while some of the papers in Damm's volume do investigate Gandhi's knowledge of Canada, the teaching

---

[3] Charles Chatfield (ed.), *The Americanization of Gandhi: Images of the Mahatma*, New York: Garland, 1976.

[4] C. Seshachari, *Gandhi and the American Scene: An Intellectual History and Inquiry*, Bombay: Nachiketa, 1969.

[5] Heimo Rau (ed.), *Mahatma Gandhi as Germans See Him*, Bombay: Shakuntala, 1976.

[6] Alex Damm (ed.), *Gandhi in a Canadian Context: Relationships between Mahatma Gandhi and Canada*, Waterloo, Ontario: Wilfrid Laurier University Press, 2017.

Background: Gandhi and the World

of Gandhi in Canadian Religious Studies programmes, and Gandhi festivals held in Canada, in the main they are also concerned with writings about Gandhi by Canadian scholars. My task here is not to write about Gandhi or reproduce documents featuring him except by way of an introduction, so these are not models that are of particular interest to me. Rather than merely see how Gandhi was perceived, I want to examine how he was used.

Graham Freudenberg, in his study of Churchill and Australia, looks at Churchill's direct relationship with Australia as part of the British Empire, as a reservoir for the British military, and through his often fraught relationships with Australian Prime Ministers, reflecting 'Australians' mixed feelings about their place in the British Empire, loyalties and the desire for a more independent Australia'.[7] When he was in power, many of Churchill's policies directly affected Australia; of course, this could not be said for any connection that Mahatma Gandhi had with the country. Although he was a powerful political figure, Gandhi's tussle with Australia amounted to little more than a battle of words over the discriminatory White Australia policy. Therefore the Freudenberg approach is not useful as a model for this study either.

A more practical way to locate Gandhi in an Australian context is also a more indirect one, like that used by Dennis Glover in his book, *Orwell's Australia*. Orwell never visited Australia, yet his impact on left politics was considerable. Orwell's writing, as Glover makes clear, helped shape Australian attitudes from the Cold War to culture wars, or at least has been called upon to do so even by those who were against everything that Orwell stood for.[8] Did Gandhi also, in some subtle way, shape Australian attitudes? Although perhaps not as often as Orwell's, Gandhi's

---

[7] Graham Freudenberg, *Churchill and Australia*, Sydney: Macmillan, 2008, p. 5.

[8] See Dennis Glover, *Orwell's Australia: From Cold War to Culture Wars*, Melbourne: Scribe, 2003.

name occasionally comes up in political speeches and, far more often than Orwell's, at peace rallies. Gandhi is frequently referred to by those discussing human rights and environmental issues. Orwell may well have been the most influential political writer of the last century, but Gandhi was its most influential nonviolent political campaigner and conscience-bearer. To what degree does this provide any signpost to the Australian psyche?

However, prior to anything else, we need a brief sketch of Gandhi's life before we can start to look at this question. And it would also be instructive to see what part knowledge about Gandhi and his beliefs played in the consciousness of the two nations that spoke and wrote about him the most: the United States where he was the object of fascination, not only for journalists, preachers, and civil rights activists but also for the general public, and Britain, the centre of the empire he was attempting to dismantle.

Gandhi: A Brief Introduction

Mohandas Karamchand Gandhi, who as Mahatma ('Great Soul') Gandhi would later come to world prominence as one of the most famous characters of the twentieth century, was born in the Indian seaside town of Porbandar in what today is the state of Gujarat, on 2 October 1869. His father served as the Diwan (Chief Minister) in local princely states; his mother was illiterate and extremely religious. Young Mohandas went to English-run schools, but neither his scholarly performance nor social skills demonstrated any promise of future greatness. As a teenager, he experimented with meat eating and smoking and occasionally stole money or gold from servants and family members. His remorse for these actions and for deceiving his family made him a self-confessed passionate truth-teller. He was married to Kastur Kapadia at the age of thirteen. On the death of his father in 1886, the family fell on hard times. Young Mohandas may not have been an outstanding student,

Background: Gandhi and the World

but of the three male siblings (while he also had a sister, given the times and traditions, she would never have been considered), he was deemed the most capable and, at crippling expense, he was selected to go to London to study Law. It was assumed that as an English-trained barrister he would secure the financial future of the extended family. He defied caste rules forbidding overseas travel and, leaving his wife and first child behind, the shy 19-year-old embarked on a voyage that would change his life.[9]

Fully qualified as a barrister, Gandhi returned to India in 1891. However, the theoretical studies he had undertaken in London did not prepare him for the practical work of a courtroom lawyer. Too overwhelmed to conduct his first case, he fled the courtroom in embarrassment. It seemed that he would be destined to be a lowly paid drafter of petitions and applications. His salvation came when he accepted a year-long position as a lawyer assisting in a complicated case involving Indian merchants in the Natal province of South Africa in 1893. Again leaving his wife and now two sons in the care of the extended family, he set off for Africa. He (later joined by his wife and children) was to spend most of the next twenty years there in the service of the Indian community, partially in rural communes that he founded. In this time, the reserved would-be barrister flourished as a successful attorney and community leader. Having, for the first time, experienced the humiliation of racial prejudice, he became a political campaigner fighting for the rights of his discriminated against countrymen.[10]

---

[9] For Gandhi's early life, see. M. K. Gandhi, *An Autobiography or the Story of My Experiments with Truth*, Ahmedabad: Navajivan, 1940 (and many other editions); Pyarelal, *Mahatma Gandhi, Vol. 1, The Early Phase*, Ahmedabad: Navajivan, 1965; Ramachandra Guha, *Gandhi Before India*, London: Allen Lane, 2013; or any of the dozens of available, useful Gandhi biographies.

[10] Later, Gandhi was criticised for being racist in his attitude towards Black South Africans. Recent scholarship, perhaps somewhat too stridently, notes that he tried to distinguish the Indian community from that of the Africans and to ingratiate himself with the ruling Whites. See Ashwin Desai and Goolam Vahed,

He led large-scale nonviolent civil disobedience (originally called 'passive-resistance' and later *satyagraha* or 'truth force') movements against discriminatory legislation. However, as a loyal citizen of the Empire, he also raised and served in Indian ambulance corps in the Boer War and the Zulu uprising. He left South Africa in mid-1914 and, after several months in London, returned to India to a hero's welcome as Mahatma Gandhi at the start of 1915.[11] The attention he received in India was not yet reflected in other parts of the world.

His post-Africa years, up to his death on 30 January 1948, are well-documented and require little elaboration. In 1917 and 1918, he led local campaigns seeking justice and better pay for farmers and urban millworkers. In 1919 he led a campaign against the repressive Rowlatt legislation, but called it off after violence broke out. He lost faith in the fairness of the Empire following the massacre of unarmed civilians at Jallianwala Bagh in Amritsar on 13 April 1919 and threw himself into the politics of independence through the Indian National Congress. In the following year, he launched the movement of Non-Cooperation against British rule, his first major campaign for Indian independence. In 1922, following another outbreak of violence, he again called off the campaign. He was arrested and spent two years in prison.

On 12 March 1930, he set off from his *ashram* (spiritual community) at Sabarmati, on the outskirts of Ahmedabad, with seventy-eight male ashramites, and walked to the seaside village of Dandi, some 350 kilometres away. The marchers reached the ocean on the evening of 5 April, and the following morning Gandhi picked up some un-taxed salt, breaking the British salt laws. This was the

---

The South African Gandhi: Stretcher-Bearer of Empire, Stanford, CA: Stanford University Press, 2016.

[11] For Gandhi's time in South Africa as a lawyer and champion of the cause of Indians, see M. K. Gandhi, *Satyagraha in South Africa*, Madras: Ganesan, 1928; Charles DiSalvo, *The Man Before the Mahatma: M. K. Gandhi, Attorney at Law*, Noida: Random House India, 2012; Maureen Swan, *Gandhi: The South African Experience*, Johannesburg: Ravan Press, 1985; and Guha, *Gandhi Before India*.

Background: Gandhi and the World

start of his most famous campaign, that of Civil Disobedience. He was imprisoned after midnight of 5 May, and two weeks later, his followers commenced nonviolent 'raids' on the nearby salt works at Dharasana. In January 1931, Gandhi and other Congress leaders were released from prison and, following discussions with the Viceroy Lord Irwin, Gandhi called off the campaign and attended the second Round Table Conference on India's future in London as the sole representative of Congress. He spent three months in the capital of the Empire, returning to India 'empty handed' in December. In January 1932, Civil Disobedience was resumed and Gandhi was again arrested. He was released in May 1933 following a fast for self-purification (or a hunger strike for political purposes, depending on the viewpoint of the observer).

Gandhi devoted the next several years to rural development and the cause of 'untouchables', whom he had called 'Harijans'— 'Children of God'. In August 1942, with Japanese troops threatening the country, Gandhi called for the British to 'Quit India'. He was imprisoned, but released in May 1944 because of ill health. From this time, until his death, he worked to try to avoid the partitioning of India along communal Hindu/Muslim lines as independence finally drew close. He was sidelined by the younger political leadership; however, he performed some of his most courageous and significant actions in the last months of his life. He did not attend the ceremonies for the finally achieved freedom of his country; instead, in November 1946, he embarked on a four-month walking tour of East Bengal in an attempt to bring peace to the warring communities and then fasted in Calcutta to quell communal rioting. In his final weeks, he fasted in New Delhi and this went far in restoring peace to the capital. He was gunned down by a Hindu fanatic because of Gandhi's concern over the fate of Muslim refugees.[12]

---

[12] For the life of the post-South African Gandhi, see Ramachandra Guha, *Gandhi: The Years that Changed the World, 1914–1948*, New Delhi: Penguin, 2018, or any of the other major Gandhi biographies.

Besides the more political movements that he led for the independence of his country from British colonial occupation, much of his time was spent in less spectacular or newsworthy, but for him just as important, village uplift and rural reconstruction work that he called the 'constructive programme'. The programme was concerned with the removal of untouchability, the re-establishment of rural industries, village sanitation, prohibition, basic education for all, the promotion of a national language, education in health and hygiene, and work towards economic equality.[13] He believed that these constructive efforts offered replacement for the things that the nationalists were opposing when they were opposing them. Without it, Gandhi felt that the overthrowing of the imperial masters would merely exchange one group of rulers for another, resulting in 'English rule without the Englishmen ... the tiger's nature but not the tiger'.[14]

There was another important facet to the Mahatma's life, one that was far less accessible, particularly to Western audiences: his spiritual quest with its dietetic experiments, celibacy, days of silence, fasts, prayers, listening to the 'small voice within', and calls for self-sacrifice and nonviolence even in the face of violent attack. In the introduction to his *Autobiography*, Gandhi wrote:

> What I want to achieve,—what I have been striving and pining to achieve these thirty years,—is self-realization, to see God face to face, to attain *Moksha* [salvation]. I live and move and have my being in pursuit of this goal. All that I do by way of speaking and writing, and all my ventures in the political field, are directed to this same end.[15]

What was the world to make of this?

---

[13] See M. K. Gandhi, *Constructive Programme: Its Meaning and Place*, Ahmedabad: Navajivan, 1941.

[14] M. K. Gandhi, *Hind Swaraj or Indian Home Rule*, Ahmedabad: Navajivan, 1939, p. 30.

[15] Gandhi, *An Autobiography*, p. xiv.

Background: Gandhi and the World

The Mahatma and the World

Around 1909, Gandhi undertook a campaign of self-promotion. In that year the Reverend Joseph Doke, an English Baptist minister who was one of Gandhi's close friends during his middle period in South Africa, became Gandhi's first biographer. That biography, titled *M. K. Gandhi: An Indian Patriot in South Africa*,[16] seems to have been more or less dictated by Gandhi to the writer, and it was Gandhi himself who arranged for its publication.[17] As soon as he had a printed copy, he sent it to the great Russian writer and pacifist, Count Leo Tolstoy. Gandhi had confessed that Tolstoy's book, *The Kingdom of God is Within You*,[18] overwhelmed him and left an abiding impression on him.[19] Gandhi then conducted a brief correspondence with Tolstoy, in the last months of the writer's life.[20] Gandhi asked Tolstoy to publicise his campaign in South Africa, while using Tolstoy's name to legitimise it.[21]

---

[16] Joseph J. Doke, *M. K. Gandhi: An Indian Patriot in South Africa*, London: London Indian Chronicle, 1909.

[17] See T. K. Mahadevan, *The Year of the Phoenix: Gandhi's Pivotal Year*, New Delhi: Arnold-Heinemann, 1982, pp. 159–164; and S. L. Malhotra, 'A Study of Gandhi's Biographies: Joseph J. Doke and Romain Rolland', *Gandhi Marg* 6 (12), 1985, pp. 845–861.

[18] Leo Tolstoy, *The Kingdom of God is Within You: Or, Christianity Not as a Mystical Teaching But as a New Concept of Life*, Leo Wiener (trans.), New York: Noonday, 1961.

[19] Gandhi, *An Autobiography*, p. 99. Gandhi's chief biographer and secretary in later life, Pyarelal, claims that so deeply was Gandhi's thinking 'impregnated with Tolstoy's that the changes that took place in his way of life and thinking in the years that followed [his reading of Tolstoy] can be correctly understood and appreciated only in the context of the master's life and philosophy', and that Tolstoy was the 'founder of Gandhism'. See Pyarelal, *Mahatma Gandhi*, Vol. I: *The Early Phase*, Ahmedabad: Navajivan, 1965, pp. 628, 707.

[20] See Thomas Weber, *Gandhi as Disciple and Mentor*, Cambridge: Cambridge University Press, 2004, pp. 38–42.

[21] See Guha, *Gandhi Before India*, pp. 339–341.

In November 1909, on a return trip from England to South Africa, Gandhi wrote his seminal political text, *Hind Swaraj*. In December, it was published in two instalments in the Gujarati section of his newspaper, *Indian Opinion*. In March of the following year it appeared in book form, in English translation, as *Indian Home Rule*. In May, Tolstoy received the thin volume that Gandhi had sent him and read it 'with great interest'. However, he was ailing and could do little to publicise the book. Half a year later, Tolstoy was dead and *Hind Swaraj* was banned in India. There was little international reaction to the book,[22] and it would be another ten years before Gandhi and his writings became widely known.

Gandhi came to the attention of the world outside India with his first major campaign for Indian independence from the British Raj, the Non-Cooperation movement of 1920–1921. However, in Australia he did not have a champion such as the New York pastor John Haynes Holmes who, on 10 April 1921, preached his famous sermon, 'Who is the Greatest Man in the World Today?' Many expected Holmes to speak about Lenin; instead, he introduced an almost unknown Mahatma to American audiences.[23] And Gandhi later declared his debt to Holmes and Americans in general:

> I am not unknown to you. I have in America perhaps the largest number of friends in the West—not even excepting Great Britain, British friends knowing me personally are more discerning than the American. In America I suffer from the well-known malady called hero worship. The good Dr. Holmes, until recently of the Unity Church of New York, without knowing me personally became my advertising agent. Some of the nice things he said about me I never knew myself. So I receive often embarrassing

---

[22] For a history of *Hind Swaraj*, see Anthony J. Parel (ed.), *Hind Swaraj and Other Writings*, Cambridge: Cambridge University Press, 1997, especially the 'Editor's Introduction', pp. xiii–lxii.

[23] See John Haynes Holmes, *Who is the Greatest Man in the World Today?*, New York: The Community Church, 1921.

Background: Gandhi and the World

letters from America expecting me to perform miracles. Dr. Holmes was followed much later by the late Bishop Fisher who knew me personally in India. He very nearly dragged me to America but fate had ordained otherwise and I could not visit your vast and great country with its wonderful people.[24]

The book *Mahatma Gandhi: The Man Who Became One with the Universal Being*, by the French Nobel Prize-winning pacifist writer Romain Rolland, did for Europe what Holmes' sermon did for America.[25] In the 1924 English version of Rolland's book, Gandhi comes across as more than a nationalist fighter. He is portrayed 'in the context of man's search for permanent peace'[26] and is compared, amongst others, to Saint Francis of Assisi. Even more impressively, after spelling out Gandhi's message of strength, self-sacrifice, and nonviolence, in the concluding pages of the book Rolland notes that 'the only thing lacking is the cross.'[27] As early as mid-March 1924, Rolland recorded in his diary that the book 'has now been published in nearly all languages; editions are following hard on each other's heels in France and Germany', and that 'it is making a deep impression in the religious world, particularly among Protestants. It reawakens the sleeping Christ in them. The Mahatma himself almost seems Christ reborn.'[28] Some years later,

---

[24] 'To American Friends', *Harijan*, 9 August 1942.

[25] As Malhotra points out, like the Doke biography, Rolland's was also a 'special-purpose' biography, in that it sought to support Gandhi's cause rather than to 'unfold the life of the subject'. See Malhotra, 'A Study of Gandhi's Biographies', p. 861.

[26] See Malhotra, 'A Study of Gandhi's Biographies', p. 859.

[27] Romain Rolland, *Mahatma Gandhi: The Man Who Became One With the Universal Being*, New Delhi: Publications Division, Ministry of Information and Broadcasting, Government of India, 1968, p. 124.

[28] 'Extract from Romain Rolland's Diary: March 1924', Publications Division, *Romain Rolland and Gandhi Correspondence (Letters, Diary Extracts, Articles, Etc.)*, New Delhi: Publications Division, Ministry of Information and Broadcasting, Government of India, 1976, p. 28. See also David James Fisher,

Gandhi admitted that 'All the reputation that I enjoy in the West is borrowed from him [Rolland]'.[29] Gandhi's own *Autobiography*, originally published as instalments in his paper *Young India*, finally appeared in book form in two volumes. They came out in 1927 and 1929 (and appeared in a single volume in 1940). In Indian terms, the book was a bestseller; however, it only detailed Gandhi's life up to 1921, before the campaign that first brought him to international attention. The ending was abrupt, and Gandhi's great Salt Satyagraha campaign and international renown were still in the future. However, Gandhi stated that the time had come 'to bring these chapters to a close'. He added that his life, from then onwards, 'has been so public that there is hardly anything about it that people do not know'.[30] As soon as he could after the chapters appeared in *Young India*, Holmes serialised them in his weekly paper *Unity*. And in the year of the Salt March, Holmes wrote the Foreword to C. F. Andrews' edited version of Gandhi's *Autobiography*. The English reverend Andrews was a very close lifelong friend of Gandhi's from the South Africa days. Towards the end of that year, Bishop Frederick Fisher, in the journal *The Christian Century*, commented that 'Here is an autobiography more captivating than fiction and a more revealing study of the human soul than I have ever read.'[31]

Nevertheless, as the Rudolphs point out, the book posed a puzzle for its Western readers. While they may have expected the

---

'Romain Rolland and the Popularization of Gandhi: 1923–1925', *Gandhi Marg*, 1974, 18 (3), pp. 145–180; David James Fisher, *Romain Rolland and the Politics of Intellectual Engagement*, Berkeley: University of California Press, 1988, especially pp. 112–144; and V. V. Ramana Murti, 'Romain Rolland and Gandhi', *Gandhi Marg*, 1966, 10 (1), pp. 38–51.

[29] Gandhi to C. Rajagopalchari, 28 March 1928.

[30] Gandhi, *An Autobiography*, p. 370.

[31] Frederick Fisher, 'Gandhi Himself', *Christian Century*, 5 November 1930, 47, p. 1345. For an examination of Gandhi's *Autobiography*, see S. L. Malhotra, 'A Study of Gandhi's *Autobiography*', *Gandhi Marg*, 1985, 7 (7), pp. 424–437.

Background: Gandhi and the World

life story of a political leader, what they received was 'so heavily concerned with the Mahatma's "private" activities that it might better have been entitled "Confessions".[32] This, however, did not seem to deter at least certain readers.

Recently, Sean Scalmer has charted the influence of Gandhi on British and American peace movements. He looks at Western sources and here, Britain and America are the most fruitful case studies. Britain, of course, was the colonial power that Gandhi was struggling against and London was the place of his youthful law studies and centre of the Empire. He visited the city on several occasions in the cause of his campaigns for the rights of Indians in South Africa, and later to discuss the future of a free India. America was also important, as not only was the United States 'a model of successful rebellion', but American public opinion was also an important tool for putting pressure on Britain during the struggle for freedom.[33] Americans were also the first to notice Gandhi's significance and then promote his methods.[34]

Books about Gandhi that could have introduced him to Australian audiences were obviously those written in, or translated into, English. Other than Rolland's hagiographical offering, all the major popular biographies of Gandhi, or books in which he featured large, were written by English and American backers and were published in Britain and America. By the mid-1970s, there had already been over 400 of these biographies published, with sixty-six being published up to the release of Louis Fischer's tome,[35]

---

[32] Lloyd I. Rudolph and Susanne Hoeber Rudolph, *The Modernity of Tradition: Political Development in India*, Chicago: University of Chicago Press, 1967, p. 169.

[33] See Thomas Weber, *On the Salt March: The Historiography of Mahatma Gandhi's March to Dandi*, New Delhi: Rupa, 2009, pp. 449–452.

[34] Scalmer, *Gandhi in the West*, pp. 6–7.

[35] Stephen Murphy, 'The Different "Gandhis" in Western Biographies', *Gandhi Marg*, 1990, 12 (3), p. 295.

the first complete biography of Gandhi to be published after his assassination.[36] While most of these books provided positive, and often very positive, images of Gandhi, some of them, being written by Christian clergymen, portrayed Gandhi in spiritual terms, as a saint. However, possibly the book that did the most to bring Gandhi to Western audiences was not a biography at all.

America's Gandhi

Gandhi first made it onto the pages of *The New York Times* in January of 1921, in an editorial that predicted that the already formidable Gandhi will 'attain formidable political power in India'. A year later, the paper carried a totally fabricated report of Gandhi's student days in London, where he learned that his social ambitions would never be fulfilled and so he left a 'disillusioned man'. As time went on, up until Gandhi's Salt March, while there was a trend to report on Gandhi with a greater sense of understanding, problems with misstated facts, biased commentary, and an 'undiscerning attitude towards the Eastern viewpoint' ensured that American readers had less than optimal help to gain an understanding of the Mahatma.[37] As Lloyd Rudolph points out, this may have been inevitable, given that 'Until Gandhi became America's "lens

---

[36] See Louis Fischer, *The Life of Mahatma Gandhi*, New York: Harper and Row, 1950; and S. L. Malhotra, 'Louis Fischer as Gandhi's Biographer', *Gandhi Marg*, 1986, 8 (5), pp. 259–270.

[37] Mark Hannon, 'Gandhi in the New York Times, 1920–1930', in G. Ramachandran and T. K. Mahadevan (eds), *Quest for Gandhi*, New Delhi: Gandhi Peace Foundation, 1970, pp. 164–172. For more on early American attention to Gandhi, see Chatfield (ed.), *The Americanization of Gandhi*; Lloyd I. Rudolph, 'Gandhi in the Mind of America', in Lloyd I. Rudolph and Susanne Hoeber Rudolph, *Postmodern Gandhi and Other Essays: Gandhi in the World and at Home*, New Delhi: Oxford University Press, 2006, pp. 92–139; and Guha, *Gandhi: The Years that Changed the World*, pp. 183–187.

Background: Gandhi and the World

on India", American views on Indian religion, society and politics were largely filtered through British sources.'[38] However, it was not the newspapers that were the main culprit in giving a distorted picture of India and Gandhi.

The sensationalist American author Katherine Mayo saw herself as a spokesperson for voiceless underdogs. She spent three months over the winter of 1925–1926 in India, researching a book about the conditions in the country. Mayo insisted that she was going to India to write an impartial study of the country for Americans; after all,

> what does the average American actually know about India? That Mr. Gandhi lives there; also tigers.... It was dissatisfaction with this status that sent me to India, to see what a volunteer unsubsidised, uncommitted, and unattached, could observe of common things in daily human life.[39]

A year after she interviewed Gandhi during her Indian sojourn, Katherine Mayo's book, *Mother India*, appeared. In it, Mayo championed the British presence in India, not only for political or economic stability but also, and particularly, because of what she saw as Hindu social customs resulting in the sexual abuses that stemmed from the practice of child marriage. In short, India was not ready for independence because of a basic deficiency in, particularly, Hindu culture. The book opens with a graphic account of animal sacrifice at the temple of Kali in Calcutta. From there it covers filth; disease (of such an extent, Mayo claimed, that if it became known, civilised nations would demand protection from India through the League of Nations); sex; disadvantage and illiteracy, mostly as it affected girls and women; heartless caste practices; the mistreatment of cows; untouchability; Hindu-

---

[38] Rudolph and Rudolph, 'Gandhi in the Mind of America', p. 113.
[39] Katherine Mayo, *Mother India*, London: Jonathan Cape, 1927, p. 20.

Muslim enmity; and, of course, woven through the narrative, Gandhi. Many were convinced that the purpose of the book was to slander India, bolster support for British imperialism, and to discredit the Mahatma.

The book was published in May 1927 in the US and two months later in Britain. It was a sensation, with thirty reprints in just three years. In America, the book went through twenty-seven editions by 1958, selling a total of almost 400,000 copies by the mid-1950s, becoming the most popular book on India in the first half of the last century.[40] In its first six months, the British publication went through eight impressions.[41] Gandhi's review of the book was titled 'Drain Inspector's Report'.[42]

Katherine Mayo's *Mother India* had greatly damaged the standing of Indians in the eyes of Americans. Gandhi was anxious to redress this imbalance, and the choice of the salt laws as the focus of the Civil Disobedience campaign played a part in doing so. The American press could not resist the analogy between Gandhi's gathering of illicit salt and the famous Boston Tea Party. Editorials, even in influential American papers, forecast that as Britain had lost America through tea, she was about to lose India through salt. The British were worried by the American press

---

[40] See William W. Emilsen, 'Gandhi and Mayo's "Mother India"', *South Asia*, 1987, 10 (1), p. 72; Seshachari, *Gandhi and the American Scene*, p. 51; and Murphy, 'The Different "Gandhis"', p. 313. For the impact of *Mother India* in America, see Manoranjan Jha, *Civil Disobedience and After: The American Reaction to Political Developments in India During 1930–1935*, Meerut: Meenakshi, 1973, pp. 30–33.

[41] However, Murphy, quoting Howard, notes that 'much of the impetus for this best-selling book was achieved in Britain "by sending a complimentary copy to every Member of Parliament"'. See Murphy, 'The Different "Gandhis"', p. 315; and Michael S. Howard, *Jonathan Cape, Publisher*, London: Jonathan Cape, 1971, p. 95.

[42] For a more detailed account of the Gandhi-Mayo interaction, see Thomas Weber, *Going Native: Gandhi's Relationship with Western Women*, New Delhi: Roli, 2011, pp. 121–126.

Background: Gandhi and the World

coverage and angered by what they saw as American simplification of a complex issue.

A significant example materialised with American United Press journalist Webb Miller's report of the exceedingly brutal response to the nonviolent 'raids' on the salt works at Dharasana near the village of Dandi. After the arrest of Gandhi following his Salt March, Miller witnessed the 'raids' and subsequent violence.[43] His report managed to evade British censors and his scoop eventually appeared in 1,350 newspapers around the world, and was read out in the US Senate. American Gandhi-supporters printed it as a leaflet and distributed in excess of 250,000 copies.[44]

Although papers like *The New York Times* continued to support British policy towards India, the censorship of reports by American journalists (when the Americans were assured that there was none) and sympathetic reports of peaceful non-resistance in the face of British brutality by Gandhi followers, was beginning to turn the minds of a large number of Americans towards scepticism in regards to British policy in India. American reporters were now on the scene in India, and no longer was the American press hostage to newsfeeds from London. Besides Webb Miller, there was also J. A. Mills of the Associated Press, William Shirer of the *Chicago Tribune*, and Negley Farson of *Chicago Daily News*. *Time* magazine, which referred to the Mahatma as 'Saint Gandhi' in its reporting of the struggle, made Gandhi its 'Man of the Year' for 1930. The tempting analogies and the positive publicity following an adherence to nonviolence in the face of physical attacks, according to Farson, 'rubbed out *Mother*

---

[43] For the raids on the Dharasana salt works, see Weber, *On the Salt March*, pp. 488–514.

[44] For Webb Miller's report of the Dharasana raids, see Webb Miller, *I Found no Peace: The Journal of a Foreign Correspondent*, Harmondsworth: Penguin, 1940, pp. 134–137. Originally, this was published in New York by The Library Guild in 1936.

India as easily as you clean a child's slate.'[45] And the triumphant image of Gandhi kept growing.[46]

Although it was occasionally mooted, a trip to America by the Mahatma never eventuated. Partially this was because Gandhi thought that even his most ardent American supporters tended to misunderstand his work, and that in the case of others there was too great a possibility that he would become a spectacle viewed out of idle curiosity.[47] However, in 1931 he allowed himself to be recorded by the Columbia Broadcasting System for a radio broadcast to the US. The recording was not only heard by many, but was also printed in newspapers across the country.[48] In 1938, the *Reader's Digest* carried a lengthy laudatory essay on Gandhi,[49] and while Guha takes this as evidence of 'the growing interest in, and admiration for, Gandhi in America,'[50] in fact, between 1932 and 1935, about seventy articles on Gandhi appeared in popular American magazines,[51] and Norman Cousins' edited book of reminiscences of Gandhi includes fourteen reflections on the living Gandhi written between 1930 and 1948, and close to twice that many tributes to Gandhi written in the next twenty years.[52]

---

[45] Negley Farson, 'Indian Hate Lyric', in Eugene Lyons (ed.), *We Cover the World: By Sixteen Foreign Correspondents*, London: Harrap, 1937, p. 139.

[46] See Harold R. Isaacs, *Scratches on Our Minds: American Views of China and India*, Armonk, New York: M. E. Sharpe, 1980, pp. 290–302.

[47] See Thomas Weber, 'Why Gandhi Didn't Go to Finland (or America or China)', in Thomas Weber, *The Mahatma, His Philosophy and His Legacy*, Hyderabad: Orient BlackSwan, 2018, pp. 93–125.

[48] Leonard A. Gordon, 'Mahatma Gandhi's Dialogues with Americans', *Economic and Political Weekly*, 26 January 2002, p. 346.

[49] John Gunther, 'The Incredible Mr. Gandhi', *Reader's Digest*, December 1938, 33 (200), pp. 111–126.

[50] Guha, *Gandhi: The Years that Changed the World*, p. 563.

[51] Kenton J. Clymer, *Quest for Freedom: The United States and India's Independence*, New York: Columbia University Press, 1995, p. 21.

[52] Norman Cousins (ed.), *Profiles of Gandhi: America Remembers a World Leader*, Delhi: Indian Book Company, 1970.

Background: Gandhi and the World

Gandhi had numerous American friends and interactions with Americans. He reportedly received more letters from America than anywhere else outside India, and numerous American journalists and visitors beat a path to his door. He had a long-lasting impact on the thinking of Americans and on their approach to social action.[53] And those wanting to examine the connections between Gandhi and America had a relatively easy task. For example, Seshachari's and Gordon's studies of the Mahatma and America,[54] which chart 'the course of Gandhi's impact upon the American imagination',[55] had no problem with finding examples, given the connections between the Indian leader and various well-known American writers and clergymen such as John Haynes Holmes,[56] Katherine Mayo, Webb Miller, Frederick Fisher,[57] Frazier Hunt,[58] Edgar Snow,[59] Margaret Bourke-White,[60] and Louis Fischer.[61] Others, whose writings highlighted Gandhi, such as Clarence

---

[53] See Gordon, 'Mahatma Gandhi's Dialogues with Americans', pp. 337, 344, and 346; and generally David Cortright, *Gandhi and Beyond: Nonviolence for an Age of Terrorism*, Boulder: Paradigm, 2006.

[54] Seshachari, *Gandhi and the American Scene*; and Gordon, 'Mahatma Gandhi's Dialogues with Americans'.

[55] William Mulder, 'Foreword', in Seshachari, *Gandhi and the American Scene*, p. vii.

[56] John Haynes Holmes, 'Mahatma Gandhi: The Greatest Man Since Jesus Christ', in Kshitis Roy (ed.), *Gandhi Memorial Peace Number*, Shantiniketan: Visva-Bharati Quarterly, 1949, pp. 239–256.

[57] Frederick B. Fisher, *That Strange Little Brown Man Gandhi*, New York: Ray Long and Richard B. Smith Inc., 1932. See also S. L. Malhotra, 'The American Clergy and the Mahatma: Frederick B. Fisher and John Haynes Holmes', *Gandhi Marg*, 1988, 9 (10), pp. 579–596.

[58] Frazier Hunt, *One American and his Attempt at Education*, New York: Simon and Schuster, 1938.

[59] Edgar Snow, *Glory and Bondage* [US title: *People on Our Side*], Sydney: Angus and Robertson, 1946.

[60] Margaret Bourke-White, *Halfway to Freedom*, New York: Simon and Schuster, 1949.

[61] Fischer, *The Life of Mahatma Gandhi*.

Gandhi's Australia/Australia's Gandhi

Marsh Case,[62] Richard B. Gregg,[63] Joan V. Bondurant,[64] and Gene Sharp,[65] along with America-based Indians such as Haridas Muzumdar[66] and Krishnalal Shridharani,[67] went on to have a large impact on the American civil rights and later peace movements. Two of the earliest major popular and complete biographical sketches of Gandhi, Louis Fischer's *The Life of Mahatma Gandhi* and Vincent Sheean's *Lead, Kindly Light*,[68] were written by Americans. Americans also made much of the supposed influence of Henry David Thoreau's essay, 'On Civil Disobedience', on the development of Gandhi's political activism,[69] and were well aware of Gandhi's impact on African-Americans such as Bayard Rustin and James Lawson before the advent of the civil rights movement,[70] and later on their great civil rights campaigner, Martin Luther King Jr.[71]

[62] Clarence Marsh Case, *Non-Violent Coercion: A Study in Methods of Social Pressure*, New York: Century, 1923.
[63] Richard B. Gregg, *The Power of Non-Violence*, Philadelphia: J. B. Lippincott, 1934.
[64] Joan V. Bondurant, *Conquest of Violence: The Gandhian Philosophy of Conflict*, Princeton: Princeton University Press, 1958.
[65] Gene Sharp, *Gandhi Wields the Weapon of Moral Power [Three Case Histories]*, Ahmedabad: Navajivan, 1960; and *The Politics of Nonviolent Action*, Boston: Porter Sargent, 1973.
[66] Haridas T. Muzumdar, *Gandhi the Apostle: His Trial and His Message*, Chicago: Universal Publishing, 1923; and *Gandhi Against the Empire*, New York: Universal Publishing, 1932.
[67] Krishnalal Shridharani, *War Without Violence: A Study of Gandhi's Method and its Accomplishments*, New York: Garland, 1939.
[68] Vincent Sheean, *Lead, Kindly Light*, London: Cassell, 1950; see also S. L. Malhotra, 'Vincent Sheean as a Biographer of Mahatma Gandhi', *Gandhi Marg*, 1988, 10 (6), pp. 340–349.
[69] See Weber, *Gandhi as Disciple and Mentor*, pp. 42–45.
[70] See Sudarshan Kapur, *Raising Up a Prophet: The Afro-American Encounter with Gandhi*, Boston: Beacon Press, 1992.
[71] See, in particular, Martin Luther King, Jr., *Stride Towards Freedom: The Montgomery Story*, New York: Harper and Row, 1958; and Thomas Weber, 'Gandhi and Martin Luther King, Jr: Causal Influence or Backing Support?' *Gandhi Marg*, 2003, 25 (2), pp. 191–203.

Background: Gandhi and the World

Britain's Gandhi

Rudyard Kipling's 1899 poem, 'White Man's Burden', was a call to the United States to colonise the Philippines, following the American victory in the Spanish-American war of 1898. The term encompassed the belief that the superior culture of the European Christian world had a duty to care for and uplift, and indeed civilise, their non-white colonial subjects. This concept was seen as a justification for European imperialism in the nineteenth and twentieth centuries. And for most of the British population, this was the case regarding the British Empire, and particularly as it applied to its 'jewel in the crown', India. But of course things would not stay as clear as that.

When violence broke out in the Punjab during the Gandhi-led protests against the Rowlatt Act, which maintained repressive wartime measures when liberalisation was expected, British tyranny became heavy-handed. In the city of Amritsar on 13 April 1919, a huge but peaceful gathering assembled illegally at Jallianwala Bagh, a large enclosed courtyard. Public meetings had only been outlawed the previous day, and it is probable that most of the demonstrators did not know that their actions were illegal. Unprovoked, the army, under the command of General Reginald Dyer, opened fire on the crowd. Almost 400 people were killed and over 1,000 wounded. News of the massacre did not appear in American newspapers until December, two months after the British government set up an official enquiry into the event, and the imposition of strict censorship ensured that it was several weeks before news of the massacre reached the rest of India. Even Gandhi did not know the full extent of the massacre until June.

British papers praised the brutal acts of General Dyer at Jallianwala Bagh as having prevented another 'Indian Mutiny', such as the one of 1857, whereas, ironically, the massacre 'could not have dealt a bigger blow to the Empire which he was professing to save.⁷² High-ranking English ladies stood outside men's clubs and hotels with collection tins, raising money for Dyer. British admirers presented him with a ceremonial jewelled sword, inscribed to the 'Saviour of the Punjab', and in London, the *Morning Post* invited its readers to contribute to a fund for Dyer. Consequently, he received a purse of over £26,000.⁷³ While a commission of inquiry was set up, it criticised Dyer merely for an error of judgement. Although he was recalled from his position and lost his pension and the government censured his actions, a minority in the Commons and a great majority in the Lords approved of them.⁷⁴

Gandhi, who till then was a supporter of the Empire, seeking merely to mend a problematic system of government, came to the conclusion that it had to be ended, not amended. He had lost his faith in the fairness of British rule and started his Non-Cooperation movement, the first that sought independence for India. His loyalties were no longer divided; he had become an implacable enemy of British domination, and now a traitorous figure in general British eyes. Not long after this, the publication of E. M. Forster's book, *A Passage to India*, raised questions about the justification for British rule in India, and caused concern because of its portrayal of interracial friendships.⁷⁵

The British government worked hard to justify its subjugation of India. It facilitated the work of writers (such as Katherine

---

⁷² B. R. Nanda, *Mahatma Gandhi: A Biography*, Delhi: Oxford University Press, 1958, p. 176; Chandrika Kaul, *Reporting the Raj: The British Press and India, c.1880–1922*, Manchester: Manchester University Press, 2003, p. 212.

⁷³ See Nigel Collett, *The Butcher of Amritsar: General Reginald Dyer*, London and New York: Hambledon Continuum, 2005, pp. 402–406; Alfred Draper, *Amritsar: The Massacre that Ended the Raj*, London: Cassell, 1981, pp. 236–238; and Kaul, *Reporting the Raj*, pp. 219, 222–223.

⁷⁴ H. S. L. Polak, H. N. Brailsford, and Lord Pethick-Lawrence, *Mahatma Gandhi*, London: Odhams Press, 1949, p. 130; and Kaul, *Reporting the Raj*, p. 219.

⁷⁵ E. M. Forster, *A Passage to India*, London: Edward Arnold, 1924.

Background: Gandhi and the World

Mayo) sympathetic to their rule while suppressing reporting that criticised it or gave an overly favourable picture of the Indian cause. The British and Indian nationalists were in a battle to influence Americans, and until the time of the Amritsar massacre and Mayo's book, American papers were inclined to rely on their London correspondents. Coverage of Gandhi itself tended to go in waves, peaking during and immediately after his three major campaigns (in the early 1920s, early 1930s, and early 1940s), and falling away as Gandhi seemed to fade into irrelevance, his glory days behind him. However, with the Salt Satyagraha, the Americans had their own reporters in place, no longer relying on British news feeds.

Horace Alexander, the British Quaker educationalist, writer, and friend of Gandhi, provides a general British view of Gandhi—one quite different to the Indian or American view. He tells us that to most Britishers, Gandhi appeared as a disloyal political leader, who led unreasonable campaigns that blocked reasonable British reforms. They saw him as appealing to the emotions of the 'undisciplined millions' instead of backing the British process of political evolution that would prepare India for self-government. The actions that Gandhi led 'seemed to the British to be unwise and uncalled for'.[76]

During Gandhi's most celebrated campaign, led off with his Salt March, the British tried a new tactic. Instead of lauding their civilising efforts in the country and then labelling the nationalists as treasonous, they attempted to ridicule Gandhi's strategy. Before the Salt March had begun, the British press claimed that what remained of Gandhi's influence was confined to 'the proletarian element and hare-brained adolescence', and when it was learned that a horse had been made available to the marchers, a story headlined 'Gandhi as Godiva'[77] appeared in the English press. *Time* magazine commented

---

[76] Horace Alexander, *Gandhi through Western Eyes*, Bombay: Asia Publishing House, 1969, p. vi.

[77] See Weber, *On the Salt March*, p. 448; and Glorney Bolton, *The Tragedy of Gandhi*, London: Allen and Unwin, 1934, p. 219.

sarcastically in its cover story that 'Englishmen do their best not to be afraid of St. Gandhi, and English correspondents spend thousands of pounds every year cabling from India that his influence is waning.'[78]

From mid-September, after being mobbed by crowds in Marseilles, to early December in 1931, Gandhi was in London as the sole representative of Congress at the Second Round Table Conference to discuss India's future. Thousands greeted him as his ship berthed at Folkstone. As well as attending the Conference, he met Prime Minister Ramsay Macdonald and other high-ranking political, religious, and social work dignitaries, the Aga Khan, and Charlie Chaplin; he met King George V dressed in his usual semi-body covering garb at a Buckingham Palace reception for Conference delegates, gave speeches and interviews, met with university students, pacifists, and vegetarians, attended receptions in his honour, and visited mill hands in Lancashire that his boycotting of British cloth had put out of work. During this time he was a sensation in the British press.

While most of the British public were proud of the Empire and did not question the appropriateness of the Raj, there were also dissenting voices, particularly after the Amritsar massacre. The often well-known figures who knew Gandhi and supported him included several influential religious and political persons. The ones who wrote about Gandhi, introducing him to British audiences, included Reginald Reynolds, a young English Quaker who was staying at Gandhi's ashram at the time, and who delivered Gandhi's letter of ultimatum to the Viceroy before the commencement of the Salt March. Frederick Sykes, the Governor of Bombay Presidency, described Reynolds as 'a foolish English youth, one of a number of unbalanced young people from England and America who were attracted to India at the time'.[79] His role as Gandhi's courier made

---

[78] 'India: A Pinch of Salt', *Time*, 31 March 1930.

[79] Frederick Sykes, *From Many Angles: An Autobiography*, London: Harrap, 1942, p. 383.

Background: Gandhi and the World

him a hot news item in the British press. It also gave him the standing to found the organisation Friends of India, to champion the cause of Indian independence and Gandhi, as well as to write several books on Gandhi and the situation in the subcontinent following his return to England.[80]

Leading Quaker pacifist Carl Heath, along with Horace Alexander and writer Alexander Wilson, established, on behalf of Gandhi, the India Conciliation Group to work towards a peaceful settlement between Britain and India. Another Quaker, who had been a missionary in India for over two decades, John S. Hoyland, in his 1943 book *Indian Crisis*, wrote sympathetically about Gandhi's role in the Indian freedom movement.[81]

In England, there were also several well-known women who had thrown in their lot with Gandhi and wrote about him and the case for an independent India. Muriel Lester was one of Gandhi's close supporters and hosted him at her community centre, Kingsley Hall, when he visited London for the Round Table Conference. She wrote several books about her encounters with Gandhi.[82] Agatha Harrison was another of Gandhi's strong English supporters, coming into direct contact with him during his London visit. Although Gandhi had long believed that the freedom struggle had to be won in India, his British supporters convinced him that some structure was needed to assist in the dissemination of his and the Congress point of view in England. He called upon Agatha Harrison to fill the role. Harrison, a leading figure with the Women's International League for Peace and Freedom and a close friend of the Reverend Charles Freer

---

[80] See Reginald Reynolds, *To Live in Mankind: A Quest for Gandhi*, London: Andre Deutsch, 1951; and *My Life and Crimes*, London: Jarrolds, 1956.

[81] See John S. Hoyland, *Indian Crisis: The Background*, London: Allen and Unwin, 1943.

[82] In particular, see Muriel Lester, *My Host the Hindu*, London: Williams and Norgate, 1931; *Entertaining Gandhi*, London: Nicholson and Watson, 1932; and *It Occurred to Me*, New York: Harper, 1937.

Andrews, became something of a long-distance press secretary for Gandhi and the Indian National Congress, and the backbone of the Conciliation Group.[83]

During the inter-war period, when she got to know Gandhi, Agnes Maude Royden was one of the world's best-known women pacifists. She became one of Britain's first women preachers and pastors, as well as a prominent champion of women's suffrage. She came into close contact with Gandhi over their common interests in poverty alleviation and pacifism. During the Sino-Japanese war, she was instrumental in founding her 'peace army', which in peace circles is legendary.

Gandhi maintained his contact with Royden after he left England, and she visited him in Delhi in January 1935, when she was in India to attend the All-India Women's Conference. On the eve of World War II, Royden commented on the strangeness of the fact that the 'best Christian in the world to-day is a Hindu'. She eagerly awaited copies of Gandhi's weekly paper *Harijan*, which to her were 'like a drink of pure water in a hot and thirsty land'. She wondered whether the West's belief in force 'may succeed in undermining the Mahatma's influence with his own countrymen and convince them that force alone can meet force'. However, when Britain became engulfed in the war with Nazi Germany, Royden came to the realisation that Nazism was even worse than war, and had to tell Gandhi of her change of heart.[84]

And then, of course, there was Mirabehn, Gandhi's best-known follower. Of all Gandhi's Western disciples, male or female, Madeleine Slade, whom he had named Mirabehn, was preeminent in British public consciousness. There are two main reasons why she simply could not be ignored by the British press: her defection 'to the other side', in spite of her status as an elite British woman

---

[83] For Lester and Harrison, see Weber, *Going Native*, pp. 83–98.

[84] For Maude Royden's connection with Gandhi, see Weber, *Going Native*, pp. 99–109.

Background: Gandhi and the World

whose father was an admiral in the Royal Navy; and because for twenty-odd years she was so frequently present by Gandhi's side, including during his stay in London in 1931.[85]

The pro-Gandhi voices were mainly the voices of those who knew Gandhi personally. Although some of them at times commanded reasonably large audiences, they still very much presented a minority view. The threat to Britain during the war further pushed thoughts of nonviolence into the background. The Mahatma's writings, including his *Autobiography*, had been read by 'surprisingly few' and, unlike in America, key commentaries on him and his methods of resistance either ended up out of print or had 'curiously little impact'. Scalmer notes that in Britain, Gandhi's paper *Harijan* 'could be considered only a "negligible" influence'.[86] It took some time before Gandhi's techniques were translated into ones that were locally applicable. Then the various peace and social protest movements in Britain during the 1950s and 1960s 'were led by a group of pacifists *directly inspired* by Gandhi's example'.[87] The impact of Gandhi in Australia was seemingly so negligible that Scalmer did not look into any possible connections. And given that Scalmer is an Australian, this potentially spoke volumes.

However, before tackling Australia's Gandhi, it may be instructive to examine Gandhi's Australia—what he knew and thought about the country—and then briefly identify Australians who had personal associations with him—those who knew him, visited him, and then wrote about him.

---

[85] For Mirabehn's life with Gandhi, see Mira Behn [Madeleine Slade], *The Spirit's Pilgrimage*, London: Longmans, 1960; Tridip Suhrud and Thomas Weber (eds), *Beloved Bapu: The Gandhi-Mirabehn Correspondence*, Hyderabad: Orient BlackSwan, 2014; and Weber, *Going Native*, pp. 190–217.

[86] Sean Scalmer, 'Globalising Gandhi: Translation, Reinvention, Application, Transformation', in Debjani Ganguly and John Docker (eds), *Rethinking Gandhi and Nonviolent Relationality: Global Perspectives*, New Delhi: Orient BlackSwan, 2009, p. 180.

[87] Scalmer, 'Globalising Gandhi', p. 178.

2

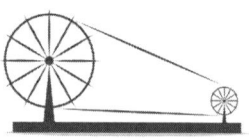

Gandhi's Australia

Mohandas Karamchand Gandhi, the young Indian lawyer working in South Africa in the cause of his countrymen, first mentioned Australia in his writings in 1896. And it was not a complimentary reference. On a brief visit back to his native India in August of that year to publicise the plight of Indians in South Africa, he published a document titled *The Grievances of the British Indians in South Africa: An Appeal to the Indian Public*. The booklet, commonly known as the *Green Pamphlet*, spelled out 'an appeal to the Indian public on behalf of the 100,000 Indians in South Africa'. However, there Gandhi also noted that: 'In Australia they are endeavouring to pass laws to restrict the influx of Indians in those parts.'[1] And he wrote a letter to his political mentor, the leading Indian politician G. K. Gokhale, where he stated that 'I have no doubt you have read the telegram about the Australian Colonies legislating to restrict the influx of Indian immigrants to that part of the world. It is quite possible that legislation might receive the Royal sanction.'[2]

By this time, Gandhi would have seen letters in the pages of Natal's papers, such as the one by 'An Australian' that stated:

> I wish for 'Colonial-born Indian's' edification he could have witnessed the reception a ship-load of coolies received in Australia

---

[1] M. K. Gandhi, *The Grievances of the British Indians in South Africa: An Appeal to the Indian Public*, Madras: Price Current Press, 1896, p. 20.

[2] Gandhi to G. K. Gokahle, 18 October 1896. See also Gandhi's speech at a meeting in Madras on 26 October 1896, where he makes a similar statement.

some years back. Like the news of a plague it spread. A ship-load of coolies were in port. The word 'coolie' was enough; crowds, in thousands, kept the wharf day and night, and not one was allowed to land. The cry from thousands echoed and re-echoed. 'Away with them to Calcutta! Back to Bombay! Away with them!' I think if they had a few more receptions like this in Natal, 'Colonial-born Indian' would have a little less self-conceit, and would think twice before making such insulting assertions. Apologising to my countrymen for deigning to reply to a coolie.

This was in response to a letter from a 'Colonial-bred Indian', who had the 'daring effrontery to compare Europeans to coolies', an assertion that was insolent and 'worthy of contempt'.[3]

A few weeks later another letter, by 'Peter Porcupine', notes that Australians

> Simply opposed the landing of Chinamen and other Asiatics in the face of all constitutions to the contrary, and when they were remonstrated with by the Universal Mother (England), they with one voice replied that the old lady must at once make up her mind whom she wants to support—Asiatics, or the Europeans. If the former, the Australians would cease to be British subjects. That carried the day.[4]

Australia was already living up to its reputation of being an exclusively white society. In a letter to the editor, the writer

---

[3] 'The Asiatic Invasion: To the Editor', *The Natal Advertiser*, 9 December 1896. From Gandhi's clippings of articles in the South African press, SN (Sabarmati Nidhi–Sabarmati Trust—*Gandhi Papers*, held at the Sabarmati Harijan Ashram, Ahmedabad), p. 1375.

[4] 'The Asiatic Invasion: Natal for the Natalians: To the Editor', *The Natal Advertiser*, SN, p. 1562. The date written on this clipping is 4 January 1897. However, this does not seem to be correct, as the printed letter is dated as having been written on 2 January 1896. It is unlikely that the letter was published a year after it had been written, especially given that 'Porcupine' was a regular correspondent.

'Boomerang', with pride rather than irony, calls Australia 'the whitest country in the world'. Boomerang was complaining that an Australian was placed on the same list of artisans entering Natal as 'Indians and other half-breeds', and finds this 'a matter that affects each and every Australian here'.[5]

Although as a subject Australia plays a very minor role in Gandhi's writings, most of what there is focuses on Australian racism, what in Australia was called the White Australia policy, a policy designed to keep out 'Asiatics'.[6]

The Issue of Racism

Less than half a year after the publication of the *Green Pamphlet*, on his way back to South Africa, Gandhi was interviewed by the *Natal Advertiser*. In answer to a question about whether Indians were currently admitted to all parts of the British Empire, Gandhi responded:

> Australia has now been endeavouring to exclude them, but the Government Bill has been thrown out by the Legislative Council, and, even if the policy were adopted in Australia, it remains to be seen whether it will be sanctioned by the Home Government. Even if the Australians were successful, I should say it would not be good for Natal to follow a bad example and one which was bound to be suicidal in the end.[7]

[5] 'Coloured Artisans: To the Editor', *Natal Mercury*, 13 January 1898.

[6] For a history of the 'White Australia' policy, see Gwenda Tavan, *The Long Slow Death of White Australia*, Melbourne: Scribe, 2005. For how it particularly affected Indians, see Kama Maclean, *British India, White Australia: Overseas Indians, Intercolonial Relations and the Empire*, Sydney: University of New South Wales Press, 2020.

[7] 'Interview to the Natal Advertiser', *The Natal Advertiser*, 14 January 1897.

The Home Government did not pass the bills. Britain was keen to maintain good relations with China, India, and Japan, and consequently urged the Australian colonies to 'adopt a less offensive and more indirect method of exclusion in the form of a dictation test in English'.[8]

Five years later, in a letter to the British Member of Parliament, W. S. Caine, Gandhi compared the situation in Australia and Canada with the one in Natal:

> In Natal, for instance, the Immigration Restriction Act, the Dealers' Licenses Act and such other Acts, of which copies have been supplied from time to time to the British Committee, are already in force. The Natal model is being followed both in Australia and Canada. Under the circumstances, it would be very difficult if not impossible to obtain repeal in Natal or altogether to frustrate the attempt of Australia and Canada to copy Natal. The key to this is to be found in Mr. Chamberlain's address to the Conference of Premiers at the time of the Diamond Jubilee..... He has met the Colonies half way, but the half way is probably more dangerous than the whole, for his sanction of indirect legislation has opened up possibilities for mischief which were never dreamt of, as you will see from my statement. Mr. Chamberlain's latest utterances are hardly reassuring. They will simply strengthen the Colonial Governments in their anti-Indian attitude. The remedy, therefore, so far as Natal is concerned, is for the Indian residents in that Colony to induce the Colonial Government to accord fair treatment, which is now more or less a matter of administration of the old laws, and where they may attempt to pass fresh restrictive measures, to appeal to the Home Government and for the friends to help them. Continued pressure from the Colonial Office and a sympathetic discussion of the Natal [question] in the Home newspapers are the chief influences that are calculated to soften the Ministers in Natal. In a measure, I think, by the aid of friends in England and India, we have succeeded there. As to Australia and

---

[8] Tavan, *The Long Slow Death*, p. 10.

Canada, the remedy is to take up the proposed measures, the text of which, unfortunately, I have not seen, and to attack the details so as to make them as lenient as possible. On the main points Mr. Chamberlain simply will not help and, if the debate is forced, he will make a speech which would embolden the Colonists in their anti-Indian attitude.[9]

Gandhi remained a keen observer of racist policies in parts of the Empire and noted the effect these can have on Indians. For example, writing about Australia's relations with Japan (which had just defeated Russia in war), he noted that

> The Government of Australia seem to have realized the strength of Japan. A Government communique recently issued says that students and traders from Japan, going on a tour of that country, will be freely admitted. They have also declared their intention so to amend their Immigration Law as not to hurt the feelings of Japan. This might benefit Indians too.[10]

However, he also noted that not all of Australia is so accommodating:

> In Western Australia, there are the same rigorous laws against Japanese subjects as against other Asiatic peoples. This has hurt Japan's feelings. The Japanese Ambassador has sent a note, demanding repeal of these laws. The Colonial Secretary, Mr. Lyttelton, has written to the Australian Government that the laws should be changed. The West Australia Minister has replied saying that the laws would be so amended that they do not hurt Japan's dignity, but that in effect they would remain unaltered. This means that the same bitter pill will now be administered to Japan with a coating of sugar.

---

[9] Letter to W. S. Caine, 26 March 1902. See also 'The Transvaal', *Indian Opinion*, 10 September 1904.

[10] 'Australia and Japan', *Indian Opinion*, 28 October 1905.

Gandhi's Australia

> What will England do in these circumstances? If the Colonies go on acting in contravention of the policy of England, the latter will either have to give up the Colonies or allow herself to be dragged along and change her own policy.
>
> What applies to Japan applies equally to India also. All the more so, because India, being a part of the British Empire, has a better claim.[11]

Half a year later, Gandhi reminded his readers of the difficulties that Japanese visitors to Australia faced: 'Though they are treated with all courtesy, inwardly the Australian feeling appears to be anti-Japanese.' On the strength of a cablegram from Melbourne, it seemed to him that Australia had rejected an invitation from the Japanese Naval Officer to visit an Australian naval vessel because 'they could not trust the Japanese', fearing that 'Japan might some day try to take possession of Australia. It appears from the leading journals of Australia that this view is held by many people there.'[12]

Sometime in 1903, Gandhi received the manifesto of the British and Indian Empire League of Australia. He called it 'important' and a healthy sign that the 'British Indians, who have settled in different parts of the world, are banding themselves in order to resist any attempt to curtail their rights as subjects of the King-Emperor.' He noted that the list of office-bearers showed not only that the Association 'evidently represents all classes of Indians', but also that 'our countrymen have been able to secure the active co-operation of some influential Europeans also'. The League aimed, in part, to 'remove certain hurtful restrictions which now operate detrimentally against natives of British India, who belong to the more enlightened classes', and sought to 'improve the social status of Indian citizens of Australia, and in doing this, will serve the dual purpose of benefiting the Indians themselves as well as

---

[11] 'Japan and the British Colonies', *Indian Opinion*, 18 November 1905.
[12] 'The Yellow Peril', *Indian Opinion*, 25 May 1906.

those with whom they are thrown in contact in their daily life'. He welcomed the foundation of the League and wished it a long and useful career.[13]

Gandhi saw Australia as a vast, underpopulated land mass where, 'The whites .... are jealous of any one landing on the island. They do not admit even men of their own race. Of Coloured peoples they are sworn enemies.' This left the north of the country almost empty and so the land remained barren, and 'must be regarded as useless wealth'. However, he noted that 'the people of Australia are now waking up to reality' and, given that Asia and Australia are neighbours, 'Asians should be allowed to settle in Australia. As such ideas spread, one may expect that Indians will eventually be able to settle in Australia.'[14]

However, until the ideas spread, Australia was making sure that non-whites would find it extremely difficult to enter the country, while 'whites have been entering in their hundreds'. Gandhi highlighted the impossible to pass tests that had to be navigated for entry: 'The test for Indians ... is so severe that not a single Indian has been able to get in so far. However, when the prejudice among the Australian people dies down, or when the official in charge is considerate, Indians may be allowed to enter after a reasonable test.'[15]

That, of course, was a possibility for some future time. While he was in the middle of his battle for Indian rights in South Africa, Gandhi saw Australia's treatment of Asians not merely as racist, but as 'wicked':

---

[13] 'British and Indian Empire League of Australia', *Indian Opinion*, 22 October 1903.

[14] 'Under-Population in Australia', *Indian Opinion*, 17 March 1906. For Gandhi's summation of the 'White Australia' policy, which he had been observing for thirty-five years, see his interview with the Australian visitor Bertram Stevens below.

[15] 'Johannesburg Letter: Confusion', *Indian Opinion*, 26 September 1908.

Gandhi's Australia

Australia has recently furnished a wicked instance of the extreme selfishness that I mentioned earlier. There, they are after the Chinese. Chinese sometimes manage to stow away to Australia. A ship is like a small settlement. It is often difficult to find a person [hiding] in the hold. To ensure that no one remains undetected, the Australian Government has ordered the hold of every steamer to be sulphurated so that the Chinese stow away is forced to come out or choke to death. Several persons have already died in this manner. The shameless and hard-hearted officials, blinded by selfishness, instead of being moved to pity by these things, gloat over them and pat themselves on the back for having so cleverly hunted out the Chinese. If anyone suggests that fumigation with sulphur be discontinued, it is not because they are anxious to save innocent lives, but because they are concerned at possible damage to the cargo. How can we accept these things about the West as civilized?[16]

While the masses may have been ill-willed, there were also more compassionate people in evidence: 'in Australia, where the other day shipwrecked men were prevented from landing because of the colour of their skin, there are Europeans who are heartily ashamed of the Colour legislation and the attitude of the masses to the question.'[17]

Those shipwrecked men need not have been trying to get to Australian shores to settle. On 3 June 1908, Gandhi wrote to Australia's Principal Immigration officer about the possibility of British Indians transhipping through Australia on their way to Fiji. On 8 July, he received a reply from the Acting Collector of Customs at the Customs Excise Office in Sydney, informing him that

> they will be allowed to land in Sydney for transhipment to the first outgoing steamer for Fiji upon Certificate of Exemption

[16] 'Johannesburg Letter: Wicked Civilization', *Indian Opinion*, 25 April 1908.
[17] 'British Indians in Australia', *Indian Opinion*, 4 February 1904.

as provided in Section 3 paragraph – h of the Immigration Restriction Act 1901–1905, provided a bond for each person in the sum of £100 with one approved surety is lodged with this office.

A copy of the relevant legislation was also sent to him. Australia was taking no chances.[18]

In 1921, Gandhi noted that 'it was Australia which led the anti-Asiatic cry'.[19] Five years later, he could still observe that racial prejudice in Australia was alive and well. He noted that for those few 'Asiatics' who had been allowed to settle in the country, there was discrimination that meant that even the well-qualified could not obtain employment.[20] This, to him, was an incomprehensible 'short-sighted policy of a nation which I otherwise admire', adding that it was bad 'on economic, ethical and political grounds'.[21]

Towards the end of his life, while talking of a living faith in God, Gandhi told his audience at a prayer meeting that people should live day-to-day and 'not stock things'. Interestingly, his assessment gave Australia as the example of the opposite. If people lived for the present, 'There would be no exploitation and no reserves as in Australia and in other countries for white men and their posterity', because 'in these distinctions lay the seed of a war, more virulent than the last two world wars'.[22] It seems that white Australian racism had left an indelible impression on him. But there were also other matters that concerned him—such as the export of Indian cows to Australia for slaughter.

---

[18] Letter from the Acting Collector of Customs in Sydney to M. K. Gandhi, 8 July 1908, SN: 4831. Gandhi's original letter is not available.
[19] 'Interview to Associated Press of India', *New India*, 2 November 1919.
[20] See 'Indians in Australia', *Young India*, 20 May 1926.
[21] 'Interview to "Stead's Review"', *The Searchlight*, 27 June 1924.
[22] 'Speech at Prayer Meeting, Amishapara', 1 February 1947, *Harijan*, 23 February 1947.

Gandhi's Australia

Cow Slaughter

Gandhi was a Hindu, and for Hindus, cows are sacred. This makes little sense in Australia where the eating of beef certainly was in Gandhi's time, and still is today, a normal and major part of the national diet. Gandhi, on the other hand, saw cow protection as one of the most wonderful phenomena in human evolution: 'It takes the human being beyond his species. The cow to me means the entire sub-human world. Man, through the cow, is enjoined to realise his identity with all that lives.'[23] Gandhi added that

> Hinduism believes in the oneness not merely of all human life but in the oneness of all that lives. Its worship of the cow is, in my opinion, its unique contribution to the evolution of humanitarianism. It is a practical application of the belief in the oneness and, therefore, sacredness of all life.[24]

And that 'my meaning of cow protection .... includes ... the protection and service of both man and bird and beast.'[25] One can only guess what an Australian cattle farmer would have made of these sentiments.

For Gandhi, there was a particular Australian connection, one that was not picked up in the Australian press. From 1929, he talked and wrote a good deal about Indian cows being sent to Australia to be butchered. Needless to say, this was not something that became a matter of local concern. It was simply a business arrangement.

In a public speech in mid-1929, Gandhi made the (for Hindus) shocking declaration that 'Nowadays, instead of protecting cows we eat them.' He continued, informing his audience and readers that

---

[23] 'Hinduism', *Young India*, 6 October 1921.
[24] 'Why I am a Hindu', *Young India*, 20 October 1927.
[25] 'Speech at All-India Cow-Protection Conference, Bombay', 28 April 1925, *Young India*, 7 May 1925.

> The reason behind a large number of cows being exported to Australia ... thanks to the Hindus of India ... is that beef worth crores [tens of millions] of rupees is being produced there. Its essence is extracted from that beef. I could make you shed tears if I described that process to you. Cows are being slaughtered there.

He notes that it is the supreme religious duty of Hindus to protect cows, stating that 'It is because we are steeped in our selfishness that we fail to see that which is there right before us.'[26] Two months later, he lamented that 'Myriads of cows are sent to Australia for being slaughtered.'[27] Some weeks later, he was again pointing the finger at wayward Hindus for allowing this situation to continue:

> Do not imagine that it is the Muslim or even the Englishman who is in the first instance responsible for this shameful state of things. We Hindus are primarily responsible for it. Cattle will be killed as they are fast becoming an economic burden on the land, and if they are not killed in India they will be shipped as they are already being shipped to Australia for its butcheries. Hindus are in the first instance possessors of the vast majority of India's cattle. It is they who sell them to butchers or their buyers.[28]

Muslims, who eat beef, are not the real culprits here because

> The number of cows sent to Australia to be slaughtered is a hundred times the number that are slaughtered in India by the Muslims. If you desire to see to it that cows are not exported abroad, you should all train yourselves in animal husbandry and act in accordance with that science.[29]

---

[26] 'Speech at Public Meeting, Kadi', 23 July 1929, *Prajabandhu*, 28 July 1929.
[27] 'Ox v. Bullock', *Navajivan*, 22 September 1929.
[28] 'The U.P. Tour – IX', *Young India*, 14 November 1929.
[29] 'Speech at Dabhan', 15 March 1930, *Prajabandhu*, 16 March 1930; *Navajivan*, 30 March 1930; and *Gujarati*; 23 March 1930.

Gandhi commenced writing a history of his ashram while in prison in 1932. The booklet was published in English in 1955. It points to a lesson that Hindus can learn from Australia's role in the slaughter of Indian cattle:

> Hindu society must discard some superstitions masquerading as religion. Hindus do not utilize the bones, etc., of dead cows; they do not care what becomes of cattle when they are dead. Instead of looking upon the occupation of a tanner as sacred, they think it unclean. Emaciated cattle are exported to and slaughtered in Australia where their bones are converted into manure, their flesh into meat extract and their hides into boots and shoes. The meat extract, the manure and the shoes are then re-exported to India and used without any compunction.
>
> This stupidity makes for the destruction of the cow, and puts the country to huge economic losses. This is not religion but the very negation of it.[30]

Finally, in a discussion on whether cow slaughter in India should be banned by law (he was against it, as the citizens of India were not all Hindus), Gandhi again reiterated the accusation, pointing out that 'some prosperous Hindus themselves encourage cow slaughter'. And, rather than doing it with their own hands, they send the cows to Australia and other countries to be slaughtered, processed, and have the products re-imported.[31]

Other Issues

The few other references to Australia in Gandhi's writing, some even praiseworthy, relate to disparate issues, including convicts, smoking,

---

[30] M. K. Gandhi, *Ashram Observances in Action*, Ahmedabad: Navajivan 1955, pp. 96–97.
[31] 'Speech at Prayer Meeting', New Delhi, 25 July 1947; M. K. Gandhi, *The Collected Works of Mahatma Gandhi*, Vol. LXXXVIII, New Delhi: Publications Division, Government of India, 1983, pp. 424–426.

and military indiscipline. In 1905, Gandhi wrote an article about the pioneer prison-reforming English Quaker, Elizabeth Fry (1780–1845). To illustrate her good works, he took Australia as his example:

> As a result of her efforts the condition of prisoners improved much. But this she considered quite inadequate. In those days, prisoners used to be deported to Australia. They were subjected to great harassment while on board ships. Even the honour of women prisoners was not safe. Elizabeth saw that all her good work was being undone on board the ships while the prisoners were being thus transported. To remedy this evil, she visited the ships at great personal inconvenience. At last she succeeded in putting an end to the sufferings of prisoners on the ships. Further, she effected some improvement in the miserable condition of the prisoners in Australia; and a law was accordingly passed to the effect that prisoners, on reaching Australia, were to be passed on to others for service after being trained there for six months. While thus sharing in the sufferings of many unfortunate persons, this good lady forgot her own suffering, and breathed her last, praying to God.[32]

Gandhi read widely and took note of activities in other parts of the world that could be of use in his campaigns. For instance, writing about the evils of smoking, Gandhi points to an Australian example:

> The Government of South Australia has noticed that smoking, besides consuming a lot of money, badly undermines the health of the people. More harm is done by cigarettes than by cigars, for the former, being smaller and cheaper, are consumed in excess. The Government therefore propose to introduce a Bill prohibiting the manufacture and sale of cigarettes.

He adds, 'When the people in a country like South Australia have begun to realise the harm done by smoking, we

[32] 'Elizabeth Fry', *Indian Opinion*, 19 August 1905.

also, we hope, will learn a lesson and come to some decision in the matter.'[33]

During World War II, Gandhi received a letter detailing rowdy and 'indecent behaviour' among Australian soldiers. A 'philanthropic lady' had invited Australian and Indian soldiers for tea, but of the over 250 Australians invited, only eight had responded. The lady, 'frantic with grief', enquired as to why her guests had not showed up. The reasons, as Gandhi fairly circumspectly spells out, do not reflect at all well on the behaviour of Australian troops. Serious indecent assault is hinted at in the Mahatma's outraged article of October 1940. When he was in Bombay, between 12 and 18 September, Gandhi had heard of the wild behaviour of the troops, but he was 'inclined to discount the stories'. However, on the 18th or 19th, when he was at Bombay station, he met some of the troops and mentioned the complaints he had heard to them, and they 'promised to set things right'. A week or so later, Gandhi even mentioned what he had heard to the Viceroy, who promised to investigate and admitted that 'the thing was serious if it was true'. Gandhi's article then becomes a tirade against the racist attitudes of whites:

> I suppose colour prejudice is as strong in Australia as in South Africa. The coloured man is dirt. There shall be no equality between the whites and the coloured races. Thus runs the South African constitution. The white man thinks that a nation containing forty crores [400 million] of people and ruled by one hundred thousand white men can only be treated as the Australian soldiers are reported to have regarded our girls, the victoriawallas and even the Indian police. The war has made no difference in the behaviour of the white man.

Gandhi questioned the steps taken to 'protect girls from the barbarity to which they were exposed', and added that if the 'facts are correctly represented' and if there was a public spirit, 'violent

---

[33] 'The Evils of Smoking', *Indian Opinion*, 21 October 1905. See also 'Juvenile Smoking', where he notes that 'in the Victorian Province of Australia', smoking for under 16-year-olds has been made illegal. *Indian Opinion*, 3 November 1906.

or non-violent', then 'no one, white or brown, would dare to touch a girl against her will'.[34] A week later, he again took up the theme, noting that the college girl who was among the first to complain to him had informed him that while the complaints were true, 'the improper behaviour stopped after a few days'.[35]

Besides the articles on racism, those on the export of Indian cows to Australia for slaughter, comments on the indiscipline of Australian troops in India, and the comparison of Australia with America (where he notes that 'Australia is peopled by those who are considered the scum of England'[36]), there is little else in Gandhi's writings and speeches about Australia. What mention there is of the country, except what we get from his discussions with a young war correspondent (see below) and the positive report of the mooted South Australian smoking ban, is generally negative. In fact, Australia featured little in his worldview and in 1924, Gandhi explained that he had 'not given much attention to Australia's problems' as he was 'too much engrossed in Indian affairs'.[37] In short, the reply to the question 'what did Gandhi think of Australia?' can be summarised as 'not much', in both senses of the answer. And this situation did not alter greatly over the next twenty-three years. The reverse, however, was not necessarily true, as a small but steady collection of curious antipodeans made their way to visit him.

---

[34] 'Disgraceful if True', *Harijan*, 6 October 1940.

[35] See 'Notes: Australian Soldiers', *Harijan*, 13 October 1940. This is not the first documented incidence of Australian troops posted overseas behaving badly. See, for example, Henry Reynolds, *Unnecessary Wars*, Sydney: NewSouth, 2016, pp. 191–195, for criminal behaviour by troops during Australia's first overseas war against the Boers in South Africa (a war in which Gandhi participated as an Indian Ambulance Corps leader); and Patsy Adam-Smith, *The ANZACS*, Melbourne: Thomas Nelson, 1978, Ch. 8, 'The Battle of Wazzir', pp. 54–57, for appalling behaviour in Cairo during World War I.

[36] Letter to Mathruadas Trikumji, 2 July 1947.

[37] 'Interview to "Stead's Review"', *The Searchlight*, 27 June 1924.

3

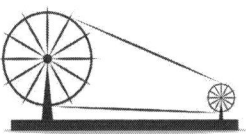

Gandhi and Australians

Gandhi had come to worldwide public attention during his anti-colonial Non-Cooperation campaign of the early 1920s. Following his spectacular Salt March in 1930, he became one of the most recognisable and famous people in the world. His correspondence, as published in the 100 volumes of his *Collected Works*, records that he received thousands of letters from (usually) well-wishers outside India (unfortunately, hardly any from Australian correspondents have been preserved). Many people also came to visit him: social reformers, peace activists, dignitaries, newspaper reporters, various faddists, and the just plain curious. Australians are relatively sparsely represented in this group, and certainly there were few as internationally well-known as the English and American personalities such as Muriel Lester, Archibald Fenner Brockway, Horace Alexander, William Shirer, Webb Miller, Margaret Sanger, Louis Fischer, Margaret Bourke-White, and Vincent Sheean, who made the trip to India to talk to Gandhi and then wrote about it.[1] However, there are noteworthy records of residents from the antipodes with personal Gandhian connections. The reports of their encounters, usually far more positive in their portrayal of Gandhi than those syndicated from the standard British or Indian sources, did make it into print in Australia. While at times providing fresh insights into the mind

---

[1] See Thomas Weber, *Gandhi at First Sight*, New Delhi: Roli, 2015.

of the Mahatma, most of these primary source materials have not been accessed by Gandhi scholars.

Some Little-Known Visitors

One of these visitors was the 28-year-old Reverend Bertram Russell Wyllie, later to become the master of Wesley College at the University of Sydney and then the University's deputy chancellor. As travelling secretary of the Student Christian Movement, he was one of the Australian representatives at the General Committee meeting of the World Student Christian Federation in India in 1928, and was Gandhi's guest for a few days.[2] He went on to speak favourably about Gandhi in public lectures (for example, to the Newcastle Rotary Club) while Gandhi was in prison during World War II.[3]

Then C. V. Thornton, an 'Australian youth', is reported to have gone to India 'recently' in order to help India 'to fight for freedom' and had joined Gandhi's volunteers during the 1930 Salt Satyagraha. He discarded his hat 'and is now wearing a homespun head covering, which is a pledge to Gandhi's cause'. Somehow, he was to violate the Salt Laws at the height of the campaign not long before Gandhi's arrest.[4]

Another young Australian interviewed Gandhi and had breakfast with him when the Mahatma was in London in 1931. H. A. Sage provided a detailed description of Gandhi's accommodation in the poor Bow district:

---

[2] 'Farmer's Son in Varsity Post', *The Herald* (Melbourne), 5 September 1932, p. 3.

[3] 'Gandhi Fights with Respect', *The Newcastle Sun*, 29 November 1943, p. 3.

[4] 'Australian in Gandhi's Cause', *Evening News* (Sydney), 21 April 1930, p. 1. This short note appeared the following day in several other papers, including *The Sydney Morning Herald* and *The Melbourne Age*.

Gandhi and Australians

I arrived at Kingsley Hall at 8.30 a.m. on September 18. Two policemen stood on guard at the entrance. I was asked to enter and take a seat, and told that Gandhi would see me in a few minutes. Several women were there, some English, with many flowers, which they hoped to present to the Mahatma, and at the same time tell him of their sympathy for his mission.

After waiting for about ten minutes a Hindu servant asked me to follow him to Gandhi's room, which proved to be situated on the roof. Here again I was obliged to wait. While waiting I looked round and discovered that Gandhi and his staff occupied three rooms....

The rooms were furnished alike with the barest of necessities—a mattress, which was on the floor, one chair, and a small mat, Gandhi's room being different only so far as it contained a radiator.

.... I was now informed that Gandhi was ready to receive me. I approached his room and bade him 'good morning'. I hesitated to enter as there was only one chair, and that was being utilised for the radiator. Gandhi mistook my hesitation for shyness and he reached and caught my arm and pulled me into the room and bade me sit next to him. I was amazed at the strength he evidently possessed. Gandhi apologised for the early interview, and told me he always endeavored to get as much business as possible done before noon.

At that moment Miss Slade entered with his breakfast, which consisted of grapes, grape-fruit, nuts, with water. He apologised again to me, saying that he could talk and eat at the same time. I noticed that the fruit was evidently the best that could be procured. He invited me to join him at breakfast.

He also gave a description of the Mahatma and his dietary habits:

> I took stock of his appearance, and found him to be very short of stature, painfully thin, with partially bald head with the usual small tuft of hair that Hindus wear, which has a religious significance. He had very few teeth. His eyes were shrewd, piercing. He was sitting on his mattress and wore a white shawl

of spun cotton. Gandhi's diet consists of fruits and nuts, with no meat, as the eating of flesh is forbidden by the Hindu religion, with goats' milk or water to drink, either plain or flavored with salt or soda.

Sage thought that Gandhi had studied Law at Oxford (it was in London) and that this resulted in his perfect, well-modulated, and distinct voice. He noted that although Gandhi had been called to the Bar, his name was later removed from the register. Consequently, 'He is prone to joke on this matter, and once signed his passport, "ex-barrister"'. He gave his visitor the 'impression of being quick and intelligent'. Sage also informed his readers about Gandhi's silent Mondays: 'by not holding conversation with any one on that day he can direct the entire resources of his mind to the formation of a plan to free his people'. This period of silence could only be broken 'in the event of a matter of paramount importance arising that needed his counsel. He informed me that he could also concentrate his thoughts on his "mission of peace" better whilst he was spinning on his spinning wheel.'[5]

Three Australian airmen also provided descriptions of Gandhi when they were taken to see him after his release from prison in 1944 by the author, journalist, and war correspondent Ronald Cecil McKie.[6] In May 1943, McKie had enlisted in the Australian Army as a gunner, but less than nine months later was discharged because he was required for the essential occupation of accredited war correspondent. He was covering the India–Burma war theatre

[5] H. A. Sage, 'If Gandhi "Fasts Unto Death"', *The Sun* (Sydney), 18 September 1932, p. 5.

[6] For biographical details of McKie's life, see Cheryl Taylor, 'Ronald Cecil McKie (1909–1991)', in Melanie Nolan (ed.), *Australian Dictionary of Biography*, National Centre of Biography, Australian National University, Vol. 19. Available at adb.anu.edu.au/biography/mckie-ronald-cecil-15568/text26780 (accessed November 2023).

when he took the airmen to see Gandhi. The air force members, 'probably the first Australian servicemen to see Gandhi', were members of 'a large group of R.A.A.F. personnel from the Middle East, who were awaiting repatriation to Australia after more than three years' service overseas'. Squadron-Leader Neville Ahern said of Gandhi that

> He looks like an aged baby in swaddling clothes, but there is nothing comic about him. I expected a doddering, untidy, and perhaps dirty old man. Instead he has remarkable presence, does not look anywhere near his 75 years, and is one of the cleanest individuals I have ever seen.

Flight-Lieutenant Lindsay Terry added that, 'I realise now why Indians follow him! What an entirely wrong impression pictures and cartoons published in Australia give of him! I expected to see a sort of Indian Mickey Mouse or Donald Duck, instead of a man for whom I would feel deep respect'.[7] And Flight-Lieutenant V. F. A. Rousseau, whom we are told is 'a descendant of Jean Jacques, famous French philosopher and writer', added that 'He impressed me as a man of tremendous dignity and terrific mental energy.'[8]

There were other, some more prominent, antipodeans who had personal encounters with Gandhi. At least three were well-

---

[7] For a selection of Gandhi cartoons published in the world's press during his lifetime, see Durga Das (ed.), *Gandhi in Cartoons*, Ahmedabad: Navajivan, 1970. For some unflattering cartoon images of Gandhi in the Australian press, see, for example, 'Exceptions to the Rule', *The Newcastle Sun*, 17 September 1931, p. 5; 'Untouchable', *The News* (Adelaide), 14 September 1932, p. 6; 'Lower, the Poor Indian, and the Truth About Drinking Water', *Smith's Weekly* (Sydney), 24 September 1942, p. 6; and 'Goosey-Goosey Gandhi', *The Argus* (Melbourne), 7 August 1942, p. 2.

[8] Ronald McKie, 'Australian Airmen See Gandhi', *The Daily Telegraph* (Sydney), 26 September 1944, p. 3.

known public figures in Australia, one was less well-known, one was anonymous, one was a famous writer, and another was in an official position in India that more or less ensured that there would be meetings between them.

Harriet Winifred Ponder

Writer Harriet Winifred Ponder was the author of *Java Pageant* and the biography of her friend, the celebrated English singer Clara Butt.[9] Although born in Kent, England, in 1884, Ponder was widely known as an Australian journalist and adventure traveller. She trained to be a singer at the Royal College of Music in London before migrating to Australia after the end of World War I for health reasons, including 'throat troubles' that ended her singing career. In Australia she worked as 'a domestic, dairy girl, secretary, music teacher, journalist and mail girl'. Then she started her journalistic life as the music critic and then editor of a Dalby, Queensland, paper.[10] She was described as 'A lady of undoubted culture and refinement. She drives her own car, dresses in somewhat unconventional style, is a musician of no mean qualifications, and a charming hostess.'[11] She was also a woman of private means and fiercely independent.

[9] Her biography of Clara Butt caused an international controversy as it claimed that before Butt's forthcoming tour of Australia, Australia's opera great, Dame Nellie Melba, had advised her to 'sing 'em muck! It's all they understand!' See 'Sing 'Em Muck! Amazing Charge: Clara Butt in Melba's Hot Denial', *The Sun* (Sydney), 5 August 1928, p. 2; 'Two Cables to Clara Butt: Melba's Query: "Possibly a Joke"', *The Sun* (Sydney), 6 August 1928, p. 8; 'Sing 'Em Muck: What Melba Said: A Painful Moment', *The Courier Mail* (Brisbane), 22 November 1933, p. 12; and Winifred Ponder, *Clara Butt: Her Life Story*, London: Harrap, 1928, p. 138.

[10] 'Items about People', *The Daily Standard* (Brisbane), 20 August 1923, p. 10.

[11] 'Like Kipling's Cat I Have to Live Alone: Bride Who Gives Hubby Something to Ponder Over', *The Truth* (Brisbane), 21 March 1926, p. 15.

Gandhi and Australians

In 1923, she was briefly back in London 'lecturing on immigration', but returned to Australia because 'women worth while are bound to get on there among the kindest folk in the world', adding that 'there was no reason why ladies of education should not accept domestic service in Australia, where no class prejudice existed'.[12] Her returned soldier-stonemason husband divorced her in 1926 on the grounds of desertion after she had left him, stating that 'I simply cannot tolerate married life. Like Kipling's cat, I have to live alone.'[13] She had not taken his name and was absent for most of their almost seven years of marriage.

A few years later, she was the first of the Australians to visit Gandhi and then provide detailed accounts of the encounter. In early 1928, while on a tour of India with Dame Clara Butt, she visited Gandhi daily for the week that she was staying with the family of a 'native merchant prince', that is, Ambalal Sarabhai, who was an intimate friend of the Mahatma.[14] She noted that Gandhi 'is more impressive than [India's great poet and intellectual] Tagore, and that he is the direct opposite to the poet in appearance, being small and ugly, but having a vivid personality and a brilliant wit.'[15] She also noted that Gandhi is 'certainly honest. He lives up to his beliefs, makes nothing out of his fame, and is one of the most charming personalities, and certainly the most interesting, I ever met. And he doesn't pose.'[16] In 1940, as Gandhi again started appearing regularly in the Australian press,

---

[12] See 'Lady Kitty's Letter', *The Saturday Journal* (Adelaide), 29 September 1923, p. 12; and 'A Spartan Girl: Many Adventures', *The Daily Mail* (Brisbane), 20 August 1923, p. 2.

[13] 'Like Kipling's Cat', *The Truth* (Brisbane), 21 March 1926, p. 15.

[14] Winifred Ponder, 'Rift in the Lute: Miss Slade and Gandhi: Will English Disciple Return to Society?', *The Telegraph* (Brisbane), 29 June 1934, p. 1.

[15] 'Miss Winifred Ponder: Well Known Writer's Return', *The Telegraph* (Brisbane), 26 March 1929, p. 5.

[16] 'Gandhi and Tagore: Impressions of Clara Butt's Biographer', *Circular Head Chronicle* (Sydney), 15 August 1928, p. 3.

Ponder gave a detailed account of her time in Ahmedabad with the Mahatma:

> He had been very ill, and we used to sit and talk with him as he lay on the bed, clothed only in a piece of homespun cotton round his loins.
>
> He was a brilliant and entertaining—often very witty—conversationalist. He was fond of making slight 'digs' at me now and then—as, for instance, in demonstrating to us the small handloom with one of which every member of the 'Ashram' (college) must do a spell every day, he turned to me with the remark, 'I do my "Whack" too—as you Australians say.'
>
> Instead of tea, Mrs Gandhi would bring us in cups of steaming hot milk, from the model farm which is the special pride of this particular teacher. Mrs Gandhi is a wrinkled bright eyed little woman with a skin only slightly darker than some English farmers' wives. Unlike her husband, she speaks no English, but her hospitable smile made us very welcome.
>
> Just before sunset the visitors would join with the remainder of the household at the service, or rather meeting, held daily on the river bank—a most impressive sight. Gandhi, who presided, walked to it from the house supported by his wife, to sit on a bank facing the groups of white cotton clad students sitting on the ground—men on one side and women on the other—with their hurricane lamps between them twinkling out more brightly in the fast-fading tropical darkness.
>
> Clara and I were provided with chairs at the back and it was an unforgettable sight—the rows of white-draped figures, the yellow glow of their lamps, the black shapes of the tall palms against the sky with the stars coming out and the light of the city of Ahmedabad across the river.
>
> Gandhi spoke in his beautifully modulated voice, delightful to listen to, although at the time weakened with illness, and in a language of which we understood no word.
>
> On one occasion Clara Butt took part, singing 'Abide with Me'—to the old hymn setting.

Surely, never in all her great career had that lovely voice of hers been in more impressive circumstances than when it rang out across the dark river. Gandhi told me next day he had lain awake for hours thinking of it, and that it was an experience he would never forget.[17]

A few months later, another and more detailed account of this visit was published in the Brisbane *Telegraph*. Ponder noted that it would be hard to 'find anyone in Australia who had never heard of Gandhi', but that few could have had the intimate contact that she and the late Dame Clara Butt were privileged to have had. Describing the convalescing Mahatma's physical surroundings, she informs readers that they were greeted by him

> lying on his bed in a bare, spotlessly clean white-washed room furnished only with bookshelves, a wooden bench or two, a chiffonier, and a bed, a rough-made wooden charpoy that looked as though it might have been knocked together in half an hour, covered with a sheet of clean coarse home-spun cotton.

Gandhi himself was a 'queer emaciated figure, naked save for a white loin cloth, with shaved head, prominent ears, and minus most of his front teeth—but with the brightest, most expressive eyes I have ever seen in the face of a human being.' She noted that Gandhi laughed often and talked incessantly. He was 'witty, entertaining, amazingly quick at the uptake and at repartee, with a command of English that few Englishmen could equal, a personality so vivid and arresting that all lack of physical advantages are forgotten.' He could talk, and do it brilliantly, on seemingly every subject without being didactic, and sometimes almost deprecatingly.

Ponder wanted to photograph Gandhi, but he had 'made a hard and fast rule' not to pose for picture takers. However, when

---

[17] 'Visited Gandhi at His Home in Ahmedabad', *The Mail* (Adelaide), 13 April 1940, p. 11.

asked, 'he gave one of his delightful impish grins, and said that if I should happen to "snap" him, "it would be quite an accident and he wouldn't notice it"'. This 'accident' occurred several times and the paper carried one of the resulting photographs.[18]

Although she wrote several books about her travels, Ponder never wrote at length about her India trip. She died in Melbourne in 1967.

Arthur H. Blacket

In March 1928, a Methodist clergyman, the Reverend Arthur H. Blacket, offered for foreign missionary work and was duly accepted and appointed to work in India.[19] His father was the respected Adelaide minister and historian John Blacket. Still only in his late twenties, Arthur sailed on 12 April and was soon ensconced at the Methodist mission in Azamgarh, working with the Dom 'untouchable' caste.[20] By March of the following year he had passed language examinations in Benares. A report on his activities in August had him organising the building of a clinic, doing the necessary paperwork to ensure that the operation ran smoothly, work for which he claimed he had no ability or liking,

---

[18] H. W. Ponder, 'Gandhi at Home', *The Telegraph* (Brisbane), 18 November 1940, p. 10.

[19] See 'Five Ministers at Wedding', the Adelaide *Mail*, 21 January 1928, p. 2; the South Australian *Australian Christian Commonwealth*, 9 March 1928, p. 4; the Adelaide *Register*, 9 March 1928, p. 14; and the Adelaide *Chronicle*, 10 March 1928, p. 47. For a more detailed life sketch of Blacket, see 'Rev. Arthur Howard Blacket', Government of South Australia, State Library, PRG 607.

[20] 'Church Notes', *The Advertiser* (Adelaide), 15 September 1928, p. 26. For Blacket's arrival in India, see the 'Diary of Rev. A. H. Blacket II', *Australian Christian Commonwealth*, 13 July 1928, p. 8; for his arrival in Azamgarh, see 'Diary of Rev. A. H. Blacket III', *Australian Christian Commonwealth*, 20 July 1928, p. 6; for his settling in at Azamgarh, see 'Diary of Rev. A. H. Blacket IV', *Australian Christian Commonwealth*, 27 July 1928, p. 13.

and preaching his first sermon in Urdu. In December 1929, he became the superintendent of the mission and besides evangelising, he was in charge of the weaving and carpet-making industries.²¹

On 3 October 1929, Gandhi visited Azamgarh. Blacket thought that those who dismissed Gandhi as a spent force—this being many years after the Mahatma's last mass movement and still a half-year before his Empire-shaking Salt March to Dandi and the enormous Civil Disobedience campaign that followed it—were mistaken. Blacket, 'very anxious to see and hear' Gandhi, attended the public meeting. He likened Gandhi to the apostle Paul and wondered at the incongruity of the scene: 'Was this, then, India's famed leader; a little man, thin, frail, stooping, clad in almost the minimum of coarse home-made cloth?' He then described Gandhi in a little more detail:

> There was a small dhoti around his legs, and a fold of cloth hanging loosely over the upper part of the body. When he turned towards me, I thought what a queer wrinkled face; but just then the wrinkles cleared before one of those illuminating smiles of his, and I did not think any more of the queerness of his face.

Gandhi spoke quietly, his message shouted to the vast crowd by a 'broadcaster'. The message itself was simple: moral preparation for the work of reform, the renewing of the heart first, then the nation, return to a simple life, help the poor, and eschew inter-communal enmity. Without these, Gandhi informed his audience, there would be no hope of achieving cherished national ideals. The thing that most impressed church minister Blacket was 'the quietness and avoidance of display which marked the great man—quietness—the seal of spiritual power'.²²

---

[21] 'Our Indian Mission', *Australian Christian Commonwealth*, 23 August 1929, p. 11; and *The Chronicle* (Adelaide), 5 December 1929, p. 59.

[22] Rev. Arthur H. Blacket, 'Face to Face with Gandhi', *The Advertiser* (Adelaide), 21 December 1929, p. 15.

Although he makes little of it, it seems that Blacket personally met Gandhi. He was on the dais with him at the public meeting and later tells his readers that he had 'the pleasure and honour of meeting Mr. Gandhi', and he had Indian friends who worked closely with the Mahatma. Further, Blacket notes that when Gandhi toured Azamgarh district, 'he stayed in the bungalow of one of my English friends, so that I have some personal knowledge of the strict simplicity of his manner of life'.[23]

While obviously in favour of much of what Gandhi stood for, in the lead up to the Salt March, Blacket dissociated himself 'from many of his political theories and methods', noting that if Gandhi 'has failed to give the country the right lead at this time, it seems, in large measure, that he has been the victim of logical necessity'.[24] Blacket wrote several letters to the editor of the Adelaide *Advertiser* on the topic of Gandhi. Although he championed British control of India and the value of Christian missionaries, he nevertheless went to great lengths to defend Gandhi against his critics. While noting that Gandhi's idealism could be impractical, he clung to his belief 'that he is one of the world's great characters'. The mission and mission school suffered boycotts during the campaign launched by Gandhi's Salt March, so he was in no mood to defend the movement. However, even with the sporadic outbursts of violence, he conceded that the 'miracle is that Gandhi's ideal was understood from his own living example by millions of Indians and won their allegiance'. He also defended Gandhi from charges that he was 'animated by Bolshevist principles', or that he lacked principles entirely, stating that such assertions betrayed abysmal ignorance as Gandhi was completely sincere in his repudiation of violence. He also deflected the charge that Gandhi was only in favour of medical

---

[23] Arthur H. Blacket, 'Mahatma Gandhi "Patriotism and Self-Renunciation,"' *Advertiser and Register* (Adelaide), 22 September 1931, p. 12.

[24] Arthur Blacket, 'Some Notes from India', *The Advertiser* (Adelaide), 21 February 1930, p. 23.

missionary work: 'the type of missionary who Gandhi does not welcome in India is the type blind to Indian sentiment and to the element of good in non-Christian religions.'[25] He added that he believed that 'Gandhi has done more than any other single man to make the principles of Jesus Christ known to Indians.'[26]

In a longer newspaper article, Blacket noted that the political movement with its speeches, processions, picketing, and threats was disastrous for the economy, and that many were coming around to the realisation that it was not 'paying the dividends they hoped for'. By this time Gandhi had already been in prison for half a year, and Blacket saw a growing spirit of bitterness, noting that there could be no resolution of the fraught situation because of the Indian people's 'utter lack of faith in the sincerity of the Englishman.'[27]

Although Blacket relayed the story of his encounter with the great man to the citizens of Adelaide through the pages of *The Advertiser*, he does not appear to have written more about the meeting and, following his final lengthy missive, his three years at Azamgarh came to an end. He did not write a book or major essay about his India and Gandhi-related experiences. Although he did write regularly for church papers and *The Advertiser*, one cannot help wondering how wide the readership of his letters defending Gandhi was.

Following his stint in India, he returned to Australia, married, and relocated to the Indo-Fijian mission in 1933, where he worked for twelve years.[28] Later, he became the principal of the Wesley

---

[25] Arthur H. Blacket, 'Gandhi in London: "One of the World's Greatest Characters"', *The Advertiser* (Adelaide), 2 October 1931, p. 22.

[26] Arthur H. Blacket, 'Gandhi's Ideals Christian in Spirit', *The Advertiser* (Adelaide), 9 October 1931, p. 22.

[27] Arthur H. Bkacket, 'India in the Melting Pot', *Australian Christian Commonwealth*, 7 November 1930, p. 11.

[28] See Kirstie Close-Barry, A *Mission Divided: Race, Culture & Colonialism in Fiji's Methodist Mission*, Canberra: Australian National University Press, 2015, p. 114.

Theological College in Adelaide, where he had studied theology in the mid-1920s. He died in 1972.

A. B. Piddington

What was a former Australian High Court judge doing visiting Mahatma Gandhi in 1929, writing a booklet about the encounter, and then titling the text *Bapu Gandhi*? (Bapu is an affectionate Hindi appellation, meaning 'father', used by Gandhi's closest followers.) The plain cover of the book lists the author as A. B. Piddington, and in brackets below his name we are informed that this author has a title: 'Mr. Justice Piddington'. A recent article about the legal and political life of the judge puts a possible dilemma encompassed in this meeting thus: 'The visit itself highlights Piddington's worldliness—one can hardly see many of his class acknowledging, still less visiting one of the exploders of the colonial world—alongside his naïve singlemindedness.'[29] What do we know about this person that would place him in Ahmedabad in early 1929? Did Piddington remember the meeting and its most important content the way that the Gandhi camp did? What may have been the significance of the meeting for both sides, and what more could have been gained from their exchange?

While not many will be familiar with the name of Albert Bathurst Piddington, even those who have heard of him will possibly know little more than that he holds the distinction of being the shortest serving High Court judge in Australia. A. B. Piddington was appointed to the Court in 1913 following the death of one of the justices and the expansion of the bench from five to seven members. Whether he was suitably qualified for the position was strongly debated at the time; however, it does seem clear that

---

[29] David Ash, 'Albert Bathurst Piddington', *NSW Bar Association News*, Summer 2009–2010, p. 54.

his elevation was a result of political manoeuvring by the Labor government of the day to stack the court with judges sympathetic to its view of the way the Constitution, in regard to the division of powers between the centre and the states in the relatively recently formed Federation, was interpreted. The Bar Associations and the newspapers in the major states ran vigorous campaigns against his appointment. A month after his elevation, Piddington resigned, never having sat on the bench.

Of course, there was much more to Piddington than this inglorious episode. He was born in 1862, won the University of Sydney's medal in classics in 1883, lectured English at the University for some years while studying Law, and was admitted to the New South Wales Bar in 1890. He was elected as an independent Liberal Member of Parliament for Tamworth in 1895. As a politician, he supported Federation but campaigned against its form. With great prescience, he believed that an upper house Senate would become dominated by political parties rather than serving State interests. As a social campaigner he championed radical causes such as free trade, the abolition of state Upper Houses and capital punishment, the right of women to vote and to retain teaching positions after marriage, and the need of a merits-based public service, and protested against mining on the foreshore of Sydney harbour. Unsurprisingly, his biography was titled *A. B. Piddington: The Last Radical Liberal*.[30] He was elected to the Council of the University of Sydney in 1910, was appointed as a Royal Commissioner by the NSW government to investigate labour shortages, the

---

[30] Morris Graham, *A. B. Piddington: The Last Radical Liberal*, Sydney: University of New South Wales Press, 1995. Besides this book, further biographical information on Piddington can be found in Ash, 'Albert Bathurst Piddington'; Michael Roe, 'Piddington, Albert Bathurst (1862–1945)', in Geoffrey Serle (ed.), *Australian Dictionary of Biography*, Melbourne: Melbourne University Press, 1988, Vol. 11, pp. 224–226; and Michael Roe, *Nine Australian Progressives: Vitalism in Bourgeois Social Thought, 1890–1960*, St. Lucia: University of Queensland Press, 1984, pp. 210–242.

working conditions of women and children, child endowment, apprenticeships, and industrial arbitration, all the while keeping up his legal practice, being appointed King's Counsel in 1913. In later years he headed several Royal Commissions (into the sugar industry and the basic wage), and, following the ending of the nation's trade and commerce-related Inter-State Commission that he chaired from 1913, in 1920 he spoke out ever more forcefully against the banks and their policies. Later, he called for higher taxes on the wealthy; castigated greedy capitalists for fomenting social conditions that would increase the likelihood of further wars; undertook the publication, in the Sydney tabloid *Smith's Weekly*, of what for the day were radical articles; and was involved in high-level political judicial cases. He died in 1945.

Although the biographical literature barely mentions his travels, Piddington also made several overseas trips during his life. He took absence from his teaching position in 1887 and travelled around Europe for a year, visiting universities. In 1912, as a representative of the University of Sydney, he attended a Congress of the Universities of the Empire in London, and then an International Eugenics Congress. Following the stay in London, he visited Spain, recording his impressions in his book *Spanish Sketches*.[31] In 1927, he briefly visited New Zealand, and in late 1928 he went to India to observe legal and constitutional developments in Calcutta (where he joined the Asiatic Society of Bengal as an ordinary member[32]) and Madras, as well as visiting Gandhi in Ahmedabad.[33]

---

[31] A. B. Piddington, *Spanish Sketches*, London: Oxford University Press, 1916.

[32] He resigned his membership in April 1930. See *The Journal and Proceedings of the Asiatic Society of Bengal*, 1930, Vol. 27, p. clxx.

[33] There seems to be some confusion as to the dates of Piddington's visit to India. He was clearly there for some weeks before his meetings with Gandhi and he sailed for home from Bombay the day after the meetings (see *Bapu Gandhi*, p. 48). The signed photograph the Mahatma gave to Piddington is dated '31-1-29'. The report of the visit was published in Gandhi's newspaper in March 1929. However, in a footnote on p. 19 of *Bapu Gandhi*, Piddington states that his

In 1929, he published a memoir titled *Worshipful Masters*, a chatty, name-dropping book detailing his encounters with, and hearsay anecdotes of, members of the political and legal fraternities.[34] The section of *Worshipful Masters* dealing with a visit to Mahatma Gandhi's ashram in India was published as a separate booklet in 1930. As with the rest of the original book, *Bapu Gandhi* is a lively description of things that Piddington had seen on his India trip, with brief asides about customs and gossipy stories about people he met or knew (again, often associated with the legal profession, and often with little relevance to Gandhi or even India). In this short fifty-four page booklet, he finally gets to Gandhi on page thirty-two, and even then, just in passing. It is only in the last few pages of the book that he records the conversations he had with the Mahatma.[35]

He notes that,

> It seemed to me in India that the fundamental origin of dissatisfaction with British rule is not anything oppressive or partial as between two races, but the same economic cause—the struggle between the Haves and the Have-nots—which is found in every modern population.[36]

But then, a little further on, discussing the deplorable living conditions of the masses, Piddington places all the blame on useless customs. The British Raj is not the cause of the 'deplorable state of

---

note that he was 'in Calcutta a month ago' was 'Written in June 1929', putting him in India in May, even though we know that he arrived back in Australia in February. 'June' must have been a typographical error, the month being January. Graham makes the point that while the photograph is dated 1929, 'there is no other mention of a journey in that year' (Graham, *A. B. Piddington*, p. 228).

[34] A. B. Piddington, *Worshipful Masters*, Sydney: Angus & Robertson, 1929. The chapter on Gandhi, 'Bapu Gandhi', which became the booklet *Bapu Gandhi*, is at pp. 160–199.

[35] A. B. Piddington, *Bapu Gandhi*, London: Williams & Norgate, 1930.

[36] Piddington, *Bapu Gandhi*, pp. 40–41.

human life', but is 'doing much to abolish it'.[37] In short, although he might be termed a liberal, he is still, as would have been usual for members of his class, an apologist for British imperialism. One wonders whether he may have read Mayo's *Mother India*.

On 21 January 1929, Piddington wrote to Gandhi from the Grand Hotel in Calcutta. The letter was addressed to 'Dear Mahatma Gandhi' and explained that he was 'very anxious' to meet Gandhi before his impending return home to Australia. He pointed out that 'It is not a visit of curiosity but I wish to speak with you about our living wage law with which I have been intimately connected in the past 6 years.' He informed Gandhi about his background and notified Gandhi that he would fit in with dates that suited the Mahatma, but that the best date for him was Thursday of the following week in Ahmedabad. He would arrive in the city on Wednesday, the 30th, and leave by the night train on Thursday.[38]

Gandhi and Piddington finally got to talk on the last day of January 1929. Piddington tells us that the 'talk was purely on labour questions'[39] and that he avoided 'every political question'.[40] He informs the reader that Gandhi was particularly interested in the provision made in NSW for a living wage and the supplementary child endowment system. The meeting ended with Gandhi noting by way of a question that the erstwhile judge had 'come all this way from Calcutta to tell me all this interesting news about the methods in the country?' Piddington explained that he would not have wasted such a great teacher's time if he had not 'thought there were some facts from our country worth his considering'.[41]

---

[37] Piddington, *Bapu Gandhi*, p. 44.
[38] Piddington to Gandhi, 21 January 1929. SN (Sabarmati Nidhi–Sabarmati Trust–*Gandhi Papers*, held at the Sabarmati Harijan Ashram, Ahmedabad): 15154.
[39] Piddington, *Bapu Gandhi*, p. 46.
[40] Piddington, *Bapu Gandhi*, p. 50.
[41] Piddington, *Bapu Gandhi*, p. 46.

Later that night, he had a final meeting with the Mahatma, where he tells us that Gandhi voiced his approval for the system of child endowment, noting that in this regard they in India 'must see what we can do'.[42]

His final greeting to Gandhi and his followers is recorded by Piddington as something of a humorous attempt at Hindustani. He had learned to recite the biblical Beatitudes from Matthew's Gospel from a Bible Society translation of the text. As Gandhi's white-robed followers crowded around, Piddington proudly proclaimed the set piece. Gandhi encouraged him to repeat it, while asking what language he was speaking. When he informed the Mahatma, Gandhi 'laughed heartily' and repeated the sentence with a different pronunciation. 'So heard,' Piddington informs us, 'the sentence received a murmured tribute of deeply felt and reverent acceptance.'[43]

The Indian transcript of the conversation is somewhat different and more detailed than the one given by Piddington. In an article in Gandhi's paper *Young India*, published on 28 March 1929 and headed 'Some Foreign Visitors', in a section sub-titled 'Blessed are the Peacemakers',[44] Pyarelal (of Gandhi's secretariat) writes:

> Lastly I come to a friend from Australia. He had been a judge there, and has served on a Government Labour Commission and played an important part in the introduction of the principle of compulsory arbitration and the minimum living wage in Australia. 'We in Australia have ended the anarchy of the unchecked self-will of the employers that prevails in Europe by adopting Justice Higgins's formula that no remuneration can be considered as reasonable so long as the employee cannot maintain himself and his family in a reasonable frugal degree of comfort,' he told Gandhiji. This led to Gandhiji's asking him as

[42] Piddington, *Bapu Gandhi*, p. 49.
[43] Piddington, *Bapu Gandhi*, p. 49.
[44] 'Some Foreign Visitors', *Young India*, 28 March 1929.

to what their conception of the normal size of a family was and whether any artificial methods were employed in Australia for restricting its size and if so with what effect. He admitted that the widespread prevalence of contraceptive methods had resulted in a deplorable loosening of the moral ties. 'Once the thing obtains a foothold among the people,' he observed, 'it becomes absolutely impossible to check or control it; it smoulders, and spreads like an underground fire.'[45]

This friend paid one more visit to Gandhiji late of an evening to bid him farewell. 'I have a request to make to you,' he said to Gandhiji at parting, 'I want you to repeat after me what I am going to say.' He had managed to pick up some Hindustani during his few months' stay in India and to Gandhiji's surprise, he began slowly to pronounce the words, *Mukarram hain jo sula karate hain*—'Blessed are the peacemakers.' 'Amen,' said Gandhiji much touched by this delicate tribute to India's great experiment in non-violence and the still greater delicacy of the friend in pronouncing it in Hindustani.

Piddington left India by ship from Bombay the day following his visit to Gandhi. He arrived back in Australia two weeks later. On his return, the Australian press informed its readership that he had been in India to observe the workings of the Statutory Commission under Sir John Simon in Calcutta, and that through the good offices of the Chief Justice of the Madras High Court he had the opportunity to observe village life and the conditions of the urban proletariat.[46] The Adelaide *Advertiser* gave a lengthy account of Piddington's views of the labour conditions in India:

---

[45] For Gandhi's views on birth control (celibacy even in marriage), see his debates with family planning advocate Margaret Sanger in Thomas Weber, *Going Native: Gandhi's Relationship with Western Women*, New Delhi: Roli, 2011, pp. 131–140.

[46] 'India Visited: Mr. Justice Piddington: Some Observations', *The Daily News* (Perth), 13 February 1929, p. 6.

while they were deplorable, he was not going to fault British rule. He noted that while it may have been natural to blame the government for these conditions, in fact, to him, it was obvious that it was not due to seventy years of British government, but 'to centuries during which most of the Indian people had been oppressed by one ruler after another'. The British government could not remedy the situation 'because of the existence of many religious doctrines, which were apt to stand across the path of social reform, to which Britain was pledged to pay respect'.[47] He did, however, note that there was great Indian interest in the Australian system of industrial arbitration and the issue of a living wage, and the related issue of child endowment.[48] These matters, of course, were areas close to his heart, but one is left wondering if the audiences to which he spoke on these matters were as passionate about them as he was.

A. B. Piddington's worldliness may have taken him to India and Gandhi, but his single-mindedness did not alter his class biases or his view that the struggles for some form of social justice that he championed in Australia would also be a panacea in India. His biographer notes that his sermonising 'points to the strength of Piddington's obsession with child endowment, but if he saw its application possible universally in poor, populous, non-unionised India he was obviously deluded'.[49] Had he engaged Gandhi in political issues, he would have perhaps been made to feel rather uncomfortable when the Mahatma explained what he saw as the main issues that concerned him about Australia—and they were not about child endowment, but about racism. At least they could agree on the evils of contraception!

[47] 'Mr. Justice Piddington: Visit to India', *The Advertiser* (Adelaide), 18 February 1929, p. 13.
[48] 'India and Australia: Interest in Our System of Arbitration', *The Age* (Melbourne), 14 February 1929, p. 8.
[49] Graham, *A. B. Piddington*, p. 169.

Bertram Stevens and a Young War Correspondent

Bertram Sydney Barnsdale Stevens was born in January 1889 in Sydney. He is best known as an Australian state politician who served as the Premier of NSW from May 1932 to August 1939. From the young age of sixteen, Stevens worked for several years in local government and in various civil service departments, including the state treasury. In this time the non-smoking teetotaller also served as a Methodist lay preacher and worked as an accountant. In 1927 he became a local councillor, and later that year he was elected as a member of the NSW Legislative Assembly. From 1929 until the fall of the Nationalist Party government following the Great Depression, he was the State Treasurer and, from 1930, deputy leader of the opposition.

In March 1932, Stevens became leader of the United Australia Party (into which the Nationalist Party had been absorbed); however, in May, the State Labor Government was dismissed by the Governor over a political dispute with the Federal Government. Stevens was appointed caretaker Premier. Immediately, he called an election which his party won in a landslide. Political infighting led to his resignation as Premier in August 1939. He left his State Assembly seat in 1940 and ran unsuccessfully for a Federal seat, his political career over.

Following his appointment as a Knight Commander of the Most Distinguished Order of Saint Michael and Saint George (or KCMG, a British honour for important service in foreign countries), between 1941–1942, the now Sir Bertram Stevens served as the Australian representative of the recently formed New Delhi-based Eastern Group Supply Council, a British India wartime body set up to coordinate the stockpiling of war material east of Suez. During this period, he called in on Mahatma Gandhi.

After the war, he resumed his accountancy practice and helped to found, and then served as president of, the India

League of Australia and wrote about Indian politics. He never again held public office and died, largely forgotten, in March 1973 in Sydney.[50]

Unlike Piddington, Stevens visited Gandhi during the war and, also unlike Piddington, was quite ready to take up political questions. During the first few days of April 1942, while Gandhi was in Delhi to confer with the Congress Working Committee about its position on the war and the Stafford Cripps proposals about India's future after its conclusion, Stevens took the opportunity to interview him.

Stevens was one of those who had no particular business matters to discuss with the Mahatma; he merely wanted to make Gandhi's acquaintance before he left his position in Delhi.[51] Gandhi, who must have been overwhelmed by those wanting of his time, was gracious enough to ask Stevens to accompany him on his early morning walk on the lawns of Birla House, the palatial residence of his industrialist supporter G. D. Birla. They talked for half-an-hour. Stevens told Gandhi that he had heard much about him from Birla, and noted that while the Mahatma had been to England and Europe and had stayed long in South Africa, he had never visited Australia. In his response, Gandhi, rather cheekily taking a dig at the White Australia policy, replied with a smile that it was no thanks to the Australian government. Stevens commented that Gandhi had made 'a very good reply'. Gandhi agreed. The Mahatma then pointed out that Australia was large enough to 'absorb millions and millions of human beings', and added that he knew what Australia was doing: 'I have followed the history of your country for over 35 years. White Australia is your policy, and as

---

[50] For biographical details of the life of Bertram Stevens, see John M. Ward, 'Stevens, Sir Bertram Sydney (1889–1973)', in Geoffrey Serle (ed.), *Australian Dictionary of Biography*, Melbourne: Melbourne University Press, 1990, Vol. 12, pp. 74–77.

[51] 'Supply Group's Future: Changed Role', *The Sydney Morning Herald*, 3 April 1942, p. 6.

a result you are without the wonderful accession of strength that would have been yours if you had followed a policy of brothering all.' In his defence of his homeland, rather than talk of deserts and poor soils, Stevens agreed with Gandhi, merely stating that the country was only 150 years old and that 'Prejudices die hard, but they are dying'. Gandhi then noted that wherever Indians had gone in the world, they were business-like and capable of taking care of themselves, adding that 'Your country with its infinite resources would have been a different country with these Indian settlers.' Although this time he did mention the low fertility of the country, Stevens again agreed with Gandhi:

> There is nothing like developing vital contacts between the peoples of different countries. During my sojourn in India I have met many people. I have found them quite capable and industrious, and the more our business people could know and come together with your business people the better for both Australia and India. And, Sir, we must not forget that the old world is already passing, old ideas are fast changing, and we are getting ready for the coming of a new world.

And to this, Gandhi gave his agreement.[52]

Five months later, back in Australia and speaking at a Constitutional Association luncheon, Stevens described Gandhi as a 100 per cent pacifist, 'whom nothing would persuade to stir the Indian nation to a military enthusiasm'. He added that Nehru, as the real leader of India's Young Nationalists, was 'obviously distressed at the suggestion that any Indian should talk of India being liberated by the Japanese.'[53]

The day before Sir Bertram Stevens had his audience with Gandhi, another Australian had also sought an interview with the 74-year-old Mahatma. While we do not know the name of

[52] Mahadev Desai, 'Two Australian Visitors', *Harijan*, 3 May 1942.
[53] 'Gandhi's Pacifism', *The Canberra Times*, 25 August 1942, p. 3.

the person, we do know that he was a young war correspondent.[54] Originally, Gandhi was not taking interviews because of his busy schedule, but, through the intercession of an unnamed friend, the correspondent was allowed to join Gandhi on his evening walk on the lawns of Birla House. They talked for about twenty minutes. In the published report of the meeting, we are given a description of the Mahatma that very much fills expectations: he walks in the garden with 'his arms on the shoulders of two beautiful young women'.[55] He is barefooted and dressed in white cotton cloth 'in the way photographers and cartoonists have made him familiar to the world'. When the reporter approached the Mahatma, one of the girls moved away so that the correspondent could walk beside Gandhi, who was given a tall cane to compensate for his missing support, and thus, walking to and fro across the lawn, began 'the strangely impressive interview'.

Gandhi refused to talk about the Cripps mission (which aimed to secure Indian cooperation during the war in exchange for full dominion status on the cessation of hostilities) or criticise the Working Committee for having a different opinion about nonviolence and his 'anti-all-war beliefs'. Talking about the evils of war, Gandhi made it personal for his interlocutor: 'I know Australians are a young and vigorous people, a race of brave men and wonderful fighters ... but I believe that it is the bravest thing of all to resist war and oppose violence.'[56] Gandhi added that this was not a new conviction for him as he had reached that conclusion in 1905, recorded it in 1908, and had continually advocated that position since. The reporter concludes his account with Gandhi's

---

[54] The Brisbane *Telegraph* merely states that the report is a 'Telegraph Special'; see 'On "Anti-All-War" Doctrine Gandhi has not Convinced Practical Indian Leaders', *The Telegraph* (Brisbane), 6 April 1942, p. 4. *The Age* says that the report is by 'The Age Special Correspondent'; see 'The Influence of Gandhi: Anti-War Beliefs Emphasised', *The Age* (Melbourne), 6 April 1942, p. 2.
[55] 'On "Anti-All-War" Doctrine', *The Telegraph* (Brisbane), p. 4.
[56] 'On "Anti-All-War" Doctrine', *The Telegraph* (Brisbane), p. 4.

assertion that 'I have proved that non-violent resistance will work—I have proved it on a small scale, but as it is worked in small things so it will work in big ones.'[57]

Writing about the Australian's visit, Gandhi's secretary Mahadev Desai asks rhetorically: 'What can a war correspondent have to do with one who is proclaiming his faith against all wars?' Nevertheless, we are informed that Gandhi received him kindly. In this case, it appears that there was little banter or serious discussion between the two of them; however, we are told that 'Gandhiji simply unburdened himself for a little while as the young man walked with him during his evening stroll'. And the unburdening that this correspondent elicited from the ageing Mahatma was very revealing of Gandhi's state of mind at the time:

> What I cannot understand is man hating brother man and thirsting for his blood. I can see no justification for the war that is going on and fast enveloping the earth. It is based on hate and vengeance and will leave a crop of hate and vengeance behind. The waste of human life and material that might have been useful otherwise for the world is appalling and sickening. Why should your country and mine be involved in this war? You are a fine resourceful people. Rather than build up your country and make it useful to the rest of the world, why should you be asked to sacrifice your manhood? And what is more painful is that it is all to no purpose. I do not know why all this fighting is going on, for whose benefit, with what great end in view.[58]

[57] 'The Influence of Gandhi: Anti-War Beliefs Emphasised', *The Age* (Melbourne), 6 April 1942, p. 2.

[58] Desai, 'Two Australian Visitors'. Of course, by this time Australia had lost thousands of soldiers as Japan overran Malaysia and Singapore. Japan had recently conquered Java, landed troops in New Guinea, and had bombed Darwin. Australia was now fighting for its life. One wonders why Gandhi was still asking questions about Australia helping the rest of the world and about sacrifices of manhood.

When the reporter whispered that he doubted if anyone knew, Gandhi responded that 'perhaps God wills peace to come as a lesson of this carnage'.

When asked about the political situation in India, Gandhi merely tells his companion that he is unable to comment. Although he attends Congress Working Committee sessions and even gives advice 'in a detached way' when he is asked for it, he has not been an official Congress member for eight years and he has differences with the Committee:

> The whole nation is not with me on the non-violence question. If the nation as a whole was absolutely peaceful, I am sure we would not be in the war, I am sure we would not have this foreign domination here. The alien rulers would not be dictating to us. We should have people here from foreign lands on terms of friendship, and we should gladly make use of their talents at our will. But I am not worrying about the nation not being with me. When I have failed to convert my nearest associates, the members of the Working Committee, I have no business to be impatient with my people. It must be my fault. It means that there is not sufficient non-violence in me to enable me to carry everyone with me. But my faith in non-violence is undimmed and unshaken. In fact it is growing every day.

In a slightly different version of this interview, Gandhi is recorded as saying,

> That the nation is not behind me does not worry me. There is no cause to be impatient. What right do I have to be impatient when I know that I cannot carry even my closest associates, the members of the Working Committee, with me? It is my fault. It means that I have not yet the necessary amount of non-violence to take everyone with me.[59]

[59] See Mahadev Desai, 'How to be Worthy of Our Heritage', *Harijan*, 12 April 1942.

The seemingly shy war correspondent got his story and it was published in the Melbourne *Age* as coming from their 'Special Correspondent at New Delhi' and the following day, as a Brisbane *Telegraph* Special'. There is no by-line to give us the journalist's name. Regardless of the titles of the pieces in the Australian press, unlike Desai's version of the encounter, which focuses on pacifism and nonviolence, the reports in the Australian newspapers emphasise the stalemate, caused by the less than practical Mahatma, with regards to the Cripps proposals.

This small encounter with an Australian also provided another insight into the Mahatma's way of navigating the world. By way of a 'very human divergence from the general theme of conversation', Gandhi smilingly declared, 'as though he knew well he was providing the sort of point Pressmen seize on enthusiastically', that 'You may be surprised to know that I have never seen a cinema and never listened to the wireless.'[60] When the amazed young man asked whether Gandhi thought that such things were bad, he was told

> that cinema films are often bad.[61] About the radio I do not know. I can certainly say that I do not care to have news from all quarters of the globe within the space of half an hour. It leaves one little time to think. And why must one have news from all quarters of the globe every half hour or so? I should be content to react to my nearest surroundings and happenings therein.

By way of parting, Gandhi told the 'Australian friend' that 'Yours is a wonderful nation.'[62]

[60] 'On "Anti-All-War" Doctrine', *The Telegraph* (Brisbane), p. 4.
[61] For more on Gandhi's thoughts on the cinema, see Thomas Weber, *Gandhi at First Sight*, New Delhi: Roli, 2015, pp. 146–147.
[62] Desai, 'Two Australian Visitors'.

Gandhi and Australians

Alan Moorehead

Another, less shy war correspondent also visited Gandhi at around this time. The writer Alan Moorehead, who was born in Melbourne in 1910, educated at Scotch College and the University of Melbourne, became a reporter for the Melbourne *Herald* in 1933. Finding Australian cultural life stifling, he left for England in 1936. He covered the Spanish Civil War and then reported on the British North Africa campaign for almost three years for the London *Daily Express*, and wrote three books about his experiences during the war in Western North Africa (later published together as *African Trilogy*), becoming one of the most celebrated war correspondents. Following the war, he published a biography of Field Marshal Bernard Montgomery and a history of the Gallipoli campaign of World War I. He was probably Australia's most famous writer of the 1950s and 1960s. Unfortunately, this great communicator suffered a major stroke towards the end of 1966 that left him unable to speak, read, or write. He died in England in 1983.[63]

Moorehead visited Gandhi 'in the very middle of the war' as a 'war correspondent to interview him in Delhi'. Rather than walking with the Mahatma, Moorehead recalled that his interview (or, perhaps better described as 'an argument'[64]) took place 'on an excessively hot afternoon', and he 'sat cross-legged on the floor sweating through' his army uniform. Gandhi was leaning on a white bolster 'wearing

---

[63] For the life of Alan Moorehead, see: Tom Pocock, *Alan Moorehead*, London: The Bodley Head, 1990; Ann Moyal, *Alan Moorehead: A Rediscovery*, Canberra: National Library of Australia, 2005; Thornton McCamish, *Our Man Elsewhere: In Search of Alan Moorehead*, Melbourne: Black Ink, 2017; and John Lack, 'Moorehead, Alan McCrae (1910–1983)', in Melanie Nolan (ed.), *Australian Dictionary of Biography*, Melbourne: Melbourne University Press, 2012, Vol. 18, pp. 172–174.

[64] See Pocock, *Alan Moorehead*, p. 124.

nothing but his cotton loincloth'. The conversations were similar to those Gandhi had with the unnamed war correspondent around the same time: Gandhi remained committed to total nonviolence even in the face of possible invasion, and he (rather than Mahadev Desai) asked Moorehead: 'What is the good of our talking? You and the people you represent are committed to violence.'[65]

Moorehead recorded the meeting in some detail in *African Trilogy*: Gandhi

> came into the room, a twist of white cotton around his loins, his black barrel of a chest quite bare, nothing on his sinewy legs or feet, steel spectacles on his nose. He shook hands, smiling, and teed himself up comfortably against his white bolster. From that moment, I could never quite catch up with the argument or bring it under control. It was not so much Gandhi's quickness or his wits. Not his really overwhelming charm and the amiable wealth and patience of his pinched little face. It was that from first to last he had the tremendous advantage of being absolutely convinced that he was right.[66]

It would appear that Moorehead and the unnamed visitor were subjected to Gandhi's then current stump speech, especially one aimed at soldiers and war correspondents. Later, Moorehead also attended one or two of Gandhi's prayer meetings just before the Mahatma's assassination. He noted that Gandhi was

> still getting up at four in the morning to exercise. He was still the nimblest (and I think the gayest) good brain in India, and he was still talking in parables on precisely the same theme. Just as the evening light was failing, the loveliest time of the day in India, the trembling old man would come out of Birla House, where he was

[65] Alan Moorehead, 'Gandhi: A Last Look', *The Observer*, 1 February 1948, p. 4.
[66] Alan Moorehead, *African Trilogy*, London: Hamish Hamilton, 1944, p. 278.

Gandhi and Australians

staying, his arms around the shoulders of two pretty Hindu girls. He looked like some great gaunt bird with long bare legs, and his little dark bird-like head poking out of his white cotton dhoti. His voice was tired but he spoke with the mind of a mental athlete.

Moorehead added that he had never come across anyone who came away from a meeting with Gandhi 'without being captivated and in a slightly elevated condition' because of his 'overpowering charm under that humility'.[67]

The reminiscences of Bertram Stevens and the two war correspondents add to the picture of Gandhi that his Australian visitors helped to create.

R. G. Casey

Born in Brisbane in 1890 and educated in Melbourne and Cambridge, Richard Gardiner Casey became an engineer before being appointed Australian Liaison Officer in London in 1924. He was elected to the Australian House of Representatives in 1931 and served in various conservative governments. The Right Honourable R. G. Casey was appointed the Australian Minister in Washington (1940–1942), the Minister of State Resident in the Middle East, and served as a member of the British War Cabinet (1942–1943) before becoming the Governor of Bengal (1944–1946), during which time he had several meetings with Gandhi.[68] In 1949 he re-entered the Australian House of

---

[67] Moorehead, 'Gandhi: A Last Look', p. 4.

[68] Initially, there was disquiet in India over Casey's appointment: Casey was an Australian and Australia had a closed-door policy towards Indians. Further, questions were raised as to the meaning of the 'British Commonwealth' if British subjects, such as those from India, were not free to enter other parts of it. See Gwenda Tavan, *The Long Slow Death of White Australia*, Melbourne: Scribe, 2005, p. 38.

Representatives and two years later became Australian Minister for External Affairs. Following his retirement from politics in 1960, a life peerage was conferred on him, giving him the title of Baron Casey. He was Governor-General of Australia between 1965 and 1969. He died in 1976.[69]

As the Governor of Bengal, in late 1945 Casey had seven lengthy meetings with Gandhi. In fact, they met so often that following a day that they did not meet, a Calcutta newspaper reported that 'Mr Casey did *not* meet Mr Gandhi yesterday'.[70] In part, it seems that Gandhi wanted to talk to Casey because he was an Australian and not part of the British establishment, rather than seek further interviews with the Viceroy. He thought that Casey could provide a channel of communication to the Viceroy in a way that would be difficult for him to manage personally.[71] Pyarelal, Gandhi's secretary and later biographer, declared that the meetings between the two were 'like an oasis in the desert of long estrangement with British officialdom since the latter had declared war on Congress'. He added that they 'took to each other at their very first meeting'.[72]

Writing in 1969, the Gandhi birth centenary year, Casey stated that Gandhi was the most 'outstanding and interesting

---

[69] For biographical information on Casey, see R. G. Casey, *Personal Experience 1939–1946*, London: Constable, 1962; W. J. Hudson, *Casey: A Biography*, Melbourne, Oxford University Press, 1986; and 'Casey, Richard Gavin Gardiner (1880–1976)', in Geoffrey Serle (ed.), *Australian Dictionary of Biography*, Melbourne: Melbourne University Press, 1993, Vol. 13, pp. 381–385.

[70] Baron Casey, 'Foreword', in Newman Rosenthal, *The Uncompromising Truth: Mahatma Gandhi 1869–1948*, Melbourne: Nelson, 1969, p. v. For a detailed account of the Gandhi–Casey meetings, see Kama Maclean, 'A Colonial in the Colonies: Governor Casey, Mahatma Gandhi, and the Endgame of Empire', *Journal of Colonialism and Colonial History*, 19 (3), 2019. Available at https://muse.jhu.edu/pub/1/article/712079 (accessed November 2023).

[71] See Maclean, 'A Colonial in the Colonies'.

[72] Pyarelal, *Mahatma Gandhi, Vol. IX, Book I, The Last Phase, Part I*, Ahmedabad: Navajivan, 1956, p. 146.

individual' that he met in India. Gandhi was 'lively and endearing', and Gandhi's 'personality, integrity and warm humanity' had a tremendous impact on him. He added that 'an admirable and unusual thing' about Gandhi was the Mahatma's refusal to make a 'harsh or critical comment' about others, even those who had criticised him.[73] Much of this is a reprise of what he had written about his meetings with Gandhi in his 1947 book describing his India years.[74] There he makes the following observation:

> By far the most outstanding and interesting individual that I met in India was Mr. Gandhi. Although I believe he is 76 years old, he shows no outward sign of the weight of years.
>
> His personality is real and lively and he has great charm. He is not, on ordinary standards, a good-looking man; yet his bearing and his appearance warm one to him. You feel that here is a human being of consequence, and likeable as well.
>
> Mr. Gandhi gave me the unusual feeling, the first time I met him, that he was a man with whom one could discuss one's most intimate personal problem, and get wise and understanding advice.
>
> He is innately courteous, tactful and a good listener. He has a good sense of fun and I think, probably, also a good sense of humour. His physical gestures are simple and dramatic. A discussion with him is enlivened by a good deal of relevant and entertaining reminiscences. [....]
>
> Mr. Gandhi is a lawyer by profession, but not, as he takes pains to point out, a man of great learning. His command of English is very good, almost perfect, but slightly coloured by the almost universal Indian habit of pronouncing certain words differently from the way we pronounce them.
>
> Mr. Gandhi is credited by many of his followers with being a Saint and a Statesman. Whilst I have a considerable regard for him, I do not believe he is either. He has protested for many years against being called 'Mahatma' (holy man), but in vain. He is

---

[73] Casey, 'Foreword', p. vi.
[74] R. G. Casey, *An Australian in India*, London: Hollis & Carter, 1947.

almost universally referred to in the Congress Press as Mahatma or Mahatmaji, the respectful and affectionate diminutive.

Mr. Gandhi is an intensively religious man. Apart from his spiritual convictions he has made more than a passing study of all religions. His daily evening prayers are attended by thousands of people, and have something of the flavour of open-air revivalist meetings. To emphasise his universal approach to religion, he introduces Muslim prayers in Arabic, hymns in English, and selections from other religions.

What claims has Mr. Gandhi to statesmanship? There is a simple criterion for determining whether a man is a statesman; the passage of time should show that he was right in his major political decisions three times out of four. I do not think Mr. Gandhi can claim this record.

Perhaps one might say that amongst saints he is a statesman, and amongst statesmen a saint.[75]

The first meeting between the two occurred on the first day of December 1945 when Casey sent a note via Gandhi's emissary Sudhir Ghosh to the Mahatma, explaining that he looked forward to meeting Gandhi when the latter had rested up following his long journey from Sevagram. Gandhi responded that he could not wait for some days, but would call on the Governor that very evening. Within an hour they were deep in conversation, with Gandhi reminiscing about his days in South Africa. Two-and-a-half hours later, at 9.30 PM, Ghosh intervened, informing Gandhi that they should leave as Casey had not had his dinner yet.

Casey escorted them downstairs, through the great hall to their car.

To Casey's surprise, they found that all the 200 servants of Government House

---

[75] Casey, *An Australian in India*, pp. 58–60. See also R. G. Casey, 'Gandhi— Outstanding Man of India', *The Herald* (Melbourne), 29 April 1946, p. 4.

were standing silently in the hall in two long rows, with their palms folded in reverence. Many of them were bare-bodied and such clothes as they had on them were not the clothes in which they were fit to be seen by the Governor. The news had gone around the servants' quarters of Government House that the Mahatma had come to see the 'Lord Sahib', and the servants thought it was their great chance to have a glimpse of the great father. But they had not counted on the 'Lord Sahib' himself coming downstairs to bid farewell to the visitor; it was not done. They looked rather sheepish when they saw the Governor. Casey was surprised. Flourishing his hand at the assembled congregation, he said to Gandhiji, 'Look at all this. I assure you I did not arrange this.'

The next day, Casey said to Ghosh: 'You know I had the shock of my life—because most of these Government House servants are Muslims! I never knew that Gandhi had that kind of a place in the hearts of Muslims in this country.'[76]

And it seems that this type of reception did not happen only on Gandhi's first visit.

Casey's wife Maie, in her autobiographical book *Tides and Eddies*, noted that whenever Gandhi came to Government House, 'all our staff, clerks, domestics, gardeners, of whatever religion or caste—all living creatures—crowded the entrance hall on his arrival and departure, greeting him reverently after their own fashion. This happened to no one else who visited us.' After the formal talks with her husband had finished, Maie 'could not keep away once I had met Gandhi'. And because she was not the Governor, her 'conversations with Gandhi flowed in unrestricted freedom'. She later recalled that 'A great man came and went and the aura of peace and patience that surrounded him remained with us for a while after he had gone.'[77]

[76] Sudhir Ghosh, *Gandhi's Emissary*, London: Cresset, 1967, pp. 58–59.
[77] Maie Casey, *Tides and Eddies*, London: Michael Joseph, 1966, pp. 155–156.

Gandhi's Australia/Australia's Gandhi

On their third encounter, two days after the first, Governor Casey experienced one of the Mahatma's eccentricities. At the meeting, Gandhi passed a note to Casey requesting a time for the following day's meeting. Casey later annotated the note with the words, 'Notes passed to me by M. K. Gandhi during our "talk", on December 3, 1945—one of his silence days—during which I talked to him for 1½ hours, he said nothing.'[78] In the next two months, Gandhi and Casey exchanged many letters (Gandhi wrote to the Governor over a dozen times). They discussed the issue of the Bengal famine and what could be done about it; home-spinning and weaving; the issue of taxation on handicrafts, salt, and milk products; irrigation; the shortage of seed potatoes; the setting up of a tuberculosis sanatorium; election problems; the plight of political prisoners and of the dismissed Calcutta Electric Supply Company workers; the relocation of villagers to areas previously bombed by the Japanese; and village violence.[79] Gandhi plied Casey with literature, including a copy of his booklet *Constructive Programme*, which provided guidelines for building a future better society while dismantling the current British regime.[80] The letters demonstrate a willingness to work together in a constructive way, and have something of the tone of friendship.

As the Governor was about to leave office and India, in his last recorded letter to Casey, Gandhi pointed to problems with the British Civil Service, which could never admit to having made mistakes, and noted that if on some future day, when Casey was no longer 'trammelled by the cares of office', Gandhi could meet him and his wife, they would 'laugh heartily over the many tragedies of

---

[78] See 'Silence Day Note to R. G. Casey', 3 December 1945.

[79] See, for example, Gandhi's letters to Casey on December 3, 6, 8 (x2), 12 (x2), 16 (x2), and 24 of 1945, and January 5 and 8 of 1946.

[80] See M. K. Gandhi, *Constructive Programme: Its Meaning and Place*, Ahmedabad: Navajivan, 1941; and letter to R. G. Casey, 6 December 1945.

Bengal', which hopefully were then in the past, and 'the ludicrous mistakes lying at the bottom of these tragedies.'[81]

During one of their meetings, Casey informed Gandhi that the shawl he was wearing was not of 'very good quality'. When Gandhi defended its quality, Casey informed the Mahatma that 'What you want is something made out of real Australian wool. I'll order some, then your hand-maidens can make you something really good.' Gandhi smiled and Casey could see that 'he was pleased' because 'He has a ready sense of humor, and can always stand his leg being pulled.'[82] To enable Casey to make the presentation of wool to Gandhi personally before he left India, on 21 January 25 lbs of scoured superfine merino wool, 'especially selected by experts to produce a shawl of incomparable quality', was air freighted by the Australian Wool Board from Melbourne to Calcutta.[83] When the wool had arrived, Gandhi thanked the Governor for the gift, promising to report on the appearance of the cloths that were to be made from the gift, and 'whether Australian wool makes better blankets than the Tibetan.'[84] Later, in a letter to the Australian Government Trade Commissioner in India, Gandhi's secretary reported that 'in regard to the wool, I have had the shawls spun in my home and woven in Simla…. The shawls are a great success— warm and soft.'[85] Ironically, it was one of these shawls that Gandhi was wearing when he was assassinated. The blood-stained cloth is exhibited at the Gandhi museum across the road from his cremation ground in New Delhi.

---

[81] Letter to R. G. Casey, 8 February 1946.

[82] 'Aust. Wool for Gandhi's Shawl', *The Daily Telegraph* (Sydney), 13 December 1945, p. 3.

[83] 'Australian Wool by Air for Gandhi's Shawl', *The Argus* (Melbourne), 19 January 1946, p. 8.

[84] Letter to R. G. Casey, 8 February 1946.

[85] 'Mr. Gandhi Likes His Shawls', *Barrier Miner* (Broken Hill), 31 July 1947, p. 7.

Gandhi's Australia/Australia's Gandhi

A decade later, on 10 August 1954, during a speech on the situation in Southeast Asia in the Australian Federal Parliament, Minister for External Affairs Casey recalled a conversation he had had with Gandhi:

> He had taken very courageous and successful action at my request, by his personal intervention in a major security problem in Bengal. Needless to say I thanked him in the most sincere terms that I could. He said that I need not thank him in such terms, and went on to speak of the personal and moral responsibility of the individual for events. He made the point that a man has to accept responsibility both for what he does and for what he does not do. He went on to say, with truth, that if a man refuses to take, or fails to take, a certain action, and if things go wrong by reason of his refusal, then he has to accept responsibility for the consequences of his inactivity.[86]

Thomas Nesbitt's Letter to Gandhi

There were also those who, while not visiting Gandhi in person, wrote to him and received replies. How many Australians were in this position cannot be determined.[87] Gandhi received countless letters from admirers and critics around the world. Many were not kept or were reused. In prison, he showed his lieutenant Vallabhbhai Patel how to fold old letters into envelopes for new mail. Long before the word was in vogue, Gandhi practised recycling—and has left historians to rue his thriftiness and the

---

[86] Commonwealth, Parliamentary Debates. House of Representatives, 10 August 1954, Question, South-East Asia, R. G. Casey.

[87] Once, when I mentioned Gandhi to a neighbour, he informed me that he had a letter from Gandhi. It seems that his father had written to the Mahatma and had received a typed letter card in response. The typing, which thanked the writer for his sentiments, was obviously done by someone in Gandhi's secretariat, but the signature was Gandhi's.

resulting loss of much archival material. After Gandhi's death, there was also a culling process, with seemingly not important correspondence being discarded. What remains is mainly in the archives at the Sabarmati Ashram. Although there were possibly hundreds, this collection contains only one readily identifiable letter written to Gandhi by an Australian.

The influential 77-year-old retired Sydney public servant, Thomas Huggins Nesbitt, wrote to Gandhi in early 1930, asking if 'with all respect he may be honoured with the autograph signature of the distinguished Mahatma Gandhi preferably on a slip of headed note paper' that he could include in his 'official representative autograph book'.[88] While Nesbitt had collected the autographs of nearly 7,000 public figures,[89] it is unknown whether he received Gandhi's autograph.

---

[88] T. H. Nesbitt to Gandhi, 21 January 1930, SN: 16515.
[89] Janet Howse, 'Nesbitt, Thomas Huggins (1853–1935)', in Geoffrey Serle (ed.), *Australian Dictionary of Biography*, Melbourne: Melbourne University Press, 1988, Vol. 11, p. 2.

4

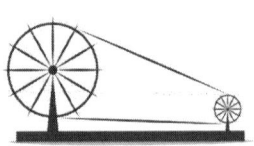

Australia's Gandhi
The Press Depictions

While generally the Australians who visited Gandhi did not have the stature of many of his American or British callers, and he did not command the interest in the press that he did in those places, nevertheless he still became known in the country through newspaper reports, through writings about him, and through the spreading of the Gandhian message by those who had an interest in his campaigns and spiritual quest, and those who had personal contact with him. As it was a time before visual mass media, the most prominent sources of knowledge about Gandhi were Australian newspapers. Very often the newspapers reproduced stories published in the British or Indian press or based their own reports on them. And often the same report, over a few days, was to appear in many Australian city and regional papers. As Kama Maclean points out, 'Overwhelmingly, reports carried in Australian mainstream newspapers came from syndicates in London, and tended to reflect an imperial righteousness and often disparaging opinions about Indian national leaders, particularly Gandhi.'[1]

---

[1] Kama Maclean, *British India, White Australia: Overseas Indians, Intercolonial Relations and the Empire*, Sydney: University of New South Wales Press, 2020, p. 176.

Australia's Gandhi: The Press Depictions

I have tried here to focus on reports from the leading papers published during Gandhi's lifetime, especially if they covered a given story before others, and particularly if the story was on the front page. However, given that there are some 60,000 reports on Gandhi in the Australian press that have been digitised on the National Library's digital portal *Trove*, many other reports and stories than those that I have included could have been used, perhaps giving a different slant to my take on Gandhi's portrayal. Further, a content analysis of the major Australian papers, looking at the number of Gandhi-related stories and the way the Mahatma was depicted in them, may demonstrate different emphases depending on the political orientation of the papers. This, however, is a task for others at some other time.

South Africa: The First Glimpses

The first mention of Gandhi in the Australian press that I could find was a record of his complaints over the treatment of Indian settlers in South Africa in the Bendigo *Advertiser* in 1895. While it might seem strange that such a story would first feature in a paper from a provincial Victorian city, rather than one from Melbourne or Sydney, in the 1890s Bendigo was still a thriving town that had come of age during the gold rush of a few decades earlier, and it still had a large Asian (mainly Chinese) population. In the report, Gandhi is described as 'one of the principal citizens among the Indian settlers in Durban', and the piece is a summary of his address to the Natal Legislative Assembly about 'the disabilities under which his countrymen suffer, and the indignities inflicted upon them by the European inhabitants of the Colony'. Gandhi talks of Indians being spat upon in the streets and pushed off footpaths, of how they were banned from riding in tramcars or using public baths. He also reminded the administration that Indian settlers were necessary and any attempt to expel them would be 'a bad day for Natal', because 'they do what the climate prevents Europeans from doing'.[2]

The most interesting part of Gandhi's account of discrimination is that he is recounting incidents that had happened to him. He tells his listeners that railway officials treat Indians as beasts and no matter how clean the Indian may be, 'his very sight is such an offence to every white man in the Colony, that he would object to sit even for a short time in the same compartment with the Indian'. And, further, that 'hotels shut their doors against them, respectable Indians having been denied a night's lodging in an hotel'. In June 1893, on the way to Pretoria to take up the legal position that had brought him to South Africa, barely a week after he arrived in the Colony, the young first-class ticket-bearing barrister, Mohandas Gandhi, was thrown off the train at Pietermaritzburg station because a white passenger did not want to share a compartment with a coloured man. This was the first overt act of discrimination that he had ever faced, and the winter's night spent shivering in the station waiting room forced him to make a decision as to whether he should fight for his rights or return to India defeated.[3] A few days later, he was beaten for not giving up his place on a stagecoach, informed that respectable hotels would not accept him as a guest, and when he did secure lodgings he was still asked to take his meal in his room because the customers were all Europeans and if he was allowed to eat in the dining room, the other guests 'might be offended and even go away'.[4] A little while later, he was kicked off a footpath. For the readers of the paper, the report seemed to be about racial discrimination in a distant colony. They could not have known

[2] 'Grievances of Indian Settlers in South Africa', *The Advertiser* (Bendigo), 4 May 1895, p. 7.
[3] M. K. Gandhi, *An Autobiography or the Story of My Experiments with Truth*, Ahmedabad: Navajivan, 1940, pp. 80–81.
[4] Gandhi, *An Autobiography*, p. 86.

Australia's Gandhi: The Press Depictions

that it was the first published episode in the life of a person they would later come to know well. Gandhi stayed in South Africa and commenced his work against the discrimination inflicted on his countrymen.

Less than two years later, Gandhi was back in the Australian press. After the publication of the *Green Pamphlet*, returning from India, he was on board the *S.S. Courland*, with Indian migrants to Natal. On 19 December, the Natal government declared Bombay, the point of departure, to be plague infected and quarantined the ship. Angry white mobs lined the docks, demanding that the passengers be sent back to India. They were not able to disembark for almost a month. When Gandhi came ashore on 13 January, he was assaulted and then blamed for having caused the trouble. Gandhi declined to have his assailants prosecuted.

In a lengthy analysis of labour issues concerning Asians in the various colonies of Britain, the Sydney *Evening News* ran a story which started off with what Gandhi had written in the pamphlet that so enraged South African whites. The report explained that Gandhi wanted the same rights for Indians as those exercised by Europeans, and that the principle that underlay the appeal would be assented to by many, and certainly more so in Britain than in her colonies. The explanation for this was:

> Suppose for the sake of argument, that there suddenly happened to Great Britain an enormous influx of Asiatics, an influx so great that all the retail trade and small handicrafts fell into their hands, and the man who now strikes on thirty shillings a week saw his work taken by a Chinaman on ten shillings a month. Would the English democracy hold forth the right hand of fellowship to these immigrants?

While Gandhi's views may 'receive considerable support not merely from philanthropists but from a large body of the public who are in no sense of the word faddists', it had to be borne in mind that 'a democracy of working people finds that if unrestricted competition is to be the order of the day, conditions will soon prevail in which there will be no room for the European working man.' While this lengthy article attempted to see matters from an Indian point of view and declared that the Boer government in the Transvaal had no right to inflict policies of extreme discrimination against Asiatic traders who had paid their dues and who had been admitted to the Colony, the government perhaps did have some right to check the free immigration of Asian traders into the Transvaal. The article concluded by pointing out that Natal and the Transvaal 'have a black labor question very like those which have troubled Australia. The upshot will be attentively watched here.'[5] The following day, the Melbourne *Age* also ran an article on the issue of Indians arriving in Durban and the protests they provoked, noting that the protesters would never let Gandhi ashore.[6]

In May 1897, Australian readers learned that Durban Indians were taking steps to oppose the Colony's immigration bills. It was mooted to send Gandhi to London to represent the Indian position to the Imperial authorities. They also learned that a petition of 5,300 signatures had been sent to Parliament by the Colonial Patriotic Union, 'asking that steps be taken to prevent the further free immigration of Asiatics.'[7] Not everything, however, went against Gandhi. In late 1899, he formed and led an ambulance corps that served in the Boer War. The readers of the Brisbane *Courier* learned that

> Mr. Gandhi, a native of India, is raising an ambulance corps of Indians in Durban. Mr. Gandhi is a lawyer, who has taken a most prominent part in the agitation of equal rights for East Indian

[5] 'A Black Labor Question', *Evening News* (Sydney), 8 January 1897, p. 4.
[6] 'Coolie Labor for South Africa: The Natal Protest', *The Age* (Melbourne), 9 February 1897, p. 6.
[7] 'South Africa: Survey of Events: Natal', *The Daily News* (Perth), 8 May 1897, p. 3.

natives in South Africa. If his corps proves a success, he will have practically won his case so far as Natal is concerned.[8]

Gandhi next featured in the Australian press in 1907. Several newspapers covered a story that garnered the headlines 'Asiatics in Revolt' and 'The Deadlock in the Transvaal'. When the Transvaal became a self-governing territory, it passed legislation requiring that Asians be registered and fingerprinted. The majority of Asians refused to obey the law and picketed registration offices, adopting the 'methods of English nonconformity' and 'have inaugurated a great passive resistance movement'. The reports noted a suggestion that a compromise might come in the form of allowing educated Indians, such as 'barristers from the Inner Temple, like Mr. Gandhi' ('the life and soul of the passive resistance movement'), to merely sign the certificates, and only the uneducated 'Ramsammy, the coolie fruit hawker', be required to give finger impressions. This is because it was difficult 'to distinguish him from a score of other Ramsammys, all as alike as two peas'. This was unacceptable to the leaders of the British Indians, who insisted that 'all must be treated alike'. The proposed system was a way for the government to know who was entitled to be resident in the Colony and to appease white fears of being swamped by Asiatics who would take their livelihoods. The papers warned that there 'is only one safe policy to pursue in dealing with the Asiatic problem, and that is to follow the lead of Australia', that if there was no compromise, either 'ten thousand Asiatics must go to gaol' or the government admit defeat. The alternatives were not pleasant and they were 'one more argument in support of a white man's country policy'.[9] Gandhi addressed a meeting of Indians on the Rand and declared that the

[8] 'War Incidents', *The Courier* (Brisbane), 9 February 1900, p. 6.
[9] See 'Asiatics in Revolt: The Deadlock in the Transvaal', *The Age* (Melbourne), 7 September 1907, p. 5. For Gandhi's own account of the campaigns against unjust laws in South Africa, see M. K. Gandhi, *Satyagraha in South Africa*, Madras: Ganesan, 1928.

sanctioning of the Act by the Secretary of State for the Colonies was a 'barbarous, savage measure', even though 'it was passed by an avowedly Christian Government'. He added that it put an undue strain on Indian loyalty. Gandhi was ordered to leave the Colony within forty-eight hours but decided to await arrest. Along with eight compatriots, he was duly arrested and then paroled.[10] A few days later, he was sentenced to two months' imprisonment without hard labour.[11] This was Gandhi's first incarceration.

Gandhi came to an agreement with General Jan Smuts, the Transvaal Colonial Secretary, regarding voluntary registration. Some of his countrymen saw Gandhi's actions as a sell-out. The Australian press, in a short report, described the aftermath: 'A number of Pathans and Punjabis at Johannesburg assaulted Mr. Gandhi and leaders of the agitation against registration by means of finger prints, as these leaders were proceeding voluntarily to register by means of affixing their signature to registration papers.'[12] There is neither sympathy nor gloating, merely a short note taken from the London papers. Gandhi then disappears from the Australian press for half a year.

In mid-August 1908, the settlement with Smuts unravelled. Gandhi is quoted as saying that while the Indians had fulfilled their part of the accord by voluntarily registering themselves, the government had breached the compact by not repealing the

---

[10] See 'Loyalty Unduly Strained', *The Daily Telegraph* (Sydney), 30 December 1907, p. 5; 'In the Transvaal: Many Indians Arrested', *The Sydney Morning Herald*, 30 December 1907, p. 5; 'Prosecution Ordered', *The Argus* (Melbourne), 30 December 1907, p. 5; 'The Lot of the Indian: Nine Ordered to Quit: All Awaiting Arrest', *The Daily Telegraph* (Sydney), 31 December 1907, p. 5; 'Indians in the Transvaal: A Deportation Order', *The Age* (Melbourne), 31 December 1907, p. 5; and many other papers.

[11] 'The Transvaal Acts: Defiant Indians Imprisoned', *The Sydney Morning Herald*, 13 January 1908, p. 7.

[12] 'The Mob's Reward: Assault on Indian Agitators', *The Sydney Morning Herald*, 12 February 1908, p. 9.

Australia's Gandhi: The Press Depictions

Act as agreed. Gandhi formally applied to have his registration papers returned to him.[13] Following mass meetings, registration certificates were burned and Gandhi 'declared that he preferred a lifetime in gaol to seeing British Indians treated like serfs'.[14] Gandhi, 'a highly educated, active-minded Indian barrister', is portrayed as the leader of the movement of resistance.[15]

After visiting Natal in connection with the agitation, Gandhi was again arrested on his return to the Transvaal for not showing his registration papers (which he had burned some weeks before) and then refusing to give a thumb impression. He was imprisoned for two months with hard labour.[16]

The first lengthy look at Gandhi as a person, and detailed analysis of the movement he led, came by way of the Launceston *Daily Telegraph*'s carriage of a story from the London *Daily Mail*'s Johannesburg correspondent, who witnessed the mass meeting and registration certificate burning on 17 August. After likening the bonfire of certificates to the Boston Tea Party, the report continues:

> Mr M. K. Gandhi [is] the acknowledged leader of something like 150,000 Asiatics in South Africa. Nervous strain was written all over the slight figure, the keen intellectual face. For a year and a half now he has been leading the passive resisters, fighting the Government, endeavoring to arrange compromises, pulling strings in India and in England. He looks back over a curious career, this Gandhi, barrister of the Inner Temple, advocate of the Supreme Court of Natal, attorney of the Transvaal, and disciple of Tolstoi. It must be more than a dozen years ago that

---

[13] 'Asiatics in Transvaal: Legalising their Status', *The Sydney Morning Herald*, 14 August 1908, p. 7.
[14] 'Transvaal Asiatics: Refusal to Register', *The Herald* (Melbourne), 18 August 1908, p. 1.
[15] 'South African Problems: Asiatics in the Transvaal', *The Daily Telegraph* (Sydney), 21 August 1908, p. 13.
[16] 'Transvaal Indians: Their Leader Sentenced', *The Age* (Melbourne), 16 October 1908, p. 5.

he went from Western India to Natal, and took up the cause of the Indians in the Garden Colony of South Africa. Anyway, he left the Prince's Dock, Bombay, on his second voyage to Natal, just at the time when plague had broken out in the Gateway of India. Two vessels, the Naderi and the Courland, sailed almost simultaneously. On arriving off the Bluff, at Durban, they were quarantined for twenty-three days. And when the Indians on board wanted to land, they found the people of Durban marching to the quays determined to repulse the immigrants by force....

Those were exciting days for Mr Gandhi. There were no bonfires then; but there were interviews with [Attorney-General] Mr Harry Escombe, and hasty escape from angry mobs. Then came the planting of the curious little colony at Phoenix, Natal—a community of Tolstoi followers who produce the paper, 'Indian Opinion,' in the intervals of cultivating the soil, and gladly work for a wage which a Kaffir house-boy would refuse.

After that the Transvaal, the fight against the Asiatic Law Amendment Act, the passive resistance movement, the ten days in gaol, and—Mr Smuts.

The Indian lawyer is proverbially keen-witted. But Mr Gandhi seems to have met his match in Mr Smuts, the Transvaal Colonial Secretary. The struggle has been very largely a personal one. That is to say, without Mr Gandhi there would have been no passive resistance; and without Mr Smuts there would have been no ground for passive resistance....

And for an audience six thousand miles away it would be foolish to attempt to explain all the details of a controversy which has become extremely complicated. But briefly—and roughly—the dispute is this. Law 2 of 1907—the Asiatic Law Amendment Act—ordered the registration of Asiatics with finger impressions. The Asiatics refused to obey it. They initiated the passive resistance movement. They went to prison. They beat Mr Smuts.... It was a moral victory for Mr Gandhi. The Indians voluntarily gave their thumb impressions....

Now the point is this. The Indians say they accepted voluntary registration on the distinct promise that Law 2 of 1907 would be repealed. Mr Smuts says that all he promised was subsequently to legalise the voluntary registration. He now proposes to do this under Law 2. But the Indians say that they have all along refused to accept Law 2, and that, therefore, they will not now acknowledge the legalisation of the certificate under it. Hence the bonfire outside the Fordsburg Mosque. The certificates to be legalised have been burnt. The Indians accuse Mr Smuts of 'slimness,' of breach of faith.... And Mr Gandhi himself and the chairman of the Indian Association have been violently attacked and almost left for dead by fanatics of their own party, because it was supposed they had consented to a compromise of an undignified character.

It is rather remarkable that both sides agree upon the main point which interests the white population. The Transvaal is determined that only Asiatics who are entitled by previous residence to be in the colony shall cross the borders. Mr Smuts has a distinct mandate from the people to insist upon this, and nothing less than this. The Transvaal has 854,000 Kaffirs to control. It has thousands of white people out of work. Therefore, it absolutely refuses to admit any more Asiatics whether they are British subjects or not, whether educated or uneducated. It claims that charity must begin at home, that what work there is going and what storekeeping there is to be done, must be saved for the white people, and not given to Asiatic strangers.

Mr Gandhi says ditto to this. But when it comes to arranging the means by which a further infiltration of Asiatics shall be prevented, trouble arises. He denounces them as insulting to British subjects. He condemns them as class legislation of the worst type—the color type. He stands for the principle of the education test instead of the color test even though in practice the principle may not be worth much.

Theoretically, academically, he is right; but the people of the Transvaal are not in the mood to discuss theories. In the first place, they say they must have protection at all costs. In the second place, they declare that the law of the land must be enforced, and that successful passive resistance will have a bad influence upon the native population.

So the struggle goes on. Who will win, it is impossible to say. Mr Smuts failed to enforce the law last time, but this time he is confident that he can succeed. But the point at issue has been so narrowed down that it does not seem impossible to arrange a compromise. Yet I fear the struggle will go on to the bitter end. It is too late to come to an agreement.[17]

Already at this stage, some of Gandhi's friends were praising him in the press and some of this was reported in Australia. For example, the well-known English Baptist pastor and evangelist, Frederick Brotherton Meyer, who had come to know Gandhi when he spent four months touring South Africa in 1908, wrote that he could

> hardly believe the evidence of my senses when I read the announcement that my friend, Mr. Gandhi, has been sentenced to two months' hard labour and to breaking stones and doing scavenger work. But I wish I were in Johannesburg that I might help him. I would count it an honour to suffer with this pure and holy soul, whom I hope to introduce to my choicest friends when he comes to England. He is not a Christian in one sense of the word, but the face of Christ hangs over his desk, and we have talked together for hours of the deepest themes that can engage the human heart. He contends only for what he holds to be the rights of the Indians who have settled in Johannesburg, many of them from before the war. His contention is retrospective for those who have entered the Transvaal and been its subjects and citizens for years.[18]

Up until the commencement of World War I, the Australian newspapers provide various small snippets of the campaigns for

---

[17] 'Transvaal Bonfire: Asiatic Defiance', *The Daily Telegraph* (Launceston), 21 October 1908, p. 8.

[18] 'News and Notes: Mr Gandhi', *The Telegraph* (Brisbane), 5 December 1908, p. 12. For Gandhi's relationship with Meyer, see James D. Hunt, *Gandhi and the Nonconformists: Encounters in South Africa*, New Delhi: Promilla, 1986, pp. 118–120.

Australia's Gandhi: The Press Depictions

Indian rights in South Africa, almost always mentioning Gandhi as the leader or director. Much is made of the arrest of members of Gandhi's family, including his daughter (even though he only had sons), following the illegal crossing of the border from Natal into the Transvaal by thousands of Indian protesters. There was another spate of reports when Gandhi was arrested several times in November 1913. And as Gandhi and Smuts finally came to an agreement concerning the issues they had struggled over for years, freeing Gandhi to finally return for good to his native India, we get a pen portrait of him quoted from the London *Evening News*, which was reproduced in the Sydney *Sun*:

> Mr. Gandhi is a man who is marked by his simplicity of attire and modest demeanor. A short, slight figure, with iron-grey hair, his whole attitude is the embodiment of gentleness and courtesy. Above all things, he is an apostle of peace.
> From the day when he was kicked on to the floor of a mail coach by a burly Dutch man who wanted his seat until that day only a few years ago when he was marched through the streets of Johannesburg in company with a chained gang of dirty Kaffirs and was afterwards herded in a cell with Chinese of the lowest order, this refined gentleman has been treated in a way that seems incredible when we realise that he was a member of the London Bar.
> In his private life Mr. Gandhi tries as far as possible to adhere to the ideals of Tolstoi. He has a refined wife and two or three children who are all fully determined to suffer with their father. He comes from an old Indian family.
> This is the man who has been sent to prison for twelve months for protesting against an unjust poll-tax of £3 and against free movement from State to State.[19]

Following his return to India in 1915, although Gandhi is the only named person in the reports of Indian unrest, the stories

[19] 'Gandhi: Leader of the Indians', *The Sun* (Sydney), 6 February 1914, p. 3.

are generally about the protests and their implications, rather than about their leader personally. The next lot of stories in the Australian press that can be regarded as featuring Gandhi were not to come until his first major campaign for Indian independence. The papers make much of the rioting that breaks out over the Rowlatt legislation and the killing of some Europeans. They also point out how this has discredited the extremists such as Gandhi, who had to call off the movement and plead for peace. However, there is very little coverage of the Jallianwala Bagh massacre. Under headings such as 'Natives Loot Trains', we learn that on 13 April 1919 'a mob defied the Viceroy's proclamation forbidding meetings. Firings ensued, and there were 200 casualties.'[20]

Non-Cooperation and the 1920s

Although Jallianwala Bagh is not mentioned in the Australian press by name until April 1923, when the British government debated the Hunter report on the massacre (referred to as an 'incident') and General Dyer gave his defence, in 1919 Gandhi was again featured regularly in reports concerning India. In April he was forbidden to go to Delhi or the Punjab, where there was unrest, and forcibly returned to Bombay when he tried to enter Delhi. As rioting broke out in several places in the country, Gandhi called off his campaign and asked followers to cooperate with the government. Gandhi's admission of a 'Himalayan blunder' in initiating a campaign that led to violence and in his underestimation of the evil in society was repeatedly proclaimed in the press. During this period of unrest, *The Sydney Morning Herald* carried a story by C. Jinarajadasa, M.A., a Cambridge scholar visiting Sydney. The readers were informed that in India, a large body of feeling wants the country to be a dominion and that

[20] 'Natives Loot Trains', *The Argus* (Melbourne), 25 April 1919, p. 7.

Australia's Gandhi: The Press Depictions

> Naturally there has been suspicion of a movement that has trained the Indians to demand the rights of colonial government, but this same movement has resolutely discouraged and discountenanced the revolutionary tactics of a very small section of extremists, who do not want to retain the link with England. Resistance to the Government is opposed by a very large section, whose influence, however, has only partly succeeded, because the influence of Mr. Gandhi has been very great amongst the masses. The crisis which found expression in the recent rioting has, however, been well settled, and the attempt which a small discontented section made to upset the settled order of things has failed.[21]

When Gandhi is mentioned in the press by religious figures, he tends to be labelled as a saint. Often ministers of religion cite his good intentions and his appeals to the words of Jesus to make his case. Often they also point out that his followers do not always grasp his ideals and violence occasionally breaks out.[22] Many other opinion pieces are not so kind. For example, an article in the Brisbane *Telegraph* informed its readers that:

> Mr. Gandhi, a well-known Indian, who has achieved notoriety as an agitator in South Africa, has recently blossomed into a Mahatma, that is, he claims to be a superman and to have religious authority over Hindus (says the 'Pioneer Mail' of 29th May). Let his adherents think as they like, but unless he is a lunatic, he must have known that passive resistance to authority of the kind he preached may be very passive indeed on the part of the well educated and intelligent, but when preached broadcast [sic] among the ignorant masses must

---

[21] 'What India Wants: Larger Share in Government: Australia as a Model', *The Sydney Morning Herald*, 11 July 1919, p. 9.

[22] See, for example, Rev. Harold Short, '"Satyagraha": "Soul Force" is Advocated by Indian Leader, Gandhi', *The Herald* (Melbourne), 21 June 1919, p. 17. Satyagraha is here defined as 'passive resistance', and it is noted that soul force is more effective than physical force and Gandhi uses the words of Christ to make this point.

invariably inflame them into very active rebellion, and require armed forces to subdue. From his recent writings, one is led to believe that Mr. Gandhi has now realised his error, but this does not excuse the mischief he has done. By proclaiming himself or allowing himself to be proclaimed as a Mahatma, he has set himself up as a guide, philosopher and friend of the Hindu public. No doubt he has been useful to those political agitators who secured his services as their catspaw, but he has done a world of mischief for which he assures us that he now is really penitent but, as his repentance is according to himself merely 'temporary' (his own word) he should be severely dealt with until his repentance is complete.[23]

Ironically, this is one of the first times he is referred to as 'Mahatma' in the Australian press.[24]

As the Non-Cooperation movement of 1920 got into full swing, the press started reporting that Gandhi's language was becoming violent. He is quoted as saying: 'When we shall use our swords again we shall warn European women and children.'[25] In fact, Gandhi had reminded his audience that they had pledged not to draw the sword, noting that while Islam permits the use of the sword, it did not countenance wanton killings, and if the audience ever did decide to draw swords, 'I am sure you would warn every European man, woman and child that their lives were not safe thenceforth. But I shall cherish the faith that you will not be obliged to come to such a decision.'[26] The shifts in the language are reasonably slight, but they distort Gandhi's meaning.

[23] 'Mr. Gandhi's Responsibility', *The Telegraph* (Brisbane), 1 August 1919, p. 2.
[24] In June 1919, an article in the Melbourne *Herald* had called him this. See Short, 'Satyagraha', p. 17. And in July, in a letter in the Melbourne paper, *Woman Voter*, the feminist, suffragist, and anti-war campaigner Vida Goldstein also refers to 'Mahatma Gandhi'. See 'Letters from Miss Goldstein', 3 July 1919, p. 2.
[25] See, for example, 'Indian Sedition: A Violent Speech', *The Sydney Morning Herald*, 18 October 1920, p. 7; and 'Sedition in India', *The Argus* (Melbourne), 18 October 1920, p. 7.
[26] 'Speech at Lucknow', 15 October 1920, *Navajivan*, 31 October 1920.

Australia's Gandhi: The Press Depictions

There was also much made of the House of Lords exoneration of General Dyer for his shooting of protesters in Amritsar the previous year and the difficulties caused by the boycott of British goods and courts as a major plank of non-cooperation. It was claimed that the movement would wreck the scheme of reform the government had instituted, 'bringing triumph to the people who uphold the methods adopted by Brigadier-General R. E. H. Dyer in suppressing the Amritsar riots.' In these reports, while Gandhi is described as 'an exalted idealist of concentrated sincerity', he is also 'deaf to all prudential argument'. His actions were opening 'the floodgate towards anarchy'. After all, if the movement develops, revenue and commerce would cease and lawyers would abandon courts, and this would engender violence. The editor of the English *Sunday Observer* is quoted as declaring that hope can be found in the fact that 'the withdrawal of nearly half the delegates from Congress before the boycott was voted, but asserts that the moderates in India must throw themselves against Gandhi's campaign if the reforms are to be saved'.[27]

Gandhi is reported as stating that India would 'pass through seas of blood before independence was attained', and that the British regime was a 'kingdom of sin'.[28] Gandhi was regularly described as the 'extremist leader' of the unrest, or as a 'violent Hindu'. However, he was also repeatedly depicted as a visionary and an idealist, but unfortunately one who was a fool with 'the dimmest notions of both his aims and the means of reaching them'. His aim seemed to be to make the country ungovernable, and somehow from that he would realise his goals. More practical Indians meanwhile could see 'in the first instalment of democratic institutions the opportunity to develop the power of a native race and achieve independence within

---

[27] 'Unrest in India: British Rule Threatened: Perilous Crisis Ahead', *The Herald* (Melbourne), 20 September 1920, p. 5.

[28] While Gandhi does call British rule 'a kingdom of sin', there is no record in his *Collected Works* of a speech or writing that mentions 'passing through seas of blood'.

the Empire'. The 'Gandhiists' may have made some progress in the cities and towns, but 'their influence upon the great inert country population is comparatively slight'.[29]

Noting that Hindus and Muslims were united in the anti-British campaign, the Melbourne *Herald* informed its readers that 'Here we have today the extraordinary spectacle of Gandhi, the violent Hindu, leading the "non-co-operation" agitation for a Moslem cause [about the position of the Sultan of Turkey as the Caliph of Islam].' The paper did, however, concede that 'native indignation at General Dyer's action, in ordering troops to fire upon the rioting mob at Amritsar, is a much more real cause of the present unrest'. It further noted that 'To the immediate future, the sinister figure of Gandhi is the chief danger. The superstitious natives regard him as a person of supernatural powers. But the educated moderates are working with success against him.'[30]

As 'Indian news is peppered with a name Gandhi', the Melbourne *Age* carried a report from the London *Daily Mail* which asked, 'what kind of a man is this?' He attracts both affection and hatred, rejects Western civilisation, and rejects modern improvements such as factories, railways, telephones, and hospitals as 'either futile or satanic'. Gandhi's genius is described as stemming from making lost causes his, adding the 'disarming sweetness of a saint' to the 'arts of an advocate'. He experiments with diet, and his asceticism is not a pose, but a 'conscious approach to the Divine'. He does not sue debtors or give evidence against an enemy and always travels third class on trains ('the acme of discomfort in India'). The question that remains is why he is known as 'Mahatma', being one 'who possesses highly spiritual, but not necessarily supernatural attributes'. The key, the paper adds, is 'wrapped in his self-revealing sentence: "Most

---

[29] No title, *The Age* (Melbourne), 22 February 1921, p. 4. See also 'India's Millions: No Menace to Australia: Missionary's Plea for Friendship', *The Sydney Morning Herald*, 16 August 1921, p. 9.

[30] 'India's Wider Future', *The Herald* (Melbourne), 12 January 1921, p. 6.

religious men I have met are politicians in disguise; I, however, who wear the guise of a politician, am at heart a religious man."'[31]

A lengthy sympathetic account of Gandhi's life and philosophy by an American correspondent in the New York *World* was also carried by Melbourne's *Age*.[32] Most accounts, however, came from British papers and were not so praiseworthy:

> Indian politicians have ... been split into two camps, those who are willing to co-operate with Britain in the good government of India and those who demand nothing short of complete self-government. Unfortunately the latter class has produced in Gandhi an agitator of amazing influence. Half political revolutionist and half religious fanatic, he has been able to play upon the ignorance and prejudices and superstitions of the semi-barbaric masses within his sphere of influence, and in passive resistance has found a weapon that is peculiarly effective against British authority. But Gandhi and his followers disturb only a small corner of a vast continent. They may easily enough be explained as the natural product of the world disturbance of the war. They are the Bolshevists of India, an evil best allowed to work out its own damnation.[33]

A regular picture of Gandhi in the press at this time is of someone who can inflame city fanatics, but is largely ignored by masses in the countryside. While he may be sincere, he is also portrayed as being extremely foolish in undertaking supposedly nonviolent campaigns that inevitably degenerate into violence, forcing him to apologise. Gandhi condemned the riots that broke out during the campaign to boycott the Indian tour of the Prince

---

[31] 'Mahatma Gandhi: The New Force in India', *The Age* (Melbourne), 26 March 1921, p. 13.

[32] 'Gandhi, the Mystic: The Newest East Indian Prophet', *The Age* (Melbourne), 2 July 1921, p. 22.

[33] No Title, *The Age* (Melbourne), 5 November 1921, p. 4.

of Wales. He undertook penance for the outbreaks by 'devoting Monday of each week to fasting and prayer'; however, much of the press described this as 'crocodile penitence'.[34] Gandhi was reported as being so upset by the Bombay riots

> that he announces his intention of swallowing nothing but water until the 'seventy and seven warring sects' [this phrase does not occur in Gandhi's *Collected Works*]—or, to be more precise, the Hindus, Moslems, Parsees, Jews and Christians—make peace with each other. Some people may doubt his sincerity, but probably without reason. For Gandhi is not the first man who, like Frankenstein, has brought into existence a monster which he is powerless to control. Visionaries like Gandhi have yet to learn that it is one thing to arouse an ignorant mob to violence and bloodshed and quite another thing to ride the whirlwind and direct the storm.[35]

A few months later, the British newspaper and publishing magnate, Viscount Lord Northcliffe, is reported as saying that after a twenty-five year absence from India, he is shocked by the changes and very worried by Hindu-Muslim unity, especially given that previously the 'Mohamedans' were 'most friendly'. He concluded that the situation has to be 'carefully handled if there is not to be disaster'. The 'Indian correspondent' who wrote the story noted that 'The outrages on the whites are so common and so serious that they are comparable to those committed during the mutiny of 1857.'[36]

The Australian press made the point that there was a pattern to Gandhi's campaigns: he stirred the masses to commence civil

---

[34] See, for example, 'Boycotting the Prince: Ghandi [sic] does Penance', *The Daily Telegraph* (Sydney), 21 November 1921, p. 7.
[35] 'Way of the World: The Man on the Box', *The Herald* (Melbourne), 22 November 1921, p. 4.
[36] 'Indian Perils: A Dangerous Situation: Natives' Increasing Temerity', *The Herald* (Melbourne), 13 March 1922, p. 6.

disobedience campaigns, insisted that they be nonviolent, the masses turned violent, deaths resulted, Gandhi had to call off the campaign, take responsibility, and fast in atonement, saying that the country had not yet achieved the level of nonviolence that he had hoped for. Then, some months later, the process would be repeated. Around the time of Gandhi's arrest, this pattern is summed up in an article where Gandhi is likened to the witches, stirring up a cauldron of trouble, in Shakespeare's *Macbeth*. He was 'leading the people of India, like Macbeth of the play, to their own destruction'. The issue was no longer which programme of political advance was better,

> but between lawlessness, with all its dangerous consequences, on the one hand, and on the other, the maintenance of those principles which lie at the root of all civilised Government. Mass civil disobedience is fraught with such danger to the State that it must be met with sternness and severity.[37]

These sentiments were also echoed by well-respected but anti-Gandhi Indian nationalists who were visiting Australia. In May 1922, Annie Besant, head of the Theosophical Society, British social reformer, and Indian resident, whom Gandhi had supplanted as the country's leading nationalist, gave an interview at the Perth headquarters of the Theosophical Society. She pronounced that Gandhi was 'hopelessly unreasonable', but deified by the common people because of the 'extraordinary amount of ignorance you have in India'.[38] And three months later, the head of the Servants of India Society (the society that Gokhale had hoped would be Gandhi's power base in India after his return from South Africa), Srinivasa Sastri, noted during a speech in Adelaide that while

---

[37] 'Wizard Gandhi: Prepares a Revolution: Stirs up Homicides', *The Herald* (Melbourne), 22 March 1922, p. 6.

[38] 'Dr Annie Besant: Arrival in Perth: Indian Ferment Discussed', *The West Australian* (Perth), 5 May 1922, p. 6.

Gandhi was admirable, his movement 'is both futile and unwise, and is foredoomed to failure'.[39]

In a similarly pro-imperialist vein, Katherine Mayo's book, *Mother India*, was extensively reviewed in the Australian press. While Gandhi is rarely mentioned—and when he is, it is as a backing for Mayo's descriptions of decadence (for example, he is quoted on the issue of child widowhood)—her book is, as she intended, a fillip for continued British domination: 'the reader is left wondering what the future can hold of races which have sunk to such an abyss of sexual depravity',[40] 'the author's conclusion will make gloomy reading for those who advocate self-government for India',[41] and the book is a 'striking vindication of British rule in India'.[42]

Following Gandhi's arrest in March 1922, not surprisingly, references to him diminish greatly in the Australian press. Until the next major civil disobedience campaign, starting in 1930, there are stories of Gandhi's release from prison following an appendicitis operation, of his waning influence, of his abandonment of political agitation in favour of social work such as the removal of untouchability and the popularisation of home spinning, discussions as to what degree he can be considered a Christian, and whether he will lose the respect of Hindus for the mercy killing of an ailing calf at his ashram. From 1924, news reports about him are occasionally accompanied by photographs.

While reporting of Gandhi had slowed, the first volume of his *Autobiography* was published in English in 1927, taking his story up to 1902. The first reference to it was by Nellie M. Scanlan, writing

[39] 'The Right Hon. V.S. Sastri: A Distinguished Indian: Visit to Adelaide', *The Advertiser* (Adelaide), 6 June 1922, p. 7.

[40] 'Indian Sociology', *The Sun* (Sydney), 4 September 1927, p. 24.

[41] 'Impotent India: Katherine Mayo's Astounding Book', *The Herald* (Melbourne), 8 October 1927, p. 19.

[42] 'Current Literature: Mother India', *The Sydney Morning Herald*, 26 November 1927, p. 9.

from Colombo, titled 'Gandhi: India's St. Francis of Assisi'. It was foreshadowing Gandhi's visit to Ceylon and wondered whether the autobiography would be published in England.[43] This was followed by long extracts in several papers from the English *Review of Reviews*, which for the first time detailed Gandhi's youthful (mis) adventures.[44] The story of his marriage at a young age and his being blinded by 'animal passion' at the time of his father's death provided a few scandalous sentences and some colourful headlines.[45]

The Salt March and its Aftermath

But of course, contrary to how it may have seemed, Gandhi was not finished. Instead, he was just about to become one of the most recognisable personalities on the planet. The decade of the 1930s provides almost half of all references to him in the Australian press. And one-third of those 1930s references were published in 1930, the year of Gandhi's most famous campaign, the one launched by his Salt March to Dandi and which saw him proclaimed as *Time* magazine's 'Man of the Year', and the following year when he attended the Second Round Table Conference in London.

Until Gandhi's pilgrimage to the sea commenced in March, reports about him were concerned with the resolution of the Congress session held in Lahore that called for independence, the boycotting of legislatures, and civil disobedience—and this was generally referred to as Gandhi's 'blunder'. These reports were also often accompanied by a picture of Gandhi in European dress, something that had not been seen for the fifteen years that he had

---

[43] Nellie M. Scanlan, 'Gandhi: India's St. Francis of Assisi', *The Brisbane Courier*, 31 December 1927, p. 18.
[44] The first being 'Gandhi: Apostle of Self-Rule: Life of Indian Leader'. *The Telegraph* (Brisbane), 26 July 1928. p. 14.
[45] See, for example, 'Married at Thirteen: The Confessions of Gandhi', *The Brisbane Courier*, 18 August 1928, p. 23.

been back in India following his time in South Africa. A report in *The Sydney Morning Herald* notes that

> A recent photograph of [Gandhi] published in Sydney, revealed him in European clothes. His doctrine makes an essential feature of Indian woven cloth for Indian backs and never in his own country has he been seen in European attire; in fact, so great is his disregard for imported clothing, that he was recently blamed for causing a large quantity of it to be publicly burned as a protest against its importation.[46]

A signed article in *The West Australian* noted that many 'armchair critics' had commented on the 'low moral tone of contemporary politics'. It was pointed out that the reverse could also be a problem when a principled leader does not realise the limitations of his disciples, this reference being to Gandhi who often had to fast to atone 'for the misdeeds of his followers'. Gandhi was universally respected, even by Europeans, for 'the sincerity of his purpose and the purity of his private life'. This perceptive article notes that the 'swaraj' (self-rule) that Gandhi sought was an internal one, not merely aimed at governments, which he regarded as satanic. And the philosophy on which Gandhi based his teachings had deep meaning for the mostly illiterate peoples of India. Now Gandhi, once 'discredited and kept on the outskirts of the political arena', was making a comeback, and 'this return to power can only appear as a calamity'. The probable dangers resulting from this 'may unfortunately be set in direct proportion to the sincerity of his convictions and the unquestionably high moral standard upon which all his actions are based'.[47]

---

[46] James H. Martin, 'Mahatma Gandhi: A Gentlemanly Rebel', *The Sydney Morning Herald*, 4 January 1930, p. 11.

[47] Fred Alexander, 'Mahatma Gandhi: A Saint in Politics', *The West Australian* (Perth), 11 January 1930, p. 4.

Other reports told the Australian reader that while Gandhi was once again a prominent figure in Indian politics, unfortunately he 'seems to be associated with certain extremists who share his political ardor more than his spiritual character.'[48] Another report on Gandhi at this time gave a similar picture of the Mahatma. A visitor to Gandhi notes that his 'almost beggar-like attitude and mildness of manner baffled those who ... had expected to find ... a firebrand, rebellious, intolerant, and thoroughly anti British. A rebel most decidedly he is, but 'a gentlemanly rebel and a sane one'; however, his 'zeal has been allowed to outrun his foresight.'[49] Further, a Mahatma who sees British rule as India's greatest curse means, in effect, that he 'would prefer to see suttee [widow burning] and thuggery still unsuppressed and child marriage regarded with no least shred of misgiving.'[50] In short, Gandhi is sometimes portrayed as a traitor or reactionary, sometimes as noble but misguided, and sometimes as an impractical idealist.[51]

Before the advent of the Salt March, the other Gandhi-related story that featured large in the Australian press was about his most prominent Western disciple, the Englishwoman Madeleine Slade, who had 'gone native' and become Mirabehn.

With the commencement of the march to the seaside village of Dandi, there to break the Salt Laws, at least in some newspapers Gandhi started appearing on the front page in the summaries of important news. Most of these reports focus on the departure of Gandhi and his ashramites from Ahmedabad ('Accompanied by 79 volunteers, Gandhi set out on his tramp, tramp, tramp to the sea coast'[52]), on the fact that the campaign would lead to violence

---

[48] 'India's Aims and Methods', *The Age* (Melbourne), 3 January 1930, p. 6.
[49] Martin, 'Mahatma Gandhi: A Gentlemanly Rebel', p. 11.
[50] 'An Indian Interlude', *The Sydney Morning Herald*, 22 February 1930, p. 16.
[51] 'Boycott in India: Growing Movement Against it', *The Age* (Melbourne), 9 January 1930, p. 8.
[52] 'Gandhi's March: Rumours of His Arrest', *The Sun* (Sydney), 14 March 1930, p. 1.

and that Gandhi knew it ('He admits there is danger of anarchy and violence'[53]), and that the start of the campaign elicited little enthusiasm and the authorities were little concerned by it (despite rumours of his arrest, the local authorities took no action other than 'posting few constables along the route Gandhi's campaign will follow'[54]), because, in effect, it was a farce ('Reports from India indicate that the opening of Gandhi's civil disobedience campaign was of a farcical nature owing to the absence of public enthusiasm'[55]). It was also pointed out that the start of the march was being boycotted by Muslims.[56] Once the Salt Laws had been broken, Australian readers were informed that Gandhi was disgusted that he and his accompanying followers had not been arrested, unlike others in the Bombay Presidency who had been, while in 'other parts of the country the opening of the campaign proved a farce'. And in any case the salt produced by Gandhi and his volunteers was 'by no means palatable, however, and comes under the Government edict of "unfit for human consumption"'.[57]

Some of these front-page stories were accompanied by photographs of Gandhi, including very old ones of him in European garb,[58] or ones that did not seem to relate to him at all. Under the caption 'Violence From Gandhi's Campaign', one paper reproduced a picture of 'native police chasing insurgents during previous outbreaks of lawlessness'. The caption to the photograph continued: 'Already clashes with the police have occurred following on the new

[53] 'The Day's News', *The Age* (Melbourne), 12 March 1930, p. 1.
[54] 'Free India: Gandhi's Aim: Wants Big Army: Fears Arrest', *Evening News* (Sydney), 12 March 1930, p. 1.
[55] 'The Day's News', *The Age* (Melbourne), 8 April 1930, p. 1.
[56] 'Gandhi's Defiant Trek: Fears Arrest: No Salt on Trail Yet', *Evening News* (Sydney), 13 March 1930, p. 1.
[57] 'Farcical Opening of Gandhi's Disobedience Campaign: Salt Salient: Disgusted over Non-Arrest; First "Honors": Public Still Unenthusiastic', *Evening News* (Sydney), 7 April 1930, p. 1.
[58] See 'Free India', *Evening News* (Sydney), 12 March 1930, p. 1.

campaign begun by Gandhi in India, rioters having been dispersed by police in two cases.'[59]

A story in the Sydney *Evening News* combined the elements of farce with a cartoon of a group of musicians happily playing the British national anthem while desperate Gandhi followers tried to stop them:

> An amusing incident occurred during a Nationalist demonstration at Bombay, pledging support to Gandhi in his disobedience campaign. A band had been hired to dispense appropriate music and to give an 'India-for-the-Indians' flavor to the proceedings, the key note of which was to be anything but British. When the Nationalist flag was hoisted in the presence of Nationalist volunteers, the hired band inadvertently played 'God Save the King.'[60]

The major newspapers also followed the progress of Gandhi's march in detail, with similar stories: Gandhi was disappointed because of the lack of hospitality and support he had received in the villages, and especially because 'A large number of village headmen who resigned under pressure from [him] have now applied to the Government for reinstatement.'[61] In government quarters, meanwhile, 'The opinion is held ... that if the authorities combine patience and firmness, Gandhi's campaign will prove a complete fiasco.'[62] The papers also reported on illness among the marchers, combining the story with a depiction of Gandhi's reactionary worldview: 'Smallpox has broken out among Gandhi's campaigners, one of whom was left behind in the village of Anand. Gandhi is a

---

[59] 'Violence from Gandhi's Campaign', *Evening News* (Sydney), 12 March 1930, p. 1.

[60] 'When Harmony Caused Discord', *Evening News* (Sydney), 14 March 1930, p. 1.

[61] 'Unrest in India: Failure of Gandhi's March', *The Sydney Morning Herald*, 27 March 1930, p. 11.

[62] 'Gandhi's Campaign: Scant Support from Villagers', *The Age* (Melbourne), 28 March 1930, p. 14.

fierce opponent of vaccination, and three children of the inmates of his settlement in Ahmedabad died of smallpox last week.'[63]

Despite all the pronouncements of the campaign developing into a fiasco, there was also some deeper analysis that backed the British position and denigrated that of those championing Gandhi and his cause:

> Following the call of a fanatic who does not present one single idea of constructive statesmanship, certain inhabitants of India are endeavouring to raise new trouble. They form a minute fraction of the mixed population of the peninsula, yet are sufficiently numerous to cause, in favouring circumstances, a great deal of perplexity. Stimulus is given them by the sinister forces which are using both them and their impracticable prophet; encouragement is also derived from the weakly, amiable tone which more than a few of the English papers and politicians adopt as befitting the occasion. That conception of sweetness and reason has not awakened the corresponding response. Gandhi, from whom at one time the best might have been expected, is now the very man who has approached the Viceroy, though in a respectful tone, with demands more extravagant than have ever been formulated save by the most irresponsible extremists. He has placed himself in line with the madmen who insist that Britain should clear out of India at a few days' notice, and has initiated a course of action which is only too likely to give the country a slight foretaste of what would ensue on the widest scale if Britain were in very truth to leave....
>
> .... He admits there is danger of anarchy and violence as the result of his campaign—a fact to which some of his followers are indifferent and many of them totally blind. But have we not always the consoling knowledge that if any such ills occur, he has promised to atone for them by fasting? ....
>
> .... Even if the demands of Gandhi and his group were reasonable in themselves, it would be out of the question to yield

---

[63] 'Gandhi's Campaign: British Troops Move', *The Sydney Morning Herald*, 20 March 1930, p. 11.

Australia's Gandhi: The Press Depictions

to the threat they imply. Such a step would bring about, more swiftly and surely than any sternness in resistance, the anarchy which Gandhi himself foresees.[64]

During Gandhi's march, a somewhat confusing letter from a resident of north Adelaide, who had lived in India and was no less critical of Gandhi and his campaign for Indian independence, was also published. 'L.A.R.O.', however, saw that the hope for it fizzling out in a fiasco was wishful thinking:

> A word about India. I was born there and lived there for years. My father put in 30 years of his military life there; my two brothers and five sisters were all born there. I served in the army there prior to and after the war. I should like to tell 'Home Rule in India' that General Dwyer was sacrificed on account of a lot of people who knew nothing then and know nothing now. The General did the only sane thing possible at Amritsar. If that riot had been allowed to go on we would have had worse trouble, and a jolly big mutiny. There was more behind the Amritsar affair than any newspaper ever published. Every country has its own internal troubles, even Australia with its Communists on the coalfields. Gandhi is working on wrong lines to obtain what he wants, but he is a big force, and has a much larger following than people give him credit for. Neither is he such a 'saint' as some people would believe. The English hold on India is very slender, and it is only a matter of time when we shall lose our oldest and richest part of the Empire. Compose the differences between the Hindus and Moslems and India would be quite fit to govern herself. In any case, the way the Europeans are behaving is one of the big primary causes of Gandhi having such a large following. Governments past or present have never carried out their promises to the Indian; all agreements have simply been treated as scraps of paper. Now that the so-called poor Indian is starting to kick against the

[64] 'Blind Leadership', *The Sydney Morning Herald*, 14 March 1930, p. 10.

many pinpricks he is the worst fellow in the world; instead of that he is one of the best.[65]

The papers reported that the government would ignore Gandhi's antics unless its hand was forced. Ironically, the central act of the breaching of the laws on the morning of 6 April was likewise ignored by the Australian press. No eyewitness reports or photographs of the drama were published. While the British press tried to belittle the event, for example by claiming that crowds wandered 'aimlessly backward and forward on the sand. There was no political demonstration of any kind and no visible elation. Indeed, the general atmosphere suggested a large size in beach picnics that have fallen rather flat,'[66] the Australian press made nothing more of the event than stating that the law had been broken and many people around the country had been arrested. The only belittling local humour came from the 'Ebb and Flow' column in the Brisbane *Telegraph* 'By D.T.H.': 'Gandhi, of course, is the man who put the salt in the sea, and, having failed to enlist the support of King Neptune, against the British Viceroy, he is taking it out again. Many people think he is not worth his salt.'[67]

Up until Gandhi's arrest just after midnight on the night of 4/5 May, press reports highlighted riots in other parts of the country, pointed out that the salt the volunteers gathered was not enough to hurt government revenues and in any case was not fit for human consumption (completely missing the point of the symbolic nature of the action), detailed Gandhi's increasing frustration at not being arrested, and his upping the ante by inciting his followers to blood-letting:

---

[65] 'The Position in India', *The Advertiser* (Adelaide), 25 March 1930, p. 18.
[66] *The Times* (London), 10 April 1930; quoted in Thomas Weber, *On the Salt March: The Historiography of Mahatma Gandhi's March to Dandi*, New Delhi: Rupa, 2009, p. 448.
[67] 'Ebb and Flow By D.T.H.', *The Telegraph* (Brisbane), 11 April 1930, p. 8.

Although several of his lieutenants were arrested, the authorities did not attempt to interfere with Mr. Gandhi, greatly to his own chagrin. Their policy was judicious. He and his cause thrive upon 'persecution.' Gandhi the 'martyr,' Gandhi starving himself to the verge of dissolution behind prison bars, Gandhi enduring the extremities of privation and hardship for the sake of Mother India, captured the imagination and attracted popular sympathy. Gandhi, ignored by the powers that be, laboriously preparing useless salt by the seashore is a less impressive figure....

He acknowledges that were the British to withdraw from India, there would immediately be an orgy of strife and bloodshed. That is the price we must pay, he says, in order to enjoy the blessings of freedom. The blessings of freedom will be imperfectly appreciated by the victims in the inevitable disturbances. Mr. Gandhi is the sort of man who is impervious to argument. His ideas are fixed, and he is sublimely indifferent to considerations, which would weigh with anyone else. The surprising thing is not that the Swarajist movement should be declining in vigour, but that any intelligent person should owe it allegiance.[68]

Gandhi was reported as no longer condemning violence and indulging in incitements to blood-letting by exhorting people 'to resist the confiscation of salt from your grips with all your might till blood is spilt.'[69] A few days later, the papers corrected themselves, reporting that Gandhi had denied that he had advised his followers to depart from 'the creed of non-violence'. Gandhi explained that 'he meant them to adopt other methods of civil resistance such as the boycott of schools and Government servants relinquishing their posts. He regards police action in taking illicit salt from volunteers as "barbarity," and urges the volunteers to refuse to surrender their salt.'[70]

[68] 'Mr. Gandhi's Fiasco', *The Sydney Morning Herald*, 9 April 1930. p. 12.
[69] 'Gandhi's New Tactics: Non-Violence Policy Abandoned: Resist till Blood is Spilt', *The Age* (Melbourne), 10 April 1930, p. 9.
[70] 'Gandhi's Campaign: Manufacture of Salt', *The Sydney Morning Herald*, 12 April 1930. p. 15.

The press also showed the civilised nature of the Raj by pointing out that 'In any other country Gandhi would have been immediately arrested, but here in India he is still free', even though, due to his campaign, 'the country from Karachi to Chittagong is a scene of numerous outbreaks designed to overthrow the Government', adding that Gandhi has 'already failed in two previous campaigns, and the Government appears confident that he will fail this time'.[71]

Reports of Gandhi's arrest and the reasons for it were printed in detail in the Australian press. *The Sydney Morning Herald* even carried a lengthy description of the event by the London *Daily Telegraph*'s Ellis Ashmead-Bartlett. Generally, the reports detailed the lawlessness and defiance of authority that resulted from Gandhi's campaign (while previously asserting that the campaign was fizzling out due to lack of enthusiasm among the masses), lawlessness that Gandhi and his lieutenants were unable to restrain, thereby forcing the government's hand. The timing of the arrest was explained by noting that there was less disorder than there would have been had Gandhi been arrested some weeks earlier, and that 'while Gandhi continued to deplore the outbreaks his protests against his followers' conduct were becoming weaker, and it was evident that he was no longer able to control them'. Gandhi also kept broadening the scope of the campaign as milder measures did not produce the desired outcome. After breaching the salt laws, he organised for the picketing of liquor shops, then the boycott of British cloth, and finally the incitement to withhold land revenue and the threat to seize the salt works at Dharasana near Dandi. While the government had 'pursued a policy of toleration even at the risk of the accusation of weakness', the events 'had shown that the history of the earlier non-co-operation movement would repeat itself if Gandhi's campaign were allowed to continue', and therefore it was decided that 'it was impossible to allow Gandhi to remain at large without grave dangers

---

[71] 'Government Calm: Has no Fear of Big Disturbance', *The Herald* (Melbourne), 21 April 1930, p. 7.

to the tranquillity of India; and considered it desirable that he be placed under restraint'.[72] And, of course, it was argued, it had to be this way given Gandhi's serious character flaws, including a reversion to his Oriental heritage over his Western side:

> The character of Gandhi presents curious contrasts. To many, his 'saintship' maintains a certain interest. Yet the simpleton in him is quite as strong as the saint, otherwise he could never have pointed straight to violent courses while persistently deploring violence. As a statesman he cannot be seriously regarded. Not once has he come forward with a single constructive proposal. His one definite demand has been that the British leave India at once—leave her, that is, to anarchy and ruin. In presenting that demand, Gandhi showed his other side, the side that is more than half Western. He abandoned for the nonce that innate instinct of bargaining which the Oriental usually shows—seen at present to perfection in the long-drawn deliberations over Egypt and the Sudan—and spoke as though he would accept no compromise. The tone of autocracy was unmistakable, but the strength which should support it was entirely lacking. None of the results which Gandhi professed to desire have occurred. All that has happened has been a partial outbreak of precisely that turbulence which he so inconsistently deprecates. This he has provoked, in the spirit of the true megalomaniac, at a time when the Simon Commission's report is almost hourly expected, itself a reminder of the serious determination with which Britain is studying the problem of India's development. Patient for long beyond all reasonable expectation, the Government has at last gently restrained the apostle of futile formulas, and has taken stern action against those who have translated his creed into murderous insurrection.[73]

Following Gandhi's arrest and imprisonment, from June onwards reports concerning him decline sharply and remain low

[72] 'Gandhi's Arrest: Official Statement', *The Sydney Morning Herald*, 7 May 1930, p. 13.

[73] 'A Turning-Point in India', *The Sydney Morning Herald*, 9 May 1930, p. 10.

until his release in the following January and his subsequent trip to England to attend the Round Table Conference on India's future. In the interim, we get repetitions of the now familiar stories of Gandhi being an idealist who is misguided or being used by extremists, or that he is something far worse. In a discussion of the second volume of Gandhi's recently published *Autobiography*, the *Evening News* informed its readers that 'between the lines it is easy enough to understand that at heart Gandhi is no Mahatma, but a politician of the crudest mould. He sought political power, but with the innumerable divisions of race, creed and culture found it impossible to obtain it in India.' However, in India '"holiness" is the one unifying virtue. Gandhi recognised this and became "holy" to order. He became a fanatic to become a power, and in short time he was one to whom the people bowed and governments deferred.'[74] The Melbourne *Herald* even carried a photograph of Gandhi at his spinning wheel with the caption, 'India's Most Dangerous Subject'. Below the picture, in a sentence the paper's readers are informed that 'This harmless-looking fanatic's campaign of civil disobedience and boycott of British cloth have lead to serious rioting and bloodshed in many Indian cities.'[75] There are also the usual stories of Gandhi's growing irrelevance (especially now that he had been imprisoned). In a reprinting of a piece by the former Home Secretary Lord Brentford, from the London *Daily Mail* of a week before, a question regarding the timing of Gandhi's arrest is raised: 'Why was there this delay in [Gandhi's] arrest—because we would have made him a martyr? Believe me, that is all nonsense. In prison he will not be a martyr; he will become a mere memory, and that not for many weeks.'[76]

[74] 'Holiness', *Evening News* (Sydney), 29 November 1930, p. 4.
[75] 'India's Most Dangerous Subject', *The Herald* (Melbourne), 6 June 1930, p. 7.
[76] 'India: Britain Must Govern: Lord Brentford's Views', *The Sydney Morning Herald*, 14 June 1930, p. 19.

Australia's Gandhi: The Press Depictions

Much of the reporting of Gandhi and the Indian independence movement at this time concerned a proposed round table conference in London to discuss India's future. The demands of Gandhi and the Indian National Congress to call off civil disobedience and attend—the framing of a constitution giving India the 'substance of Independence', a repeal of the salt tax, and the release of political prisoners—were considered too extreme by the government. Gandhi and the Congress boycotted the conference. Without the key figures from the nationalist side, the conference, which sat from mid-November 1930 to mid-January 1931, could accomplish nothing.

Gandhi was released from prison on 25 January. For three weeks, from mid-February, Gandhi and the Viceroy, Lord Irwin, negotiated terms of settlement for the ending of civil disobedience and for attendance at a second round table conference.

Sir John Monash, the heroic general of the Great War considered by many to be the greatest living Australian, was in India at the time of Gandhi's release from prison and his negotiations with Lord Irwin. He was the official Australian representative at the opening of the new Indian capital at New Delhi. Before he embarked on the trip, someone warned him by phone that Gandhi had ordered him to be poisoned. On his return to Australia in early April, Monash gave several talks on his impressions of India. He declared that Indian Home Rule had to be opposed not only because it was premature, but also because it could lead to the creation of a potential enemy on Australia's trade route. He also declared that he was not sure that Gandhi was not a humbug.[77] This elicited a

---

[77] See 'Problems of India: Importance to Australia: Sir John Monash's Return', *The Argus* (Melbourne), 1 April 1931, p. 6; 'Indian Problem: Sir John Monash's Views', *The Sydney Morning Herald*, 1 April 1931, p. 20; and a few days later, in all the other major Australian papers. On the 'humbug' statement, see especially 'If India Secedes: Good-bye to Australia: Sir John Monash's Address', *The Sydney Morning Herald*, 11 August 1931, p. 9; 'India's Future: Effects of Secession: Is Gandhi a Humbug?', *The Argus* (Melbourne), 11 August 1931, p. 6; and Geoffrey Serle, *John Monash: A Biography*, Melbourne: Melbourne University Press, 1982, pp. 519–522.

response from the Reverend Selwyn Evans by way of a letter to the editor of the monthly pacifist journal *Peacewards*. Evans wrote that Monash 'does not understand Gandhi, and never could'. After all, an army officer 'living in the atmosphere of military bounce and arrogance cannot be expected to possess a spiritual insight even to understand, much less to appreciate, this Indian saint'. He added that 'When a man calls this saint's piety and humility "humbug," he proves that he understands neither.'[78]

Before Gandhi sailed to England in August to attend the Conference as Congress' sole representative, there was much speculation in the press about what he would wear in London. Several Australian papers reported Gandhi as saying that if he in fact went to London, he would appear in his 'national attire', because it 'would be an act of discourtesy to the King if I appeared in any dress other than national', adding that 'If the weather permits I shall dress in England exactly as I dress in India, wearing a loincloth',[79] or 'He will wear a woollen long skirt reaching the ankles and a shawl.'[80] Later, this revelation was expanded upon. Gandhi was reported as saying that as he represented, through Congress, 'the very poorest, semi-starved and almost naked villager, he would wear only a loincloth, with whatever additions the English climate might demand.' Further, he added,

> I should be guilty of discourtesy to the English ... if I deceive them by not appearing as I am. I would fail in my mission if I commenced by deception. If I am to win their hearts, as I want to do, I can only do so by being cent per cent truthful.[81]

[78] 'Correspondence', *Peacewards*, 1 September 1931, p. 3.
[79] See, for example, 'Gandhi in Talkie: Will Wear National Dress in London', *The Age* (Melbourne), 2 May 1931, p. 11.
[80] 'London Conference to be Attended by Gandhi', *The Sydney Morning Herald*, 3 August 1931, p. 10.
[81] 'When Gandhi Goes to London: Will Wear Only Loincloth Unless Climate is Cold', *The Age* (Melbourne), 11 July 1931, p. 11.

Australia's Gandhi: The Press Depictions

The theme was carried forward in a lengthy interview by Nell Murray—the 'Herald Woman Writer in London'—with Muriel Lester of the Kingsley Hall settlement where Gandhi was to reside during his visit. Following talk of the problem of keeping goats so that Gandhi could have his required milk, Lester was asked if Gandhi would attend the Conference dressed only in his loincloth, his customary dress in India. Lester's given response was that 'Mr. Gandhi is a sensible man, and if he found the English climate caused him any discomfort, I am sure that he would adopt European clothing.'[82]

This fascination with Gandhi's eccentricities was to take on massive 'fake news' proportions. One story noted that officers of the P and O line of cruise ships, which presumably would be transporting Gandhi to London, were 'perturbed at the prospect of the Indian fanatic Gandhi as a passenger from Bombay to the United Kingdom'. As Gandhi would be on official government business, a 'cabin de luxe' would be placed at his disposal; however,

> if he is true to his fanatical beliefs he will spurn shipboard comforts, and continue his simple mode of living in the security of the fo'castle, or, clad in his symbolic loincloth, brave the rigors of the variable weather on the liner's broad decks. This much-discussed passenger has already intimated to representatives of the shipping line that his ablutions must be made in the holy water of India, and gallons of murky liquid drawn from Mother Ganges will be taken on board at Bombay to supply his drinking and infrequent washing requirements.[83]

Nevertheless, this also indicates a different way of presenting Gandhi to the Australian readership. His eccentricities now become endearing. Rather than being presented as a dangerous fanatic, his

[82] Nell Murray, 'When Gandhi Goes to London: East End Welfare Worker Will Be His Hostess', *The Herald* (Melbourne), 10 August 1931, p. 6.
[83] 'About People', *The Age* (Melbourne), 29 July 1931, p. 7.

humour is emphasised and he is portrayed as a celebrity. While his participation in the Conference is reported upon, there is much more about his daily activities and habits: what he ate, where he slept, who he talked to (including Charlie Chaplin), and what he said. Interviewed en route on the *S. S. Rajputana*, Gandhi is quoted as saying that he was anxious to meet his critics, such as Winston Churchill, and was sure that he could convince them 'of the justice of India's cause'. On board, he was 'huddled on a wooden bench in the stern, hidden from head to foot in a shroud-like garment'; as it was his day of silence, he had more time to sleep. In the Red Sea, 'Gandhi went to the bridge under the captain's direction, and took the helmsman's place. He navigated the liner for 10 minutes,'[84] and joked that 'I hope I don't capsize the boat and drown everybody', as he 'sharply twisted the wheel from starboard to port'.[85] The readers were also informed that Gandhi 'has made friends with the ship's cat, with which he shares his goat's milk (his chief food) and his mattress at night'.[86]

In Marseilles, Gandhi was greeted by 200 journalists and photographers[87] and when he finally landed in Folkestone in pouring rain, he remarked, 'This is proper English weather.'[88] He was 'attired in a loin-cloth and shawl, and walked bareheaded and barefooted [in fact, he wore sandals] through the puddles of rain-water. He refreshed himself with goat's milk and orange juice before attending the reception.' When he was asked if he would

---

[84] 'Gandhi's Mission: Justice of India's Cause', *The Sydney Morning Herald*, 5 September 1931, p. 12.

[85] 'Mr. Gandhi's Voyage: How He Spends His Day of Silence', *The Age* (Melbourne), 5 September 1931, p. 11.

[86] 'Gandhi Shares Milk with Cat: Ship Mates: Will Try to Convince English Critics', *The Herald* (Melbourne), 4 September 1931, p. 9.

[87] 'Gandhi in London: On a Mission of Peace: Enthusiastic Reception', *The Sydney Morning Herald*, 14 September 1931, p. 9.

[88] 'Non-Violence: Gandhi's Advocacy: Freedom for India', *The Brisbane Courier*, 14 September 1931, p. 13.

Australia's Gandhi: The Press Depictions

not 'be ashamed to appear before the King clad in a loin-cloth', Gandhi allegedly chuckled and replied that while 'The British wear plus fours', he preferred 'to wear minus fours'. And, at customs, when he was asked if he had anything to declare, he is said to have replied, 'I am a poor mendicant. My earthly possessions consist of six spinning wheels, a can of goat's milk, six homespun loin-cloths, and my reputation, which is not worth much.'[89]

Small incidents were made much of. For example, in a committee room in Parliament at Westminster where Gandhi was addressing a group of Labour members, he informed them that he had to leave and return to Kingsley Hall unless 'he could be allowed to say evening prayers there'. When there was no objection,

> On the stroke of 7 o'clock the Gandhis, father and son [Gandhi's youngest son Devdas was part of the entourage], Mrs. Naidu and Miss Slade, all in Indian clothing, squatted on the cushions on the floor and chanted Hindu scriptures and invocations, surrounded by a few interested members of the House of Commons.[90]

Gandhi also visited Lancashire, where his friendly reception bewildered French newspapers. *Le Journal* was reported as saying, tongue firmly in cheek, that

> One would have expected that the special protection given Mr. Gandhi in France would have been doubled when he was among the mill hands who are unemployed owing to his campaign in India, but instead he was fraternally acclaimed. The fact only re-emphasises the view that the Englishman's esteem and friendship can but be won by attacking him to his face and telling him disagreeable truths.[91]

---

[89] 'Gandhi in London', p. 9.
[90] 'On the Stroke of Seven: Gandhi's Evening Prayers: Unprecedented Scene at Westminster', *The Age* (Melbourne), 18 September 1931, p. 11.
[91] 'Gandhi in Lancashire: French Press Bewildered', *The Age* (Melbourne), 29 September 1931, p. 7.

Of course, there were still the odd jabs. An Australian Press Association report pointed out that Gandhi had received a 'good press' and 'is the most photographed visitor in London for a long time. His pictures are in every paper [including Australian ones from October onwards], though here and there are suggestions that his eccentricities in his clothing, diet and asceticism are mere showmanship.'[92] And then there were some stories that totally departed from the now usual script:

> Mahatma Gandhi, the Indian Nationalist leader, has 'fallen flat' in England. His insistence on his outlandish garb is largely responsible for his failure to impress political circles in London comparably with the influence he exerted in India. People who expect visiting diplomats to conform to sartorial usage get a shock similar to seeing a coolie in a drawingroom when Gandhi appears in his slovenly shawl, sandals and loin-cloth at the Round Table Conference meeting and other official occasions.[93]

And along with H. G. Wells' quip that 'I have no use for him, nor for his loincloth, nor for his mental obliviousness to dentistry' that was carried in several Australian papers,[94] some stories continued to denigrate Gandhi. For example, a long unsympathetic article about him finishes with the prediction that

> The greatest peril to Gandhi's reputation is that his life should be long. Every day new millions find him out. Every day the squatting saint loses some of his impressiveness. *Not far off,*

---

[92] 'Non-Violence: Gandhi's Advocacy: Freedom for India', *The Brisbane Courier*, 14 September 1931, p. 13.

[93] 'Gandhi Fails to Impress: London Indifferent: Outlandish Garb Largely to Blame', *The Herald* (Melbourne), 26 September 1931, p. 7.

[94] See, for example, 'Wells on Gandhi: Oblivious to Dentistry', *The Herald* (Melbourne), 29 October 1931, p. 10; and 'Mr. H. G. Wells: Makes a Political Prophecy', *The Sydney Morning Herald*, 30 October 1931, p. 9.

Australia's Gandhi: The Press Depictions

perhaps, is the gale of world-laughter that will blow Gandhi down from his perch.[95]

Of course, other stories were far more positive and provided quite a different perspective on his reception in London. While some critics had called Gandhi a 'hypocrite and a poser', these stories talk of the crowds in both the East End and the West End who waited to catch a glimpse of him.

> When he takes his early morning walk through the cheerless streets of Bow and Bromley, groups of dock workers gather to see him pass, and give him a cheer, 'Good old Gandhi!' Smiling a smile which reveals a gap in his front upper teeth, the Mahatma acknowledges the greeting with a wave of the hand.

And in this way, 'Gandhi the showman, has become the showpiece of the Round Table Conference.'[96] Gandhi, after all, was attempting to go over the heads of the politicians and appeal directly to the English people. The wishful thinking that he was an overnight wonder, or how he was alienating those in power through his sartorial choices, was beside the point.

While the papers carried short daily reports of the happenings at the Conference, often predicting its collapse because of a stalemate brought about by different perceptions of India's future held by the different Indian interest groups, the picture presented of Gandhi at the sessions is humanising:

> Mr. Gandhi's personality surmounts in some strange manner his lack of physical significance. One close observer of him put his curious impressiveness down to the fact that when he is still he

---

[95] 'Gandhi: The Biggest Bluff in History: Impudent Humbug Falls Flat in London', *The Sun* (Sydney), 4 October 1931, p. 13.
[96] 'Gandhi Smiles: The Simple Life in London', *The Herald* (Melbourne), 20 October 1931, p. 6.

is genuinely still. He does not fiddle about with a pencil or paper or cross and uncross his legs; he remains perfectly immobile, and in some way this very lack of movement hints at hidden reserves of thought and character—an impression that is strengthened, when he speaks, by his soft and extremely deliberate tones.[97]

The Round Table Conference petered out without anything concrete being achieved. Gandhi demanded complete independence, and believed that differences between various communities could be more easily settled if the British were no longer present. Other representatives had different views. Four days after the Conference concluded, Gandhi headed for home via Paris, Switzerland—where he spent several days as the guest of Romain Rolland—and Rome. The Italian press carried an alleged interview with Gandhi where he stated that he would resume civil disobedience as soon as he returned home. Gandhi strenuously denied ever having given such an interview, but the press gave it extensive coverage. Reports of the cuddly Mahatma evaporated. He was blamed for the deadlock in the Conference and was again, more and more, portrayed as the fanatic who was happy to countenance any amount of violence as long as Britain left India. A week after he had landed at Bombay, in early January 1932 he was back in prison.

For those who were tired of reading about the doings of the Mahatma in far-off India and England, there was always the relief of the sports pages and the turf guide. In June 1931, it was announced that sportsman and horse trainer Eric Connolly had bought the 'top-hole colt of the year so far as looks go', the Queensland-bred 475 guinea bay colt who 'will race as Gandhi'. For the next several years, punters could follow the fortunes (or more often the misfortunes) of the four-legged Gandhi on the track.[98]

[97] 'London Gossip', *The Age* (Melbourne), 31 October 1931, p. 18.
[98] See, for example, 'Pars From All Parts', *The Advocate* (Burnie), 20 June 1931, p. 3; 'Consistent Juveniles', *Sporting Globe* (Melbourne), 10 October 1931, p. 1, and 'Victorian Juveniles Succeed: From the North', 21 October 1931, p. 6;

Towards the End

During the rest of the 1930s the coverage of Gandhi in the Australian press again was slight, except for the expected occasional spike. For example, much was made of Gandhi's 'fast unto death' over the issue of the setting up of separate electorates for 'untouchables'. Gandhi took no food for five days and, as his health deteriorated, a compromise was arrived at with the leaders of the oppressed castes, resulting in the cancellation of the decision and the ending of the fast. Interestingly, the press stories generally did not delve into the complex politics surrounding the fast. Rather, they stated that in an interview on 20 September 1932, Gandhi had expressed his wish for the complete eradication of caste and of untouchability.[99] From here on, the press interest in Gandhi is fairly scant, increasing whenever he went on a fast or when he was released from prison (and these were regular occurrences during the early 1930s), or when there were demonstrations against the Mahatma by orthodox Hindus enraged by his anti-untouchability campaigning. These reports were accompanied by much wishful thinking about Gandhi's growing irrelevance. Perhaps the most extreme report in this regard was relayed to Australian audiences in the pages (including the front page) of the Sydney *Sun*, where it was announced that Gandhi had astonished India by returning to his Ahmedabad ashram (something he vowed at the start of the Salt March not to do until Indian independence had been attained[100]), and this was taken to mean that 'he has decided to give up politics and devote the rest of his life to meditation and prayer'. This was because he could see that his

---

'True! Form of Colt: Vauntry Wins', *The Sun* (Sydney), 11 October 1931, p. 36; and 'V.A.T.C. Meeting: Notes and Anticipations: Ceilidh or Phocis', *The Australasian* (Melbourne), 16 July 1932, p. 16.

[99] This was an exaggeration as Gandhi had only spoken about eradicating untouchability, 'root and branch'. See *The Times of India*, 21 September 1932.

[100] In fact, Gandhi merely visited an ill ashramite. He did not stay at the Ashram and announced the disbandment of the establishment.

influence was waning, leading him to make a strategic retreat. 'As a political force he is dead, but there is always a chance that he will think out a new scheme and emerge again from his retirement.'[101] A story on the inside of the paper was humorously anti-Gandhi:

> The news that Mr. Gandhi has retired from the world and gone into a monastery will be received by intelligent British people with no particle of regret.
>
> This little Hindu with bad teeth, in spite of the fact that the English people took him as a joke, did enormous harm to the prestige of British rule in India. The extraordinary welcome which he, one of Britain's worst enemies, received in London must have amused him as much as it surprised those who understood his significance.
>
> He has spent a good deal of the last few years in gaol, making gestures to advertise his fast-fading prestige among his own people. His choice of a monastery instead of gaol shows a shrewdness which it is hard to reconcile with the sainthood that was claimed for him, not only by his own people, but by admiring British intelligentsia. Perhaps the goat's-milk is better in the monasteries, and they may not have given him orange-juice in gaol. At all events, once in the monastery it is to be hoped that he stays there.[102]

After Gandhi's retirement from Congress and active politics in 1934 to devote himself to rural uplift and anti-untouchability causes, some reports were even more outlandish, declaring that he would retire to the Himalayas to study 'the ancient system of Aryan yoga' and then tour Germany, 'where he will establish Yogic centres to inspire Europeans with ancient Aryan ideals of life'.[103]

---

[101] 'Will Go Away: Gandhi to Enter Monastery: Politics Ended', *The Sun* (Sydney), 20 July 1933, p. 1.

[102] 'An Enemy Retires', *The Sun* (Sydney), 20 July 1933, p. 16.

[103] See 'Gandhi Will Turn Yogi', *The Sun* (Sydney), 19 November 1936, p. 25; and 'Gandhi Leaving Politics for Yoga', *The Herald* (Melbourne), 20 November 1936, p. 7.

Australia's Gandhi: The Press Depictions

Gandhi re-emerged in the Australian press in 1939. First there was his fast in March for constitutional reform in the tiny princely state of Rajkot, where his father had served as Diwan and where he had lived as a child. This was followed by the serialisation of John Gunther's book *Inside Asia*, then still unavailable in Australia.[104] The chapter on Gandhi reprinted in the Sydney *Daily Telegraph* (and several other papers) employed the headline, 'One-fifth of the Human Race would Revolt at his Call', and added that the chapter was about 'the scrawny man who will be worshipped as a god when he dies.'[105]

However, it was the start of Germany's war with Britain that again brought Gandhi into the headlines. There was relief that he seemed to back Britain's war effort, but there was also concern about how far that support would go, given that Gandhi was not satisfied with the vague promises in the Viceroy's declaration of what would happen in regard to Indian independence after the war.[106] Gandhi issued a statement that while he could not speak on behalf of Congress, 'his sympathies were with Britain and France from a humanitarian standpoint. He could not contemplate without being stirred to the depths the destruction of London.' Gandhi, who broke down, disclosed that he had sent a letter to Hitler in July, begging him to listen to the appeal of one 'who deliberately shunned the method of war and not without considerable success.' He added: 'I do not think that India's deliverance will be worth anything if Britain and France fall. Nevertheless, it appears that Hitler knows no God but brute force.'[107]

---

[104] John Gunther, *Inside Asia*, New York: Harper, 1939. The chapter 'Mr. Gandhi' is at pp. 364–389.

[105] 'One-Fifth of the Human Race would Revolt at his Call', *The Daily Telegraph* (Sydney), 26 June 1939, p. 9; and 'Gandhi: The Incredible', *The Argus* (Melbourne). 30 June 1939, p. 9.

[106] 'All India Opposed to Germany: Gandhi Looks for Concessions', *The Sun* (Sydney), 19 October 1939, p. 9.

[107] 'Gandhi Stands for Britain: Force is Hitler's Only God', *The Courier Mail* (Brisbane), 8 September 1939, p. 5. On Gandhi's relationship with Hitler,

Gradually, the papers started voicing a concern that Gandhi would give up his seemingly unconditional support for Britain and perhaps give the signal for the commencement of a civil disobedience campaign, given the more forceful position on the question of Indian independence held by the Congress.[108] The talks between Gandhi, who was not authorised to speak for the Congress, and the Viceroy Lord Linlithgow reached a deadlock over the question of whether India's future should be determined by Britain or by the Indian people themselves. Nevertheless, Gandhi noted that he did not doubt the Viceroy's sincerity and that 'the hour for civil disobedience has not yet been reached'.[109] It was also reported that Gandhi did not blame Britain for the past. On the contrary, Indians admired 'the bravery, skill, and spirit of adventure of Britons'. However, they could not 'conscientiously pray for the success of British arms if it meant a further subjection of India'. He added that 'Britain must give India her due. She must trust India's sense of justice, not her own strong arm.'[110] Still, Gandhi is portrayed as a restraining influence on the more radical politicians who were not happy with dominion status, but demanded complete independence and the commencement of immediate civil disobedience to achieve it. This view of Gandhi as friend rather than enemy led to the occasional positive humorous portrayal. For example, a resident of Armidale sent a version of a rhyme on the 'dissertation on shirts and the men who wear them', to their local paper:

---

see Thomas Weber, 'The Mahatma and the Fuhrer: "Dear Friend" vs "Shoot Gandhi"', in Thomas Weber, *The Mahatma, His Philosophy and His Legacy*, New Delhi: Orient BlackSwan, 2018, pp. 195–222.

[108] 'Position of India', *The West Australian* (Perth), 23 February 1940, p. 16.

[109] 'Nearer Our Goal: Statement by Gandhi', *The Sydney Morning Herald*, 12 February 1940, p. 12; and 'Negotiations to Continue', *The Age* (Melbourne), 12 February 1940, p. 9.

[110] 'Gandhi's India Admires Britain', *The Daily Telegraph* (Sydney), 19 February 1940, p. 3.

Australia's Gandhi: The Press Depictions

> Oh, some may wear a black shirt
> In Rome or Terrancini,
> And shout a lusty 'viva'
> In praise of Mussolini.
> Or some may choose a brown shirt
> And march along in style,
> Saluting Adolf Hitler
> And crying 'Hitler Heil'.
> And some prefer a blue shirt,
> Making speeches in the Dail,
> And hold big demonstrations
> Against Fianna Fail.
> Yet others favour red shirts
> And find their Alma Mater
> In Bolshevist Utopia,
> With Stalin as dictator.
> But I am not attracted
> By these great leaders' call,
> I'll choose Mahatma Gandhi,
> And wear no shirt at all.[111]

Gandhi's moderating influence on the left of the Congress Party was commented on again and again in the Australian press. Much was made of Gandhi's refusal to cause problems for Britain when it was 'a question of life or death for them', ruling out mass civil disobedience. However, he warned the government that 'he was considering alternative methods, perhaps a spectacular single act by himself in order to convince the British Government of India's right to determine her future.'[112]

Before this could happen, Gandhi was again in the news when he advised Britain to 'let Hitler in', to take possession of

---

[111] 'Tale of a Shirt', *The Armidale Express and New England General Advertiser*, 24 April 1940, p. 4.
[112] 'Gandhi Against Mass Civil Disobedience', *The Telegraph* (Brisbane), 29 April 1940, p. 2.

'your beautiful island and your homes. Allow yourselves to be slaughtered but refuse to owe allegiance to them [Hitler and Mussolini].' According to Gandhi, 'Non-violence has achieved considerable success in India and England with greater skill could make perfect this matchless weapon.' He added that the appeal was prompted by his love for Britain and the British people.[113] Perhaps surprisingly, this suggestion was not met with immediate outrage. In fact, after reporting Gandhi's obviously preposterous advice, it was ignored by the Australian press—whether this was because there were simply more pressing important issues to focus on, or because no one wanted to engage in a debate around the issue, or because it was the sort of statement that could be expected from the Mahatma, is unclear.

At this time, the press noted with some satisfaction that the 'All-India Congress Committee rejected by 91 votes to 63 Gandhi's contention that the principles of non-violence should be extended to India's national defence.'[114] On the question of Indian independence, Gandhi claimed that 'a free India alone can render effective help to Great Britain,'[115] and the press pointed out that while Gandhi would happily 'stalk the battlefield' to convince soldiers 'that their methods were outraging the best instincts of the human race', he did not want to embarrass Britain during the war because he realised 'that Nazism is far more sinister than anything inherent in British imperialism'. Other Congress leaders, however, were 'not sure that the principles for which [Britain] is fighting in Europe will be applied to India.'[116]

When some Congress members were arrested for making seditious speeches, Gandhi stated that 'the Government is inviting

[113] 'Policy of "No Violence": Urged by Gandhi', *The Age* (Melbourne), 4 July 1940, p. 7.
[114] 'Gandhi Out-Voted', *The Age* (Melbourne) 29 July 1940, p. 7.
[115] 'A Free India: Gandhi's Demand', *The Sydney Morning Herald*, 8 July 1940, p. 7.
[116] 'Talks on India Held Up', *The Herald* (Melbourne) 12 August 1940, p. 4.

the party to start civil disobedience. It is a pity.'[117] Although no mass movement was commenced, single individuals sequentially courted arrest over the government's lack of resolve to spell out its position on India's future. In a piece, carried by several papers, the well-known Australian academic and essayist Walter Murdoch wrote that 'We may think Gandhi a nuisance at the present moment, but we ought to feel proud that our rule in India has been such as to make Gandhi possible, however inconvenient the result may be for ourselves.'[118]

Because of Gandhi's attitude of not wanting to embarrass Britain, and only calling for individuals to court arrest rather than a mass civil disobedience campaign to keep India's independence struggle alive, he received little coverage for the next two years, and what there was tended to be factual statements of his movements or summaries of what he wrote in his papers, or occasionally longer sympathetic pieces. Early in 1942, three regional papers carried such an (unattributed) article on Gandhi:

> At 70 years, in a time of persistent political crisis engendered in India by Europe's war, Mohandas Gandhi is still one of his country's most active leaders....
>
> Advancing years have undoubtedly left an impress on his personality and mode of life. Deeper furrows line his face, he sleeps much more than before, and nuts have practically disappeared from his diet. But he is even now an astonishingly early riser and never misses the community prayers at 4 o'clock. Indeed, all his best thinking and writing is generally done between the hours of 2 and 4 in the morning....

[117] 'Road to India: Birdwood on Dangers', *The Age* (Melbourne), 26 August 1940, p. 7.
[118] Walter Murdoch, 'Shame or Pride? The Empire', *The Herald* (Melbourne), 16 November 1940, p. 10; *The Advertiser* (Adelaide), 16 November 1940, p. 12; and 'The Empire: Shame or Pride?', *The West Australian* (Perth), 16 November 1940, p. 6.

There is something gripping about this old man as one watches him in the quiet of his home at Sewagram (meaning the 'village of service'), surrounded by a band of workers who share his enthusiasm and subscribe to his philosophy of life. Strange as it may seem, there are few politicians, as a rule, living in his colony. His main interests are not political, but human: rural development, the abolition of untouchability, a new system of education for India's villages, a better diet for her poverty-stricken population—these touch the main springs of his life far more than politics.

India's freedom means, of course, everything to him. But the struggle from his standpoint is not essentially political, as most of the Indian Nationalists would regard it, but only an expression of the two principles he cherishes most—non-violence and truth.

The war found him last year in a position of considerable embarrassment, for the conflict was the very negation of all that he stood for. Moreover, within the Congress party there had developed in the last two years powerful elements which looked upon his technique with suspicion, some even with decided hostility.

But Gandhi, with rare courage and insight decided in September last year to take his own line. Convinced that Hitlerism was a menace to the world's security and to civilisation, he committed himself to a position of almost unconditional support of Britain and France. India's deliverance, he thought, was bound to come, sooner or later; but 'what will it be worth,' he wrote, immediately after an interview with the Viceroy, Lord Linlithgow, 'if England and France fail, or if they come out victorious over Germany ruined and humbled?'

At any time during the past months Gandhi could have started civil disobedience and caused great embarrassment for the British. If he has refrained from taking the plunge, it is not only because of his diffidence in keeping civil disobedience free from violence. Another and even greater consideration is that he will not embarrass the British while they are engaged in a life-and-death struggle against ruthless aggression. He would rather wait until the end of the war to assert India's claims than act on the principle that Britain's difficulties are India's opportunity.

Gandhi has the supreme advantage of being singularly free from all trace of bitterness. He has remained unmoved before an angry audience and has laughed in perfect good humour at savage criticisms of himself. He has a unique capacity for detaching himself from the problems that are engaging his attention. It is the result of long practice based on the central teaching of his favourite Hindu scripture, the Bhagavad Gita.

Will he live to see the fulfilment of his hopes? 'If India achieves freedom in my life-time,' he says, 'and I have energy still left in me, I will take my share, though outside the official world, in building up the nation on a strictly non-violent basis.'....[119]

As an invasion of India by the Japanese became ever more likely, Gandhi proposed that India should adopt the surrender suggestion that he had made to Britain almost two years earlier. In an interview with Australian Alan Moorehead, then a correspondent of the London *Daily Express*, that was carried by several Australian papers, Gandhi said that 'I would not surrender India. I would let the Japanese land and then fight them with non-violence.' He pointed out that the Chinese 'made the mistake' of fighting the Japanese, 'and fighting still goes on in China'. If they had 'simply refrained from co-operating with the Japanese, then the Japanese would have been defeated'. He added that he did not think that this would 'have meant the death of the last Chinese' as the Japanese would have stopped, as it 'is not human killing where there is no resistance'. He added, 'There are 350,000,000

---

[119] See 'Gandhi will not Embarrass Britain', *Nambour Chronicle and North Coast Advertiser*, 30 January 1942, p. 5; 'Who is Gandhi? Indian Leader's Life: Free from Bitterness', *The Armidale Express and New England General Advertiser*, 4 February 1942, p. 2; and 'Who is Gandhi? Indian Leader's Life: Free from Bitterness', *The Inverell Times*, 2 March 1942, p. 6.

Indians and the Japanese cannot destroy them all.'[120] Not only did the Congress leadership not back Gandhi in this proposal, but the report also appeared at the time that Darwin was being bombed by the Japanese air force and Australian soldiers were fighting the Japanese army just north of Australia in New Guinea—yet it elicited no immediate ridiculing response.

A month later, however, Gandhi's position was tackled in an editorial in the Brisbane *Telegraph*. The paper stated that 'passive resistance' to a Japanese attack, or in the 'unrealistic prattle of the Indian leader', to employ 'non-violent non-cooperation with invading forces', is the 'most dismaying development in the Far Eastern war theatre since the fall of Singapore.' That Gandhi 'should turn in distrust and bitterness from Britain and imagine that they can play a game of pacifist "postman's knock" with the most brutally realistic military nation on earth seems to be the height of incredible stupidity.' This is because the 'decision amounts to an invitation to the Japanese to walk in and take possession of the country.'[121] As the likelihood of Japanese invasion became more real, the papers wrote about Gandhi's vacillation on the question of whether British troops should remain in India.

In July, the press made much of Congress' appointment of Gandhi as leader of a new anti-British campaign that would aim at political but not military withdrawal of the rulers from India. Gandhi was reported as saying that 'There is no room left for negotiation. Either they recognise India's independence or don't. There is no question of one more chance. After all, this is open rebellion.'[122] The press, as

---

[120] 'Gandhi's "No-Fight" Creed', *The Herald* (Melbourne), 6 April 1942. p. 1. For another account of this encounter, see Alan Moorehead, *African Trilogy*, London: Hamish Hamilton, 1944, pp. 278–280.

[121] 'Editorial: India Arms Itself with a Loin Cloth', *The Telegraph* (Brisbane), 5 May 1942, p. 4.

[122] 'Gandhi Talks of Open Rebellion', *The Daily Telegraph* (Sydney), 16 July 1942, p. 3; and see also 'No Compromise with Gandhi: "Open Rebellion"', *The Age* (Melbourne), 16 July 1942, p, 2.

could be expected, accused Gandhi of wanting to 'hand over India, lock, stock, and barrel to the Japanese'.[123] Then, a few weeks later, the next piece of sensationalist news regarding Gandhi was published by the government from papers it had seized, which showed that the Mahatma was prepared to negotiate with the Japanese as a first step if India received her freedom. Gandhi claimed that while he did not want the Axis powers to win the war, he added that 'Japan's quarrel is not with India. She is at war with the British Empire.'[124] This caused an outrage.

Soon thereafter, the papers reported the motion for Britain to 'Quit India', giving Gandhi authority to proclaim a mass civil disobedience campaign if Congress' demand for the immediate withdrawal of British rule was not granted. Gandhi and other Congress leaders were instantly arrested.[125] With Gandhi safely behind bars (or, more accurately, in the 'luxury prison' of the Aga Khan's palace in Poona[126]) and the gradual subsidence of the rioting which had broken out with the arrest of the Congress leaders, Gandhi again faded from the press reports.

Gandhi next entered the spotlight when he commenced a twenty-one day fast ('unto capacity' rather than 'to the death') on 10 February. The fast was to highlight the lack of progress regarding a settlement of the questions surrounding Indian independence, and because of the government's allegation that Congress was

[123] 'Gandhi's Plea is Suspect: Rejection Certain', *The Herald* (Melbourne), 17 July 1932, p. 4; and see also 'Government Prepared to Stop Gandhi Forfeiting India', *The Courier-Mail* (Brisbane), 18 July 1942, p. 2.

[124] 'Gandhi "Quisling" in India's Grave Crisis', *The Sun* (Sydney), 5 August 1942, p. 1.

[125] For details of the arrests, see 'Swift Action Saved India', *The Herald* (Melbourne), 10 August 1942, p. 2; 'Dawn Arrest of Gandhi was Without Incident', *The Telegraph* (Brisbane), 10 August 1942, p. 2; and 'Gandhi, With 53 More, Arrested; Swoop in India', *The Courier-Mail* (Brisbane), 10 August 1942, p. 1.

[126] See 'Luxury Prison for Gandhi: Closely Guarded in Palace', *The Age* (Melbourne) 15 August 1942, p. 2.

responsible for the violence that swept the country after the call to 'Quit India'. At first, the papers made the point that Gandhi had refused to accept freedom for the duration of the fast (which at times was labelled a 'hunger strike' and 'political blackmail'), 'preferring to remain under the eye of British medical men in comfortable conditions'.[127] This was followed by daily bulletins of Gandhi's failing health, what the fast was doing to his body,[128] the many appeals for his release from imprisonment, whether the fast was genuine, given that he was taking some fruit juice or glucose,[129] and discussions of what would happen if he died in prison because of the government's intransigence in the matter.[130] The papers announced the breaking of the fast on 4 March.[131]

Many of the reports of Gandhi's fast seemed to show genuine concerns over his suffering and seemed to will him to live. There were reports of Indians, Americans, and Australians going on sympathetic fasts, and even those claiming to have saved Gandhi's life. For example: 'It was I who saved Gandhi,' claimed Mr Samuel Rosenberg, Sydney-based prison reform activist and secretary of the Howard Prison Reform League. 'The death of Gandhi because of his fast would have struck a blow at democracy. That is why I willed him to live.' Rosenberg apparently did this by praying for the Mahatma, who was his 'twin soul', in 'trams, motor cars, at his office, and when at home, in shorts and a yellow chrysanthemum'. With

---

[127] 'Gandhi the Poseur: Fasting in Comfort', *Mudgee Guardian and North West Representative*, 11 February 1943, p. 1.

[128] 'Fight Against the Toxins', *The Sydney Morning Herald*, 27 February 1943, p. 9.

[129] 'Gandhi Near End of "Phoney Fast"', *The Herald* (Melbourne), 1 March 1943, p. 2; 'Recovery of Gandhi: Aid of Glucose', *The Sydney Morning Herald*, 5 March 1943, p. 6; and 'Glucose, Not God, Saved Gandhi', *The Daily Telegraph* (Sydney), 5 March 1943, p. 4.

[130] 'Rioting Expected if Gandhi Dies', *Examiner* (Launceston), 23 February 1943, p. 1.

[131] 'Gandhi's Fast Ends: No Celebrations', *The Sydney Morning Herald*, 4 March 1943, p. 6.

his hands 'clasped in prayer', Rosenberg whispered: 'Mahatma, you will live', 'Thou shalt not fail me and thy country in its hour of need.' And his prayers grew stronger as Gandhi grew weaker. 'Had Gandhi died, the outcry would have echoed round the world, he said.' He added that 'I myself would then have been forced to go on a record-breaking fast as a protest on behalf of the spirit of India.' Although he had been to India, Rosenberg had never met Gandhi—something he was going to set right: 'He intends to go there again soon, shake hands with Gandhi, and give him the yellow chrysanthemum.'[132]

Following Gandhi's fast, the papers reported on whether the fast was a failure,[133] ran longer analyses examining the 'Gandhi Myth',[134] and then detailing the charges in a London White Paper that blamed the recent riots squarely on Gandhi and Congress, noting that Gandhi knew that the Indian masses would not remain nonviolent when he launched the campaign of civil disobedience.[135] They also ran numerous factual reports on the failing health, and then death, of Gandhi's wife Kasturba, and the imprisoned Mahatma's own incapacitation with malaria, anaemia, and low blood pressure.[136]

Given his poor health, Gandhi was released unconditionally from prison on 6 May 1944. In the months following his release, the papers speculated on whether the Viceroy, Lord Wavell, would grant Gandhi an interview. They also reported at length on his differences with Muslim leader Muhammad Ali Jinnah over the

---

[132] '"I Saved Gandhi," Says Mr. Samuel Rosenberg', *Truth* (Sydney), 7 March 1943, p. 17.

[133] 'Gandhi's Fast a Failure', *The Age* (Melbourne), 17 March 1943, p. 1.

[134] 'Authority Explodes "The Great Gandhi Myth"', *The World's News* (Sydney), 20 March 1943, p. 3.

[135] 'Gandhi Had Deep Laid Plans to Wreck India', *The Telegraph* (Brisbane), 25 March 1943, p. 1.

[136] In fact, Gandhi suffered from high, not low, blood pressure. See Thomas Weber, 'Rauwolfia: Gandhi's Favourite Tranquiliser?', *South Asia* 41 (3), 2018, pp. 567–578.

structure of a future free India,[137] then on his lengthy and ultimately unsuccessful September negotiations with Jinnah over the Moslem League's plan to subdivide a free India into Hindu and Muslim states,[138] and his relationship with Jawaharlal Nehru, 'undoubtedly India's number two man.'[139]

There was also some assessment of Gandhi's life and achievements. The *Age*'s 'special correspondent in India' informed the paper's readers that Gandhi, 'still unchallenged as No. 1 public figure in India', had turned seventy-five and was the cause for celebration in the country, even though 'it followed closely upon one of Gandhi's biggest political flops', the breakdown of his negotiations with Jinnah. While some saw him as 'an implacable idealist', others 'refuse to look upon him in any other way than as a shrewd politician who alone is fit to lead the country out of the mess'. According to this report, Gandhi had been portrayed as a 'humbug, obstructionist, humanist, genius, saint'. 'When Gandhi travels he is the guest of millionaires, but he keeps to the simple life as far as possible, and adheres to a frugal diet of goat's milk, dates and raisins.' And, as a result, it is 'unquestioned that all classes personally revere Gandhi':

> I saw evidence of this when I attended a prayer service which the Mahatma (Great Soul) arranged one evening at the spacious grounds of a big home on Malabar Hill, Bombay. All types of people were there—wealthy and lowly, old and young—and all evinced the same attitude of intense devotion toward Gandhi, who sat huddled up on a raised platform like some ancient god.

---

[137] See 'Rebuff to Gandhi: Plan Rejected by Moslems', *The Sydney Morning Herald*, 1 August 1944, p. 3; and 'Hindu-Moslem Deadlock: Widespread Surprise at Jinnah's Blunt Rejection of Formula: Gandhi Again in Spotlight', *The Sydney Morning Herald*, 2 August 1944, p. 2.

[138] See 'Complete Racial Deadlock: Hindu-Moslem Talks', *The Sydney Morning Herald*, 30 September, p. 3.

[139] 'A Mysterious Message', *The Sydney Morning Herald*, 8 August 1944, p. 3.

Australia's Gandhi: The Press Depictions

Gandhi remains an enigma even to some men who have studied him for a lifetime, but these men grant him the quality of intense idealism, especially to the cause of the downtrodden of India. They say it is difficult to understand some of his traits and easy to misunderstand them. Take Satyagraha, for example. Satyagraha literally is 'insistence on truth,' but it is generally employed as meaning non-violent non-co-operation. In this doctrine, which Gandhi originated while practising as a lawyer among the Indian colony, in South Africa, the Mahatma aims to employ a weapon bringing moral influence as distinct from brute force against the wrongdoer. So say his closest adherents. The exponent of Satyagraha is prepared to suffer in a spirit of sacrifice.

Gandhi's doctors say he is suffering, from many ailments, and needs careful nursing and plenty of rest. But when I saw him daily at the conference at Dr. Jinnah's home I was repeatedly struck by his appearance and sprightliness, especially when he swung off down the hill, sometimes carrying a bamboo staff, and always with his Swiss watch swinging from his loin cloth.

Cartoonists have not done Gandhi justice. He has a great deal of personal charm, and his toothless smile is a winner. His well-creased, gleaming white loin cloth served to heighten the color of his brown skin, which usually is shining as a result of almond oil massage, which contrasts with the stern, immaculate Dr. Jinnah's sallowness.

The general feeling among Indians is that the failure of the Gandhi-Jinnah talks is one of tragic disappointment. It is felt that the collapse of the conference represents a staggering set back to the Indian Nationalist hopes of achieving independence in the manner desired.

Mr. Jinnah's summary: 'I've failed in the task of converting Gandhi,' puts the case clearly.

Publication of the letters that passed between Gandhi and Jinnah shows that Gandhi would not budge from the proposal that any separate state decided upon by plebiscite should come as soon as possible after India was free 'from foreign domination,' nor would Jinnah move from the League's plan that there should be a communal settlement before any united efforts to secure the freedom and independence of the peoples of India.[140]

In a mid-1945 review of India's parties and political leaders, T. L. Goodman, whose piece was carried in several papers, noted quite correctly that 'Mr. Gandhi is almost daily "news"' and that every one of his public statements and activities 'is reported, and although there are those who declare that India now needs more dynamic and realistic political leadership, Gandhi keeps on his throne.' He holds court in his mud-floored hut in Sevagram and in the 'gilded halls' of one of his millionaire supporters, or 'at some other admirer's palatial residence at a hill resort' to where people come 'hundreds of miles to seek the counsel of this oracle'.[141] For the rest of the year, the Australian papers carried many reports regarding Gandhi's personal meetings with the Viceroy Lord Wavell in Simla (Gandhi did not attend the conference on India's future held there, acting merely as an adviser to Congress), followed by reports of his meetings with the Bengal Governor, the Australian Richard Casey.

With the defeat of Nazi Germany, the press informed its readers that the Mahatma was not enthusiastic over the victory. The Australian papers made much of Gandhi's statement that he 'could not enthuse over the Allied Victory in Europe'; however, he did add 'that the Axis victory would have been far worse' because 'The Axis accepted violence as its creed. The Allies won because of their superior arms and manpower but at least paid lip service to peace, truth and non-violence.'[142]

[140] 'Unchallenged as Public Figure: Gandhi —"Humbug and Saint"', *The Age* (Melbourne), 3 October 1944, p. 2.
[141] T. L. Goodman, 'The Men Who Count in India's Bid for Independence', *The Sydney Morning Herald*, 9 June 1945, p. 2.
[142] 'Gandhi is Not Enthusiastic Over Victory', *The Telegraph* (Brisbane), 11 June 1945, p. 1.

Australia's Gandhi: The Press Depictions

The war having finished, political prisoners freed, and with Indian independence obviously close, the elderly Gandhi's appearance as a newsmaker in the press was greatly diminished. He was no longer part of the forthcoming leadership of the country. During 1946, reports had him denouncing riots; being attacked by 'untouchables' as not being their representative when he decided to stay in low-caste quarters, instead of in a more comfortable setting when visiting Delhi; his discussions with various British officials; and his comments on plans put forward concerning India's future. However, by this time he was well-known enough for longer retrospective biographical features on him to become more common.[143] His views on various subjects, often quoting articles from Gandhi's newspaper *Harijan* or from his regular prayer meetings, such as the atomic bomb, communism, and racial issues in South Africa, were routinely reported. And there were frequent references to him or his habits to conjure certain images, for example describing someone's physique or sartorial sense as being Gandhian, or noting that some proposal was as relevant in the modern world as Gandhi's spinning wheel, or that a hotel was so simple that Gandhi would revel in it. Photographs of him were frequently carried—even when there was no story, other than a caption, to go with them.

But there was still space for the odd dig at the sainted Mahatma: 'Gandhi nowadays does his contemplating squatting on a large hollow rubber mat, like a hot water bag, but filled with crushed ice', his 'quarters, in the so-called "sweepers' colony," are sumptuous with carpets, colored awnings, punkas, and a radio—things which the average sweeper has not seen in all his life.'[144] Other reports add 'a loud speaker system, with telephones and typewriters', to Gandhi's chattels.[145] However, perhaps the worst example was a report

---

[143] See, for example, 'A Holy Man in Politics', *Western Mail* (Perth), 23 May 1946, p. 3.
[144] 'Gandhi Sits on Ice', *The Herald* (Melbourne), 9 October 1946, p. 10.
[145] 'Gandhi Meditates in Comfort', *News* (Adelaide), 10 October 1946, p. 2.

by the vehemently anti-Gandhi journalist and radio personality, A. M. Pooley. As late as June 1947, he could still write that 'From the time I met him in 1921 I have always considered this man as a hypocritical publicity hunter, an inverted snob.' His column in the Sydney *Sun* went on to note that Gandhi had a police record in South Africa and that he 'was expelled from Johannesburg for molesting white women'.[146] It appears that Pooley had somehow perversely interpreted the allegation that Gandhi had broken South African laws because he, as a coloured person, had employed a white woman in his legal office as molestation. This caused outrage and something of an international incident, with objections even from Nehru in India.[147]

With the mass killing in the East Bengal district of Noakhali in October, the papers announced that Gandhi would tour the affected areas in a peace mission and soon he was back in the news spotlight—but more as a commentator rather than main player. When Mountbatten became the new, and last, Viceroy of India, one of the first things he did was to invite Jinnah and Gandhi for talks amid growing communal clashes around the country. Pictures of the Mahatma and Lord and Lady Mountbatten were regularly featured in the press; however, substantive pieces on Gandhi were replaced by small reports of his statements concerning his strong objection to the partition of India that Jinnah and the Moslem League demanded, of his warnings against violence and threats to go on a fast if violence continued, and on his probable retirement and possible move to Pakistan after partition.

There was, however, a more sympathetic human interest story about Gandhi at this time. His well-known, cheap fob watch, one of his 'most prized possessions', which 'for 25 years has dangled from his loincloth', was reported to have vanished on a train journey

---

[146] A. M. Pooley, 'Gandhi: He can wreck the new India plan', *The Sun* (Sydney), 8 June 1947, p. 8.

[147] See Maclean, *British India, White Australia*, p. 224.

between Bihar and Delhi. This watch was 'the only foreign article he permitted himself to use'.[148]

When independence came to a divided India, Gandhi was not in Delhi taking part in the celebrations. He was in a riot-torn part of Calcutta on a peace mission. The press reported that angry mobs threw stones at his residence demanding that he leave, but soon he was being hailed as a hero who brought peace to the worst affected parts of the city, his presence producing 'miraculous' results.[149] When rioting again broke out, Gandhi went on a fast that was to end 'only if and when sanity returns to Calcutta'.[150] Gandhi proclaimed that 'Fasting is a weapon which has hitherto proved infallible to me.' He added that 'What my word in person cannot do, my fast may.'[151] McKie, who visited Gandhi with three airmen in 1944, provided an informed analysis of Gandhi's fasts, noting that in India they are taken seriously because of their religious significance. While Australians may think that Gandhi is 'an old fool', when he starts a fast it makes complete sense to Indians.[152]

Gandhi had never fasted for a worthier cause. He was reported as having been 'groping in the dark for some time, and is now happy that God has shown him the way' and he would be 'happy even if the fast meant death to him'.[153] Gandhi broke his fast after three days when he had obtained an undertaking signed

---

[148] 'Gandhi Loses His Watch', *The Advertiser* (Adelaide), 28 May 1947, p. 1.

[149] '"Miracle" by Gandhi Brings Peace to Indian Riot Area', *The Sydney Morning Herald*, 29 August 1947, p. 1.

[150] 'Will Fast to "Restore" Sanity—Gandhi', *The Herald* (Melbourne), 2 September 1947, p. 1.

[151] 'Gandhi in Dramatic Bid for Peace', *The Sydney Morning Herald*, 3 September 1947, p. 3.

[152] Ronald McKie, 'Fasts Aren't a Joke in India', *The Daily Telegraph* (Sydney), 10 September 1947, p. 8.

[153] 'Peace Hopes on Gandhi's Fast: Challenge to India Terror', *The Herald* (Melbourne) 4 September 1947, p. 1.

by the leaders of the warring communities that 'they would be responsible for the preservation of peace—at the cost of their own lives, if necessary'. After he had ended his fast, 'Gangs of youth laid hand grenades, Sten guns and other weapons at Mahatma Gandhi's feet.'[154] It was proclaimed that the Calcutta 'miracle', whereby 'a week which began amid lawlessness has just finished with an astonishing all-round display of faith, hope and charity, will have a chapter to itself when Gandhi's life is written.'[155] Gandhi was now being portrayed as some sort of saviour, this being evident in the stories published when he went to Delhi to attempt to bring peace to the new nation's capital:

> Even greater than the power of troops and modern planes is the power of the mystic Gandhi. All India was startled but immensely relieved last month when the 78-year-old spiritual leader of the Hindus made a decision to virtually mortgage his life as a guarantee to the unhappy, uncertain minorities whose unhappiness and uncertainty became the excuse for mass slaughter.[156]

On 12 January, amid continued massacres in the country, Gandhi announced at his evening prayer meeting that he would undertake another fast for an indefinite period for Hindu-Muslim unity. While some papers made the point that the fast was to be undertaken 'in the luxurious home of the Delhi millionaire, G. D. Birla',[157] and others made light of the announcement, noting that Gandhi, 'the world's champion faster', was 'on another hunger

---

[154] 'Indians Surrender Weapons to Gandhi', *The Sun* (Sydney), 5 September 1947, p. 7.

[155] 'Gandhi Gets Miracle by Publicity', *The Herald* (Melbourne), 8 September 1947, p. 5.

[156] 'Was India Ripe for Partition? Racial Enmity Barrier to Development', *The Herald* (Melbourne), 13 September 1947, p. 14.

[157] 'Gandhi Fast in Luxury', *The Courier Mail* (Brisbane), 14 January 1948, p. 1.

strike',[158] most reports were factual in their comments, detailing Gandhi's failing health. Others were hopeful of a positive outcome for Gandhi's action, announcing that 'there has been a remarkable response'.[159] When Gandhi broke his fast after five days with the signing of a peace pledge by government and community leaders, the press was quick to announce Gandhi's success.

Under the heading 'Gandhi's Heroic Blackmail', the *Sydney Morning Herald* proclaimed that

> The courage and determination of a frail old man, without rank or office, seem likely to succeed, where Government parleys and appeals have failed, in halting India's drift to disaster. In Western eyes the response to Mr. Gandhi's heroic blackmail has been nothing short of astounding. No event since the granting of independence has stirred India's leaders and masses alike so deeply.... Mr. Gandhi has not only achieved a great personal triumph but has also given new hope for his country's future.[160]

And the papers noted the mass celebrations that followed.[161]

In a detailed examination of Gandhi's achievements, the well-known Hungarian-Australian journalist Dr Emery Barcs declared that 'with five days of fasting, 78-year-old Mahatma Gandhi has done what the outstanding men of India and Pakistan couldn't do in five months.' He added that while to a few Indians Gandhi's fast was 'political blackmail', to most 'it is a significant act by a saint'.[162]

---

[158] 'Peace for India or Death for Gandhi: World's Champion Faster on Another Hunger Strike', *Singleton Argus*, 14 January 1948, p. 1.

[159] 'Gandhi May Succeed: Response to Fast', *The Sydney Morning Herald*, 16 January 1947, p. 3.

[160] 'Gandhi's Heroic Blackmail', *The Sydney Morning Herald*, 19 January 1948, p. 2.

[161] See, for example, 'Joy Sweeps India When Gandhi Ends Fast', *The Sun* (Sydney), 19 January 1948, p. 7; and 'Enthusiasm in Delhi', *The Sydney Morning Herald*, 19 January 1948, p. 1.

[162] Dr Emery Barcs, 'He Opposes All Violence: How Gandhi's Fasting Stops Bloodshed', *The Daily Telegraph* (Sydney), 20 January 1948, p. 8.

Two days after the ending of the fast, a bomb exploded during Gandhi's prayer meeting. No one was injured and the bomb thrower was apprehended. Reports of the incident were carried widely in the Australian press and there was also reporting on police efforts to track down the ringleaders of the attempt on Gandhi's life. And then it happened. On 31 January 1948, the press was blanketed with front page reports about the assassination of the Mahatma the day before by a Hindu fanatic.

Gandhi after Gandhi

In the following days the Australian press expressed shock at Gandhi's death, lauded him as a saint, detailed his last movements, published tributes from world leaders, worried about riots in India, and even reported that the killing was part of a Communist plot to plunge India into a bloodbath.[163] There were descriptions of the Mahatma's cremation on the day after his slaying, and editorials and letters in praise of Gandhi, as well as reminiscences, became common in the days following his death.[164] Analyses of the reasons for the killing were published[165] and there was speculation over whether the fifth cricket test match would go ahead.[166] There were reports of the large memorial service that was held the following Sunday at the Melbourne Assembly Hall, attended by the Indian

---

[163] 'Plan to Plunge India into War: Gandhi's Death Part of Red Plot: Danger of Bloodbath', *Truth* (Brisbane), 1 February 1948, p. 3.

[164] 'Gandhi Once Aided Bassendean Man', *The Daily News* (Perth), 6 February 1948, p. 3.

[165] See, for example, Hal Colebatch, 'Why Was Gandhi Killed?', *The West Australian* (Perth), 7 February 1948, p. 18.

[166] '5th Test in Doubt', *The Age* (Melbourne), 2 February 1948, p. 3.

[167] 'Test Cricketers Weep at Gandhi Service', *The Sydney Morning Herald*, 9 February 1948, p. 3; and 'Packed Congregation Pays Tribute to Gandhi', *The Argus* (Melbourne), 9 February 1948, p. 3.

Australia's Gandhi: The Press Depictions

cricket team,[167] and of the flags at half mast and the minute of silence at the Melbourne Cricket Ground when the test did go on. This story was frequently accompanied by photographs of the Indian team wearing black arm bands.[168]

Perhaps the final significant news of Gandhi's achievement was the relative peace that descended on the country following his death: '... in the fortnight since Gandhi's assassination there has been a remarkable change in the political atmosphere in India.' Reports added that 'Gandhi, by his death, has gone far towards achieving what he could not bring about in his lifetime— communal tolerance.'[169]

Then, as could be expected, Gandhi gradually faded from the press reports. Books about Gandhi were noted and reviewed, and readers were informed that the Mahatma's picture would replace that of the King on one rupee notes in India, and that his picture would appear on Indian commemorative stamps. News shifted to the trial of Gandhi's assassins, and the feverish reporting about Gandhi ended.

Gandhi in the Australian Parliament

Besides the press accounts, there was also the odd mention of Gandhi in the Australian Federal Parliament. Over the years, politicians of all stripes have used the name of Gandhi in their speeches, often in their maiden speech, generally quoting some well-known aphorism attributed to the Mahatma. However, serious speeches concerning Gandhi are rare, and where he was mentioned, it was often in the context of point scoring from the opposition. For example, in 1935 during the second reading of a bill concerning sanctions against Italy for its invasion of Abyssinia (Ethiopia) under

[168] 'Cricketers Mourn Gandhi', *The Age* (Melbourne), 7 February 1948, p. 3.
[169] 'Check to Fanatics', *The Age* (Melbourne) 17 February 1948, p .1.

the covenant of the League of Nations, the Attorney General, Robert Menzies, noted that while Gandhi was 'the leading pacifist in the world', he had 'organised a boycott against the British Government for the purpose of securing independence'.[170] The following day, the conservative Country Party politician, Archie Cameron, stated that John Curtin, the Opposition Leader, had a position similar to Gandhi's, that is, bury his head in the sand and bring shame to the country.[171] A decade later, Labor Minister Arthur Calwell, in a debate over a suggested medical plan, in a putdown of the then opposition leader, stated that Menzies was like Gandhi, in that he 'communed with himself'.[172] Another decade later there was a serious question raised about the erection of a statue to Gandhi in Canberra.[173]

While Gandhi never achieved the celebrity status that he had in Britain and America, he and what he stood for were certainly not unknown to Australian audiences, as the coverage in the Australian press and mentions in the Parliament attest. But how was this knowledge utilised in this country? Did he have any impact that was more than as a newsworthy foreign political figure during his lifetime?

---

[170] Commonwealth, Parliamentary Debates. House of Representatives, 31 October 1935, Sanctions Bill, second reading, Robert Menzies.

[171] Commonwealth, Parliamentary Debates. House of Representatives, 1 November 1935, Sanctions Bill, second reading, Archie Cameron.

[172] Commonwealth, Parliamentary Debates. House of Representatives, 9 March 1945, Question, Suggested Medical Plan, Arthur Calwell.

[173] Commonwealth, Parliamentary Debates. House of Representatives, 11 November 1954, Question, Mahatma Gandhi, Anthony Luchetti.

5

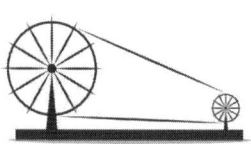

Australia's Gandhi Organisations

The American and English experience suggests that the place to look for Gandhian connections is in peace organisations and movements and in environmental campaigns, and possibly in religious groups that may have felt an affinity with Gandhi. The Australian Quakers lived up to these expectations, while peace and environmental campaigns generally did not. Aid organisations are not typically bracketed with Gandhi; however, in Australia the most prominent aid organisations had clear Gandhian underpinnings.

Gandhi, Peace Movements, and Environmental Campaigns

Much of the focus on Gandhi in the West came from peace movement activists who looked to him for inspiration, and, later, to provide a framework of tactics that could be used in campaigns. From the time Gandhi made it to international prominence, the peace movement literature in Britain and America was resplendent with references to Gandhi. Perhaps oddly, this was not the case in Australia: here, Gandhi does not even make it into the index of Saunders and Summy's *The Australian Peace Movement*;[1] is only briefly mentioned in Summy's lengthy article on Australia in the encyclopaedia of nonviolent action, *Protest, Power, and Change*, and then only in connection with relatively recent environmental campaigns;[2] and is only mentioned in passing in Eleanor Moore's 1948 book, *A Quest for Peace*. Moore informs her readers that Miss A. Lambrick, 'for some years president of W.I.L.P.F. [Women's International League for Peace and Freedom] in Australia', had a special interest 'in the peoples of Asia, their problems and customs'. As a result, 'She gave helpful addresses on Gandhi, Kagawa, Tagore and Krishnamurti', people who 'showed a marked sense of spiritual responsibility, for which it was difficult to find a parallel among Occidental leaders'. She added that she was captivated by some words of Gandhi's on ends and means, which 'struck us as an admirable definition of our own belief in peace and freedom, not only as an end, but as a method.'[3] While Gandhi is mentioned as one of several Orientals who may have been inspirational, and although the word 'method' is also mentioned, there is no connection made in her writing about Gandhi being someone who is to be followed in any tactical sense. And, given the reporting of Gandhi in the Australian press, this was not because of any absence of information about the Mahatma or his praxis.

While peace history books are relatively silent on Gandhi connections, Gandhi does make it into the pages of Australia's premier peace publication around the time of the Mahatma's

[1] Malcolm Saunders and Ralph Summy, *The Australian Peace Movement: A Short History*, Canberra: Peace Research Centre, Australian National University, 1986.

[2] Ralph Summy, 'Australia: A History of Nonviolent Action', in Roger S. Powers and William B. Vogele (eds), *Protest, Power, and Change: An Encyclopedia of Nonviolent Action from ACT-UP to Women's Suffrage*, New York and London: Garland Publishing, 1997, pp. 25–32. There is no mention of Gandhi in Summy's article 'Australia, Peace Movements In', Nigel J. Young (ed. in chief), *The Oxford International Encyclopedia of Peace*, Vol. 1, Oxford: Oxford University Press, 2010, pp.155–160.

[3] Eleanor Moore, *The Quest for Peace as I have Known it in Australia*, Melbourne: Wilke & Co, 1948, p. 107.

greatest fame in the early 1930s. The Reverend Dr Charles Strong, editor of the newsletter/magazine of the Melbourne branch of the London Peace Society and the Australian section of the WILPF, *Peacewards*, wrote sympathetically about Gandhi on several occasions. Under the heading 'India to-day gives cause for anxiety to the workers for peace', he noted that in India there were those who would accept dominion status within the British Commonwealth, such as the Princes and the Moderates, and those who wanted immediate independence, such as Gandhi and the 'violence party'. He added that Gandhi 'may probably be swept aside by the nationalists who believe in violence.'[4] Although some of his facts of Gandhi's life are incorrect, Strong also wrote a front page piece on Jesus and Gandhi[5] and a lengthy and considerate review of Charles Freer Andrew's recently published book on Gandhi, *Mahatma Gandhi's Ideas*. The review ends with: 'Gandhi was brought up as a Jain, Jains who regard it as a sin to hurt even a snake. He feels himself to be but clay in the hands of the Eternal, and hopes, through reincarnation, to be finally united with his God.'[6] While there was the occasional letter to the editor concerning Gandhi and an article on Gandhi's trip to Switzerland on his way home from the Round Table Conference by Strong's namesake, the American pastor Dr Sydney Strong,[7] most of the mentions of Gandhi were reports on Gandhi's activities by Strong himself. Others did not seem to engage with Gandhi's nonviolence, and there was little to demonstrate that Gandhi had any influence on the local peace movement at that time.

---

[4] Charles Strong, 'India to-day gives cause for anxiety to the workers for peace', *Peacewards* XIII (9), 1930, p. 6.
[5] Charles Strong, 'Jesus and Gandhi', *Peacewards* XIV (1), 1930, p. 1.
[6] Charles Strong, 'Mahatma Gandhi's Ideas', *Peacewards* XIII (11), 1930, p. 2. Although there was a strong Jain influence in the area where Gandhi grew up, he was not brought up as a Jain and he spoke very little about reincarnation, and then not as a way of being united with God.
[7] Sydney Strong, 'Gandhi in Switzerland', *Peacewards* XV (5), 1932, pp. 4–5.

While Gandhi did get the odd mention in articles discussing overseas peace movements and peace education, he is surprisingly absent from articles about local peace actions. When Summy and Saunders examined themes in the Australian peace movement, they pointed out that the country has had a long and vibrant history of peace campaigning, but that other than the anti-conscription movement during World War I and the opposition to the Vietnam War, it had generally been ignored by journalists and had little impact on policymakers. Gandhi was not mentioned in relation to the peace movement or in the Summy and Saunders article.[8]

However, Gandhi's name was mentioned in the defence statements of young men who had been taken before the courts for refusing to register for the military draft or refusing to enter service when they had been conscripted in the 1960s and early 1970s, during Australia's involvement in the Vietnam War. One of the young anti-war, anti-draft activists who had been imprisoned three times for his efforts, Michael Hamel-Green was strongly influenced by 'Gandhi's approach and philosophy'.[9] He explained that

> Early in 1968, in an effort to discover how apathy and indifference had been overcome in other times and in other places, I studied Gandhi's campaigns in India, the Civil Rights Movement in America and the CND movement in Britain. I rapidly became convinced of the efficacy of non-violent direct action techniques to mobilise people out of apathy. Such action works not by violent coercion and intimidation but by an appeal to people's conscience and rationality (not necessarily of those in power so much as of those who might join a movement in opposition to those in power). Such action is distinguished from bourgeois notions of 'non-violence' by virtue of the fact that it is not afraid, where necessary, to transgress the legal and institutional boundaries set

---

[8] Malcolm Saunders and Ralph Summy, 'Salient Themes of the Australian Peace Movement', *Social Alternatives* 3 (1), 1982, pp. 23–32.

[9] Personal communication from Michael Hamel-Green, 3 December 2018.

to dissent (and this is nearly always necessary). Gandhi and King had at least demonstrated the feasibility of such methods, even if they had not succeeded in creating a genuine revolution in their respective societies.[10]

The Peacemaker, the paper of the Federal Pacifist Council of Australia, was the venue for the publication of anti-conscription and anti-Vietnam War sentiments and where the arrest and trial outcomes of resisters were reported. The paper carried articles about nonviolence theory, often as extracts from American and British activists, which included references to Gandhi. However, while there was the occasional exception—for example, Christopher Campbell, who, while refusing to register for National Service, noted that 'in the Gandhian tradition' his actions were 'the last resort to be used in the pursuit of an attainable objective; the way of carrying on when legal means have failed, the acceptance of suffering is necessary'[11]—it is clear from the reproduced statements by local conscientious objectors that Gandhi generally played little part in their thinking.

Some radical student groups took a direct action Maoist approach to their activism, and for some others Gandhi provided not only strategies of nonviolence, but also a governing spirit. How much this influenced the power holders and onlookers, as opposed to the activists themselves, is an open question. In its overview of legal avenues to obtaining conscientious objector status, and thus being exempted from military service, an unsigned article in the University of New South Wales student paper, *Tharunka*, noted that 'The teachings of Mahatma Gandhi are often used as well [as religious affiliation]. Applicants on these grounds are almost never successful in gaining an indefinite deferment but are sometimes

[10] Michael Hamel-Green, 'Vietnam: Beyond Pity', *Australian Left Review* April–May 1970, p. 56.
[11] 'Christopher Campbell Replies to Mr. Bury', *Peacemaker* 29 (4&5), April–May 1967, p. 6.

declared to be "non-combatants".[12] Nevertheless, occasionally religious beliefs demonstrating pacifism were enough to exempt objectors from having to comply with the National Service Act.

When peace activist Quakers Diana and Barrie Pittock wrote about nonviolent social change, they noted that the Movement for a New Society in the United States grew out of Gandhian and activist Quaker traditions, and that African Americans were profoundly influenced by the Indian Gandhian movement. However, they could not point to any local movement with the same lineage.[13]

Charles Perkins was an Aboriginal activist who came to public attention as the leading figure of the 1965 Freedom Rides—a bus tour of outback New South Wales to protest against the discrimination that the local indigenous population was subjected to. Thirty or so volunteers protested outside Returned Soldiers' League establishments that would not allow Aboriginal ex-servicemen inside and invaded segregated swimming pools. The Freedom Rides achieved huge press coverage and forced local councils to abandon their blatantly segregationist policies.[14] Perkins does not mention the American Freedom Riders of 1961 in any detail other than to say that he and a few others went to see Reverend Ted Noffs of the Wayside Chapel in Sydney to ask about the idea of a freedom ride. Noffs informed them about the 'American situation'.[15] The US Freedom Riders saw their action as a way of demonstrating the superiority of Gandhian nonviolence over the use of violence. While Gandhi was the backdrop to the American movement, he was not mentioned as a source of

---

[12] 'Conscientious Objection', *Tharunka*, Kensington: UNSW, 26 April 1966, p. 12. See also Verity Burgmann, *Power and Protest: Movements for Change in Australian Society*, Sydney: Allen and Unwin, 1993, pp. 190–191.

[13] Diana and Barrie Pittock, 'Building an Alternative to the War System: Towards Nonviolent Social Change', *Social Alternatives* 3 (2), 1983, pp. 7–12.

[14] For a history of the Freedom Ride, see Charles Perkins, *A Bastard Like Me*, Sydney: Ure Smith, 1975, pp. 74–91.

[15] Perkins, *A Bastard Like Me*, p. 74.

Australia's Gandhi: Organisations

inspiration by the Australian participants, despite the fact that leaders such as Perkins clearly knew of Gandhi; in a 1974 national radio broadcast, Perkins reminded his audience that Gandhi considered the treatment of minorities as the primary test of a society's claim to be truly civilised.[16] Aboriginal academic John Maynard notes that earlier on there may have been some influence of the American Black activist Marcus Garvey and his Universal Negro Improvement Association (UNIA) on the Australian Aboriginal Progressive Association in the 1920s. While the UNIA was influenced by Gandhi, he could find no evidence of any direct Gandhian influence on Aboriginal activists.[17]

This lack of significant coverage seems to have been something of a puzzle even to the historians of the peace movement.[18] They suspect that while Australian peace movement leaders were aware of Gandhi, he did not appear to be relevant to them. This may have been because the Australian peace movement was overwhelmingly 'pacific-ist' (that is, aspirationally pacifist) rather than 'absolute pacifist', and for them Gandhi may have been too much of a pacifist ideologue. Gandhi may also not have been seen as relevant because the local peace movement was concerned with issues around conscription, disarmament, and protesting against wars that Australia was involved in, while Gandhi was seen as being involved with Indian national independence.[19]

---

[16] Peter Read, *Charles Perkins: A Biography*, Melbourne: Penguin, 2001, p. 193.

[17] John Maynard, '"Be the Change You Want to See": The Awakening of Cultural Nationalism—Gandhi, Garvey and the AAPA', *Borderlands e-journal* 4 (3), 2005.

[18] Personal communications from Hilary Summy, 22 and 23 February 2018.

[19] Personal communication from Malcolm Saunders, 23 February 2018, and Carolyn Rasmussen, who published a book on the Australian peace movement in the 1930s (see *The Lesser Evil? Opposition to War and Fascism in Australia, 1920–1941*, Melbourne: The History Department, The University of Melbourne, 1992), 23 February 2018.

Looking at Western peace literature generally, it soon becomes clear what a large part the example and philosophy of Mahatma Gandhi play in it. American and British notables wrote about them, and set up organisations based on them. That Gandhi played such a minor part in the Australian literature could at first be put down to the fact that Australia was such a small pond that naturally those surveying the literature would focus on key areas, the seemingly most important and most influential sources. On further investigation, a different picture emerges. That Gandhi did not feature in the Australian survey literature was not merely because there were more important players to focus on, but because, for some reason, Gandhi played such a miniscule part in Australian peace writings and peace movements.

While Gandhi seems to be more to the fore in Australian environmental campaigns, something similar can be said about their connection with Gandhi: he was something of a shadow figure, one whose name came up in stirring speeches but, with the exception of the activism of the Melbourne Rainforest Action Group (see below), was not explicitly looked to in the formulation of long-term strategic goals or even directly in tactical choices. Many campaigns took nonviolence seriously. Campaigners talked about nonviolent sustainable lifestyles, discussed the efficacy and limits of nonviolence, and held workshops where nonviolence was role-played. The issue at hand was nonviolence, not necessarily Gandhian nonviolence. Nevertheless, Gandhi was often used as a rhetorical tool in environmental campaigns.

Although Gandhi is mentioned only once in his partial autobiography[20] and not at all in his authorised biography,[21] in his speeches Dr Bob Brown, the founder of the Australian Greens, frequently referenced the Mahatma—in particular the statement

[20] Bob Brown, *Optimism: Reflections on a Life of Action*, Melbourne: Hardie Grant, 2014, p. 199.
[21] James Norman, *Bob Brown: A Gentle Revolutionary*, Sydney: Allen and Unwin, 2004.

Australia's Gandhi: Organisations

attributed to Gandhi that 'The Earth provides enough to satisfy every man's need but not for every man's greed', and his alleged answer that 'It would be a good thing' when asked what he thought of Western civilisation.[22]

Robert James ('Bob') Brown is an iconic figure in Australian environmental and political circles. He was born in Oberon, a small New South Wales country town just after Christmas of 1944. He graduated as a medical doctor from the University of Sydney in 1968 and then worked in hospitals in Canberra, Darwin, and Alice Springs. During those years, he refused to certify those conscripted during the Vietnam War as being fit for military service. Between 1970 and 1972 he worked in hospitals in London and then, after travelling home as a ship's doctor on a passenger liner, as a general practitioner in Launceston in Tasmania, where he joined the ultimately unsuccessful but lesson-rich campaign to save Lake Pedder from being flooded. In 1976, he fasted for a week to protest against the arrival in Hobart of the gigantic American nuclear-powered and armed aircraft carrier, the *USS Enterprise*. Earlier that year, he had rafted down the Franklin River to the Gordon River, an adventure that he maintains altered his life.[23]

From 1979 until 1984 he served as director of the Tasmanian Wilderness Society and then led the campaign to stop the damming of the wild Franklin River. This led to his arrest, along with almost 1,300 others. He was jailed for nineteen days in Hobart, joining close to 500 others who were also imprisoned. Brown entered State politics in 1983 and served as the Member for Denison for ten years. Between 1996 and 2012, when he retired, he was a Tasmanian Senator in the Federal Parliament, campaigning for peace, human rights, and environmental causes. After his retirement from public office, he set up the Bob Brown Foundation to promote environmental awareness.

---

[22] Personal communication from Bob Brown, 24 January 2019.
[23] Brown, *Optimism*, p. 29.

Before the commencement of the Franklin River campaign, Australia's most celebrated environmental protest, Brown wrote that,

> The direct defence of wilderness will take courage and restraint by a great number of people. *Most of all, we must be peaceful.* There is aggression in the air. The State government will hope to divert attention from the absurdity of its scheme by creating a 'law and order' issue out of our campaign to defend the wilderness. They hope to achieve aggression and confrontation. We will win where they fail.
> There are clear guidelines to the peaceful blockade. Firstly we must act without threat or harm to anyone or any living thing. That is an absolute. To be successful in depriving the authorities of the violent confrontation they seek, we must not only be peaceful ourselves, but do all we can to avoid them harming us. That will require good planning, flexibility and, at times, rapid change of tactics.[24]

While in this explanation for the necessity of nonviolence Brown does not mention Gandhi by name (and of course there is no reason why he should), it demonstrates a very Gandhian form of action and he later assessed that Gandhi's 'example on peaceful direct action has been pivotal in Tasmania's great environmental protests.'[25] The protest to save the Franklin River from being dammed entailed two days of nonviolence training at the frontier town of Strahan before activists were permitted upriver to the protest site. For some, this was constraining, while for others it was enlightening.

In any case, while Gandhi and Gandhian nonviolence may have provided something of a guiding principle to some groups and

---

[24] Quoted in Jeni Kendal and Eddie Buivids, *Earth First: The Struggle to Save Australia's Rainforest,* Sydney: Australian Broadcasting Corporation, 1987, pp. 106–107.

[25] Personal communication from Bob Brown, 24 January 2019.

organisations, the impact was small. Again, as was the case with the peace literature, the histories of environmental campaigns, and protest campaigns generally, Gandhi either did not feature at all or was merely mentioned in passing as a historical antecedent.[26]

Gandhi and the Quakers

Eventually Gandhi became better known as his name was mentioned in conscientious objector trials, through the various 'principled' nonviolent campaigns, movies, and books, and through the efforts of Australian Quakers. Gandhi and members of the Society of Friends had a natural affinity. They both had strong beliefs about the importance of nonviolence and the presence of God in everyone, and shared a practical approach to social problems. Gandhi's method of satyagraha 'vividly recalled the peaceful, open disobedience of seventeenth-century Quakers in Britain to laws which their consciences could not accept'. And the same could be said about the quest for Truth, which for Gandhi and for Quakers had to 'irradiate all the business of daily living, and bring justice and mercy, righteousness and peace, into the common intercourse of humanity'. Further, they both believed that 'the use of outward weapons', however righteous, was not to be condoned, and that social justice, which was essential to peace, had to 'be fought for with "the sword of the spirit" alone'.[27] Quakers became Gandhi's closest supporters in Europe and America. He was sent a parcel of Quaker books by his friend Horace Alexander[28] and he knew about the Quaker practice of silence.[29]

---

[26] See, for example, Drew Hutton's introductory essay, 'What is Green Politics?', in Drew Hutton (ed.), *Green Politics in Australia*, Sydney: Angus and Robertson, 1987, p. 19.

[27] Marjorie Sykes, *Quakers in India*, London: Allen and Unwin, 1980, pp. 2–3, 128.

[28] Gandhi to Horace G. Alexander, 25 January 1929.

[29] See Gandhi to Mirabehn, 22 June 1932.

This dialogue with Gandhi's Truth and his nonviolence had proved to be attractive to many members of the Society of Friends, and his close associates included Reginald Reynolds, as well as Carl Heath, John S. Hoyland, Horace Alexander (who spent time with Gandhi during his Noakhali pilgrimage), and Agatha Harrison, the leading members of the Indian Conciliation Group, formed during his stay in London for the Round Table Conference to act as the go-between for British and Congress politicians and, in effect, as Gandhi's press consultants. Marjorie Sykes, known as a Gandhian Quaker because of the way she lived her Quaker belief, and a Quaker Gandhian because of the way she practised Gandhian philosophy, noted that 'By the time Mahatma Gandhi visited London for the Round Table Conference of 1931 he had several trusted Quaker friends; before he left London he had many more.'[30] However, as Hallam Tennyson notes, 'Quakers have been working on more or less Gandhian lines for several centuries.'[31] This natural affinity was evident in Australia.

One of Australia's main connections with Gandhi was through the Quaker Donald Groom. He was born in February 1913 in England into a religious pacifist family and, unusually for the time, the family was vegetarian and teetotaller. Just before the war commenced, his parents, 'perturbed by the Methodists' refusal to reject war,'[32] became Quakers. Groom's father worked at the local cooperative society.

When he had left home, Groom undertook a degree in accounting but retained 'his love of unionism, cooperative ventures,

---

[30] Sykes, *Quakers in India*, p. 1. For her personal reminiscences of Gandhi, see Jehangir P. Patel and Marjorie Sykes, *Gandhi: His Gift of the Fight*, Rasulia: Friends Rural Centre, 1987.

[31] Hallam Tennyson, 'Preface', in Patel and Sykes, *Gandhi*, p. viii.

[32] Victoria Rigney, *Peace Comes Walking*, Carindale, Qld: Glass House Books, 2002, p. 3. For biographical sketches of Groom, see 'Donald Groom: Biographical', *The Australian Friend*, October 1979, p. 2; and Donald Groom, 'Looking Back—Looking Forward', *The Australian Friend*, June 1970, pp. 2–4.

and workers' education programs'. His biographer informs us that 'The more that he studied economics, the greater became his conviction that he had to engage in social change if he was to make a difference in the world.'[33] He was elected Secretary of a Workers' Education Committee on International Affairs and, at the time of Hitler's showcase Berlin Olympic Games, he went to Germany to study international socialism. Two years later, at the age of twenty-five, he resigned and took up an accounting position with a Quaker aid organisation that was engaged in relief work in Spain during that country's civil war.

While continuing his relief work in Paris, Groom attended a meeting of the International Fellowship of Reconciliation and heard Gandhi's London host, Muriel Lester, speak about the Mahatma and his philosophy of nonviolence. This changed the course of his life. After the 'horror of Bonn, and the misery of Barcelona', Groom heard about the positive example set by Gandhi in India from an Indian friend studying in Paris, and decided that he had to go to India to learn more. He returned briefly to England, married his soul-mate Erica Hodgkin, and prepared for service in India.

Donald and Erica were assigned to service Hoshangabad in central India and he and his now pregnant wife sailed for Bombay at the beginning of August 1940. In India, one of Groom's first trips was to see Gandhi, whom he was to get to know well. In 1943 the Grooms took responsibility for the Friends Rural Centre in Rasulia, which had been a Quaker centre for rural development since 1875. The Centre established emergency work schemes to provide income for the surrounding villagers, a cooperative where grains could be bought at fair, not black market, prices, and a model farm where they could experience different methods of cultivation. For the next several years, the Centre occupied their lives. However, the education of their children became a concern for Erica, and the two eldest

---

[33] Rigney, *Peace Comes Walking*, p. 11.

were sent to missionary boarding schools. In 1956 Groom joined Gandhi's spiritual heir, Vinoba Bhave, on his Bhoodan 'land gift' marches and Erica returned to England with their three children.[34] Marjorie Sykes became the new interim director at Rasulia.

For twenty-one years, the last five with Vinoba, the 'walking saint', Groom had devoted his life to India with visits of various lengths back to England and to his family, from which he was becoming slowly estranged. In 1961, he returned to the now also estranged country of his birth. There he spoke regularly on the messages of Gandhi and Vinoba, but spent much of the following years moving between the two countries. In that time he undertook two lecture tours of America, was for four years the Field Secretary of the Friends Peace Committee, and then served as the General Secretary of the National Peace Council.[35]

At the end of 1969, he was invited to go to Australia, to where his now grown children had all emigrated, to be the first full-time paid Secretary of the Yearly Meeting of the Australian Religious Society of Friends. Just before leaving England, at the Summer Conference of the Fellowship of Reconciliation in Chichester, he spoke on the 'Inspiration and Challenge of Gandhi's Life' and on 'Non-Violence According to Gandhi'.[36]

He and Erica arrived in Australia at the beginning of April 1970. After some months in Sydney, they moved to Melbourne. For the next two years, Groom worked to improve communication between Australian Quaker groups, and between Quakers and the rest of the Australian population. He spoke on Gandhi and nonviolence and, as Martin Luther King Jr. had 'constructed an

---

[34] For Groom's involvement in the Bhoodan Movement, see Donald G. Groom, *With Vinoba*, Varanasi: Sarva Seva Sangh, 1969.

[35] See 'Around the Churches', *The Canberra Times*, 12 September 1970, p. 15; and 9 October 1971, p. 16.

[36] Both Donald Groom, 'Gandhi's Challenge', and Constance Willis, 'Non-Violence According to Gandhi', are in *The Peacemaker* 32 (112), January/February 1970, p. 8.

Australia's Gandhi: Organisations

American version of non-violence from Gandhian *satyagraha*, ... Donald recognised the importance of finding a version relevant to Australians.'[37] He became a major force in translating Gandhian philosophy to young peace activists.

He organised schools for nonviolence training and became involved with those resisting the Australian National Service Act. He also 'endeavoured to bring an understanding of Asia—and particularly of India—and what India has to teach us—to Friends and to others limited in their vision by an exclusively European inheritance.'[38] And this, to a large extent, meant what he had learned from Gandhi and the Indian Gandhians.

In mid-1972, Groom attended the fourteenth triennial conference of War Resisters' International in Sheffield. On the way back to Australia, during a visit to India, on 11 August, along with seventeen others, he was killed in a plane crash at New Delhi. Although he had only been in Australia for two-and-a-half years, he had a significant impact on the organisation of local Quaker practice and the peace movement more generally.

Aid Organisations and Gandhi

Community Aid Abroad grew out of the organisation Food for Peace (FFP). Father Gerard Kennedy Tucker, an Anglican priest who founded the Brotherhood of Saint Laurence in the 1930s to work with the poor, first in Newcastle and then in Melbourne, inspired the setting up of Food for Peace in 1951[39] when he sent

---

[37] Rigney, *Peace Comes Walking*, p. 244.
[38] 'Donald Groom', *The Australian Friend*, March 1973, p. 11.
[39] There is debate about the date: some sources put it at 1951, others at 1952 and even 1953. See 'Brotherhood Timeline: Through the Decades: 1950: Community Issues', fn10. Available at bsltimeline.pbworks.com/w/page/27549149/Through%20the%20decades%3A%201950 (accessed November 2023).

the first food parcel to India in order to help those suffering during a famine.[40] From 1953, when the first sum of money was sent to a poverty-stricken hospital in a rural north Indian village via local Quakers, regular collections of money were then forwarded to a Quaker working in India who had links with Indian Gandhian self-help projects. One of the chroniclers of this history noted the similarities between Tucker and Gandhi as both 'resorted to strategies of civil disobedience and non-violent resistance in their respective battles to overcome injustice and indifference'.[41] Tucker lived by the principles of 'demonstrating on a small scale what needs to be done on a large scale', 'putting a fence at the top of the cliff instead of an ambulance at the bottom' and 'arousing the conscience of the community'.[42]

In 1961, Tucker's nephew David Scott was seconded to Food for Peace as its first staff member.[43] In 1962, Scott, 'the young man who used to help at weekends, went to India to see what had been achieved by "The Society of Friends", in New Delhi, a reliable organisation which handled the original Food for Peace donations and came back to become FFP's first Director.'[44] The name of the organisation was changed to Community Aid Abroad

---

[40] For the life of Gerard Tucker, see John Handfield, *Friends and Brothers: A Life of Gerard Kennedy Tucker, Founder of the Brotherhood of St. Laurence and Community Aid Abroad*, Melbourne: Hyland House, 1980; Gerard Tucker, '*Thanks Be': The Autobiography of Gerard Kennedy Tucker*, Melbourne: Brotherhood of St. Laurence, 1954; and I. R. Carter, *God and Three Shillings: The Story of the Brotherhood of St. Laurence*, Melbourne: Lansdowne Press, 1967.

[41] Bill Deane, *The Earth Has Enough: The Story of Community Aid Abroad*, Melbourne: Community Aid Abroad, 1978, pp. 10, 37–38.

[42] David Scott, *He Got Things Done: A Memoir of Gerard Kennedy Tucker, Anglican Priest*, Melbourne: Brotherhood of St. Laurence, 2000, p. 5.

[43] For the early history of the Brotherhood of St. Laurence and Food for Peace, see Ben Bennett, *G. K. Tucker Settlement: An Historical Record 1935–1995*, Melbourne: Brotherhood of St. Laurence, 1995.

[44] Bennett, *G. K. Tucker Settlement*, p. 20.

Australia's Gandhi: Organisations

(CAA), so as not to be seen merely as a food providing agency. It became the first Australian non-governmental international aid and advocacy agency outside missionary societies and the Red Cross. The emphases became the uplift and development of whole communities.[45] CAA took up working with Third World groups in ways that aimed to develop entire communities rather than merely provide emergency aid to the groups they partnered in an effort to bring a greater level of justice to the world. And initially, these groups were Indian Gandhians.

Susan Blackburn, the chronicler of CAA, notes that 'India was an easy place for CAA to find project partners' because there could be found 'a host of Indian village development workers who proved to be a constant source of inspiration about new ideas and methods. In the 1960s most of those Indian partners were Gandhians, part of an already well-established network of voluntary social workers.'[46] CAA's first full-time Indian field representative, Roshan Lal Agarwal, explained that the reason for working with Gandhians was that he sought partner organisations where the workers 'were absolutely reliable', and where it was clear that all the money that came from Australia 'was spent the right way'. In this regard, 'Gandhian people who had given their lives to service could be depended on.'[47]

Eventually, as partner groups matured and as thoughts about the type of groups and projects evolved, Gandhian organisations became an ever smaller part of CAA's India programme. However, the CAA/Gandhi connection was far more than the fact that most of CAA's early work focussed on India and there, on Gandhian organisations. It also flowed the other way. Gandhi's name was often employed by Scott, who was influenced by the Gandhian social worker Sugata Dasgupta, whom he considered a mentor.

---

[45] For the history of CAA, see Susan Blackburn, *Practical Visionaries: A Study of Community Aid Abroad*, Melbourne: Melbourne University Press, 1993.
[46] Blackburn, *Practical Visionaries*, p. 45.
[47] Blackburn, *Practical Visionaries*, p. 57.

Gandhi's Australia/Australia's Gandhi

Although Gandhi's name is not mentioned explicitly in many CAA documents, early policy papers certainly came across as having the 'flavour' of Gandhian principles and Gandhi's approach to development and the formulation of appropriate approaches to aid. In his autobiography, written in the third person, Scott informs his readers that 'He was particularly influenced by the concept and articulation of community development promoted by Gandhi in India in the 1960s, taking the concept and fostering its application in community projects in inner-city Melbourne in the 1960s and 70s.'[48]

The Queensland social work academic and ex-student of Dasgupta, Anthony Kelly,[49] had long been involved with CAA as the academic advisor to the Community Leadership Program that was sponsored jointly by the University of Queensland and CAA, and managed by Mike Dendle. The Program had conducted many guided tours of India, showing the participants on the ground development work. This exposure programme was conducted twice a year and continued for more than a decade. It was profoundly influenced by Gandhian thinking and Gandhian projects.

For the month of October 1998, CAA advertised a dedicated tour of India, 'In the Footsteps of Gandhi'. It was to take in various Gandhian sites in New Delhi (the Gandhi Peace Foundation), Ahmedabad (the Sabarmati Ashram), Pune (Aga Khan Palace and Yerwada Prison), Wardha (Sevagram Ashram), and Mumbai (Mani Bhavan). The prospectus for the tour announced its aims as providing those with an interest in Gandhi with insights 'into the application of [Gandhi's] ideas in India as well as enabling consideration of their relevance to Australian life and society', providing 'valuable perspectives on social change' and 'new

---

[48] David Scott (with Carrie Hutchinson), *Always Say Yes: The Life of David Scott*, Sydney: Pier 9, 2014, p. 230.

[49] Not to be confused with Anthony Kelly the Melbourne-based nonviolent activist, Peace Brigades International trainer, and founding member of Pt'chang, a 'Nonviolent Community Safety and Peacekeeping Group'.

Australia's Gandhi: Organisations

perspectives and challenges' for those 'more concerned with exploring their personal philosophies', and, finally, 'Australians with a genuine interest in international development and global issues will gain a broader perspective on matters of aid and development and the international context within which we live in Australia.' The trip was to be led by Dave Andrews, who had engaged in social work with disillusioned travellers in India for many years and was deeply influenced by Gandhi, and Don Gobbett, who was one of the founders of the 'post-Christian' intentional community, Cennednyss, in the Adelaide Hills and who also acknowledged his debt to Gandhi.[50] Unfortunately, due to a lack of participants, the trip never went ahead and, while there were other trips to India, no further explicitly Gandhi-related tours eventuated.

Oxfam Australia, as CAA is now known,[51] is one of Australia's largest aid and development enterprises (having merged with the Australian Freedom from Hunger Campaign in 1991). It has grown far beyond the vision of Tucker and the Food for Peace volunteers of the mid-twentieth century. It has development projects in thirty countries, it is an important channel for emergency aid in cases of natural disasters, it engages in campaigning for Aboriginal and Third World worker rights, it operates shops selling goods produced ethically for fair pay by Third World producers, and organises fundraising events such as the annual Walk Against Want. In short, while it has expanded the scope of its work significantly, its origins were clearly Gandhi-inspired.

---

[50] See Estelle and Don Gobbett, 'From Mission Field to Potato Patch', in Bill Metcalf (ed.), *From Utopian Dreaming to Communal Reality: Co-operative Lifestyles in Australia*, Sydney: UNSW Press, 1995, pp. 84–98.

[51] For how CAA became linked with Oxfam, see Maggie Black, *A Cause for Our Times: Oxfam: The First 50 Years*, Oxford: Oxford University Press, 1992, p. 170.

6

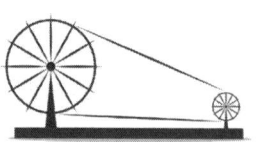

Australia's Gandhi People

Several of what may be seen as people's movements that did have a Gandhian underpinning were to a large extent the personification of their founder or leading light. For example, it is unlikely that the Melbourne Rainforest Action Group would have operated on Gandhian principles as it did without the guidance of Robert Burrowes, the most well-known activist in the organisation; and, despite years of struggle, the Australian Gandhian Movement remained little more than the efforts of its founder, Stephen Murphy. The key person in the Sydney-based International Centre of Nonviolence is Gambhir Watts, who founded and has run the organisation from the time that he was inspired by Gandhi's South African granddaughter, Ela Gandhi. And in Perth, the Love Makes a Way organisation is to a very large extent the activities of the pastor Jarrod McKenna. Here, I want to look at these Gandhi-inspired individuals who personify the organisations that encompass them, to try to see what it was that brought them to Gandhi and what they took from Gandhi's philosophy. I also want to briefly refer to Allan and Wendy Scarfe, who went to India to do Gandhian work and then gave Australians a unique view of the post-Gandhi Gandhian movement.

Australia's Gandhi: People

Nonviolent Activism

Generally, nonviolent action in Australia was seen as a useful tactic rather than a philosophy or way of life.[1] However, in his account of nonviolent action in Australia, Ralph Summy notes that 'a few leading activists were committed to nonviolence as a way of life. Influenced by Gandhian ideals, they have gathered in groups like Melbourne's Rainforest Action Group.' He adds that MRAG campaigns 'are conducted according to a principled conception of nonviolence, in which secrecy and sabotage are renounced', and efforts are taken to build genuine positive relationships with various protagonists. He then singles out Robert Burrowes (who was the inspiration for Gandhian nonviolence within the group) as the prime example of those practising 'principled', that is, Gandhian, nonviolence.[2]

When Robert J. Burrowes turned fourteen in 1966, he came to a turning point in his life. He 'decided that I would devote my life to answering two questions—Why are human beings violent? How can this violence be ended?'[3] Following the completion of an Economics and Politics degree at Monash University in Melbourne in 1973, a Master of Arts in 1984, and, as a highly qualified lifesaver, a five-year stint as the Honorary Secretary of the Victoria branch

---

[1] Peter Jones, Margaret Pestorius, and Bryan Law, 'The Story of the Australian Nonviolence Network', *Nonviolence Today* 43, March/April 1995, pp. 16–19.

[2] Ralph Summy, 'Australia: A History of Nonviolent Action', in Roger S. Powers and William B. Vogele (eds), *Protest, Power, and Change: An Encyclopedia of Nonviolent Action from ACT-UP to Women's Suffrage*, New York and London: Garland Publishing, 1997, p. 31.

[3] For a summary of Burrowes' life, see Robert J. Burrowes, 'Robert J. Burrowes: If You Live Your Dream, You Have Lived'. Available at robertjburrowes.wordpress.com (accessed November 2023). Links to Burrowes' publications can be found on this site.

of The Royal Life Saving Society Australia, Burrowes completed the writing of a Gandhi-related Ph.D. dissertation under the supervision of Ralph Summy at the University of Queensland in Brisbane in 1993, and lectured part-time at the Royal Melbourne Institute of Technology in a course on War and Peace in the Nuclear Age.

During 1982 and 1983, Burrowes participated in the Franklin River Blockade in western Tasmania, and for the next several years was engaged in many other environmental and anti-military campaigns. This led to around twenty-five arrests and fifteen periods of imprisonment. In 1985, he volunteered for three months with a Community Aid Abroad refugee health team in the Sudan. Here, he was confronted with the aftermath of war and famine. Throughout his activist years, references to Gandhi were common in his writings and speeches.[4]

Of the many campaigns Burrowes was associated with, three stand out. Since the 1982–1983 tax year, as someone who refused to kill, he started redirecting part of his taxes to nonviolent, environmental, human rights, and development causes as a matter of conscience, rather than allowing his money to support killing in the form of military expenditure. He refused to pay for others to do any killing for him. In his first tax withholding action, in November 1983, he presented the Taxation Office in Melbourne with a cheque for $1,344.49, being 90.2 per cent of his assessment, that being the portion of the previous federal budget that was not allocated to military spending.[5] In following years he attempted to pay his tax bills 'in kind' with non-lethal goods (such as shovels, which would have been useful for farming purposes in famine-stricken countries,

---

[4] For Gandhian influences on Burrowes' life, see Josephine Flanagan, 'Protesting can be Fun', *The Herald* (Melbourne), 21 July 1989, p. 10.

[5] 'Refusal to Pay Tax for Military Spending', *The Canberra Times*, 22 November 1983, p. 3.

dirt representing rent for our presence on Aboriginal land, and water tanks and trees for the welfare of a dry continent), rather than in 'legal tender'.

A debt action was brought against him by the Commonwealth of Australia in August 1989 to recover just over $4,700 in withheld taxes and charges for lateness in payments. The magistrate ordered Burrowes to pay the outstanding amount plus interest and further court costs. On 27 November 1991, in the Federal Court of Australia, Burrowes was declared bankrupt so that the money owed by him by way of unpaid taxes (there being no other creditors) could be collected by the taxation authorities.[6] In December, he received a formal letter from the Official Receivers Office Insolvency and Trustee Service Australia, informing him of his obligations as a bankrupt. He wrote back, declaring that his conscience would not allow him to comply with the directives of the Court.[7] This meant that what was originally a debt action had moved into the sphere of criminal law. Now Burrowes was not only withholding money, but he was also facing contempt of court charges for refusing to obey a court order which directed him, as a bankrupt, to cooperate with the public trustee. Imprisonment is a standard outcome of a conviction of contempt.

On Wednesday, 22 April 1992, the long saga of Burrowes' war tax resistance campaign came to a head when he was back in the Federal Court on contempt charges. Surprisingly, a half-hour after the proceeding began, he walked out of the court with a conviction for contempt, but without additional penalty. In a manner akin to Gandhi's asking for either the highest penalty from the judge trying him for sedition in 1922 if the judge thought that Gandhi was wrong in following his conscience, or for the judge to resign

---

[6] For Burrowes' defence statement, see 'Defence Statement of Robert J. Burrowes, Tax Resister, before a Federal Court of Australia in Melbourne 27 November, 1991', *Social Alternatives* 11 (2), 1992, pp. 43–48.

[7] See Robert J. Burrowes, 'Bankrupt Tax Resister Refuses to Cooperate', *Nonviolence Today* 24, January/February 1992, p. 12.

from his post if he did not, Burrowes put it to Mr Justice Northrop that there were two possible outcomes:

> On the one hand, if you are not convinced that my conscience should be the basis of my behaviour on this matter or that there is not adequate merit in my intellectual, moral and conscientious convictions regarding my absolute abhorrence of military violence, and if you believe totally in the adequacy of the law as it applies in this case, then you must, in accord with your own conscience, impose a penalty as the law prescribes. In these circumstances, no other course of action would be appropriate.
>
> On the other hand, your conscience may well tell you that what I am saying entails a sense of justice that goes beyond the law as it stands and your judgement today could reflect that. In any case, you must be willing to make an imaginative decision that may be viewed initially with some scepticism by your legal colleagues but which I can assure you will be viewed by many people, and certainly future generations, as both enlightened and visionary.[8]

He then invited the judge to join him in the struggle to create a new world civilisation of peace and justice. Not surprisingly, Burrowes was ordered to pay costs (the judge made no response to the defendant's statement that he would refuse to pay), but no further order was made and Burrowes was free to leave the court. The issue of his war tax resistance has not been raised since.

Several Australian capital cities had rainforest action groups, groups that operated by consensus and eschewed hierarchy. The Melbourne group was the largest and most prominent, and the ex-lifesaver Burrowes was its leading figure. Between 1989 and 1990 MRAG was at its peak, conducting its actions in the spirit of Gandhi. The goal of the group was to end Australia's imports

---

[8] Thomas Weber, 'War Tax Resister Convicted of Contempt', *Nonviolence Today* 27, July/August 1992, p. 7. See also Kay Ansel, 'Activist Not Punished for Contempt', *The Age* (Melbourne), 23 April 1992, p. 5.

of rainforest timber from Southeast Asian sources, and thus to curtail rainforest destruction. The most newsworthy of the nonviolent actions involved blockading the ships bringing in the timber from berthing, by activists—either swimming or in kayaks or on surfboards—interposing themselves between the ships and the wharf, painting the sides of docked ships with anti-logging messages, and attempting to reload timber onto ships that had unloaded their cargo. MRAG members always maintained strict nonviolent discipline and informed the police and other authorities about their actions in advance.[9]

MRAG was even praised in the pages of the police magazine *Police Life* for being so forthcoming in their notifications of action plans to police: 'With not a hint of violence at any action, the group now has the confidence of police to be trusted to be responsible and co-operative.' In turn, the police even alerted MRAG to the arrival of rainforest timber carrying ships that may have skipped their attention, and Burrowes and activist Alexandra Perry 'could only praise the police for their assistance and professional conduct during the dispute.'[10] In an analysis of the trials of arrested MRAG members, legal academic Roger Douglas concluded that 'when the protestors are committed nonviolent activists, the demand on resources is minimal. Police can safely assume that there are not going to be attacks on life and property, and that if arrests are to be made, they will arouse minimal resistance.'[11] And, at trials, this has led to police prosecutors coming close to assuming the role of the defence.

---

[9] The magazine *Nonviolence Today* carried several articles by Robert Burrowes describing the actions and lessons learned from them. See, for example, 'Nonviolent Struggle for the Rainforests', *Nonviolence Today* 15, June/July 1990, pp. 3–6.
[10] Geoff Callcott, 'The Greening of the Thin Blue Line', *Police Life*, May 1990, pp. 20–21.
[11] Roger Douglas, 'Timber Cutting on Trial: Police, Courts and the Rainforest Action Group', *Interdisciplinary Peace Research* 2 (2), 1990, p. 83.

Under Burrowes' guidance, the campaign of MRAG utilised an 'ideological-strategic' approach rather than the more typical 'tactical-pragmatic' one of most previous campaigns.[12] In his more detailed writings on nonviolence theory, Burrowes sees the first type (later termed 'principled-revolutionary') as epitomised by Gandhi's salt satyagraha, and the second (later termed 'reformist-pragmatic') as being represented by the campaign to save the Franklin River.[13]

However, Burrowes' Gandhian principled approach to nonviolence was not always applauded. He notes that activists whose approach to nonviolence utilises an ideological, strategic, and structural approach will relate to State functionaries with courtesy and respect, and that this attracts 'considerable criticism from some quarters.'[14] The approach of MRAG, which entailed openness with the police and the avoidance of property damage,[15] was condemned by other, less ideologically driven activists as being part of the 'church of nonviolence'. This led to fierce debates in the pages of the left-wing journal *Arena*[16] and *Nonviolence Today*,[17]

---

[12] Robert J. Burrowes, 'Rainforest Pickets', *Nonviolence Today* 17, October/November 1990, p. 10.

[13] See Thomas Weber and Robert J. Burrowes, 'Nonviolence: An Introduction', Victorian Association for Peace Studies, *Peace Dossier* 27, 1991, p. 2; Robert J. Burrowes, 'The Dimensions of Nonviolent Struggle', *Nonviolence Today* 18, December/January 1990/91, p. 18, and *The Strategy of Nonviolent Defense: A Gandhian Approach*, Albany: State University of New York Press, 1996, p. 101.

[14] Burrowes, 'Rainforest Pickets', p. 12.

[15] For Burrowes' reasoning in this matter, see 'Monkeywrenching and Nonviolent Action', *Nonviolence Today* 12, December/January 1989/90, p. 7.

[16] See Andrew Nette, Kate Tempany, and Ian Wilson, 'Nurrungar: Giving Warning', *Arena* 89, 1989, pp. 38–44, and 'Rainforest Action', *Arena* 92, 1990, pp. 139–145; and Rob Burrowes and Tom Weber, 'The Strength of Nonviolence', *Arena* 90, 1990, pp. 164–168.

[17] See, for example, Robert J. Burrowes, 'Nurrungar—A Theoretical Reflection', *Nonviolence Today* 11, October/November 1989, pp. 8–10; Denis Doherty, 'Nurrungar—Theory in Magnificent Practice', *Nonviolence Today* 15,

Australia's Gandhi: People

following disagreements about how to behave at the protest camp at the joint Defence Space Communications Station at Nurrungar in South Australia at the end of September 1989. MRAG was accused of trying to impose its Gandhian version of nonviolence on other groups that utilised different approaches.

The Iraqi invasion and annexation of Kuwait in August 1990 and the resulting build-up of the United States-led, United Nations-sanctioned military forces in neighbouring Saudi Arabia resulted in the formation of the Gulf Peace Team (GPT). The central focus of the GPT was a camp on the border between the two States, containing seventy-three people from fifteen countries who sought to prevent the 1991 Gulf War. Eight of them, including Burrowes, were from Australia. The aim of the GPT was to oppose 'any form of armed aggression ... by any party in the Gulf ... by setting up one or more international peace camps between the opposing armed forces', and thereby 'withstand nonviolently any armed aggression by any party to the present Gulf dispute'.[18] In the early morning of 17 January, the day after the UN Security Council deadline for Iraq to withdraw from Kuwait expired, the war started. Bombers flew over the camp and supplies became increasingly scarce. Camp members argued about what further actions to take until, ten days later, they were evacuated by Iraqi forces back to Baghdad. While there was nothing particularly Gandhian (or indeed successful in terms of stopping hostilities) about this first on the ground interposition by activists between two warring armies,[19] for Burrowes it was

---

June/July 1990, pp. 8–11; and Felicity Ruby and Ian Cohen, 'All the Way with NVA', *Nonviolence Today* 18, December/January 1990/91, pp. 14–17.

[18] See Gulf Peace Team *Policy Statement*, released in London in October 1990.

[19] For the history of such attempts, see Thomas Weber 'A History of Nonviolent Interposition and Accompaniment', in Yeshua Moser-Puangsuwan and Thomas Weber (eds), *Nonviolent Intervention Across Borders: A Recurrent Vision*, Honolulu: Spark M. Matsunaga Institute for Peace, 2000, pp. 15–41;

lesson-rich and helped him to think more strategically about his approach to nonviolence.[20]

Following several more years of committed environmental and anti-military activism and teaching potential nonviolent leaders in intensive workshops, Burrowes shifted his orientation and started changing the 'personal components' of his life. With his developing realisations, he noted that his 'commitment to reshaping the world' meant that he had to be 'equally determined to reshape' himself. And this, in turn, meant the inner work of getting in touch with his emotions, spirituality, and 'inner voice'.[21] In late 1996, Burrowes informed his friends that he was 'disengaging as fully as possible from civilisation', and that he would from then on be incommunicado, working on his own emotional healing.[22]

Of course nonviolent activism did not disappear with the departure of Burrowes from the public arena. Nevertheless, what may be classed as a Gandhian approach to nonviolence became far less visible. However, more recently there was a small visual depiction of Gandhi in a peace-related protest. In September 2005,

---

and Thomas Weber, 'From Maude Royden's Peace Army to the Gulf Peace Team', *Journal of Peace Research* 30 (1), 1993, pp. 45–64.

[20] See Robert J. Burrowes, 'The Gulf War and the Gulf Peace Team', *Social Alternatives* 10 (2), 1991, pp. 35–39, and 'The Persian Gulf War and the Gulf Peace Team', in Moser-Puangsuwan and Weber (eds), *Nonviolent Intervention Across Borders*, pp. 305–316.

[21] Robert J. Burrowes, 'Nonviolence as a Way of Life', *Nonviolence Today* 38, May/June 1994, pp. 4–6, and 'Nonviolence and the Inner Voice', *Nonviolence Today* 47, November/December 1995, pp. 8–10. See also 'The Phases of My Nonviolent Activism', *Nonviolence Today* 48, January/February 1996, pp. 4–5.

[22] Perhaps the best example of Burrowes' thinking from this period is contained in his web article, 'Why Violence?'. Available at tinyurl.com/whyviolence (accessed November 2023). This document is now in its ninth edition and has been greatly expanded. It is available online at https://dkeenan.com/RJB-WhyViolence.pdf (accessed November 2023).

Australia's Gandhi: People

Scott Parkin, a visiting American nonviolence activist, was arrested and then deported from Australia because he presented a 'threat to national security'. Following his arrest, Parkin's friends and peace activists protested in most of the state capitals, and a short time later, at a function in Melbourne, the Attorney-General, Phillip Ruddock, was confronted by activists in handcuffs, wearing Gandhi masks and carrying placards which read, 'Would You Deport Gandhi Mr Ruddock?'[23]

Jarrod McKenna, an ex-dreadlocked Perth-based pastor and social change educator, works for the welfare of refugees, the education of peacemakers, protests against war and environmental destruction—and regularly gets arrested for his efforts. His aim appears to be not merely to preach Christ's gospel, but actually to live it, or, as he puts it, 'rolling up our sleeves and just getting on with the practical work of loving our neighbours'.[24] And very often his statements and writings reference Gandhi.

Perhaps McKenna's life trajectory can be partially understood when his family background is considered. His father had been a monk in an Irish Catholic order that cared for the sick and dying. His mother was from a non-religious family of Jewish heritage, and, influenced by Martin Luther King Jr's civil rights movement, dedicated her life to Jesus at her local Baptist church.[25] His parents were of the belief that 'in serving the poor, you serve God'.[26]

McKenna was born in the Perth suburb of Balcatta in 1980, and educated at the prestigious boys' Anglican Hale School, and

---

[23] Brian Martin and Iain Murray, 'The Parkin Backfire', *Social Alternatives* 24 (3), 2005, pp. 46–49, 70.

[24] Bron Sibree, 'Young Pastor at the Forefront of Social Change in Australia', *Sojourners*, 18 May 2012. Available at sojo.net/articles/young-pastor-forefront-social-change-Australia (accessed November 2023).

[25] Ann Lim, 'The Dreadlocked Minister with a Heart for Refugees', *Eternity*. Available at www.eternitynews.com.au/charity/the-dreadlocked-minister-with-a-heart-for-refugees/ (accessed December 2023).

[26] Sibree, 'Young Pastor at the Forefront of Social Change in Australia'.

at the Uniting Church's St. Stephen's School. He was dyslexic and had attention deficit disorder, and

> dealt with not doing all that great at school by being quick with my tongue, and when that didn't work, I was quick with my fists. I was depressed as a child and it was a huge thing for me realising that I had value, that God loved me and that that love which saves me is also something that we can live.[27]

At the age of thirteen, he was baptised in the family swimming pool as members of the house church his parents belonged to sang 'I've Decided to Follow Jesus'. From then on, 'my early experiences of following Jesus were breaking up fights that I would otherwise have been in'.[28]

He went on to study fine arts at Curtin University, study for ministry at the Australian College of Ministries, and then, with a scholarship, went to the US to study theology at a liberal arts Christian college, Lipscomb University, in Nashville, Tennessee. There he became acquainted with the Christian radical peace traditions of groups such as the Catholic Worker movement, Quakers, Anabaptists, and Mennonites, for whom 'following Jesus means rejecting violence and making God's love practical'. However, being in America during the 9/11 terrorist attacks brought him face-to-face with 'a very sentimentalized Christianity that had more to do with patriotism, militarism, race and privilege than it had to do with Christ.' And this led to a turning point in his life:

> 'Am I going to opt out of this?' because frankly, I was horrified by a lot of what passed for Christianity. But, ironically, it was the year I started reading Gandhi for the first time.... Gandhi had this

---

[27] Justin Brierley, 'Profile: Jarrod McKenna', *Premier Christianity*, 14 September 2015. Available at www.premierchristianity.com/Past-Issues/2015/October-2015/Profile-Jarrod-McKenna (accessed November 2023).

[28] Brierley, 'Profile: Jarrod McKenna'.

challenge that we must be the change we wish to see in the world, and I realize if this Hindu can take Jesus that seriously why not the Church? That gave me the courage to seek to be part of this brilliant, untold story of Christianity that does look like Christ.[29]

Back in Perth, in 2004 he was one of the founders of the group Empowering Peacemakers in Your Community, which used music, art, and the media to encourage students to, among other social justice and spiritual aims, explore the very Gandhian 'themes of nonviolent education not merely as a tactic of social change but as a chosen lifestyle'.[30] In 2006, this led to the then 26-year-old Jarrod McKenna becoming the youngest ever recipient of the Donald Groom Peace Fellowship. Since then, as a social justice advocate, McKenna has opposed the federal government's pernicious policies towards refugees and asylum seekers. As 'one of the founders of Love Makes a Way, a movement of Christians who seek a return to more humane asylum-seeker policies through prayer and non-violent protests (such as occupying government offices)', he has been arrested repeatedly.[31] However, as one writer has said, he is 'the sort of God botherer that you don't mind being bothered by':

> Most churches would consider it both a moral calamity and a PR disaster if their pastor was arrested and detained for any reason. The opposite is true for Jarrod McKenna's Westcity Church in Perth. The media attention has resulted in a wave of young, unchurched Australians turning up on Sundays, intrigued by the activities of McKenna and his fellow activists and the Jesus they say they represent.[32]

---

[29] Sibree, 'Young Pastor at the Forefront of Social Change in Australia'.
[30] Adrian Glamorgan, 'Jarrod McKenna, Peace Fellow', 7 December 2006. Available at wecan.be/beencouraged/123/ (accessed November 2023).
[31] Lim, 'The Dreadlocked Minister with a Heart for Refugees'.
[32] Brierley, 'Profile: Jarrod McKenna'.

Although one cannot necessarily call him a Gandhian activist, his speeches and writings are resplendent with references to the Mahatma and his activism reflects a form of nonviolence conversant with Gandhian philosophy. For a year he posted a blog titled 'Wednesdays with Gandhi', where he has made comments such as 'Jesus gave us the means, Gandhi showed it was possible', and,

> Gandhi freed a nation from the biggest superpower of his day without a militia, without weapons, without running for parliament or holding a political position. How? By the sheer force of his character that had become obedient to Jesus' teachings in the Sermon on the Mount. The politics of love are practical. Oddly enough I think Gandhi as a Hindu had a better understanding of the Christian paradigm for political engagement than most Christians seem to.[33]

And further:

> Gandhi famously refused to become a Christian yet daily spent 2 hours meditating after reading the Jesus' Sermon on the Mount. (Anybody know any Christians who spent 2 hours meditating on Christ's teachings today?) Repeatedly when asked for the inspiration of his nonviolent revolution in India he would not fail to mention Jesus and his teachings. Gandhi's dedication to Jesus and practice of his teachings cannot be doubted, nor can his dedication to his Hinduism (albeit a Hinduism that looks like Jesus. So much so Gandhi was often accused of 'Christianising' Hinduism and was finally shot by someone who believed he was corrupting Hinduism.)[34]

---

[33] Jarrod McKenna, 'Backyard Missionary voting for Jesus (today!)', 17 October 2007. Available at www.backyardmissionary.com/author/jarrod-mckenna/page/2/ (accessed November 2023).

[34] Jarrod McKenna, 'Jesus bigger than Christianity?', 12 September 2007. Available at www.backyardmissionary.com/author/jarrod-mckenna/page/2/ (accessed November 2023).

Australia's Gandhi: People

Sometimes the evangelist McKenna even seems to use Gandhi to validate a contextual understanding of Jesus, informing his readers that Gandhi had pointed out that 'Jesus was the most active resister known perhaps in history. His was nonviolence par excellence.'[35] And as a Christian social justice activist and international social change educator, while Jarrod McKenna may not be a card-carrying Gandhian, nevertheless his is a voice that has introduced many thousands of young people to the life and strategies that the Mahatma insisted were as old as the hills.

As with his young friend McKenna, Gandhi also featured in several of the books written by the Brisbane-based Christian anarchist and social activist and, for some, 'prophet', Dave Andrews. For example, in *Crux*, a book about the meaning of Jesus' crucifixion at the time and for now in the present, Andrews examines Gandhi's connection with and criticism of Christianity and his prescriptions for the conduct of political campaigns, and of satyagraha as being in essence a Christian way of life.[36] In another of his books, *Building a Better World*, he contrasts Gandhi with his mentor Tolstoy, pointing out that the Mahatma did not only think of changing the world, he also changed himself.[37]

Given his background, the Gandhi connection is unsurprising. Born in 1951, Andrews was brought up in a Baptist Church household, committed himself to Christ as a youngster, and married Angie Bellas at age twenty. Soon thereafter they went to Afghanistan and then India, where they worked for the next twelve years with disturbed travellers, drug-dependent locals, and the poor. After their visas were not renewed, in 1984 they returned to Australia and started an organisation known as the Waiters'

---

[35] Jarrod McKenna, 'Imagination fit for the larrikin Jesus', 19 September 2007. Available at www.backyardmissionary.com/author/jarrod-mckenna/page/2/ (accessed November 2023).

[36] Dave Andrews, *Crux: The Place of the Cross in the Process of Transformation*, Melbourne: Mosaic, 2013, pp. 72–73, 93–98.

[37] Dave Andrews, *Building a Better World*, Sydney: Albatross, 1996, p. 195.

Union to work with the poor in West End, an inner city suburb of Brisbane. Besides his voluminous writing and frequent public speaking engagements, Andrews worked with the Christian aid agency Tear Australia and teaches community development at various theological colleges.[38]

The Australian Gandhian Movement

Stephen Murphy was born in Adelaide in 1958. At the age of seventeen he commenced a career in journalism, initially writing on tennis-related topics. Five years later, 'having been deeply influenced by an Indian friend and colleague' and becoming 'aware of the flaws in Western politics and culture', he embarked on what might be called a journey of self-discovery. He travelled, coached tennis in West Germany, became involved in Third World development work through the Australian Freedom from Hunger campaign, explored socialist and Marxist ideology, and discovered Mahatma Gandhi in 1984 after reading Gandhi's *Autobiography* and seeing Richard Attenborough's movie, *Gandhi*.[39] He completed a Bachelor of Arts degree at the University of Adelaide with majors in International Politics and Asian History, and a Gandhi-focussed honours dissertation ('The Relevance of Gandhi in Independent India'). Calling himself a Western Gandhian 'of Hindu religious orientation', on the anniversary of Gandhi's assassination in 1988, he launched the Gandhian Movement of Australia (GMA).

---

[38] For life sketches of Dave Andrews, see www.daveandrews.com.au/bios (accessed November 2023).

[39] This information comes from personal communications from Stephen Murphy; from the dust jacket of his book, *Why Gandhi is Relevant in Modern India: A Western Gandhian's Personal Discovery*, New Delhi: Gandhi Peace Foundation, 1990; from a brief biographical note in the 1998 edition of the introductory pamphlet to the International Gandhian Movement; and from various newsletters that he published.

Later, he worked to bring into being an international Gandhian movement that linked Gandhian organisations, such as the GMA and other similar entities, around the world.

The reasons for the founding of a GMA were that 'Gandhi's teachings can contribute much to the tasks of understanding and reforming Australian society, in which violence and untruth have taken such a strong hold', and therefore its 'materialistic ethos must be challenged'. Its aim was to build 'a network of part-time volunteer "Workers" as well as "Supporters" throughout Australia'. Through the fledgling organisation, Murphy aimed to 'increase awareness and understanding of Gandhian ideas in Australian society', and to 'create an awareness of Gandhism's relevance to various [peace, women's, Aboriginal, anti-nuclear] movements.'[40]

In March 1991, Murphy mooted the formation of a worldwide network of Gandhian organisations as the International Gandhian Movement (IGM). Murphy explains that

> The origins of the IGM lay in a belief that the world is evolving in such a way that shows Mahatma Gandhi's teachings and philosophy to be highly relevant for our times. The ideas and ideals contain a tremendous potential, yet to be fully realised, for bringing great benefit and moral uplift to the world.[41]

Murphy spelled out the meaning of the IGM thus:

> The name was deliberately selected. It is, firstly, 'international'. The I.G.M. is far from the first Gandhi organisation outside of India, but we believe it was the first to be conceptually international. We are aware of the maxim, 'think globally, act locally'.... But there is a strong and fundamental universal dimension to Gandhi which,

---

[40] Stephen Murphy, 'Gandhian Movement of Australia', *Nonviolence Today* 15, June/July 1990, pp. 18–19.

[41] Stephen Murphy, *The International Gandhian Movement: An Introduction*, Canberra: The International Gandhian Movement, 1998, 3e, p. 3.

in a world becoming ever more interdependent, we feel has to be acknowledged. Therefore, as an international body the I.G.M. expresses this fundamental universality of Gandhi.

'Gandhian' means we maintain a strictly Gandhian identity and approach, rather than being a general 'peace', or even 'Sarvodaya' [Gandhian welfare], organisation. The I.G.M. strives to practice and embody the principles it advocates. Although the principle of compromise is an important one in Gandhian thought, on the fundamental principles of Gandhi's approach we will not compromise. 'Gandhian' also implies the opportunity to develop Gandhi's ideas in the context of today through experimentation.

'Movement' signifies that the I.G.M. is intended to be dynamic and activist. We regard the organisation as an expression of the spirit of *karma yoga*, as idealised in Hinduism's *Bhagavad Gita*. The organisation exists to serve God through work and action. What it will achieve we do not know, nor are we even concerned. The *Gita* ideal is simply to serve through devoted action. The fruits of our labours God will determine.[42]

The organisation did not aim to deify Gandhi, and was supposedly concerned more with his ideas than with Gandhi as a historical figure. Being realistic, Murphy noted that there was no aim of making the organisation big, adding that 'we have been less concerned about numbers and size than about integrity, about adhering to truthful and nonviolent—Gandhian—means, as well as striving for Gandhian ends.' He added, 'Our development is bound to be relatively slow.'[43]

From July 1990, these efforts were supplemented by the production of a quarterly newsletter magazine, *Global Conscience* (which, after fifteen issues, was superseded by a smaller quarterly newsletter, *Gandhian Opinion*, in 1994). The publications carried selections from Gandhi, commentary from Murphy, and news from other Gandhian centres around the world. In 1992, Stephen

---

[42] Murphy, *The International Gandhian Movement*, p. 5.
[43] Murphy, *The International Gandhian Movement*, p. 6.

Australia's Gandhi: People

Murphy completed a Master of Arts degree in the Department of Politics at Melbourne's La Trobe University, with a dissertation on the changing portrayal of Gandhi in the writings of his early Western biographers.[44]

Over the years, Murphy wrote tirelessly about Gandhi, contributing to major newspapers and journals. However, perhaps his most lasting contribution to popularising a Gandhian ethic was his book on the relationship between the Mahatma and India. It grew out of his research trip to India for his B.A. Honours thesis. There, in a third person account, Murphy briefly chronicles his three-month travels in India in late 1986 and early 1987, where 'the young Gandhian' went 'to learn for himself what has become of Gandhi's land and his relevance in it'.[45] He provides an outline of Gandhi's philosophy, looks at possible negative interpretations of Gandhism, explores the argument that Gandhi has become irrelevant, and puts forward arguments that counter these views. The book was published by a Gandhian publishing house in Delhi and included a Foreword by the eminent Gandhian, ex-senior politician and author, R. R. Diwakar, who was obviously impressed with the contents of the book and by Murphy personally, calling him 'a seeker of truth' and a 'serious logical thinker'.[46]

The book was based on Murphy's travel around Gandhian sites in India, mostly by train on an Indian Railways pass, and on interviews with several leading Gandhians. Initially, he was 'somewhat despondent' because a 'newly-arrived Gandhian in India longs to feel something of Gandhi's spirit. But it seems rarer than a fresh cool breeze in any of the cities he so disliked.'[47] He visited

---

[44] Stephen Murphy, 'Constructing the Mahatma: The Evolution of Gandhi's Image in His Western Biographies, 1909–1954', Master of Arts dissertation, Department of Politics, School of Social Sciences, La Trobe University, 1992.

[45] Murphy, *Why Gandhi is Relevant in Modern India*, p. 13.

[46] R. R. Diwakar, 'Foreword', in Murphy, *Why Gandhi is Relevant in Modern India*, p. x.

[47] Murphy, *Why Gandhi is Relevant in Modern India*, p. 11.

Gandhi's Australia/Australia's Gandhi

Porbandar, Gandhi's birthplace; Mani Bhavan, where Gandhi stayed when he was in Bombay (now Mumbai); the Satyagraha (Sabarmati) Ashram in Ahmedabad which was Gandhi's headquarters before he set off on the Salt March; Sevagram Ashram in the centre of India, the Mahatma's headquarters following the Salt March; Birla House, where Gandhi was assassinated; and Rajghat in Delhi, where Gandhi was cremated.

Murphy explains that the journey to India was a personal one: 'the search for the will to make a commitment to the Gandhian way'. The focus became 'the search for the "Gandhi" within'. It seems that the personal turmoil of his previous years and of his ambivalence about and often horror of his engagement with the land of Gandhi brought him to an epiphany of sorts:

> It seemed a crossroads was approaching. However, one evening as another train journey was underway an intense clarity descended. In a few minutes of profound creativity there was a dramatic turning point. A vow of commitment to the Gandhian way was subsequently taken. Thus the period in India represented not only the most difficult three months of my life, but to date the most creative and important as well.[48]

While the book was well-written and readable, and contained sharp observations and a sustained argument for Gandhian praxis, it did not make much of an impact in the Gandhian literature and probably very few copies made it to an Australian audience.

Stephen Murphy's commitment and drive kept the organisations and projects he conceived in the name of Gandhi going. However, as he candidly noted in 1991,

> The I.G.M. is beginning life with few advantages. Its workers number just two, myself and my wife, and its supporters or members, zero. We have other commitments with which to

---

[48] Murphy, *Why Gandhi is Relevant in Modern India*, p. 137.

contend currently. There is little experience in the running of organisations and almost no money.[49]

Besides the meagre amounts that came in from membership fees, subscriptions, and donation, the bulk of the funds needed to print newsletters and serve other expenses of the various IGM projects came directly from the personal funds of the Murphy household.

In 1993, Murphy began looking into the possibility of establishing 'a truly Gandhian ashram', called Gandhi Farm, in Australia. A teetotalling vegetarian who strived to live by the 'Gandhian ideals of non-possession, bread labour and voluntary poverty', and was 'progressing towards veganism and brahmacharya' (celibacy), Murphy and his family were 'progressively giving the household a Gandhian character and routine' in anticipation of their life at Gandhi Farm. However, the funds raised for the project were not enough to bring the enterprise into existence.

Eventually, the historical Gandhi book collection that Murphy had accumulated was disbursed, and from mid-1999 the IGM wound down. In reality, although it had well-known international supporters, it never achieved a take-off point. With fewer than fifty members, it was Murphy's personal efforts that kept the organisation going for a decade. In short, it remained not much more than Stephen Murphy's personal project. It became clear that Freedom from Violence Australia, a charitable organisation that Murphy had set up to do good works and provide him with employment and an income, was not bearing the desired fruits either. At the age of forty, with a family and little wealth, Murphy moved to Queensland and went back to his previous occupation of coaching tennis, and a major chapter in the Australia/Gandhi connection came to a close.

---

[49] Stephen Murphy, 'First Steps of the International Gandhian Movement', *Global Conscience* 2 (1), July–September 1991, p. 7.

The International Centre of Nonviolence

The most recent Australian Gandhi-related organisation appears to be the International Centre of Nonviolence (ICON), and possibly the strongest populariser of Gandhi in recent times has been its founder, the prominent Indian businessman and 'Taxation Guru', Gambhir Watts. Watts met Gandhi's granddaughter, Ela Gandhi, in South Africa while attending the 'Roots to Fruits: Nonviolence in Action' conference, organised by the Gandhi Development Trust at Durban University of Technology in mid-2012. Inspired by her work in promoting Gandhian nonviolence, Watts announced the setting up of the International Centre of Nonviolence Australia on Gandhi's birth date, the second of October of that year. The aim of the organisation was spelled out as:

> Our vision is of a nonviolent society based on the celebration of our common humanity and of the natural environment that sustains us. We will work to make strategic interventions in education—development of educators and curricula, teaching and writing—that challenge structural violence, enable learning untainted by violence and advance a culture of nonviolence. It works through reflective practice and focussed research to develop and disseminate its understanding, and to build networks of education with a similar vision and commitment.[50]

It was formally launched with the attendance of Ela Gandhi on 27 February 2013 at the New South Wales Parliament House, in the presence of distinguished religious leaders, academics, and politicians. Like its South African namesake, the Centre was strongly Gandhi-focussed and, just as the South African

---

[50] Gambhir Watts, 'Education on Action in Nonviolence', 27 February 2013. Available at www.nonviolence.org.au/educatioon-on-action-in-nonviolence/ (accessed November 2023).

organisation had Ela Gandhi as its leading light, the Australian equivalent was Gambhir Watts.

Gambhir Watts was born on 7 August 1949 in Bombay in a more or less anti-Gandhi neighbourhood. He was educated in his home city, obtaining degrees in economics and commerce, and started his career as a bank officer in 1969 at the Bank of India and then as branch manager at the Oriental Bank of Commerce and Industries in Bombay, a position that he held until 1980.[51] He then served as the Managing Director and Chief Consultant for the business consultancy company Bee Gee Holdings in Mumbai, until he decided to migrate to Australia because of local corruption and a desire to do something different.[52] With his scientist wife and two young children, he arrived in Sydney in 1992. On 28 June 2013, in an interview with *The Indian Sun*, one of Australia's leading South Asian news magazines, Watts described the difficulties of settling in a new country and finding employment. After shuttling between India and Australia on work projects for a year-and-a-half, he upgraded his qualifications and worked pro bono with emerging community organisations, before he finally landed a job as a finance officer with the NSW Institute of Psychiatry. After two-and-a-half years, he started his own tax agency business in 1996. Although he had had no contact with Indian officialdom in Australia, his work with the local community brought him to the notice of the then Consul General of India in Sydney, Madhusudan Ganapathy, who was working to bring a chapter of the Mumbai-based Bharatiya Vidya

---

[51] This information comes from personal communications from Gambhir Watts; from his self-published autobiography, *The White Queen*, and self-published book on Gandhi, which details his connection with Bharatiya Vidya Bhavan and his discovery of Gandhi in a prologue titled 'My Tryst with Karmayogi Mahatma Gandhi'; and from various interviews conducted with him and published online.

[52] See Gambhir Watts, *The White Queen*, published by the author, 2019.

Bhavan to Australia. Watts was approached to assist, and this is where his interest in Gandhi originated.

In 2005, Gambhir Watts was asked to make a speech on Gandhi at the launch of a 'Gandhi/King/Ikeda' exhibition in Sydney. Still knowing little about the Mahatma, he asked the World President of Bharatiya Vidya Bhavan for advice. He was sent four books on Gandhi, which he 'studied day and night, as if I had to appear for my university examination and made notes for my speech. This reading made me fall for Gandhi and since then there is no going back.'[53]

The Indian educational and cultural trust Bharatiya Vidya Bhavan, one of the world's largest non-government organisations (NGO), was set up by the Gujarati writer, lawyer, and nationalist, Gandhi's acquaintance K. M. Munshi, in 1938. In August 2003, a Sydney chapter was added to the organisation's many overseas centres and Watts was asked to be Executive President. The organisation celebrates the Hindu festival of Holi, encourages the learning of Hindi and Sanskrit, and promotes the maintenance of Indian traditions in Australia through various cultural events.[54] Since July 2005, the Bhavan has also published a monthly journal, *Bhavan Australia*, a cultural/religious magazine aimed at an international and a local, particularly Hindu, Indian readership. The electronic version of the journal is sent to over 5,000 recipients, mostly those in significant public positions in Australia and around the world. Printed hard copies go to Bhavan's headquarters in India, to High Commissioners and ambassadors of different countries represented in Australia, and to the organisation's local sponsors and members. The magazine often carries articles about Gandhi,

---

[53] Gambhir Watts, *Karmayogi Mahatma Gandhi*, published by the author, 2020, pp. 10–11.

[54] 'Interview: Gambhir—India's Culture Ambassador in Sydney', *The Indian Sun*, 28 June 2017. Available at www.theindiansun.com.au/2013/06/28/gambhir-indias-culture-ambassador-in-sydney/ (accessed December 2023).

and publisher and general editor Watts' introductions generally refer to the Mahatma. It is rare for an issue not to devote significant space to Gandhi. Since 2004, the local Bharatiya Vidya Bhavan's Gandhi-related activities went on to include an interfaith prayer meeting on 30 January at Hyde Park and then Parliament House in Sydney, and, since 2004, the conducting of an essay competition, with generous prizes, on the relevance of Gandhi, which is open to all Australian university students. The prizes included a return ticket to Mumbai to enable the winner to visit the Sabarmati or Sevagram ashrams, a laptop computer, and a book voucher. Unfortunately, in some years there were fewer entries submitted than there were prizes, and the standard of the essays was not always of the quality to warrant the prizes received. When lecturers involved in Gandhi-related courses brought the essay competition to the notice of their students, the number and quality of the entries increased.[55] Since 2007, the Bhavan has also organised celebrations of the International Day of Nonviolence in Sydney on Gandhi Jayanti (Gandhi's birth date, 2 October).

Besides his role in Bharatiya Vidya Bhavan, Watts is also a commissioner with the Community Relations Commission for a Multicultural NSW and was the chairperson of the Northern Regional Advisory Council between 2009 and 2012. He championed the introduction of daily Hindi news on SBS television and is deeply involved with the local Indian community. In 2012, he was honoured with the Medal of the Order of Australia for his outstanding services in multicultural relations in NSW. Much of his non-professional time is now taken up with ICON. Watts

---

[55] See, for example, 'M. K. Munshi Essay Competition: Prize Winning Essays', *Bhavan Australia*, October 2009, pp. 16–50, for the winning essays of 2009. Due to this general lack of response, the essay competition has remained inactive since 2016; however, there are plans to relaunch the competition with targeted promotion in the universities.

explained that he was 'personally greatly influenced by Mahatma Gandhi's concept of Satyagraha and nonviolent active resistance', and that the task of ICON was to 'spread this Gandhian concept through our publications and events as can be seen from the list of our events.'[56]

In October 2013, one of the first major efforts of ICON was to put out a quarterly digital magazine, *Nonviolence News*, again published and edited by Watts, dedicated to presenting 'scholarly contributions towards explaining and developing the concept, philosophy and practice of non-violence in action from the ancient to the current times.'[57] The initial issue, with Gandhi on the cover, contained a Foreword message from Ela Gandhi and several Gandhi-related articles. This continued in later issues, which generally carried a number of such articles, often of considerable length, reproducing Gandhi's own words or those written about the Mahatma and his approach to nonviolence reprinted from other sources.

The following May, ICON inaugurated the Mahatma Gandhi International Prize for Social Responsibility at the Soka Gakkai International Victoria Community Centre in Melbourne. The initial prize went to Daisaku Ikeda, the President of SGI, 'an ardent follower of Mahatma Gandhi's values of nonviolence and peaceful reconciliation'. The prize was accepted on Ikeda's behalf by the General Director of the organisation, Yoshitaka Oba. Then, on 2 October, a 'Nonviolence Month' was launched at the University of New South Wales. Proceedings started with a speech by Watts, emphasising the role and importance of Gandhian values in combating all forms of violence. The audience received educational

---

[56] 'Enduring Legacy', in *India Empire Magazine*, January 2013.
[57] Gambhir Watts, 'President Page: Non-violence', *Non-Violence News* 1 (1), October 2013, p. 7. Available at www.nonviolence.org.au/news-magazine (accessed November 2023). In 2016, the hyphen was dropped from the title of the news magazine. It is now *Nonviolence News*.

material highlighting Gandhi's stress on truth and nonviolence as the twin pillars sustaining his life.[58]

The degree to which the work of the organisations he heads relies on him is clearly revealed in the 'President Page', for the first time written not by Gambhir Watts but by editorial committee member Anna Andriiashina. It is headed, 'How to Overcome Pain and Let Hope into Your Life':

> Sad news has come to us on the 3d of February 2018. Mr. Gambhir Watts OAM was hit by the car. Because of this terrible accident Mr. Watts had lost his both legs and seriously hurt his shoulders. Luckily, there were no spine or head injuries. Mr. Watts spent one month in the hospital struggling with pain, stress and depression but was still highly determined to organise our most loved Holi Festival as he has always been mainly responsible for putting it together and organizing finances. However, in mid-March Bharatiya Vidya Bhavan Australia Organisation has decided to cancel Holi 2018 as we all believe that Mr. Watts needs all his strength, energy and vital power to fight with the physical and mental consequences of the accident. Today Mr. Watts remains in the Rehabilitation Centre and makes progress in his recovery. We extend our best wishes for him and keep him and his family in our prayers.[59]

In fact, Watts was in the Royal Prince Alfred Hospital for three months with broken bones in his legs and shoulder. For a year, he got around with the aid of a walking frame and then crutches. Not long after, while walking with the aid of a cane, he was back at work and at the helm of Bharatiya Vidya Bhavan

---

[58] See 'Mahatma Gandhi International Prize for Social Responsibility—10 May 2014'. Available at www.nonviolence.org.au/10-May-2014/ (accessed November 2023).

[59] Anna Andriiashina, 'President Page', *Bhavan Australia*, March–April 2018, p. 3. Available at bhavanaustralia.org/upload/Bhavan_Australia_March-April_%202018.pdf (accessed December 2023).

and ICON almost full time, and finalising his documents-based book on Gandhi's youth and experiences in South Africa on his journey to mahatmaship. Recently, Gambhir Watts has had issues with the Tax Practitioners Board which terminated his tax agent registration;[60] nevertheless, his fascination with Gandhi does not seem to have dimmed.

Doing Gandhian Work in India

In 1956, while working in English schools, the young Australian teachers Allan and Wendy Scarfe befriended an Indian merchant, who suggested that they visit India on their way home and wrote an introduction for them to meet the senior Gandhian and once leading politician, Jayaprakash Narayan. Their meeting with JP (as Narayan was known) in Bombay is beautifully described in their book, *Remembering Jayaprakash*. When JP asked them what their motives behind coming to India were, they noted that it was not to join the Gandhian land-gift to the poor movement, of which they knew little, but told him that 'We want to do something to help people who are less fortunate than ourselves.'[61]

JP invited them to come to his ashram school in the village of Sokhodeora in India's poorest state, Bihar. The Scarfes, still only in their mid-twenties, accepted the challenge and for half a year they undertook voluntary work there. Two-and-a-half years after their return to Australia, they headed back to India and JP's ashram. They sailed in December 1960 and embarked

[60] See 'AAT decision backs TPB finding on grounds of public interest', 10 September 2019. Available at https://www.tpb.gov.au/aat-decision-backs-tpb-finding-grounds-public-interests application to stay termination decision'. Available at accountantsdaily.com.au/regulation/13508-aat-knocks-back-senior-cpa-s-application-to-stay-termination-decision (accessed December 2023).

[61] Allan and Wendy Scarfe, *Remembering Jayaprakash*, New Delhi: Siddharth, 1997, p. 4.

on a two-and-a-half year stint as teachers and founders of JP's Experimental Rural School. Those years were detailed in their insightful first book *A Mouthful of Petals: The Story of an Indian Village*, published in 1967.[62]

Of course, all of this happened after the death of the Mahatma, but there are some interesting Gandhian elements to the Scarfes' story. In 1958, after they had returned to Australia from their first Indian sojourn, the Australian Broadcasting Corporation interviewed them for a radio programme. Wendy clearly remembers how surprised they were when they were told that they were not to mention Gandhi by name, and that if they did, the programme would not go to air.[63] Whether this was the action of a disgruntled producer or interviewer or was—less likely—ABC policy, cannot be determined. Unfortunately, unlike talks which are normally scripted, interviews are unscripted and, during the time in question, transcripts were generally not made *ex post facto* and little of this type of radio output was retained as recordings.[64] Further, as the warning was not part of the interview itself, but part of a preliminary instruction, there would be no record in any case. It appears that in some circles, Gandhi was not only ignored but also actively shunned.

It must have come as something of a shock to the notable-packed Gandhi Centenary Celebrations Committee when their esteemed guests, JP and his wife Prabhavati, headed off to the Scarfe's home town of Warrnambool soon after their arrival in Australia in September 1969 for the Gandhi birth-centenary celebrations. JP had informed the Scarfes that he would gladly accept the invitation to visit Australia on the condition that 'time

---

[62] Wendy and Allan Scarfe, *A Mouthful of Petals: The Story of an Indian Village*, London: Heinemann, 1967.
[63] Personal communication from Wendy Scarfe, 13 March 2018.
[64] Personal communication from Guy Tanter of the ABC Document Archives, 21 March 2018.

Gandhi's Australia/Australia's Gandhi

must be set aside for at least two to three days private visit with you'. Before they could leave Melbourne for the drive to Warrnambool, the Scarfes, JP, and Prabhavati were provided an expensive lunch at the high-status Southern Cross Hotel, paid for by the Australian government. However, it was 'something of a national humiliation for us because the hotel had no vegetarian food. Jayaprakash finally had to compromise with an omelette but when it arrived it was full of pieces of ham. He picked them out. Prabhavati ate fruit.'[65]

During the Narayans' stay with them, the Scarfes mooted the idea of a biography of JP. He was not overly enthusiastic; however, Prabhavati was concerned about her husband's health and 'pressed' the Scarfes 'anxiously' to undertake the task. In the end, JP acquiesced.

During the Australian Christmas (summer) holidays, Allan and Wendy Scarfe returned to India in December 1970 to gather material on JP's life for the biography. The resulting 460-page book, probably still the best biography of JP, was published in 1975.[66] The book had detailed JP's life up until the end of 1973; however, some of the most momentous events in JP's life happened in his final years. On the very day that Mrs. Gandhi's 'Emergency' was declared, a copy of the book arrived on the desk at *The Times of India* for review. The editor later noted that, 'Quick on the heels of the book came a frantic note from the publishers suggesting, euphemistically, that the review be "held over for the moment".' An abridged and updated version was published in 1997.[67] If one wants to understand the post-Gandhi Gandhian movement and one of its towering figures, the writings of Allan and Wendy Scarfe are essential resources.

[65] Scarfe and Scarfe, *Remembering Jayaprakash*, p. 273.
[66] Allan and Wendy Scarfe, *J.P.: His Biography*, New Delhi: Orient Longman, 1975.
[67] Allan and Wendy Scarfe, *J.P.: His Biography (Revised Edition)*, New Delhi: Orient Longman, 1997.

7

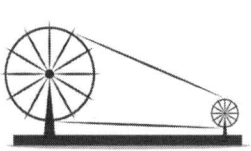

Australia's Gandhi
The Academy

When Indian and other overseas Gandhian guests came to Australia to lecture on Gandhi, the venue for the addresses was often a university hall. This was not only because public lectures are regularly delivered at universities, but also, at least in part, because there were Gandhi-related courses being taught in Australia that such lectures complemented—and for many of the young, the university provided the avenue via which they came to know something about Gandhi. The University of Queensland was pioneering in this process. The Indian scholar Sugata Dasgupta encouraged Ralph Summy and Anthony Kelly to give their respective courses in Peace and Development Studies a truly Gandhian focus.

Partially due to population differences, and partially because of seemingly less interest, there were far fewer books on Gandhi published in Australia than there were in Britain or America. However, a much larger proportion of the books that were published here were academically important and broke more new ground than could have been expected, given their numbers. Here, the names of Mark Thomson (on Gandhi's ashrams), Robert Burrowes (on a Gandhian nonviolent approach to national defence), Jos Jordens (on Gandhi's approach to religion), Sean Scalmer (on Gandhi's influence on radical protest in the West), and perhaps me (on Gandhi's Salt March), deserve special mention. Universities also hosted Gandhi conferences and orations.

Gandhi in the Academy

In 1977, Ved Mehta's book, *Gandhi and His Apostles*, was published in England.[1] In 1983, around the time of the first Australian screening of Attenborough's movie *Gandhi*, it was placed on the Higher School Certificate syllabus as a reading in biography and, in 1989, as a non-fiction reading in Victorian high schools. Rather than being a text suggested or mandated for students of History or Asian Studies, who may have had access to other materials that offered a different picture from Mehta's account of the Mahatma, it was a required text for students of English. Mehta, after all, was a well-known critic and novelist and an admirable wordsmith. This meant that the knowledge a generation of Victorian students had about the Mahatma came either from the movie or from Mehta's account, an account that portrayed Gandhi, and particularly his followers, in a mostly unsympathetic way. While informative and well-written, the book accented the sexual and scatological.[2]

In his sections on 'Gandhians', which bookended the central section of *Gandhi and His Apostles*, when he is not describing their clothing, their physical appearance, or the setting in which the meeting took place, Mehta seems to be poking fun at them. Unselfish helpfulness on the part of his interviewees is rewarded with criticism, with character assassination, and negative interpretations of ambiguous circumstances or statements. Most of those who gave of their valuable time to Mehta are portrayed as eccentrics, or made

[1] Ved Mehta, *Gandhi and His Apostles*, London: Andre Deutsch, 1977.
[2] For his review of the book, or, more accurately, his mixed thoughts on Gandhi, see Australia's most cerebral politician, the Labor Member of Parliament, lawyer, and writer Barry Jones, 'India's Father and Mother Figure', *The Age* (Melbourne), 28 January 1978, p. 25.

Australia's Gandhi: The Academy

to appear like fools or worse. And the 'Gandhians' he talks to are generally elderly big city-dwelling individuals well-known for some past association with the Mahatma. Almost none of them are village constructive workers labouring with and for the downtrodden. None are youthful idealists. It seems he simply had no idea where to look for real Gandhian work and Gandhian workers; instead, he focuses on a collection of 'Gandhian' personalities. Mehta was in the forefront of those presenting admirably anti-hagiographical analyses of Gandhi, but also of those who take pride in debunking 'the myth of the Mahatma'. Gandhi's own eccentricities are made to seem worse than they were because of the mental state of his interviewed followers. And here, there is often the intentional application of current standards and worldviews to a time when they were simply not held, or insinuating that the customs of others are perverse or at least quaint, or the taking of statements out of context. And in the case of Gandhi, there is not enough credit given to him changing his mind, or for personal growth.

The book provided a totally different picture of Gandhi than the film. And it was not difficult to determine the source of those attitudes: when the topic of Gandhi came up in my courses, the most frequent first question students asked about the Mahatma was whether it was true that he slept with young women. And this question could not have been formulated by viewing the movie.

Besides the knowledge about Gandhi that high school students have gained through the literary route of Mehta's book, there have also been some experiential approaches: for example, Margaret Hepworth's workshops. Hepworth is a Melbourne-based teacher and peace educator who presents workshops, particularly for teenagers, on how to become global citizens. She recalls that after attending a 'Making Democracy Real' conference in India in 2014, she travelled to Gandhi's Sabarmati Ashram and was inspired to use Gandhi to bring out the good that everyone has somewhere inside. On her return to Australia, she started inviting student groups to tell her about Gandhi. Later that year, at Birla House

(Gandhi Smriti) in Delhi, the name for the new project she was to dedicate herself to came to her: 'The Gandhi Experiment'. Later, she added the sub-heading, 'World Peace Through Education'. The idea behind the project was to teach 'teenagers global citizenship, conflict resolution, anger management, forgiveness and how to enact their thoughts for a more positive future'. While the 'Gandhi Experiment' was not specifically about Gandhi the person, it was, in her view, about 'the essence of his message', that is, about nonviolence, social action, personal responsibility, and living one's life through one's values. Anecdotes from Gandhi's life are often key starting points for discussion and reflection. Since then, Hepworth has been running the workshops in several countries and, as part of her programme, she has produced a book 'of mindful activities and lessons for parents and teachers'[3] to provide tools and strategies for peace-building.

University Courses and Gandhi

Perhaps the most important connection between Gandhi and Australians in educational settings has happened in universities. While many academics have dealt with Gandhi in their various university courses, the names of Sugata Dasgupta, Ralph Summy, and Anthony Kelly stand out.

Born in 1929 in Pennsylvania, Summy was an American who had majored in economics at Harvard and served as a mid-shipman in the navy reserve (a requirement of his Harvard scholarship).[4] Following graduation, he worked as a journalist with the *Houston Post*, but was soon drafted into the US Army and sent to Germany with the American occupation troops. He was assigned to the

---

[3] Margaret Hepworth, *The Gandhi Experiment: Teaching our Teenagers how to Become Global Citizens*, New Delhi: Rupa, 2017.

[4] For the life of Ralph Summy, see Hilary Summy, 'Ralph Summy: A Journey in Pursuit of Nonviolence', *Social Alternatives* 37 (2), 2018, pp. 41–44.

Australia's Gandhi: The Academy

Public Information Office of the 16th Infantry Regiment to write a history of the Regiment's landing at Normandy during D-Day in 1944. This experience forced him to consider the slaughter and human waste of war. Following his discharge from the military, Summy found work in a leading Boston bank and, in 1960, became the main organiser for a rally of the anti-nuclear Sane Nuclear Policy organisation in the city. The bank gave him an ultimatum: either he leave SANE or the bank. His banking career was over, but because of his radical activities he came to the attention of the Senate Internal Security Sub-committee. His refusal to comply with their requests led to problems with the SANE executive committee, resulting in his resignation, and ensured that he was unable to find full-time employment. At age thirty-three, in early 1962, he migrated to Australia. He pursued teaching qualifications and completed a Masters in Politics degree at the University of Sydney with a dissertation titled, 'Australian Peace Movement 1960–67: A Study of Dissent'. He had found his calling as a teacher. After two years in Sydney, he became an academic at the University of Queensland, tutoring in courses on Australian and American politics while maintaining his peace activism with local peace committees that focussed on issues around the Vietnam War, nuclear weapons, and civil liberties in Queensland, then Australia's most repressive state.

On sabbatical leave in 1974, Summy met the American scholar Gene Sharp, who had recently produced his three-volume magnum opus, *The Politics of Nonviolent Action*. Back at the University of Queensland, after overcoming some resistance from his colleagues, he introduced a subject, 'The Politics of Nonviolent Change'. In 1977, he founded the journal *Social Alternatives*, which aimed to 'provide a forum for discussing and analysing problems, with an emphasis on formulating nonviolent alternatives in a quest for peace and social justice'.[5]

[5] Hilary Summy, 'Ralph Summy', p. 41.

Indian academic Sugata Dasgupta's time at the university brought large Gandhi-related changes. Born in 1926, he had a broad education in the arts and social work. In 1964, he became the joint director (and later director) of the Gandhian Institute of Studies at Rajghat in Varanasi, an institute founded by the ex-socialist politician and later leading Gandhian, Jayaprakash Narayan. He held that post and served as professor of social work until 1976. During that time, the Institute was a world-class centre for intellectual scholarship that worked to apply the philosophy of Gandhi to practical problems.[6] The Institute also attracted important scholars from outside India, and seems to have inspired them to produce seminal works. For example, Johan Galtung, the Norwegian sociologist known as the 'father of modern peace research', refined his ideas about structural and direct violence there in 1969 and wrote the groundbreaking paper, 'Violence, Peace and Peace Research', on the roof terrace of the Institute.[7] Following Prime Minister Indira Gandhi's declaration of an 'Emergency' and the closing of the Institute and the jailing of JP, its chairman, in 1976, Dasgupta left India and joined the staff of the School of Social Work at the University of Queensland as a senior lecturer in community development and social planning.[8] In his three years

---

[6] Such as facilitating the surrender of criminal gangs in the Chambal valley. See Thomas Weber, *The Shanti Sena: Philosophy, History and Action*, New Delhi: Orient BlackSwan, 2009, pp. 120–131, and *Gandhi's Peace Army: The Shanti Sena and Unarmed Peacekeeping*, Syracuse: Syracuse University Press, 1996, pp. 108–115.

[7] See Johan Galtung, 'Violence, Peace and Peace Research', *Journal of Peace Research* 6 (3), 1969, pp. 167–191; and Thomas Weber, *Gandhi as Disciple and Mentor*, Cambridge: Cambridge University Press, 2004, pp. 210–211. E. F. Schumacher, of 'small is beautiful' fame, also did much of his groundbreaking work at the Institute.

[8] See Ngaire Chant, Sue Cochrane, and Robyn Kennedy, 'Foreword', in Sugata Dasgupta, *Towards a Post Development Era: Essays in Poverty, Welfare and Development* (Ngaire Chant, Sue Cochrane, and Robyn Kennedy [comp. and eds]), Delhi: Mittal, 1985, p. xi. See also Ralph Summy, 'Nonviolent Politics:

Australia's Gandhi: The Academy

in the country, Dasgupta influenced many people, including David Scott of Community Aid Abroad, with his critiques of development and visions of alternative strategies for implementing social justice. After the ending of the 'Emergency' and the release of JP from prison, he returned to India and established the Jayaprakash Narayan Institute for Social Change in Calcutta and founded the social policy journal, *Continuum*.

Not long after Sugata Dasgupta arrived at the University of Queensland, he inquired whether anyone was working in the area of nonviolence and so came into contact with Ralph Summy. Dasgupta thought that Summy's nonviolence subject 'fell short of Gandhian ideals' as it 'overlooked Gandhi's constructive program and its application to the problems of development in the marginalised countries'. Believing Dasgupta to be right, Summy asked him to prepare a syllabus with a more Gandhian flavour. The resulting course, 'Nonviolence and the New Society',[9] was the first Australian university-level subject to specifically engage with Gandhi as more than a leading political actor in a course on South Asian history.

Summy's original 1976 nonviolence subject concerned itself with an

> intensive examination of the technique of nonviolence as a means for controlling political power and effecting social change. Analysis focuses on nature of power, its sources, function of consent, meaning of nonviolence, dynamics and mechanisms of nonviolence, civilian defence, and efficacy of various methods in terms of the circumstances.

It used case histories extensively. In short, it closely reflected Sharp's major work; *The Politics of Nonviolent Action* was the main text.

From Praxis to Research to Classroom to Praxis to Research to Classroom', *Ahimsa Nonviolence* 1 (4), 2005, pp. 319–326.
[9] Ralph Summy, 'Nonviolent Politics', p. 322.

Gandhi's Australia/Australia's Gandhi

Dasgupta's course outline for Summy's Gandhi-based 1978 subject stated that the new subject would examine the principles and design of a nonviolent society and examine the concepts of decentralisation, conflict, organisation, truth, love, and ahimsa (nonviolence). These concepts were related to ways of 'bringing nonviolent society into being while reducing the "violence" content of existing society'. The subject covered the areas of 'violence, development and tensions', 'Gandhism's meaning of violence', and 'education for a nonviolent society'. It was a course concerned with a Gandhian view of the world and the possibility of a society based on the Gandhian ideal. Many of the examples and references related to India and the writings of Gandhi, JP, and Dasgupta.

Summy taught political science at the University of Queensland for thirty-three years. He was instrumental in establishing an interdisciplinary major in Peace and Conflict Studies at the university, and went on to consolidate the University of Queensland as one of the world's premier academic centres for peace and conflict resolution studies. Hundreds of students came across Gandhi and nonviolence as a result of having attended Summy's classes. In mid-1996, he coordinated the 16th Biennial Conference of the International Peace Research Association, with the theme of 'Creating Nonviolent Futures'. After his retirement from the university the following year, he became Director of the Spark M. Matsunaga Institute for Peace at the University of Hawai'i in Honolulu, a post he held for three years before returning to Australia. In retirement, he continued to write on the topics of nonviolence and the peace movement.

Sugata Dasgupta did not only influence Ralph Summy during his time at the University of Queensland. While he may have had a profound bearing on the teaching of Peace Studies, he had a similar impact on courses related to community development through his work at the university and his influence on his student

Australia's Gandhi: The Academy

Anthony Kelly, who was to take over Dasgupta's position when he returned to India.

Born in Adelaide in 1943 and educated in Douglas Park south of Sydney, Kelly joined an order of priests, studied philosophy at a Seminary in Canberra for three years, and theology in Melbourne for two—which left him 'totally disillusioned'. He then completed a social work degree at the University of New South Wales, focussing on the participatory development model espoused by Saul Alinsky. After his studies, he was appointed Director of the Queensland Council of Social Service (QCSS). This was during the Whitlam years when much was done to implement development programmes in the country. Following the sacking of the Whitlam government, Kelly notes that 'he was ready for a real change' and 'wanted to really re-think what professional approaches were possible in the development domain', ones that fit better with Australian conditions than the Alinsky model.[10]

Kelly was Director of the QCSS when he first met Dasgupta. He wanted to be exposed to international experience in the field and Dasgupta wanted to get to know the local and national scene better, and thus a fruitful working relationship developed. Kelly left his Queensland Council post to undertake a Masters degree in community development under Dasgupta. Immediately after graduating, Kelly worked with the Northern Territory government to establish an indigenous community development programme. When Dasgupta returned to India following the lifting of the 'Emergency', he asked Kelly to apply for his position and wrote him a reference. Kelly was successful in his application and ended up teaching in the Social Work Department at UQ from 1980 until his retirement in 2005. He taught subjects with the titles of 'Community Development', 'Peace Work in the Community', and 'Working with Indigenous People'. He notes that his ideas 'have

[10] Personal communication from Anthony Kelly, 1 March 2019.

been deeply influenced by the Gandhian tradition, and someone who knew Gandhi personally taught him these practices.[11] From that time on, Kelly worked with Dasgupta at local, national, and international levels until Dasgupta's death.

Kelly's book, *Participatory Development Practice*, was jointly authored with fellow Queensland academic Peter Westoby. Detailing practices of participatory development and their Gandhian connections, it summarises Kelly's Gandhian approach to development practice and community work, which had been the focus of his teaching for decades. It also tells us that he proudly belongs to a people-centred 'Gandhian tradition' and that Gandhian soul-force sits at the heart of this tradition. The authors quote a passage from the 'Introduction' in Gandhi's autobiography to epitomise this approach, to illustrate the ways of practice of the good community worker:

> I hope and pray that no one will regard the advice interspersed in the following chapters as authoritative. The experiments narrated should be regarded as illustrations, in the light of which every one may carry on his own experiments according to his own inclinations and capacity. I trust that to this limited extent the illustrations will be really helpful; because I am not going either to conceal or understate any ugly things that must be told. I hope to acquaint the reader with all my faults and errors. My purpose is to describe experiments in the science of Satyagraha, not to say how good I am. In judging myself I shall try to be as harsh as truth, as I want others also to be.[12]

Since his retirement from academia, Kelly has been involved internationally with mining companies, sharing this tradition, so

---

[11] See the author's note in Anthony Kelly and Peter Westoby, *Participatory Development Practice: Using Traditional and Contemporary Frameworks*, Ruby, Warwickshire: Practical Action Publishing, 2018, p. ix.

[12] M. K. Gandhi, *An Autobiography or the Story of My Experiments with Truth*, Ahmedabad: Navajivan, 1940, pp. xv–xvi. See Kelly and Westoby, *Participatory Development Practice*, pp. 168–169.

that they can tailor their activities to work more constructively with people whose lives they disrupted.

For the Fifteenth International Peace Research Association General Conference, held in Malta in early November 1994, leading peace educationalist Robin Burns and I wrote a joint paper examining the prospects for and results of developing courses with theoretical bases provided by Mahatma Gandhi and Brazilian educator Paulo Freire. We concluded that 'Gandhi and Freire have a place on campus. And a dialogue which develops their ideas, key concepts, analysis and actions, within contemporary settings, and with appropriate learning processes, provides a fruitful basis for a peace studies or peace education program.'[13]

Gandhi had featured strongly in Indian History and Indian Politics subjects at La Trobe University (as he obviously does in all the few such remaining courses in our tertiary institutions), and the Peace Studies subject, taught at the university since 1988, contained one session on Gandhi (out of a total of twenty-six in the course) by the Indian History lecturer. In 1992, the subject was reorganised. Instead of a range of guest lecturers speaking on various self-contained topics introducing diverse perspectives on the problem of war and negative peace with little theoretical coherence, I took over the teaching and the emphasis of the course shifted to include large sections on nonviolence and peace activism. Besides a lecture on Gandhian satyagraha, in seminars the students tackled questions such as: 'What is "passive resistance"?, Why did Gandhi dislike the term?', 'In the light of Gandhi's fasts and his writings on the practice of fasting, is satyagraha really about conversion or coercion?', and 'How important is the concept of God in Gandhian satyagraha? Why is it so important?'. Gandhi was not featured as an Indian politician, but rather as someone who was a

---

[13] Robin Burns and Thomas Weber, 'Gandhi and Freire on Campus: Theory and Practice in Tertiary Peace Studies Programs', *Peace Education Miniprint no. 76*, March 1995, Malmo: School of Education, p. 38.

primary model of peace activism, a Gandhi of potential personal relevance to class members.

Between 1998 and 2011, I introduced another subject, 'The Politics of Nonviolent Activism', with a heavier Gandhi emphasis. A quarter of the course concerned Gandhi and an examination of his campaigns and the views of his critics directly, and much of the rest of the subject matter (nonviolence, Gene Sharp, nonviolent activism, and 'people power') had strong Gandhian overtones. The students discussed questions such as: 'Why did Gandhi become a nonviolent activist?', 'What does satyagraha mean and how does it "work"?', 'What tactical and strategic lessons for nonviolent political action can be gleaned from Gandhi's campaigns?', 'What have been the main feminist reactions to Gandhi's nonviolence?', and 'What have been the main criticisms of Gandhi's nonviolence from the Left?'

These subjects lapsed after my retirement and Gandhi went back to being an important Indian politician. From Peace Studies, he returned to Politics and History. However, Gandhi-focused Peace and Development Studies courses continued to be taught. For example, the University of New England in Armidale in New South Wales has a long history of teaching Peace Studies. From the late 1980s until 2010, Howard Brasted taught a third-year History subject, 'Gandhi and Non-Violent Action in the Twentieth Century', that was devoted almost entirely to Gandhi. He continues to teach this at the Masters level. Later, Rebecca Spence taught a Peace Studies subject, 'The Philosophy and Practice of Nonviolence', and, at the time of writing, Marty Branagan was teaching an updated version of this unit, titled 'Active Resistance: Contemporary Nonviolence'. Here, deeply principled conceptions of nonviolence are examined through a study of Gandhi, 'one of the best-known and most written-about exponents of this framework of nonviolence'. The subject explores 'the way in which Gandhi saw nonviolence as an approach to all of life and especially as related to the social context surrounding him', with a focus on conversion

Australia's Gandhi: The Academy

(rather than coercion) as a struggle for truth, ahimsa, and the interconnectedness of all beings, and the 'constructive program' and its meaning for peace-building. And academic, researcher, and West Papua human rights activist Jason MacLeod teaches a Masters-level unit, 'Nonviolence: Philosophy and Practice', with a significant Gandhi component, at the Peace and Conflict Studies programme at the University of Sydney.

Gandhi obviously still features in the few extant Asia/India Politics and History subjects, and other courses that highlight Gandhi come and go in Peace Studies and Development Studies offerings. However, it is very rare that a university-level subject focuses its main attention on Gandhi.

Writings on Gandhi

While Australian academics did write major works on topics concerning modern Indian history in which Gandhi obviously featured strongly (and even had a picture of the Mahatma on the cover[14]), very few focussed specifically on Gandhi himself.

A great many books about Gandhi appeared after his Salt March, and again in 1969, his birth centenary. In the latter case, the Gandhi Centenary Committee of Victoria commissioned Newman Rosenthal, an academic who visited India frequently, to write a biography to celebrate the occasion.[15] Although there were other smaller Gandhi tracts, such as Hugh Owen's contribution to the University of Queensland's 'Leaders of Asia' series,[16]

---

[14] See, for example, Jim Masselos, *Nationalism on the Indian Subcontinent: An Introductory History*, Melbourne: Nelson, 1972; and also Robin Jeffrey, Lance Brennan, Jim Masselos, Peter Mayer, and Peter Reeves (eds), *India: Rebellion to Republic: Selected Writings 1857–1990*, New Delhi: Stirling, 1990.

[15] Newman Rosenthal, *The Uncompromising Truth: Mahatma Gandhi 1869–1948*, Melbourne: Nelson, 1969.

[16] Hugh Owen, *Gandhi*, St. Lucia: University of Queensland Press, 1984.

Rosenthal's seems to be the only book-length biography of the Mahatma aimed at the 'average reader' to be published in Australia. In other words, it was an easy to read introductory biography that did not aim to add anything new to the Gandhi story or break any new research ground.

In the following year, Sibnarayan Ray, the well-respected Indian scholar and then head of Indian Studies at the University of Melbourne, edited an international symposium of academic essays about Gandhi and his philosophy, with contributions by Australian scholars Hugh Owen (on the 1920–1922 Non-Cooperation movement), I. W. Mabbett (on Gandhi and Nehru), Jim Masselos (on Gandhi and Tilak), and J. T. F. Jordens (on the Hindu heritage of Gandhi's religion), as well as internationally renowned scholars of Indian history, and Gandhi scholars and activists such as Dennis Dalton, Arne Næss, Nirmal Kumar Bose, and Jayaprakash Narayan.[17] The chapters covered such areas as Gandhi's moral development and its relation to Hinduism and Jainism; his relations with his leading contemporaries Tilak, Gokhale, Tagore, Nehru, and Roy; Gandhi's role in Indian politics; and basic aspects of Gandhism, such as decentralisation, approaches to the economy, and violence and satyagraha.

In his Foreword to the book, the renowned Australian scholar of ancient India, A. L. Basham, noted his happiness that the book had been edited and produced in Australia. He saw it as 'an indication of the great development of Australian interest in Asia in general, and in India in particular'. He thought that the 'coming years will see many more works of this kind, on India and other parts of Asia, coming from Australian scholars and Australian presses'.[18] However, this volume appears to be the extent of substantial work on the Mahatma to be published in the country before the 1990s.

---

[17] Sibnarayan Ray (ed.), *Gandhi, India and the World: An International Symposium*, Melbourne: The Hawthorn Press, 1970.

[18] A. L. Basham, 'Foreword', in Ray (ed.), *Gandhi, India and the World*, p. 12.

Australia's Gandhi: The Academy

In 1988, my first Gandhi-related book—an examination of the Gandhian roots of the Indian Himalayan tree-hugging Chipko movement—was published.[19] The book did not provide a deep analysis of the movement (I could speak neither Hindi nor Garhwali, the local language, and I did not mention the role of leftist agitators in the development of the movement), but it did provide a link to Gandhi by highlighting the connection of some of the Mahatma's Western women disciples who were important in the background history of anti-logging protests in the hills, as well as discussing the movement's methods of activism in terms of satyagraha, Gandhi's practice of nonviolent action.

In 1990, the Gandhi Peace Foundation in New Delhi published Stephen Murphy's book, discussed above, and the following year, after much delay, they published my Master of Arts dissertation under the title *Conflict Resolution and Gandhian Ethics*.[20] That book presented a detailed analysis of satyagraha as the Gandhian approach to conflict resolution, looking at concepts fundamental to it, principles on which it was based, and the processes involved. The book then examined the way an individual could employ Gandhian methods in interpersonal, legal and industrial, social and international conflicts. It concluded with an examination of Gandhian ethics and why, according to Gandhi, satyagraha might be more than an effective method of conflict resolution: it had the possibility of providing the framework for a life worth living. Large sections of this book went into informing my Peace Studies courses taught at La Trobe University.

The writing of my Ph.D. dissertation, 'Unarmed Peacekeeping and the Shanti Sena', was completed early in 1991. It was published in 1996 as *Gandhi's Peace Army: The Shanti Sena and Unarmed*

---

[19] Thomas Weber, *Hugging the Trees: The Story of the Chipko Movement*, New Delhi: Viking, 1988. The book was published as a Penguin paperback the following year.

[20] Thomas Weber, *Conflict Resolution and Gandhian Ethics*, New Delhi: The Gandhi Peace Foundation, 1991.

Peacekeeping. While the book was mostly concerned with a section of the post-Gandhi Gandhian movement, it also examined the historical background to the idea as formulated by Gandhi and the Gandhian philosophy on which the Sena was founded. In 2009, a substantially re-written Indian edition of the book was published as *The Shanti Sena: Philosophy, History and Action*.

In 1997, after many years languishing with various publishers, HarperCollins in New Delhi brought out what I think is my most important book: the close to 600-page tome detailing Gandhi's celebrated Salt March to Dandi and my own walk retracing the route of the Mahatma's political pilgrimage.[21] It covered the day-to-day experiences of the marchers through the collection of oral history remembrances of those along the route; newspaper reports, both nationalist and pro-government, covering the event; government files, including those of police officers observing at close quarters; diaries of the marchers; and interviews with most of the ex-marchers who were still alive. It has become the standard work on the march itself.

Mark Thomson wrote only one book and several articles on Gandhi; nevertheless, his contribution to Gandhi scholarship is huge. Thomson was born in Sydney and spent his early years in Papua New Guinea, where his father worked at a senior level in the colonial administration from 1949 until 1973. He completed a Bachelor of Arts degree, which included an Indian History course under Jim Massellos, at the University of Sydney in 1974. Massellos convinced him to undertake a Master of Arts degree, with a dissertation on Gandhi's Sevagram ashram. It was completed in 1976. Taking a fairly unorthodox step for an Australian postgraduate, the following year Thomson applied for a scholarship as an Australian Exchange Scholar under the Commonwealth Scholarship and

---

[21] Thomas Weber, *On the Salt March: The Historiography of Gandhi's March to Dandi*, New Delhi: HarperCollins Publishers, 1997. A paperback version was published in 2000, and a revised edition was published by Rupa in 2009.

Fellowship Plan to complete a Ph.D. at the University of Bombay. He lived in Bombay from 1978 until 1982 and in 1983 received his doctorate for a dissertation on Gandhi's settlements, titled 'Gandhi and His Ashrams: An Enquiry into the Social Dynamics of Nonviolence'. For the first time, the biography of Gandhi's four ashrams, Phoenix Settlement and Tolstoy Farm in South Africa and Sabarmati and Sevagram Ashrams in India, had been written.

While still a postgraduate student in Bombay, Thomson wrote the first article to come out of his research, noting that 'The establishment of the Sevagram *ashram*, and the experiments subsequently carried out there are one aspect of Gandhi's life which has received scant attention from the many historians drawn to the study of this phenomenal individual.'[22] Thomson examined the Mahatma's experiments with alternative approaches to village life at Sevagram, where Gandhi had settled to provide a living laboratory where 'public focus' was directed to 'Gandhi's programme rather than the veneer of his press image.'[23]

Following his graduation, Thomson served as a public servant with the Australian International Development Assistance Bureau. Between 1986 and 1989, he was the Second Secretary in the Australian High Commission in Mauritius. During his tenure in Mauritius, in October of 1989, Thomson delivered a lecture titled 'The Gandhi Ashram from Phoenix to Sevagram: An Experiment in Living' at the Mahatma Gandhi Institute in Moka, and during the late 1980s he had several other works on Gandhi published.[24] In 1993, while he was serving as the First Secretary, Development Assistance, at the Australian High Commission in New Delhi, his key book, *Gandhi and His Ashrams*,[25] was published.

---

[22] R. M. Thomson, 'Gandhi at Sevagram: "India in a Village"', *Gandhi Marg* 2 (8), 1980, p. 431.

[23] Thomson, 'Gandhi at Sevagram', p. 437.

[24] The most significant of which was Mark Thomson, 'Hind Swaraj and the Constructive Work Programme', *South Asia* 9 (2), 1986, pp. 37–54.

[25] Mark Thomson, *Gandhi and His Ashrams*, Bombay: Popular Prakashan, 1993.

Although a great amount had been written about Gandhi by the time Thomson's book came out, most of it was centred on the personality of Gandhi himself, as politician, saint, and prophet. Now, finally, we had a scholarly (but eminently readable) account of how Gandhi had attempted to shape his ashrams as examples of a way to live a life of truth and nonviolence, and how, in turn, they had shaped him. Thomson explains that the

> book is a contribution to the ongoing quest to rediscover the nonviolent alternative. It tests the strength of Gandhi's claim that the ashrams were his finest achievements, and that the successes and failures of these communities were merely reflections of his own strengths and weaknesses.[26]

In short, Gandhi's ashrams 'were living laboratories wherein he and his colleagues experimented with ways and means of enabling India's villages to live in dignity and freedom'.[27]

The book was launched by the Maharashtra Governor and the Australian High Commissioner in Bombay, and the following year, Thomson was awarded the Bharat Mitra Samman (Friend of India Honour) for it by National Press India.

Another substantial academic work, this time investigating Gandhian techniques of nonviolence, by the nonviolent activist Robert Burrowes, was published in 1996. *The Strategy of Nonviolent Defense: A Gandhian Approach*[28] was the published version of Burrowes' Ph.D. dissertation. The aim of the book was to provide a strategic theory and framework for use in the planning of nonviolent defence, and tackled the issue of whether nonviolent defence can be effective against violent military aggression. Burrowes analysed several nonviolent struggles and described a way of conducting

---

[26] Thomson, *Gandhi and His Ashrams*, p. 2.
[27] Thomson, *Gandhi and His Ashrams*, p. 276.
[28] Robert J. Burrowes, *The Strategy of Nonviolent Defense: A Gandhian Approach*, Albany: State University of New York Press, 1996.

Australia's Gandhi: The Academy

struggle not only non-violently, but also in a way that is highly principled, recognising the suppression of human needs as the cause of conflicts. While the book does not limit itself to Gandhi as the source for his argument, Burrowes includes a chapter detailing the Gandhian conception of nonviolence. He analyses the causes of conflict and, in a Gandhian way, searches for an outcome that will benefit all parties. The book was highly praised by leading academics as a breakthrough and a major contribution to the alternative defence and nonviolence literature.

J. T. F. (Joseph Teresa Florent, known to his Australian friends as Jos) Jordens also wrote a significant Gandhi-related text. The 'Introduction' to the Indian edition of *Gandhi's Religion: A Homespun Shawl* by Ramachandra Guha declares that 'This is one of the best books I had read on Gandhi', and 'whenever friends asked me for a short list of good books on Gandhi I always placed Jordens's book in the first five'.[29] This is high praise, given that Guha is himself a gifted biographer of Gandhi and one of the best known Indian public intellectuals. The book, about Gandhi's religion, was originally published in 1998, but Jordens had been working in the area of Hindu religions for a long time before its publication. In 1978, he had published an authoritative account of the life of Dayananda Saraswati, the Hindu reformer and founder of the Hindu advancement organisation, the Arya Samaj. Three years later he published the biography of another of the great Hindu reformers, Swami Shraddhananda.

Jordens was born in Belgium, in 1925. After completing high school, he joined the Jesuit order, which had a long tradition of scholarship in Indian studies. In 1947, he enrolled in the faculty of Oriental Studies at the University of Louvain, where he studied Sanskrit and wrote a Ph.D. dissertation on the *Bhagavad Gita*.

---

[29] Ramachandra Guha, 'Introduction to the Indian Edition: Gandhi's Faith and Ours', in J. T. F. Jordens, *Gandhi's Religion: A Homespun Shawl*, New Delhi: Oxford University Press, 2012, pp. xii–xiii.

These studies were supposed to prepare him for educational work in India and so, in 1953, the year after his graduation, he set off for the subcontinent to personally experience something of what he had been studying intellectually. However, the years there convinced him that he would rather be an academic than a priest, and consequently he migrated to Australia in 1957.

In Melbourne in 1959, he obtained a Diploma of Education and taught languages and Indian History at prestigious private schools before being appointed as the first head of Indian Studies at the University of Melbourne in 1961, the first such department in an Australian tertiary institution. In 1970, he joined Basham at the Department of Asian Civilisations at the Australian National University. During his time at the ANU, he published his two influential books and served six years as Faculty Dean. But Gandhi was also starting to occupy his mind. In 1990, he presented the Tenth Annual A. L. Basham Lecture, titled 'Gandhi: Conscience of Hinduism and Scourge of Orthodoxy'.[30] This was a summary of the much larger project he was working on, the one that became *Gandhi's Religion*.[31]

In researching the book, Jordens did not go to secondary sources. Almost all the references come from a close reading of the ninety substantive volumes of Gandhi's *Collected Works*. There were none of the shortcuts that are often employed in the Gandhi literature: finding a few relevant quotations from compendia of Gandhian thoughts and then elaborating. In this chronological spiritual biography, Jordens allows Gandhi to speak for himself. In comparing Gandhi's religion to a large, bulky, homespun woollen shawl, Jordens notes that

---

[30] J. T. F. Jordens, *Gandhi: Conscience of Hinduism and Scourge of Orthodoxy*, Canberra: Faculty of Asian Studies, The Australian National University, 1991.

[31] This biographical information comes from Guha's 'Introduction' to Jordens' book on Gandhi's religion; and Anthony H. Johns' obituary 'Joseph Jordens (1925–2008)' in the Australian Academy of the Humanities, Proceedings 33, Canberra, 2008, pp. 71–74.

at first it looks very plain to the eye, but we can detect the beauty of the strong patterns and the contrasting shades of folk art. With its knots and unevenness, it feels rough to the touch; but soon we can experience how effective it is in warming cold and hungry limbs. Gandhi combined in his frail body the ideals of total renunciation and of total dedication.[32]

Jordens' writings were an antidote for those who saw Gandhi as little more than a wily politician. Gandhi's personal spiritual life, which was of central importance to him, is illustrated in a way that shows a vastly different Mahatma than the one that generally emerges from popular (largely political) biographies.

Every year, still, a great many books are published onGandhi. And many of those add nothing new to our knowledge of the Mahatma. However, the 2011 publication of Sean Scalmer's book about Gandhi's influence on American and British peace movements was not only well-informed, well-documented, and accessible, but was also an important addition to the literature. As one reviewer put it, the book 'provides a masterly synthesis of historical and socio-political structural analysis'. Through *Gandhi in the West*,[33] the reader gains a deep understanding of Gandhi's reception in England and America, and how his version of nonviolence became so compelling, particularly to those who were engaged in civil rights and anti-nuclear campaigns. Scalmer examined the background to this phenomenon: how Gandhi's struggle for Indian independence was perceived, the degree to which Gandhi was viewed through racist stereotypes, how newspapers reported the Mahatma, and how early pacifist groups attempted to incorporate Gandhian techniques into their campaigns—campaigns that 'are now mostly forgotten, but they provided the leadership, institutional

---

[32] Jordens, *Gandhi's Religion*, p. 276.
[33] Sean Scalmer, *Gandhi in the West: The Mahatma and the Rise of Radical Protest*, Cambridge: Cambridge University Press, 2011.

base, and political repertoire of the more famous campaigns of the 1960s'.³⁴

Sean Scalmer came from a working-class family, which gave him a strong interest in trade unions and socialism. He first became aware of Gandhi through Attenborough's movie and, sometime later, via Gandhi's *Autobiography*, which, he says, repelled him in parts but also left him intrigued.³⁵ He studied Politics and Political Economy at the University of Sydney prior to undertaking a Ph.D. on intellectuals and class in the Australian labour movement. A year of his Ph.D. studies was spent working under the guidance of the leading American sociologist and political scientist, Charles Tilly, at the Center for Studies of Social Change at the New School of Social Research in New York. The globalisation protests of the early 2000s led to an interest in direct action, including nonviolent direct action, which, in turn, led to *Gandhi in the West*. Following research and teaching positions at Macquarie University, in 2007 he took up a position teaching History at the University of Melbourne. His research on social movements, class, and democracy led to the publication of several books in these fields.

It is noteworthy that although relatively few books about aspects of Gandhi's life or thought were written by Australians, most of the ones that were made significant contributions to the literature on Gandhi.

The books listed above were all sympathetic to Gandhi and championed his version of nonviolence. There were, however, also voices critical of Gandhi, particularly from the left. In his history of communism in the 1930s and early 1940s, Ralph Gibson, the communist organiser, writer, and sometime editor of the Party's newspaper the *Guardian*, relates communist movements around the world to those in Australia.³⁶ However, his chapter on the situation

---

³⁴ Scalmer, *Gandhi in the West*, p. 7.
³⁵ Personal communication from Sean Scalmer, 16 October 2018.
³⁶ Ralph Gibson, *The People Stand Up*, Melbourne: Red Rooster Press, 1983.

Australia's Gandhi: The Academy

in India is not so linked. There he examines Gandhian campaigns, and while using the Indian communist Rajani Palme Dutt as his main source,[37] he is not totally scathing in his assessment of the philosophy of, and campaigns led by, the Mahatma. In 1982, Alec Kahn, ex-Monash University student radical, former editor of the International Socialist paper, *The Battler*, and member of the Socialist Workers' Action Group, took this further in a pamphlet titled 'Gandhi .... Hero or Humbug? How "Non-Violence" Failed in India'.[38] It was reprinted as a more professionally produced 'Socialist Worker Pocket Pamphlet' under the title of *Gandhi and the Myth of Non-Violent Action* in 1996. The analysis of Gandhi's campaigns was largely based on the writings of two early Indian Marxist interpreters of Gandhi: E. M. S. Namboodiripad[39] and Dutt. The pamphlet concluded that

> Gandhi cannot take credit for the departure of the British, but he probably can take some credit for the wretchedly unequal society that they left behind. For by ruining the popular worker/peasant upsurges of the 1919–1934 period, he guaranteed that the Indian capitalist class would remain intact to receive the reins of power from the British. They continue to wield those reins ruthlessly to this day, invoking Gandhi's name as they go.[40]

Besides books, there were also shorter pieces on Gandhi published in Australia. As noted above, the Indian community journal, *Bhavan Australia*, carries a substantial Gandhi content, as does Gambhir Watts' *Nonviolence News*. Before them, the

---

[37] R. Palme Dutt, *India Today*, London: Gollancz, 1940.

[38] Alec Kahn, 'Gandhi .... Hero or Humbug? How "Non-violence" Failed in India', n.p., An International Socialist Pamphlet, 1982.

[39] E. M. S. Namboodiripad, *The Mahatma and the Ism*, New Delhi: People's Publishing House, 1959.

[40] Alec Kahn, *Gandhi and the Myth of Non-Violent Action*, Sydney: Bookmarks, 1996.

country's premier nonviolent activist journal, *Groundswell*,[41] and its continuation *Nonviolence Today*,[42] was where one would anticipate the greatest coverage of matters Gandhian in an Australian activist-focussed publication. Nonviolence is far broader than Gandhi; however, even though he is mentioned in passing on several occasions, there is probably less serious analysis of his campaigns and what can be learned from them than could be expected. While the fifth issue of the journal contained a review of Attenborough's movie *Gandhi*,[43] it was not till the twenty-ninth issue that *Groundswell* (December/January 1987/1988) carried a reprint of an article in *Peace News* (of November 1987) on 'Gandhians After Gandhi', by the American writer Mark Shepard. This was a description of well-known Gandhians and their organisations, not an investigation of Gandhian praxis.[44]

The second number of *Nonviolence Today* brought its readers a reprinted piece by Christopher Kruegler on the intellectual antecedents of civilian-based defence. This was a survey of nonviolence literature, much of it based on others' (for example, that by Richard B. Gregg and Krishnalal Shridharani) examinations of Gandhian campaigns. It also featured a review of Geoffrey Ostergaard's book, *Nonviolent Revolution in India*, on the Indian post-Gandhi Gandhian Movement.[45] In the following two years

[41] First published every two months from October 1982 as *Groundswell: Newsletter for a New Society*, and then from August 1985 as *Groundswell for Nonviolent Revolution*.

[42] Published every two months or so from February/March 1988 until it folded following its May/August 2000 number.

[43] Allan Beesey, 'Gandhi the Film', *Groundswell* 1 (5), 1983, pp. 9–10. This review was originally published in the La Trobe University student paper *Rabelais*.

[44] This, in turn, was excerpted from Shepard's book, *Gandhi Today: A Report on Mahatma Gandhi's Successors*, Arcata, CA: Simple Productions, 1987. Perhaps tellingly, while the spelling is correct in the article, the cover of *Nonviolence Today* lists the piece as 'Ghandians After Ghandi'.

[45] See Christopher Kruegler, 'Civilian-Based Defense: The Intellectual Antecedents', *Nonviolence Today* 2, April/May 1988, pp. 13–16 (originally

Australia's Gandhi: The Academy

I wrote three articles that looked at the meaning of Gandhian satyagraha, the reasons for employing Gandhian forms of nonviolence (not only because it works, but because it is also right), and a critique of American social activist Saul Alinsky's suggestion that Gandhi's nonviolence was a result of his lack of weapons.[46] The most prolific contributor to *Nonviolence Today* was Robert Burrowes. While he does not explicitly mention Gandhi in most of his articles, the Gandhian 'flavour' is unmistakeable. In his final published pieces, where he talks about his journey in nonviolence, Gandhi is front and centre.

The other journal where one could have expected fairly regular articles on Gandhi and his nonviolence was *Social Alternatives*, the journal founded by Ralph Summy. Its first issue was published in December 1977, with the Gandhian Sugata Dasgupta as one of its five original editors. The themes that were to be an 'ongoing concern of the journal' included, as first in a list, 'Peace Studies and Peace Research'. The lead article of the first issue was an extract of about one-fifth of Jayaprakash Narayan's prison diary, written while he was incarcerated during Mrs. Gandhi's dictatorial 'Emergency'.[47] With the picture of JP on its cover, the scoop in obtaining the rights to publish the diary extracts immediately gave the journal international cachet. This was possible because Dasgupta was a close friend of JP, India's preeminent Gandhian activist. It all boded well for serious discussions of things Gandhian; however, after the ending of the 'Emergency', not long after the publication

---

published in *Civilian-Based Defense: News & Opinion* 4 (3), 1988, pp. 1–4); and Brian Martin, 'The Pitfalls of Nonviolent Revolution', *Nonviolence Today* 2, April/May 1988, pp. 16–17.

[46] See Thomas Weber, 'Satyagraha', *Nonviolence Today* 10, August/September 1989, pp. 3–4, 'Nonviolence: The Other Reasons', *Nonviolence Today* 13, February/March 1990, pp. 4–6, and 'Alinsky and Gandhi on Means and Ends', *Nonviolence Today* 16, August/September 1990, pp. 8–10.

[47] 'Loss of a Friend and Dedicated Peace Worker', *Social Alternatives* 4 (3), 1984, p. 61.

of the initial issue of *Social Alternatives*, Dasgupta returned to India, and with his departure Gandhi lost his primary promoter at the journal.

Ten years after its founding, *Social Alternatives* carried a section on 'Nonviolent Political Action', but none of the articles said anything about Gandhi. It was not until 1996 that the journal published its first specifically Gandhi-related article. Michael Salla, a former Ph.D. student of Ralph Summy, then teaching Politics at the Australian National University in Canberra, took a postmodernist look at Gandhi's nonviolence and argued that it was about far more than a way of securing India's independence: 'nonviolence referred to a lifestyle, a normative outlook' in the search for 'Truth' (rather than 'truth'), and that there can be no nonviolent future as nonviolence is something that had to be created in the present.[48]

The following year, in his 'Guest Editor's Introduction' to a special issue on global nonviolence, Summy started off by saying that 'A spectre haunts the world. The spirit of Gandhiji is alive and well.'[49] The papers in this issue of *Social Alternatives* described nonviolent actions around the world; however, none related to Australia or had much to say about Gandhi or his approach to nonviolence.

To mark the twenty-fifth anniversary of the journal, a special issue on nonviolence theory and practice was published. The only paper specifically discussing Gandhi was my 'Gandhi's Nonviolence and the Salt March'.[50] In 2010, a themed issue of *Social Alternatives* (with Gandhi's image on the front cover), featuring papers presented at the Asia-Pacific Peace Research Association's conference held in Hualien in Taiwan in September 2009, was published. In his

---

[48] Michael Salla, 'There is No Nonviolent Future', *Social Alternatives* 15 (3), 1996, pp. 41–43.

[49] Ralph Summy, 'Nonviolence Around the World: The Triumph of Gandhi', *Social Alternatives* 16 (2), 1997, p. 4.

[50] Thomas Weber, 'Gandhi's Nonviolence and the Salt March', *Social Alternatives* 21 (2), 2002, pp. 46–51.

Australia's Gandhi: The Academy

'Editor's Introduction', John Synott noted that 'the philosophy and strategy of Mahatma Gandhi underpins much of the scholarship in Peace Studies and the methods of practical work in peacebuilding around the region'. Synott went on to observe that

> after a period of a few decades from the 1960s onwards when Gandhi's work was discovered and promoted in courses in peace and conflict studies in Western universities, that same work is now being discarded and ignored. New generations of students are not being provided the opportunity to study or examine Gandhi's work…. Gandhi's writings and knowledge have been framed within universities as obsolete. The whole discipline of peace studies that places Gandhi as a central figure has been rendered as 'unscientific' by university managers in their quest to satisfy research indicators and impact identifiers in competitive academic environments where gaining research funding and meeting performance targets have come to dominate academic research and teaching.[51]

In the introductory essay, Indian academic Ravindra Kumar explained Gandhi in terms of nonviolent non-cooperation, providing an analysis of the principles and history of nonviolence through traditions established by Gandhi and the social and political values and tactics involved.[52] That Kumar admired and commended Gandhi's nonviolence, and the fact that Gandhi-related courses were being taught at the University of Queensland since the mid-1970s, from the late 1980s at the University of New England, and from the early 1990s at La Trobe University, did little to contradict Synott's conclusions.

Nevertheless, Australian academics wrote several important papers and book chapters on Gandhi and nonviolence. For example, the La Trobe University philosopher John Fox presented a paper at the 'Non-Violence—Christian Perspectives Convention' in

---

[51] John Synott, 'Editor's Introduction', *Social Alternatives* 29 (1), 2010, p. 3.
[52] Ravindra Kumar, 'Nonviolent Non-Cooperation: An Effective, Noble and Valuable Means for Peaceful Change', *Social Alternatives* 29 (1), 2010, pp. 5–10.

Melbourne in July 1967. This became a lengthy and influential article titled 'Theory and Practice of Non-Violent Action', published in *The Peacemaker* during the height of the conscientious objector movement and several years before Gene Sharp made 'nonviolent action' an important subject in the peace lexicon. Following a summary of Gandhi's life and campaigns, campaigns in other parts of the world, and Richard Gregg's formulation of satyagraha as 'moral ju-jitsu', he provided an analysis of the strategy and techniques of nonviolence: 'One's attitude should be that of love and of complete respect for the other as a person. Therefore one must use the most persuasive and least coercive means available. If these fail in turn, one should use only the least injurious types of pressure.'[53]

As something of a follow-up to Sibnarayan Ray's international virtual symposium on Gandhi that led to his 1970 edited book, in 2004 a real-time Gandhi symposium was held at the Australian National University, which also resulted in a substantial book. Arranged by Debjani Ganguly, the head of the Humanities Research Centre at the university, and John Docker, the Adjunct Senior Research Fellow at the Centre, a conference titled 'Gandhi, Nonviolence and Modernity' was convened at the beginning of September. The conference participants included international Gandhi scholars such as Ajay Skaria, Charles DiSalvo, Tridip Suhrud, Makarand Paranjape, and Anjali Roy, as well as several local academics. The keynote address, titled 'Ahimsa and other Animals: The Genealogy of an Immature Politics', was delivered by Leela Gandhi, a great-granddaughter of Gandhi, then teaching at the School of English at Melbourne's La Trobe University.

Several of the papers from the conference were reprinted in a special issue of the *Borderlands* e-journal[54] a year after the

---

[53] John Fox, 'Theory and Practice of Non-Violent Action', *The Peacemaker* 30 (4), April 1968, pp. 4–5.
[54] John Docker and Debjani Ganguly (eds), 'Gandhi, Nonviolence & Modernity', *Borderlands e-journal* 4 (3), 2005. Available at https://webarchive.

Australia's Gandhi: The Academy

symposium, and about half of the papers were later edited by Ganguly and Docker into a book published in America three years after the conference[55] and in India two years after that.[56] The aim of the book was to look at Gandhi not only as an '"Indian" figure, but as an activist thinker whose transcultural nonviolent ethics of the everyday eminently translates across a range of political sites'. The blurbs on the various editions of *Rethinking Gandhi and Nonviolent Relationality* explain that the 'volume also gives us vignettes of Gandhi's more eccentric aspects—his vegetarianism, his fasts and medical practice, and his experiments in communal living. Without deifying Gandhi, the volume sensitively explores the sheer worldliness and embodied nature of Gandhi's thought, practice and legacy' by combining 'historical, philosophical and textual readings of different aspects of the leader's life and works'. The book also covered areas such as Gandhi's political development through his legal practice, his relevance to global peace movements, and his relations with Dalit leader B. R. Ambedkar. The Australian scholars who participated in the conference and contributed to the published work were John Docker ('Josephus: Traitor or Gandhian'), Debjani Ganguly ('Vernacular Cosmopolitanism: World Historical Readings of Gandhi and Ambedkar'), Sean Scalmer ('Globalising Gandhi: Translation, Reinvention, Application, Transformation'), and me ('Gandhi Moves: Intentional Communities and Friendship').

In mid-March 2015, the ANU Humanities Research Centre organised a one-day event titled 'Gandhi: A Workshop on the Nature of his Enduring Influence'. The workshop mission statement noted:

---

nla.gov.au/awa/20060820141236/http://www.borderlandsejournal.adelaide.edu.au/issues/vol4no3.html (accessed December 2023).

[55] Debjani Ganguly and John Docker (eds), *Rethinking Gandhi and Nonviolent Relationality: Global Perspectives*, London: Routledge, 2007.

[56] Debjani Ganguly and John Docker (eds), *Rethinking Gandhi and Nonviolent Relationality: Global Perspectives*, New Delhi: Orient BlackSwan, 2009.

Gandhi's Australia/Australia's Gandhi

An oscillation from Gandhi as a Mahatma to Gandhi the shrewd leader to Gandhi the deliberate obscurantist, and back, can distract from interesting and problematic aspects of Gandhi's work that continue to inform our understanding of the environment, literature, philosophy and history across the world.

The workshop was introduced by leading Indian scholar and writer about Gandhi, Ashis Nandy, followed by six papers by Australian academics: Debjani Ganguly ('M. K. Gandhi: The 'Inconsistent' Thinker as Moral Icon'), Kama Maclean ('A Funny Little Man: Cartoons and Jokes about Gandhi in the Empire'), myself ('The Cooption of Gandhi [Because of his Enduring Influence] for Non-Gandhian Causes: Or 101 Uses for a Dead Mahatma'), Assa Doron ('Gandhi's Vision, Modi's Broom'), Peter Friedlander ('Gandhi and Hindustani'), and Meera Ashar ('Belonging and Nation: Thinking with Gandhi').

Over the years, several Australian academics have also written well-received scholarly papers on Gandhi. One of them was Kenneth Rivett, an ex-lecturer at the University of Melbourne and then, until his retirement in 1984, an Associate Professor in the School of Economics at the University of New South Wales, who wrote on pacifism, immigration, and refugee issues as well as campaigning against the White Australia policy. He penned an article examining Gandhian economics in terms of Western economic theory,[57] and another comparing and contrasting Gandhi's satyagraha with Tolstoy's nonviolence.[58] A. L. Basham, the author of the groundbreaking book *The Wonder That Was India*,[59] also wrote a

---

[57] Kenneth Rivett, 'The Economic Thought of Mahatma Gandhi', *The British Journal of Sociology* 10 (1), 1959, pp. 1–15; published in booklet form in India as *Economic Thought of Mahatma Gandhi*, Bombay: Allied, 1959.

[58] Kenneth Rivett, 'Gandhi, Tolstoy and Coercion', *South Asia* 11 (2), 1988, pp. 29–56.

[59] A. L. Basham, *The Wonder That Was India*, London: Sidgwick and Jackson, 1954.

chapter on traditional influences on the thought of Gandhi.[60] Michael Salla wrote on Gandhi's views of human nature, his conception of an ideal society ('Ramarajya'), his formulation of nonviolence, and how this related to the possible formation of 'Satyagraha brigades'.[61] Besides the Gandhi-related books that I have published, I have also written numerous articles and book chapters on Gandhian themes. Many of the more substantial of these were collected in two volumes: *Gandhi, Gandhism and the Gandhians* (2006)[62] and *The Mahatma, His Philosophy and His Legacy* (2018).[63]

The renowned Indian scholar of comparative religion, Arvind Sharma, who has spent most of his academic career teaching in American universities, lectured at the University of Queensland in the late 1970s and then at the University of Sydney during the 1980s until the mid-1990s. Early on in his time at UQ, in a volume of Australian essays on world religions, his important contribution on Gandhi's interpretation of the *Bhagavad Gita* was published. While through Krishna's urgings to the uncertain prince Arjuna that it is his duty to fight in the fratricidal war that is about to commence, the *Gita* seems to imply that violence can be commended, Sharma explains that Gandhi's seemingly unique interpretation says the opposite: that the battle of the *Gita* is in fact an allegory of the battle of good against evil within a person, and the message is actually one of nonviolence, and there may have been some historical precedent to this effect in ancient allegorical interpretations of the *Gita*.[64]

[60] A. L. Basham, 'Traditional Influences on the Thought of Mahatma Gandhi', in R. Kumar (ed.), *Essays on Gandhian Politics: The Rowlatt Satyagraha of 1919*, Oxford: Clarendon Press, 1971, pp. 17–42.

[61] Michael Emin Salla, 'Satyagraha in Mahatma Gandhi's Political Philosophy', *Peace Research* 25, 1993, pp. 39–62.

[62] Thomas Weber, *Gandhi, Gandhism and the Gandhians: Essays by Thomas Weber*, New Delhi: Roli, 2006.

[63] Thomas Weber, *The Mahatma, His Philosophy and His Legacy*, Hyderabad: Orient BlackSwan, 2018.

[64] Arvind Sharma, 'Some Early Anticipations of the Gandhian Interpretation of the Bhagavad-Gita', in Victor C. Hayes (ed.), *Australian Essays in World*

Other academics, such as Brian Martin, one of the leading theorists of nonviolence at the University of Wollongong, and Stuart Rees, ex-Director of the Centre for Peace and Conflict Studies at the University of Sydney and Chair of the Sydney Peace Foundation, regularly refer to Gandhi in their writings and speeches.

It is not just academic publications that feature Gandhi. He has also made an appearance in Australian fiction. Early in his short story writing career, Frank Moorhouse, one of the country's most celebrated writers, penned a piece featuring the Mahatma. 'The Girl from the Family of Man'[65] was used by Scalmer as a way to introduce Gandhi in his book on Gandhi's reception in the West. Where Moorhouse, the ex-journalist, editor, union organiser, and champion of authors' rights, came into contact with Gandhi is not clear, especially as 'Gandhi' is written as 'Ghandi' throughout and 'satyagraha' as 'satyagrapha'. The story is about Angela, an idealistic American contract teacher who likes Gandhi and Joan Baez, and her lecherous and somewhat vulgar local would-be lover, Kyle. For her, Gandhi is a symbol of peace and a non-aggressive approach to the usual 'stand over' relationships that are so common. For Kyle, being sympathetic to Gandhi is not much more than a method of seduction. Fortunately for him, Gandhi's attitude to celibacy did not need to be taken too seriously, as Angela noted that 'He's a little crazy there.'

Gandhi Orations

Orations in the name of Gandhi and speeches on Gandhian topics are not rare occasions. For example, the Fijian writer and politician and later Australian academic, Professor Satendra Nandan, delivered a lecture titled 'The Making of the Mahatma:

Religions, Adelaide: The Australian Association for the Study of Religions, 1977, pp. 66–72.

[65] Frank Moorhouse, 'The Girl from the Family of Man', *Westerly*, July 1970, pp. 25–31.

Australia's Gandhi: The Academy

The Markings of the Outsider-Writer'[66] at the National Press Club in Canberra on 3 October 2017. The oration was given under the auspices of the Canberra-based Australian Centre for Christianity and Culture to mark the United Nations' International Non-Violence Day, celebrated on Gandhi's birthday. It drew some interesting parallels between the lives of Gandhi and the Australian writer Patrick White. Gandhi orations are also regularly organised by the Canberra chapter of the Indian welfare establishment, the Global Organization for People of Indian Origin. Many other such events could be listed; however, the foremost Gandhi orations are the ones delivered at the University of New South Wales in Sydney.

Since 2012, on India's Martyrs' Day, the anniversary of Gandhi's assassination, the UNSW has organised a celebration, starting with a remembrance ceremony on the University library lawn by the bust of Gandhi and culminating in a Gandhi Oration. The oration need not necessarily be on an explicitly Gandhian theme, but it is delivered by 'a person whose life's work exemplifies Gandhi's ideals'. Orations have been delivered by the Aboriginal statesman Senator Patrick Dodson (2012), the writer Tom Keneally (2014), the journalist Peter Greste (2016), and the social researcher and author Hugh Mackay (2017). However, occasionally they are explicitly about Gandhi.

In 2011, the American Pulitzer Prize-winning author Joseph Lelyveld published a partial biography of Mahatma Gandhi[67] that outraged public opinion in India and served as a vehicle for the self-promotion of leading politicians who railed against the supposed contents. Although the book was not yet available on the

---

[66] Satendra Nandan, 'The Making of the Mahatma: The Markings of the Outsider-Writer', Charles Sturt University, 3 October 2017. Available at cdn.csu.edu.au/__data/assets/pdf_file/0011/2876339/The-MAKING-of-the-Mahatma-The-MARKINGS-of-the-Outsider-Writer-.pdf (accessed December 2023).
[67] Joseph Lelyveld, *Great Soul: Mahatma Gandhi and His Struggle with India*, New York: Knopf, 2011.

subcontinent and so had not been read by the politicians, populist calls for its banning came thick and fast. The writer was accused of portraying Gandhi as 'a sexual weirdo, a political incompetent and a fanatical faddist',[68] not to mention a homosexual and a racist; things the book itself did not say. One of Australia's best-known jurists and former Justice of the High Court of Australia, the human rights campaigner and leading ethicist, Michael Kirby, took up this theme in the second Gandhi Oration in 2013. Later that year, it was published as a 'Penguin Special' short book titled, *What Would Gandhi Do?*[69] The back cover of that book promises to show the reader 'how remarkably useful Gandhi's insights remain when confronting the world's challenges'.

Kirby is neither a Gandhi scholar nor an anti-Gandhi revisionist (as are many recent Gandhi evaluators, who see it as their mission to discover something new about Gandhi, often something of a sexual or racist nature, in order to expose the 'fairy tale' of a saintly Mahatma). After making the point that Gandhi was generally, but unnaturally, disgusted with sex, Kirby makes several strong insinuations concerning Gandhi's probable homosexuality without actually 'outing' the Mahatma.[70] For Kirby, this is not an exercise in Gandhi defamation. He views possible evidence of Gandhi's homosexuality as a positive, one that supports the normalisation of varying sexualities.

As a good jurist, Kirby would probably insist that he is merely engaged in a process of examining available evidence. However,

---

[68] Andrew Roberts, 'Among the Hagiographers', *The Wall Street Journal*, 26 March 2011. For a more detailed account of this controversy, see Thomas Weber, 'How Outrage Gripped Gandhi's Recalcitrant Nation', *Inside Story*, 27 July 2011. Available at insidestory.org.au/how-outrage-gripped-gandhis-recalcitrant-nation (accessed December 2023). It was reprinted with references in Thomas Weber, *The Mahatma, His Philosophy and His Legacy*, Hyderabad: Orient BlackSwan, 2018, pp. 265–274.
[69] Michael Kirby, *What Would Gandhi Do?* Melbourne: Penguin, 2013.
[70] See Kirby, *What Would Gandhi Do?*, pp. 35–53.

he had neither the time nor the expertise to do the necessary and independent research. Nor did he have quite enough familiarity with the Gandhi story to fully understand the context of various reported events or fragments of correspondences. Instead, in his oration and essay he has relied on Lelyveld and given some of Lelyveld's possible insinuations more weight than they warrant. Often the text reflects Michael Kirby's views rather than lessons from a counterfactual twenty-first century Mohandas Gandhi.

The allusion to Gandhi's homosexuality is based on the Mahatma's relationship with the architect Hermann Kallenbach. Kirby's speculations aside, in trying to understand the young South African resident Gandhi, even Lelyveld warns that in an age 'when the concept of Platonic love gains little credence', details of the relationship and quotation from letters 'can easily be arranged' to reach a conclusion that is not necessarily warranted. Lelyveld notes that the relationship described 'a strong mutual attraction, nothing more'.[71] Kirby is unconvinced.

As Gandhi's latest biographer, the extremely competent archivist Ramachandra Guha, points out, Kallenbach was a confirmed heterosexual and the relationship between the two was that of brothers.[72] A reading of Gandhi's own letters to family members and friends clearly confirms his revulsion to sex of any kind. Kirby focuses on a letter by Gandhi in London to Kallenbach in South Africa that has reference to Vaseline and cotton wool. Overlooked by Kirby and his source Lelyveld, that sentence also refers to 'corns'. Knowledge of the exercise habits of the almost fanatical walkers and a careful reading of the letter, as well as another of Gandhi's references to Vaseline, indicates that the issue was problems with Gandhi's feet, nothing more.

---

[71] Lelyveld, *Great Soul*, p. 88.
[72] Ramachandra Guha, *Gandhi Before India*, London: Allen Lane, 2013, pp. 600–601, 607.

In any case, Gandhi's sexual orientation is not relevant to his greatness or otherwise, and the sexual orientation of a writer should be of no consequence in judging their work. But things are not always that simple (the personal *is* political). Kirby came out as being gay in 1999 and since then, has often spoken in support of gay rights. Here, he is not speculating about Gandhi's sexuality to denigrate Gandhi. While his cause is far nobler, Kirby probably tells us more about himself than his subject. And on his subject, a good story aside, he is almost certainly wrong.

Probably the part of this oration and essay that was of most interest to the majority of the audience and readers was the section on sex and Gandhi's sexuality. In a cursory way, Kirby also touched on Gandhi's and his own attitudes to the issues of women's rights (Gandhi would fight for them), climate change (Gandhi would recommend ecological restraint), and animal rights (Kirby and Gandhi both care about animal welfare and recommend vegetarianism). It is a pity that he did not develop these themes further.

Although Kirby's speech, and the book that resulted from it, was the best known and the most controversial of the Gandhi Orations held at the UNSW, it was not the only one with a strongly Gandhian theme. In 2015, the Mahatma's granddaughter Ela Gandhi delivered the oration, noting that the teachings of Gandhi are more relevant than ever, given Islamophobia, terrorism, and climate change, and stressing the Mahatma's philosophy of nonviolence and example of a simple lifestyle; and more recently, in 2018 the award-winning Indian journalist and political commentator, Shoma Chaudhury, spoke about 'The Significance of Gandhi in a Post-Truth World', noting that 'At a time when public conversation is defined by appeals to hyper emotion and facts don't matter, we need Mahatma Gandhi more than ever.' She added that 'Gandhi was not just a saviour of the past, he offered a diagnosis of the present and was a prophet of the future.'

Australia's Gandhi: The Academy

In the 2019 oration titled 'Justice in Action', the Chief Advocate of World Vision, Tim Costello, reminded the audience that the issues Gandhi was most concerned about almost a century ago—poverty, hunger, violence, war, and injustice—were still with us, noting that 'Gandhi's ideal of self-sacrifice over self-interest, individual obligations over individual rights, renunciation over consumption, and self-sacrifice over violence still ring true.' He spoke of how Gandhi inspired others as a peaceful revolutionary who fought against injustice with justice and against violence with nonviolence. Costello posed a question about the relevance of Gandhi's message in today's 'post truth' world and concluded that he is still incredibly relevant. His conclusion, following a lengthy examination of issues concerning justice and our responsibility as a country and as individuals, led him back to the Mahatma as a beacon of hope.

Other than Kirby's, the UNSW and other orations have had little impact on Australia's Gandhi knowledge base. The small-dimensioned booklet that came out of Kirby's speech, with fifty-six pages of well-spaced text, can easily be read in one short sitting. This leaves the question of how much Kirby has contributed to introducing Gandhi to Australian audiences, and whether this introduction is in the vein of Mehta's book on Gandhi. Australians have not produced a detailed non-polemical popular book about Gandhi, and no overseas book seems to have garnered the attention of a local readership that Mayo's 1927 book *Mother India* did. Nevertheless, public audiences still attend public lectures, go to the cinema, and view visual museum displays. And, for them, they are probably more important in shaping perceptions than the written word.

8

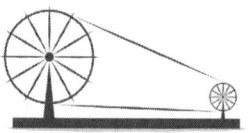

Australia's Gandhi
The Public

When talking about the Australian public in relationship to Gandhi, I am not thinking of the elite few who sought out the Mahatma in India, or those who belong to issue-based organisations that may employ Gandhian rhetoric, or those who teach Gandhi-related subjects in the universities or attended their lectures, or indeed those who have written learned works about Gandhi that very few Australians will ever read. I am thinking of the ordinary public that goes to public lectures by overseas Gandhians because of interests in peace, or to the cinema to see a movie that features Gandhi, or has a picnic in a park with a Gandhi statue and reads the inscription, or wanders into a museum to check out an exhibition that features photographs of Gandhi. And in particular, I am thinking of members of the large Australian Indian, particularly Hindu, community that tries to keep Gandhi alive as part of its heritage.

Overseas Gandhian Visitors

While the senior Gandhians Jayaprakash Narayan and Dr K. Arunachalam, renowned Gandhian academics Sibnarayan Ray and Sugata Dasgupta, and the well-known Gandhi-inspired Quaker personalities Marjorie Sykes and Reginald Reynolds, had

Australia's Gandhi: The Public

visited Australia in the decades after Gandhi's death, there were also others, and even earlier ones. Several of these Gandhian individuals provided first-hand accounts of Gandhi, Gandhian movements, and Gandhian philosophy in action to those members of the public who came to listen to them.

Charles Freer Andrews

Born in 1871, the Anglican Reverend Charles Freer Andrews took up a position teaching philosophy at St. Stephen's College in Delhi in 1904. In 1913, Gopal Krishna Gokhale asked him to go to South Africa to help the Indian community in its struggle, led by Gandhi, against discriminatory legislation. There he came into contact with the Mahatma to be, and they forged a firm, lifelong friendship. While he was known as *Deenabandhu*, 'Friend of the Poor', in India, Gandhi called him 'Christ's Faithful Apostle' after his initials, and Andrews was the only figure to refer to Gandhi by his first name—Mohan—instead of as Mr Gandhi by his opponents, or as Gandhiji, or Mahatmaji, or Bapu by his followers. Theirs was a relationship of equals.

In 1915, the Indian government asked Andrews to go to Fiji and investigate the alleged mistreatment of indentured Indians there. On the way, he visited Australia, where it seems that he 'felt uncomfortable among Australians whom he thought brash and vulgar, although kind enough'. On 15 October, he wrote a letter to his other close Indian friend, the poet Rabindranath Tagore, explaining that 'allowance had to be made for national immaturity' because 'Australia is passing through the raw stage of youth. Otherwise the vulgarities,—the gambling, drinking, extravagance, & worldliness,—would be too openly offensive. I have found beneath all these a wistful tenderness,—and there is very little veiled hypocrisy.' Four days later, in another letter to Tagore, he was a little more conciliatory, noting that there is a generosity here which redeems the sins of youthful pride. I have more hope for the Australian than for the Englishman. The Australian has vices, but hypocrisy is not one of them.... The Englishman has become hardened in self-deception by long years of compromise with conscience. The Australian is young & generous. He may act flagrantly against his conscience—as a young man often does—but he will be too candid & honest to deceive himself.[1]

Following another trip to Fiji in 1917, Andrews travelled extensively in Australia, challenging Australian Christians by asking if there was not 'something to repent of' where 'the wealthiest company in the land [the Australian headquartered Colonial Sugar Refining Company] is now grown rich and prosperous out of this very indentured labour with its terrible fruits?' On his journeys in Australia he gathered volunteers and allies, and women friends who 'mended his ragged coats and shirts and replenished his stock of socks and handkerchiefs; but so absorbed was he in his work that he never noticed the difference!'[2] Andrews' findings in Fiji resulted in the ending of indentured labour.

In 1929 *The Australian Christian Commonwealth* paper ran the first part of a lengthy laudatory piece by Andrews about his 'friend' Gandhi,[3] and following that there were many reviews of Andrews' biographies: *Mahatma Gandhi's Ideas*, *Mahatma Gandhi: His Own Story*, and *Mahatma Gandhi at Work*.

In July 1936, the saintly Andrews was back in Australia under the auspices of the Australian Student Christian Movement to address students in Sydney, Melbourne, Adelaide, and Perth.

[1] J. H. Bloomfield, 'C. F. Andrews in New Zealand', *The New Zealand Journal of History* 7 (1), 1973, p. 71.
[2] Benarsidas Chaturvedi and Marjorie Sykes, *Charles Freer Andrews*, New Delhi: Publications Division, Ministry of Information and Broadcasting, Government of India, 1971, p. 141.
[3] C. F. Andrews, 'Gandhi as I Know Him', *The Australian Christian Commonwealth*, 10 May 1929, p. 6; and 17 May 1929, p. 6.

He spoke about his reminiscences of Gandhi and Tagore, about 'Gandhi: The Man and his Mission', and talked about what Gandhi had taught him about Christianity in their time in South Africa in 1913–1914. During his visit, he was often asked why Gandhi was not a Christian. His reply included the story about how, in his company, Gandhi was turned away from a church door because of his colour. He would then challenge the audience about the white Australia that he disliked intensely, telling them that 'You younger generation must change all this.'[4]

Deenabandhu Andrews died in 1940 at the age of sixty-nine in Calcutta. His friend Marjorie Sykes co-wrote his biography, for which Gandhi had written a brief pre-publication Foreword six weeks before he was assassinated: 'Charlie Andrews was simple like a child, upright as a die, and shy to a degree. For the biographers the work has been a labour of love. A life such as Andrews' needs no introduction. It is its own introduction.'[5]

Muriel Lester

Muriel Lester was a well-known British Christian pacifist author, eloquent preacher, and social worker. She was born in December 1883 into a wealthy home with the privileges of a good education, travel, and a full cultural life.[6] From her father she acquired a strong

---

[4] 'Reverend Mr. Andrews' Plan for Right Personal Attitudes Towards War', *The Telegraph* (Brisbane), 14 July 1936, p. 2. For Andrews' observations of the 'White Australia' policy, see Kama Maclean, *British India, White Australia: Overseas Indians, Intercolonial Relations and the Empire*, Sydney: University of New South Wales Press, 2020, pp. 125–129.

[5] Chaturvedi and Sykes, *Charles Freer Andrews*, p. vi.

[6] For the story of Lester's life, see her autobiographical volumes, *It Occurred to Me*, New York: Harper and Brothers, 1937; and *It So Happened*, New York: Harper and Brothers, 1947; as well as the biography by Jill Wallis, *Mother of World Peace: The Life of Muriel Lester*, Enfield Lock, Middlesex: Hisarlik Press, 1993; and Thomas Weber, *Going Native: Gandhi's Relationship with Western Women*, New Delhi: Roli, pp. 83–92.

religious faith and social conscience and from her mother, a love of nature, books, music, and travel. In her youth, she realised that everyone was not as privileged as her, that many members of the working class lived in slums and worked in appalling conditions in factories—and decided to do something about it.

With her sister Doris, she set up boys' clubs, nursery and adult schools and in 1915, they founded the first iteration of Kingsley Hall, which became a teetotal pub to provide a congenial evening gathering place for the residents of the local crowded slum houses. Gandhi was a guest of Muriel at a newer Kingsley Hall when he came to London to attend the Second Round Table Conference.

Lester first went to India in 1926, and arrived at the Sabarmati Ashram on Gandhi's fifty-seventh birthday. At her first meeting with him, she explained that it would be important for Gandhi to come to England. Gandhi responded by noting that he had nothing to teach people like her. She interrupted him by explaining that she did not want him to 'come to England in order to teach us. I want you to come and learn from us.' Gandhi burst out laughing and they became close friends.[7]

It was to be another five years before Gandhi could make it to England. However, when Lester heard that he was coming to the Conference, she wrote to him:

> Now you're coming, don't forget this is the place where you will be happy, Kingsley Hall. You'll find we live extremely simply, you'll find we have cell-bedrooms on the flat roof, little tiny places, you can have one of them and whoever you bring will be treated the same way and you will find that we have our days punctuated by times of prayer just as you have.[8]

---

[7] Lester, *It Occurred to Me*, p. 135; and see also Muriel Lester, *My Host the Hindu*, London: Williams and Norgate, 1931, pp. 49–55.

[8] Francis Watson and Hallam Tennyson, *Talking of Gandhi*, New Delhi: Sangam, 1976, p. 78.

He replied, 'I would rather stay at your settlement than anywhere else, for there I will be living among the same sort of people as those for whom I have spent my life.'⁹

Following travels in China and Japan for the International Fellowship of Reconciliation (IFoR), she joined Gandhi's gruelling anti-Untouchability (*Harijan*) tour in early 1934 and visited earthquake-devastated Bihar with him. She visited Gandhi in India several times in the later 1930s, her last during the chaos of Partition in 1946.

In the 1930s, Lester spent more and more time working with IFoR and turned over the leadership of Kingsley Hall to Doris after returning from her 1934 India trip. From the end of World War II until she was in her eighties, Muriel Lester devoted her life to the IFoR cause as its travelling secretary, completing nine around-the-world trips, lecturing and writing and even being imprisoned in that capacity. Lester visited Australia in May–June 1949 on a packed lecture tour. Although generally she was not talking specifically about Gandhi but rather on international peace and religion, Gandhi was often referenced in her talks. For example, in Hobart she pointed to the Mahatma as 'one whose power for peace came from allowing God to work through his body'.[10] She gave ninety addresses in the country during her two-month visit.[11]

Reginald Reynolds

Reginald Reynolds was a British pacifist, left-wing writer, teacher, salesperson, broadcaster, regular poet for the *New Statesman*, anti-colonial campaigner, critic of British imperialism in India, and partner in a socialist book centre who 'loved to sing, dance, drink rough cider, watch horror films, lay bricks, cleave wood and, in

---

[9] Gandhi to Muriel Lester, before 5 July 1931.
[10] 'Prominent British Social Worker in Hobart', *The Mercury* (Hobart), 2 June 1949, p. 7.
[11] Wallis, *Mother of World Peace*, p. 237.

fancy dress, to caper with a pantomime horse, and whose 'appeal was magnetic'.[12] He was also a collaborator with Gandhi and Horace Alexander. Reginald Reynolds was born in 1905 into a Quaker family. He studied at Woodbrooke College in Birmingham where he met fellow Quaker and friend of Gandhi, Alexander, who suggested that he visit Gandhi in India. The 24-year-old Reynolds arrived at the Sabarmati Ashram on 24 October 1929.

Having entrusted him with the delivery of his pre-Salt March ultimatum letter to the Viceroy, Gandhi explained that he was 'having it specially delivered by a young English friend who believes in the Indian cause and is a full believer in non-violence and whom Providence seems to have sent to me, as it were for the very purpose.'[13] Later, Gandhi added that 'I selected an English friend as my messenger, because I wanted to forge a further check upon myself against any intentional act that would hurt a single Englishman,'[14] and that by

> choosing Reginald Reynolds as my messenger, I sealed the bond between [the British] and me. For my enmity is not against them, it is against their rule. I seem to be born to be an instrument to compass the end of that rule. But if a hair of an English head was touched I should feel the same grief as I should over such a mishap to my brother.[15]

Reynolds has an interesting recollection of his role in a major event in Indian political history:

> Before I went, Gandhi insisted that I should read the letter carefully, as he did not wish me to associate myself with it unless

---

[12] Robert Huxter, *Reg and Ethel: Reginald Reynolds: His Life and Work and His Marriage to Ethel Mannin*, York: Sessions Book Trust, 1993, pp. 7–8.
[13] Gandhi to Lord Irwin, 2 March 1930.
[14] 'About that Letter', *Young India*, 6 March 1930.
[15] 'Speech at Broach', 26 March 1930, *Navajivan*, 30 March 1930.

Australia's Gandhi: The Public

> I was in complete agreement with its contents. My taking of this letter was, in fact, intended to be symbolic of the fact that this was not merely a struggle between the Indians and the British. By using an English courier instead of a postage stamp Bapu has deliberately dramatised this fact for all the world to know. But symbolism would have been false had I merely taken the letter without completely associating myself with what it contained.... I could easily have endorsed a document less generously worded.[16]

Due to ill health, he returned to England in the summer of 1930. Reynolds then served as the General Secretary of the No More War Movement between 1933 and 1937, married the leftist novelist Ethel Mannin in 1938, was a conscientious objector during World War II, working in a mobile hospital unit, and wrote tirelessly on the oppression of India, most notably in his book *The White Sahibs in India* (that contained a laudatory Foreword by Jawaharlal Nehru),[17] and was involved in several pro-Indian nationalist groups in England. Following Gandhi's assassination, in 1949 he returned to India as a delegate to the World Pacifist Conference and then travelled the world as Field Secretary to the British Friends Peace Committee.

In 1958, Reynolds visited Australia in that role as a guest of the Melbourne Monthly Meeting of the Society of Friends. Although he was in physically poor shape, he felt that he had to go to Australia because he was 'wanted there and ordinary working people had paid for his passage'. This meant that he travelled by the cheapest class, hoping to 'give those good people some change out of what they've put up for me.'[18]

---

[16] Reginald Reynolds, *To Live in Mankind: A Quest for Gandhi*, London: Andre Deutsch, 1951, pp. 51–52.
[17] Reginald Reynolds, *The White Sahibs in India*, London: Secker and Warburg, 1937.
[18] Quoted in Huxter, *Reg and Ethel*, p. 229.

Reynolds arrived by ship in Freemantle on 1 December. After starting his lecture tour, in a letter to Ethel, he noted that he had never been 'so lionised. I seem to have made a hit with almost every department of the University; and the University Extension Organiser, who arranged two lectures for me, has written to his colleagues in Melbourne and Sydney, urging them to use me to the full.'[19] He made a broadcast, examined the plight of Aborigines, and addressed the Perth Fabian Society. Following his stay in Perth, he boarded a train for Adelaide, where he was to stay until the eighteenth of the month. After that, he was scheduled to visit all Monthly Meetings and Canberra, and then stay in Melbourne for a public meeting on 4 January 1959.

His tour was scheduled to last until 24 February; however, on his way to the General Meeting of Australian Quakers in Melbourne, which was to be held at the start of January,[20] Reginald Reynolds died in Adelaide on 16 December 1958[21] of a cerebral haemorrhage. He was fifty-three years old. Even in death he struck a blow for the liberation of women. In a piece in the *Australian Women's Weekly*, headed 'His Wife has Full Say', published a month after his death but obviously written just before, the readership is informed that he 'gives his wife full say' in his affairs. 'AND he does what she says.' Further, they 'never travel together' as 'one has to be home to deal with the other's correspondence', and while he is away, 'my wife handles my business'.[22] One wonders what the readers made of such an equal relationship.

His obituary in the London Quaker journal, *The Friend*, described him as an eccentric, a visionary, and a prophet:

---

[19] Quoted in Huxter, *Reg and Ethel*, p. 230.
[20] 'Visit of Reginald Reynolds', *The Australian Friend*, 20 October 1958, p. 4.
[21] Most sources give this date; however, Huxter maintains that he collapsed the following day, was taken to hospital, felt better, and did not die until two days later. See Huxter, *Reg and Ethel*, p. 231.
[22] 'Worth Reporting: His Wife has Full Say', *The Australian Women's Weekly*, 14 January 1959, p. 45.

Australia's Gandhi: The Public

To him life was a continual plea for honesty, tolerance, racial equality, justice, truth and spiritual treatment for man. His protesting spirit and inquiring, amazingly versatile, mind took him at one moment to the American South into the heart of the Negro problem and the next moment to Japan to support a protest against hydrogen bombs; to India, Africa—and at last to Australasia, his physical resources spent to a degree not fully realised until now. He would have gone anywhere for the truth.[23]

Jayaprakash Narayan

By the time he came to Australia for the Gandhi Centenary Celebrations and to visit his friends the Scarfes, Jayaprakash Narayan had been a Marxist intellectual, a celebrated anti-British revolutionary, founding member of the Congress Socialist Party, and a prisoner. In 1954, he turned his back on party politics and devoted his life to Gandhian constructive work, joining Vinoba's Bhoodan land gift movement, and in essence became Gandhi's political heir and, with Vinoba, the leading figure in the Indian Gandhian establishment. Later, in 1974 he challenged the corrupt political rule of Prime Minister Indira Gandhi that led to her dictatorial 'Emergency', which saw him back in prison and, after elections which Mrs. Gandhi lost, the senior figure behind the short-lived Janata government of Morarji Desai. JP died in 1979.

During the ten days JP spent in Australia, from 16 September 1969, he gave several addresses. Although not a Member of Parliament, he was an extremely well-known and important Indian political figure. This meant that his formal itinerary kept him from small groups and meant he was more or less limited to attending receptions and larger functions in remembrance of Mahatma Gandhi, along with various organised tourist excursions. The Indian High Commissioner to Australia instigated the

---

[23] Ian A. Hyde, 'Man of Vision', *The Friend* 116 (52), 26 December 1958, p. 1664.

setting up of the Gandhi Centenary Celebrations Committee to 'stimulate a study of the life and worldwide influence of Mahatma Gandhi'. The Victorian Committee was comprised of important diplomats, academics, and leaders of aid organisations, as well as Wendy Scarfe. It was chaired by Dr Hari Sinha of the Australia–India Society. Besides the insisted upon stay with the Scarfes in Warrnambool, the programme for JP and his wife Prabhavati was in the hands of the Department of External Affairs and the Indian High Commissioner.[24]

After their country sojourn, the Narayans addressed, at the Melbourne Town Hall, high school students who were taking Asian Studies. This was followed by a lecture at La Trobe University on 'Gandhi and Modern India' on the 18th and a lecture at the University of Melbourne on 'Gandhi's Relevance to our Time' the following day. On the 20th, JP participated in a seminar at La Trobe University on 'Gandhi and the Politics of Nonviolence' with representatives of the Australia–India Society, the Institute for International Affairs, and Community Aid Abroad.[25] The Indian High Commissioner A. M. Thomas delivered the inaugural address. During that seminar, Professor Hugo Wolfsohn argued with JP about the efficacy of nonviolence.[26] For the university's programme to honour Gandhi, from 20 September there was a week-long Gandhi photograph exhibition. Between various lecturing engagements, the Narayans were taken to the Dandenong Ranges, and to the Healesville wildlife sanctuary.

From Melbourne they flew to Canberra, where JP gave a public lecture on 'Gandhi and Modern India' at the Australian National University on 22 September.[27] Later, in a national broadcast as

---

[24] See Allan and Wendy Scarfe, *Remembering Jayaprakash*, New Delhi: Siddharth, 1997, pp. 265–284.

[25] See 'Seminar on Gandhi', *La Trobe University Record Newsletter* 3 (5), 8 September 1969, pp. 6–7.

[26] Scarfe and Scarfe, *Remembering Jayaprakash*, p. 280.

[27] 'Riots Could be Prevented', *The Canberra Times*, 24 September 1969, p. 11.

the ABC's guest of honour, JP talked about regional security and the war in Vietnam, but also reminded his audience of the continuing relevance of Gandhi: 'Gandhi's message was universal and proclaimed the dignity and autonomy of the individual. By decrying narrow, selfish nationalism and preaching a world human community, Gandhi left behind him a heritage that transcended time and space.'[28] JP also spoke in Brisbane before flying home to India from Sydney.

Marjorie Sykes

As a tribute to Groom, the Donald Groom Peace Fellowship was set up by the Australian Yearly Meeting in 1974. The aim of the Fellowship, which was awarded until 2012, was to assist selected persons to research and undertake trainings in nonviolence, to help defray the travel costs of Friends in the Asia-Pacific region, and to assist with the publication of materials on nonviolence. The first Fellow was Marjorie Sykes who, during her 1974–1975 world tour, visited Southeast Asia and Australasia. From March 1975, she spent over seven weeks in Australia, giving talks in Sydney, Melbourne, Brisbane, Canberra, Adelaide, and Perth on religious and educational issues, the search for a just society, the connections between Quaker and Indian thought, simple living, the search for peace, and of course on Gandhi and his continuing relevance.[29]

Marjorie Sykes' Gandhian pedigree was impeccable. She was born to not overtly religious schoolteacher parents in May 1905 in Yorkshire. In 1923, she entered Newnham College at Cambridge University with a scholarship to study English. At the university, she mixed with Indian students and came to know something about Gandhi through them, and also started to seriously read the Bible

[28] '5 Nations "Need Link"', *The Canberra Times*, 6 October 1969, p. 3.
[29] Martha Dart, *Marjorie Sykes: Quaker Gandhian*, York: Sessions Book Trust, 1993, p. 117.

under the influence of some of her teachers. After graduating with honours in 1926, she spent another year earning her Cambridge Teacher's Diploma and then placed her name on a list for those interested in teaching in Africa as some of her student friends had done. No position was immediately available and she was advised to gain further experience at home first, so she took a junior teaching post on the outskirts of Liverpool. In May 1928, Sykes received an urgent request to go and teach at the Bentinck School for Girls, run by the London Missionary Society, in Madras. In October, the 23-year-old teacher set sail for India.

Early on in her teaching position, Sykes displeased her superiors by riding her bicycle around the streets, travelling on 'ordinary native buses', and starting to wear khadi, hand-spun, hand-woven, clothes.[30] She also became a vegetarian and inquired further about Gandhi.

Although Bentinck had been an ideal home for Sykes, by the mid-1930s she was beginning to have second thoughts about the entire educational system. She started to wonder whether 'she could not make a contribution as a teacher in a more independent and more fully Indian setting'.[31] Through friends she met Quakers, and soon felt that this was where she belonged. During a trip to England in 1936, she formally became a member of the Religious Society of Friends. Back in India, in August of 1937, she read a short article by Gandhi on his vision for the educational system that he wanted for Indian children.[32]

During the Christmas holidays of 1938, she went on a pilgrimage to visit Gandhi's school at Sevagram and then Shantiniketan, where Tagore invited her to join his staff. She became aware of the similarity in the educational ideals of the two institutions and of the

[30] Pat Barr, *The Dust in the Balance: British Women in India 1905–1945*, London: Hamish Hamilton, 1989, p. 131.
[31] Jehangir P. Patel and Marjorie Sykes, *Gandhi: His Gift of the Fight*, Rasulia: Friends Rural Centre, 1987, p. 47.
[32] See 'Criticism Answered', *Harijan*, 31 July 1937.

frequent exchange of personnel between them. She secured funds from the London Quakers and accepted Tagore's offer, arriving at Shantiniketan in early July 1939. Over the next few years, she taught there and at the Women's Christian College in Madras.

In 1945, she visited Gandhi to consult the files at Sevagram to assist her with a biography of her friend Charlie Andrews, which she was working on. Gandhi asked her to consider coming to the ashram to help with the basic education programme. She agreed to do so after the biography was finished. By that time, Gandhi was dead and India had achieved independence. Sykes was now forty-four years old. She decided to stay on in India as a citizen of the newly formed republic and joined Sevagram with the responsibility for training Gandhian teachers in 1949. She was based at Sevagram for the next ten years as the head of the Teacher Training Section.[33]

Sykes spent the rest of her life writing, travelling, and teaching, dividing her time between various Quaker centres in India and England. With advancing age, Marjorie Sykes settled into the Quaker retirement community 'Swarthmore' near London in 1991, where she died in August 1995 at the age of ninety.

Lanza del Vasto

Joseph Jean Lanza del Vasto was born to a French-speaking Sicilian noble family in 1901. He led a privileged early life, studying in Paris, Florence, and Pisa. He obtained a Ph.D. for a dissertation on the question of the Christian Trinity. However, academic life did not suit him and his scholarly reading led him to become a dedicated Catholic. He turned his back on high society and embraced voluntary poverty and the life of a vagabond. During his student days at Florence, he was given a copy of Romain Rolland's

---

[33] For Sykes' connections with Gandhi, see Weber, *Going Native*, pp. 121–126.

biography of Gandhi, which sparked a desire to learn from the Mahatma personally.

In 1936, he travelled to Asia. The trip is detailed in his classical work, *Return to the Source*.[34] There, he lyrically described being 'delivered' of his trousers, jacket, and shirt in Madurai. He donned a loincloth and 'stepped into the field of human relations unimpeded' as people for whom a foreigner was little more than easy prey, 'vanished into space', and he found himself invited into the confidences and homes of many Indians.[35]

In 1937, the writer, philosopher, musician, and devout Christian set out for Wardha 'to learn how to be a better Christian.'[36] He met Gandhi at Sevagram Ashram, where the Mahatma gave him the name Shantidas (servant of peace) and introduced him to nonviolence, convincing him that it was the central truth of Christianity. That encounter was to prove to be the turning point of his life. He stayed with Gandhi at Sevagram for three months, doing manual work and learning from his master. As an outgrowth of what he learned, he formulated his 'axioms of nonviolence', which held that

1. You do not have the right to return evil for evil.
2. The end does not justify the means.
3. Fear, constraint, and force will never establish justice.
4. It is not true that violence is justified in self-defence.
5. It is not true that murder is justified when the 'common good' demands it.
6. It is false that technology, economy, and politics are morally neutral.

---

[34] For his travels in India and meeting with Gandhi, see Lanza del Vasto, *Return to the Source*, London: Rider, 1971. For Gandhi's influence on him, see Thomas Weber, *Gandhi as Disciple and Mentor*, Cambridge: Cambridge University Press, 2004, pp. 173–180.

[35] Lanza del Vasto, *Return to the Source*, pp. 35–36.

[36] Lanza del Vasto, *Return to the Source*, p. 97.

7. It is completely false that the established order represents justice.[37]

In 1939, he returned to France and, following the War, set up a Christian/Gandhian rural, unmechanised community known as the 'Community of the Ark'.[38] The Community became a centre for nonviolent activism against the French use of torture during the Algerian war of independence, against the internment camps for Algerians living in France, for the recognition of the right to conscientious objection to military service, and against the French production of nuclear weapons.[39] He fasted for his causes, and became known as the person who 'keeps Gandhi alive in the West'.

During March and April of 1980, Shantidas toured Australia, speaking to various organisations and conducting nonviolence workshops for young activists. The imposing, charismatic patriarch, who looked as if he had just stepped out of a medieval monastery, had a powerful influence on those who attended those talks and workshops. He died in early January 1981, just a few months after his visit to Australia.

Sugata Dasgupta

As already noted, Sugata Dasgupta was a Gandhian social worker and academic who wrote on the themes of Gandhian economics, nonviolence, and social change. He worked at the University of Queensland in 1976–1979, where he influenced the course of Ralph Summy's and Anthony Kelly's academic work. Subsequently, Dasgupta came to Australia almost yearly on speaking tours. In late August 1984, he came for a three-week speaking commitment

---

[37] Lanza del Vasto, Joseph Jean, *Warriors of Peace: Writings on the Technique of Nonviolence*, New York: Knopf, 1974, pp. 53–57.
[38] See Mark Shepard, *The Community of the Ark*, Arcata, CA: Simple Productions, 1990.
[39] See, generally, Lanza del Vasto, *Warriors of Peace*.

that was to take in Brisbane, Canberra, Melbourne, Hobart, and Launceston. Following a five-day workshop on Gandhian thinking (Gandhian economics, Gandhian political action, Gandhian spirituality, and Gandhian community organisation) that he led in Brisbane, he travelled to Canberra. On 5 September, *The Canberra Times* announced that he would speak that night at 8 PM at the meeting of the Canberra Catholic Social Justice Group.[40] Three days later, the paper announced that he had died of a heart attack the following day.[41]

His life's work was summarised in his obituary in *Social Alternatives*:

> His life was dedicated to advancing Gandhi's concept of the 'constructive programme'. Like his mentor he aimed to *create* the nonviolent society—not just to *oppose* exploitation and repression with nonviolent methods. His positive approach invariably brought him around to the starting point of Western development theory which he saw as a fundamental cause of domestic and global violence. Maldevelopment led to peacelessness led to overt violence. The only way to arrest the vicious cycle was for the radical to intervene nonviolently at all levels of human endeavour: the intra-personal, the inter-personal, the societal, the environmental, and the international. He developed an analysis and programme that attempted to realize the now popular slogan 'To act locally and think globally'.[42]

The legacy of this thinking resided in courses taught by his friends and colleagues Ralph Summy and Anthony Kelly, in the activism of some of the students of those courses and others who heard him speak, and his association with the early theoretical

---

[40] 'Talk by Indian', *The Canberra Times*, 5 September 1984, p. 24.

[41] Bill Goodall, 'The Words of Men of Peace Deserve to Live on After Them', *The Canberra Times*, 8 September 1984, p. 2.

[42] 'Loss of a Friend and Dedicated Peace Worker', *Social Alternatives* 4 (3), 1985, p. 61.

development of Community Aid Abroad. As the obituary notes, 'his greatest legacy is the inspiration he instilled in those people fortunate to have heard him at first hand. He communicated his complex ideas with great clarity and simplicity.' And this is what he was doing in Canberra in September of 1984.

K. Arunachalam

Another Gandhian visitor was the venerable Indian Dr K. Arunachalam, who had recently retired after twelve years as chairperson of the Gandhi Smarak Nidhi (Gandhi National Memorial Trust) in India. The 80-year-old Tamil Gandhian constructive worker with an impressive white beard visited Australia in late 1990. He came to 'investigate the nature and extent of the Gandhian legacy and nonviolent struggle in this part of the world.'[43] He was originally invited to the country by Stephen Murphy of the Gandhian Movement of Australia and was later hosted by Robert Burrowes. In his two months in the country, he toured the main cities in Australia, speaking to activists, natural healers, university students, and members of the Indian community. In November in Melbourne, he participated with seventy others in a picket organised by the Melbourne Rainforest Action Group to 'Save the Rainforests' by blockading the timber ship, the *Alam Teladan*. His photograph as part of the picketing group at Victoria Dock appeared in *Nonviolence Today*.[44]

Burrowes summed up his visit thus:

> While in Australia and New Zealand, Arunachalam made a deep impression. People he met were touched by his integrity and humility. He was always willing to share his profound knowledge

[43] Robert J. Burrowes, 'Gandhian in Australia', *Nonviolence Today* 18, December/January 1990/1991, pp. 7–8.
[44] See Robert J. Burrowes, 'Rainforest Ship Blockaded and Picketed', *Nonviolence Today* 18, December/January 1990/1991, p. 11.

of Gandhian thought and nonviolent revolution in India. More personally, he was willing to share his stories of Gandhi (with whom he worked for twenty years) and about his own rich and meaningful life as a satyagrahi.[45]

Arunachalam was born in 1910 in the Madurai district of Tamilnadu in south India, into a large traditional family. He received an upper-class education at the well-respected English-language St. Xavier's College, Palayamkottai, graduating with a B.A. degree in 1931. Gradually he became interested in Gandhi's philosophy and constructive programme, assuming a life of voluntary poverty and simplicity. Although of a high caste himself, under the inspiration of Gandhi, he commenced working with 'Untouchables' in his local area. After falling in love with Manomani, a young Christian teacher and Gandhian activist, he married, but in the Gandhian way, took a vow of lifelong celibacy.

In 1933, Arunachalam spent a week at Vinoba's ashram and a week at Sabarmati Ashram. In 1940, he graduated from teachers' college with a degree in teaching, and in 1952 he obtained an M.A. degree in teacher education from the State University of Iowa in the United States. On his return to India, he trained and taught in various Gandhian institutions and then participated in Vinoba's Bhoodan movement. He established a department of Gandhian studies at Madurai Kamraj University (where he was still teaching postgraduate students at the time of his Australia trip), and then held high posts in various Gandhian organisations. He worked for prohibition, cow protection, khadi, basic education, and was briefly imprisoned during Mrs. Gandhi's 'Emergency'. During the 1980s, he was a member of the State Legislative Council of the Government of Tamilnadu. In 1985, the Gandhigram Rural University honoured him by conferring on him the degree of Doctor of Philosophy. Following the death of his wife in December

---

[45] Burrowes, 'Gandhian in Australia', p. 8.

1986, he grew the substantial white beard that distinguished him on his Australian tour. In late 1987 he made a return visit to America to lecture on Gandhian thought and in 1989 visited Canada and Brazil to attend seminars on spiritual and yogic matters, and later in the year to Denmark to study the educations system and folk high schools.[46]

Coming from the south of India, Maharishi Dr K. Arunachalam only managed to meet Gandhi in person once. However, he spent much of his life working with or overseeing major Gandhian organisations. Following a lengthy illness, he died on 8 August 1996 at the Gandhi Memorial Museum campus in Madurai, aged eighty-seven.

Rajmohan Gandhi

Rajmohan Gandhi and his siblings (Tara, born 1934; Ramchandra, 1937–2007; and Gopalkrishna, born 1945) came from the most illustrious of Indian families. Their father was Devadas, Mahatma Gandhi's fourth and youngest son. Their mother Lakshmi was the daughter of the leading south Indian nationalist (known as 'Gandhi's conscience keeper') and the first (and last) Governor-General of independent India, Chakravarti Rajagopalachari. Devadas spent most of his working life, from 1937 until his death in 1957, as the editor of the English-language nationalist paper, *Hindustan Times*. The children grew up in a flat on the top floor of the *Hindustan Times* building. Rajmohan later recalled that 'The smell of ink, the clack of Linotype, the roar of the presses, the traffic in and out of the family apartment during the ferment of pre-independence India, gave his childhood "a certain tempo".'[47] And

---

[46] See C. Periyathai, *Quest for Immortality: Biography of Maharishi Doctor K. Arunachalam*, Madurai: Tamilnadu Sarvodaya Mandal, 1994.

[47] Marie Arana-Ward, 'Rajmohan Gandhi', *The Washington Post*, 15 October 1995.

in the number of journalistic columns and books he has produced, the tempo has been maintained in Rajmohan's life.

Rajmohan was born in New Delhi in 1935 and received a B.A. and then an M.A. degree in economics in 1956 from St. Stephen's College. Following his graduation, he went to Edinburgh to work as a trainee reporter at *The Scotsman*. There he became associated with the Moral Re-Armament (now Initiatives for Change) movement, and toured the world spreading its message until he returned to India in 1964 and founded the journal *Himmat* ('Courage'). In 1981, he became editor of the Madras *Indian Express*. Between 1990 and 1992, he served in the upper house (the Rajya Sabha) of the Indian Parliament, and more recently he joined the Aam Aadmi Party where he unsuccessfully contested elections on an anti-NDA (National Democratic Alliance, the current government in power in India), anti-corruption platform. In his life, he has also been a biographer (writing about, among others, his grandfathers), a historian, a research scholar, an academic (including several years as a professor in the United States at the University of Illinois at Urbana-Champaign), and public speaker. He has received many Indian and international awards and has worked untiringly for India-Pakistan and Hindu-Muslim reconciliation.

He has also toured Australia several times on speaking tours as a Moral Re-Armament worker, for the first time at the World Conference of Moral Re-Armament in Canberra in January 1966, and again at a Moral Re-Armament conference in Melbourne in late December 1968 and early January 1969. He was in Australia in March 1997 to attend a communications conference in Sydney, and in 2000 to attend an environmental conference in Melbourne. While these visits were not strictly Gandhi-related, the Mahatma was the subject of interviews and press reports. In March of 2013, he was again in Australia as a guest of the ANU's Research School of Asia and the Pacific as a Distinguished Visitor. He lectured to students on the partition of the Punjab and a comparison between India's 1857 revolt against British domination and the American Civil War, and recorded videos and podcasts on the topics. On 18 March he presented a public lecture in Bendigo on the topic 'What would Gandhi do?'

Ela Gandhi

Mahatma Gandhi's second eldest son, Manilal, was born in India in 1892, not long after his father had returned to his homeland following his law studies in London. In 1893, Gandhi went to South Africa on a legal assignment that was to last a year. In the end, Gandhi spent most of the next twenty years there. In 1897, his family, including the 5-year-old Manilal, joined him in Durban. They moved to the Phoenix Settlement in 1904. As part of his father's civil disobedience campaign, Manilal was arrested for the first time in 1910. In 1914, the Gandhi family returned to India; however, in 1917, Gandhi sent Manilal back to South Africa to help with the publication of *Indian Opinion* and with the continuation of the political work he had started there. Manilal carried on as the editor of the paper for the next thirty-six years and actively participated in the defiance campaigns against apartheid laws, serving his last six-month imprisonment with hard labour in 1954. Manilal married Shushila Mashruwala in 1927, and they had three children: Sita, born in 1928, Arun in 1934, and Ela in 1940.[48]

Born in Durban, Ela Gandhi grew up on the Phoenix Settlement, Gandhi's first ashram. She had the opportunity to finally meet her grandfather on family trips to India in 1946 and 1947, when they stayed for some months at Sevagram Ashram. Following in the footsteps of her grandfather and father, after completing her university degree in social work, Ela became a social worker, political activist (which resulted in almost nine years of banning and five years under house arrest), and is the founder of the

---

[48] For the life of Manilal Gandhi, see Uma Dhupelia-Mesthrie, *Gandhi's Prisoner? The Life of Gandhi's Son Manilal*, Cape Town: Kwela, 2005.

Natal Organisation of Women. She was also a politician, serving as the African National Congress representative for the Phoenix area in the South African Parliament between 1994 and 2004. She is still promoting Mahatma Gandhi's ideals through the Gandhi Development Trust that she founded in 2002 and as the founder and vice-chairperson of the International Centre of Nonviolence, a Centre she had set up four years before at Durban University of Technology to promote nonviolence through education. She is the eldest member of the Gandhi family in South Africa.

In recent years, Ela Gandhi has visited Australia on several occasions. She came first in February 2013 to launch ICON Australia in Sydney.[49] During her six days in Melbourne and Sydney, she undertook many media interviews. On 26 February, she spoke at the University of Melbourne's Australia-India Institute on the theme of 'If Gandhi were Alive Today?', spoke on ABC radio's *Life Matters* programme with Natasha Mitchell, and under the auspices of ICON and Soka Gakkai International Australia at Sydney's Olympic Park, she spoke on 'Human Security and Sustainability'. She was also interviewed on DKTV (the leading Australian Indian television show, Desi Kangaroo TV). During the days she spent in Melbourne she visited a children's farm, a homeless shelter, the University of Melbourne's Early Learning Centre, and the Victorian Women's Domestic Crisis Service. In December, she was back in Australia as a guest speaker at the tenth anniversary celebration of Perth's Curtin University's Centre for Human Rights Education. She talked on human rights and the death of Nelson Mandela. She was interviewed on ABC Radio in Perth.

On 30 January 2015, Ela Gandhi was invited to deliver the annual University of New South Wales Gandhi Oration. On

---

[49] See her interview with SBS News, 'Gandhi: Education Key to Combating Violence', 3 September 2013. Available at https://www.sbs.com.au/news/article/gandhi-education-key-to-combating-violence/z7x0r5kmn (accessed December 2023).

the following day, she gave a public lecture on 'The Power of Nonviolence as a Means of Inspiring Change'. A few days after that she spoke at the Sydney Museum of Contemporary Art in conversation with the UNSW academic Laura Shepherd, and gave an interview to the youth-focussed digital publication, *The Point Magazine*.[50] On 1 May 2018, Ela Gandhi spoke before an audience of 300 people for the opening of the Melbourne Immigration Museum's interactive Gandhi exhibition. Her talk was broadcast live on the ABC on Jon Faine's Conversation Hour.

Ela Gandhi is an important figure in her own right, but the fact remains that she is the granddaughter of Mahatma Gandhi, and so her speeches often reference Gandhi and, in the case of interviews, interviewers cannot refrain from asking her about her iconic grandfather. In addition to relating stories of growing up in Phoenix Settlement and finally getting to meet Gandhi on visits to India when she was a 7-year-old child, the message from these speeches and interviews is about Gandhian values and how we can try to live up to them (summed up by the attributed to Gandhian aphorism to 'Be the Change you Wish to See in the World'), about truth, nonviolence, equality (and particularly gender equality), and living in harmony with nature. She states that her aim in life is to take Gandhi's message forward in the world, something she has been actively doing on her visits to Australia.

Others

Of course, there were also many others. Occasionally Indian academics came and gave Gandhi-related lectures, for example Dr Suman Khanna, Professor Uma Dhupelia-Mesthrie, and Professor Bindu Puri, or attended a Gandhi-themed conference (for

---

[50] See 'Gandhi Brings Non-Violence to Australia', *The Point Magazine*, February 2015. Available at http://thepointmagazine.com.au/post.php?s=2015-02-05-gandhi-brings-non-violence-to-australia (accessed December 2023).

example, those who participated in the 'Gandhi, Nonviolence and Modernity' conference held at the Australian National University in September 2004). Sometimes younger Gandhian activists, such as Swati Desai, came for nonviolence conferences or to meet fellow campaigners, and others, such as Shobhana Radhakrishna, came simply to extol the virtues of the Mahatma.

Dr Suman Khanna, a philosopher and peace researcher at the University of Delhi, who authored the book *Gandhi and the Good Life* and founded the Gandhian NGO Shanti Sahyog that works in Delhi's urban slums, was in Australia on a speaking tour in December of 1996. Professor Uma Dhupelia-Mesthrie, an academic historian at the University of the Western Cape in South Africa and Gandhi's great-granddaughter (who chronicled the life of her grandfather, Manilal Gandhi), gave public lectures on Gandhi in October 2019 in Sydney and Melbourne as a guest of the Australian Indian Overseas Congress.

Swati Desai, a trained physicist from a Gandhian activist family, with her husband Michael Mazgaonkar, also from a Gandhian activist family, has for the past thirty years been engaged in constructive work in the tribal area of rural Gujarat. They are part of the team that heads up the Gujarat Gandhian organisation, the Gujarat Sarvodaya Mandal. In the summer of 1992, as the Donald Groom Peace Fellow, Desai toured Australia and addressed over thirty social justice groups committed to nonviolence, sharing her experiences of Gandhian work in India.

Shobhana Radhakrishna, whose father, Radhakrishna, was a senior Gandhian and Secretary of the Gandhi Peace Foundation, spent part of her youth at Sevagram ashram and has since devoted her life to Gandhian causes. She is the founder and 'Chief Functionary' of the Indian government-sponsored Gandhian Forum for Ethical Corporate Governance. In this role, she works to (re)introduce Gandhian values to business leaders through lectures to large Indian corporations and to audiences around the world. As part of a lecture tour encompassing twenty-one countries, in the first two weeks of April 2019 she gave public lectures on 'Mahatma Gandhi's Leadership and its Relevance in the Contemporary World' and 'Leadership and Corporate Governance' at various Australian universities and Indian Consulates in Melbourne, Canberra, and Sydney.

In April 2023, as a visiting Gandhi scholar at the University of Melbourne's Australia India Institute, Jawaharlal Nehru University Professor Bindu Puri spoke on 'Gandhi: On the Good Human Life', 'Gandhi: Truth and Non-Violence', and 'Gandhi's Alternative Understanding of Justice'.

Gandhi in the Movies

Although it took many years full of setbacks to get the movie made,[51] when it finally hit the cinemas *Gandhi* was a phenomenal success around the world, making 'Gandhi' a household name. In his Australian National Press Club address a few days after its local premiere (three months after its international release in Delhi and London), director Richard Attenborough noted that the film not only drew big audiences in the American heartland, 'the bastion of insularity in which any film not about familiar subjects has to work hard to survive', but that it also recovered its costs almost completely in American screenings.[52] This success could partly be attributed to the fact that its release (in March 1983 in Australia) coincided with a very tense period of the Cold War, a time when nuclear Armageddon seemed to be a frightening possibility. As an Australian reviewer put it,

---

[51] For the making of the film, see Richard Attenborough, *In Search of Gandhi*, London: The Bodley Head, 1982.

[52] See Dougal MacDonald, 'Gandhi has Immense Impact', *The Canberra Times*, 19 March 1983, p. 14. The film went on to win eight Oscars, including Best Picture, Best Actor (Ben Kingsley), and Best Director (Richard Attenborough).

with the Cruise missiles intended for Europe at the end of the year and the Trident submarine already prowling the Pacific, a film which tells the west that non-violence was once a powerful mass movement is sorely needed. The millions joining the peace movements of Europe and America can do with some inspiration towards direct action. If it takes a tasteful, BBC2 Gone with the Monsoon to introduce Gandhi's activities to modern masses, so be it.[53]

The film was dubbed 'the movie that became a movement'. As one reviewer pointed out a year after the film's release, it had become one of the most widely seen films in history and formed part of a renaissance of interest in Gandhi.[54] While the film bordered on the hagiographical, paradoxically it also fostered something of a backlash among conservatives who feared that the sentiments promoted by the film could 'weaken the will of the free world' to fight a war if that was required, so a campaign of picking faults with the movie and 'ridiculing and belittling' Gandhi was commenced.[55] In other words, Gandhi has been attacked as both a lackey of the ruling class and as a sop to the left. A particularly virulent attack on the movie came from the film critic Richard Grenier, for the American magazine *Commentary*.[56] As Nanda pointed out, 'the very elements in the film that jar on historians and biographers [and there were several chronological inaccuracies, telescoping of events,

[53] Martha Ansara, 'Gandhi or Gone with the Monsoon', *Filmnews*, 1 March 1983, p. 15.
[54] See Mark Juergensmeyer, 'The Gandhi Revival—A Review Article', *Journal of Asian Studies* XLIII (2), 1984, p. 293.
[55] B. R. Nanda, *In Search of Gandhi: Essays and Reflections*, New Delhi: Oxford University Press, 2002, p. 9. See also Jason DeParle, 'Why Gandhi Drives Neoconservatives Crazy', *Washington Monthly* 19, September 1983, pp. 46–51.
[56] See Richard Grenier, 'The Gandhi Nobody Knows', *Commentary*, March 1983, pp. 59–72. See Nanda's response in B. R. Nanda, *Gandhi and his Critics*, Delhi: Oxford University Press, 1984, pp. 1–3.

oversimplifications, and fictionalised events] have contributed to its popularity.'[57]

Australia again seemed to be somewhat isolated from the politics of Gandhi. The country's major film journal presented a lengthy and very sympathetic account of Gandhi's life and philosophy, rather than a review of the film itself or any disparagement of the Mahatma.[58] Nevertheless, there were some quibbles in the Australian press. Professor of History at South Australia's Flinders University, R. J. Moore, noted that the film 'warps history to ... achieve the support of the present Congress Government of India ... and for commercial gain.' Not only was the space given to American reporters disproportionate, but the film was wrong in making it out that Gandhi's mass movements freed India from British rule, when in reality it was a 'welcome escape from empire by a war-weary Britain.'[59]

Of course, Attenborough's classic has not been the only Gandhi-related movie screened in Australia. Indian films, including those featuring the Mahatma, are screened at various festivals and are often available for purchase at Indian grocery stores. The most prominent of these have been Rajkumar Hirani's hilariously over-the-top Gandhi-channelling romantic comedy *Lage Raho Munna Bhai* and Feroz Abbas Khan's thoughtful biopic *Gandhi My Father* (which was the opening film for the Fifth Australian Indian Film Festival held in Sydney in October 2007). And documentaries about Gandhi, or about Indians living in the West returning to India on Gandhi quests (for example, Mishal Husain in the BBC production *Gandhi: The Life and Legacy of India's 'Father of a Nation'*), are periodically screened on Australian television.

---

[57] Nanda, *In Search of Gandhi*, p. 244.
[58] See Arnold Zable's review 'Gandhi' in *Cinema Papers* 43, May/June 1983, pp. 159–161.
[59] R. J. Moore, 'Gandhi Criticised', *The Canberra Times*, 17 June 1983, p. 10.

Gandhi's Australia/Australia's Gandhi

Gandhi Statues and Exhibitions

In Federal Parliament in November 1954, with India's High Commissioner General K. M. Cariappa present in the diplomatic box, Labor politician Anthony Luchetti asked the following question of Prime Minister Robert Menzies:

> With the direct object of maintaining and developing friendly relations with our Asian neighbour, India, which is a member of the British Commonwealth of Nations, will the right honourable gentleman give favourable consideration to the erection of a suitable monument or edifice to honour the work of the late Mahatma Gandhi in the fields of peace and British Commonwealth unity?[60]

Menzies promised to give the matter 'some thought'.[61] One paper quite perceptively reported that what Menzies had said meant that the suggestion would be considered 'in that perfunctory manner which means consideration but no action'. The story, by the Adelaide *News*' 'staff man in Canberra', added that the suggestion obviously 'deserved better treatment', and that

> Such a tribute from a white nation to an Indian leader would have a tremendous impact in Asia. In terms of ultimate security and goodwill, it might even be a better investment than the £100,000 spent on the American War Memorial which now dominates Canberra's northern skyline.[62]

---

[60] Commonwealth, Parliamentary Debates, House of Representatives, 11 November 1954, Question, Mahatma Gandhi, Anthony Luchetti. See also 'Monument for Gandhi Suggested', *The Advertiser* (Adelaide), 12 November 1954, p. 5.

[61] Commonwealth, Parliamentary Debates, House of Representatives, 11 November 1954, Question, Mahatma Gandhi, Robert Menzies.

[62] 'They'll Hush Up the Budget Next', *News* (Adelaide), 16 November 1954, p. 2.

Australia's Gandhi: The Public

In fact, Australia did not officially get its first Gandhi statue until 2002 when the then Governor-General, Peter Hollingworth, unveiled the bronze effigy of the often depicted striding Mahatma with stick in hand. The statue is in Glebe Park in Civic, the centre of Canberra. It was created by the Indian sculptor Ram V. Sutar (who since has had several of his Gandhi statues erected in different parts of the world) and funded by members of the local Indian community. The statue is atop a large plinth which carries the text of what has become known as Gandhi's seven social sins: Politics without principles; wealth without work; pleasure without conscience; knowledge without character; commerce without morality; science without humanity; and worship without sacrifice; as well as Albert Einstein's assessment of Gandhi: 'Generations to come, it may well be, will scarce believe that such a one as this ever in flesh and blood walked upon this earth.'

The Indian High Commissioner to Australia, Gopalaswami Parathasarathy (1995–1999), had tried to find a suitable position for a Gandhi statue in an Australian city, but was not met by any favourable response. Eventually, the moving force behind this project was the Canberra businessman, marriage celebrant, and Hindu temple trustee Niranjan Aggarwal. From 1996, he had been agitating to have a Gandhi statue erected in Canberra. He travelled to India to find an appropriate sculptor to create the statue and conducted lengthy discussions with ACT and Commonwealth bureaucrats as to its placement. Canberra's main thoroughfare, Northbourne Avenue, was considered, but it was realised that people would merely drive past, and negotiations concerning the Peace Park behind the National Library eventually came to naught. Glebe Park, with its many lunch-time civil servant visitors, was settled on. The statue was installed in 2000 and it was hoped that the Indian Prime Minister Atal Bihari Vajpayee would officially perform the unveiling during his visit to Australia to attend the scheduled Brisbane Commonwealth Heads of Government Meeting in 2001. Following the 11 September terrorist attacks in

New York and Washington, the meeting was cancelled. The task was undertaken by Hollingworth the following year.

Following Canberra's example, recently several Australian cities have been graced with statues of the Mahatma. The next was Sydney, where at the University of New South Wales a bust of Gandhi was unveiled on the Library Lawn by the Sydney Consul-General of India Amit Dasgupta, the NSW Treasurer Eric Roozendaal, and the university's Vice-Chancellor Professor Fred Hilmer on 1 September 2010. The bust carries the (mistakenly attributed to Gandhi) quote, 'An eye for an eye only makes the whole world blind.' The idea for a Gandhi monument came from Dasgupta following the attacks on Indian students in Melbourne and Sydney the year before.[63] The Vice-Chancellor agreed and the Indian government presented the bust to the people of NSW and the university. For the university, which has a large Indian student population, the bust became a rallying point for tolerance and understanding. Following the inauguration of the memorial, annual ceremonies on 30 January and 2 October have been conducted beside the bust. Dasgupta went on to suggest an oration in the name of Gandhi. Hilmer thought that it could be an annual event.[64] The UNSW now has the most prominent focus on Gandhi of any Australian tertiary institution[65]—and this cannot be detrimental in attracting fee-paying Indian students to the campus.

[63] For the political repercussions of the attacks, see Meg Gurry, *Australia and India: Mapping the Journey 1944–2014*, Melbourne: Melbourne University Press, 2015, pp. 198–201. The Indian Gandhi-promoting business personality Gambhir Watts notes that he was working to get a Gandhi statue installed in Sydney for four years before the project was taken over by Dasgupta. See Gambhir Watts, *The White Queen*, n.p.: the author, 2019, pp. 250–251.

[64] This information comes from various social media reports and personal communication from Amit Dasgupta, 13 February 2019.

[65] The UNSW can boast of another Gandhi connection: On a trip to India to attend an Australia-India Skills Conference in Delhi in April 2017, Australian Prime Minister Malcolm Turnbull presented the Indian Prime Minister Narendra Modi with a replica pair of Gandhi spectacles made from

Australia's Gandhi: The Public

On 19 January 2012, the South Australian Premier, Jay Weatherill, unveiled a bust of Gandhi, created by the famous Indian sculptor Gautam Pal, at the University of Adelaide. The sculpture was a gift to the university from the Government of India, represented by Amit Dasgupta. The 2-metre tall sculpture is in the hidden away garden, known then as the Garden of Serenity and henceforth as the Garden of Contemplation, outside the library. The plinth is inscribed with the attributed to Gandhi quote: 'Be the Change You Wish to See'. The university's Vice-Chancellor, Professor James McWha, remarked that a constant reminder of Gandhi and his life on campus was in keeping with the university's mission and values.[66]

Two years later, it was Brisbane's turn. Just six months after his election as India's Prime Minister, Narendra Modi was in Brisbane for the G20 (the 'Group of Twenty' forum for world leaders and bankers to promote international financial stability) summit. On 16 November he unveiled a statue of Gandhi, again created by Delhi sculptor Ram Sutar, in the scenic Roma Street Parklands in central Brisbane. At this stage Modi had rock star status and it was reported that the event 'was something like Beatlemania', with a throng of Indian supporters from among the city's 80,000 Indian community present. In attendance at the unveiling were the Brisbane Lord Mayor Graham Quirk and the Governor of Queensland, Paul de Jersey. In his speech, Modi talked about Gandhi and global warming.[67]

---

recycled materials in a process pioneered by researchers at the UNSW. Gandhi's spectacles were the symbol of Modi's Swachh Bharat ('Clean Up India') campaign.

[66] See 'Premier Unveils Sculpture of Mahatma Gandhi', University of Adelaide, News & Events, 19 January 2012. Available at https://www.adelaide.edu.au/news/news50561.html (accessed December 2023).

[67] Tony Moore, 'Indian PM Narendra Modi unveils Gandhi statue', *Brisbane Times*, 16 November 2014. Available at www.brisbanetimes.com.au/national/queensland/indian-pm-narendra-modi-unveils-gandhi-statue-20141116-11nwf9.html (accessed December 2023).

Gandhi's Australia/Australia's Gandhi

In 2016, there was the making of a potential international incident when students and staff at the University of Ghana in Accra insisted that a statue of Mahatma Gandhi, a gift of the Indian government, be removed. The reason was that Gandhi had been declared a racist, who had denigrated blacks as being inferior to his Indian co-nationalists while he was fighting for Indian rights in racist South Africa.[68] This accusation presumably came as something of a shock to the many who saw the Mahatma as the epitome of fairness and inclusiveness. While nothing quite like this has occurred in Australia, in mid-2018 a statue-related controversy occurred in Melbourne's Dandenong, home to a large South Asian and particularly Indian population. The Federation of Indian Associations of Victoria proposed the setting up of a life-size bronze statue of Gandhi opposite the Dandenong railway station in the Indian Cultural Precinct. The Greater Dandenong City Council conducted a survey of the local community to gauge its response to the proposal and of the 963 responses (of which 87 per cent came from those with an Indian background), unexpectedly, and to the great disappointment of the FIAV, 65 per cent said no to the erecting of the statue. No reasons for the survey answers were recorded; however, possible political disagreements within the community may have been the cause. A temporary mural was painted on a wall instead.[69] Three years later, the Australian Indian Community Charitable Trust in Rowville,

---

[68] The statue was finally removed in 2018. See the Australian editions of *The Guardian* of 23 September 2016 ('Petition calls for Gandhi statue to be removed from Ghana University'); 7 October 2016 ('"Racist" Gandhi statue banished from Ghana university campus'); and 14 December 2018 ('Statue of "racist" Gandhi removed from University of Ghana'). Protests over the appropriateness of Gandhi statues have also occurred in Ottawa, Canada, and in several Californian cities.

[69] See Avneet Arora, 'Community says "No" to Gandhi's Statue in Melbourne's Dandenong', SBS Punjabi, 31 July 2018. Available at www.sbs.com.au/yourlanguage/punjabi/en/article/2018/07/31/community-says-no-gandhis-statue-melbournes-dandenong (accessed December 2023).

Australia's Gandhi: The Public

Melbourne, was still working to install a life-size bronze Gandhi statue in their recently acquired Community Centre building. On Friday, 12 November 2021, Prime Minister Morrison finally unveiled the statue, a gift of the Indian government. It was vandalised the following night. No suspect has ever been identified.

Yet another iteration of the familiar Ram Sutar statue of the purposefully striding Gandhi, clad in a short dhoti, with a shawl around his shoulders and staff in hand, was unveiled in Sydney in 2018. During a three-day State visit, India's President Ram Nath Kovind, the first Indian Head of State to visit the country, unveiled a Gandhi statue in Jubilee Park in Parramatta, the heart of Sydney's Indian community. On 23 November, as part of the upcoming 150-year anniversary of Gandhi's birth, an audience of 500, mostly Indians, watched and listened to speeches by Kovind, who said that Gandhi treasured many values that Australians hold dear, including multiculturalism (which certainly was not evident in Gandhi's time), and by Prime Minister Scott Morrison who also lauded the country's multiculturalism, likening it to a 'good garam masala'. Following the unveiling, Kovind presented Morrison with a copy of Gandhi's *Hind Swaraj*.[70]

It is doubtful if the proliferation of Gandhi statues, gifted to the country by the Indian government, will do anything towards orienting the public to seek a greater understanding of the Mahatma and what he stood for. However, the statue inaugurations make for wonderful photo opportunities for dignitaries and seem to be a source of pride for the local Hindu Indian diaspora.

Besides the bronzed permanence of the various Australian Gandhi statues, there have also been several more ephemeral representations of the Mahatma over the years. During the Gandhi

---

[70] See '"Like a Good Garam Masala": PM Hails Multiculturalism at Gandhi Statue Unveiling', SBS News, 23 November 2018. Available at https://www.sbs.com.au/news/article/like-a-good-garam-masala-pm-hails-multiculturalism-at-gandhi-statue-unveiling/1jk9kabp5 (accessed December 2023).

birth centenary year of 1969, the High Commissioner for India, A. M. Thomas, came to Melbourne on 19 October to attend the opening by Lord Casey on the following day of a Gandhi exhibition at the State Savings Bank of Victoria.[71]

More formal exhibitions have also been organised. For example, Museums Victoria hosted an exhibition of Gandhi's South Africa days and how his experiences there transformed him, at the Immigration Museum in Melbourne from mid-April to mid-July 2018. The exhibition, titled 'Mahatma Gandhi: An Immigrant', contained artefacts, photographs, archival film footage, voice recordings, and interactive digital technology which allowed museum visitors to navigate their way through the immense amount of material—and a booth where they could take selfies with Gandhi! The exhibition, which was on loan from the Mahatma Gandhi Digital Museum in Hyderabad, India, was visited by Gandhi's South African granddaughter Ela.

Not long after the Melbourne Gandhi exhibition, another was opened in Perth. Peter Rühe, a collector of Gandhi memorabilia, restorer and distributor of Gandhi photographs, and head of the German GandhiServe Foundation, commissioned the colouring of hundreds of black-and-white photos of Gandhi and, through the Indian arm of GandhiServe, published them in book form. The book, over 7 kilograms in weight and almost 700 pages in length, contained over 1,280 photographs[72] and became the source for the latest 'Borderless Gandhi' exhibition.

Perth resident Gandhi enthusiasts Nilesh Makwana (from a Mumbai-based Gujarati family who was educated in London) and his Norwegian wife Lene discovered their passion for community projects and Gandhi's teaching and founded 'Borderless Gandhi' in 2014 to promote Gandhi's 'ideology of peace, equality and

---

[71] 'Diplomatic Diary', *The Canberra Times*, 15 October 1969, p. 16.
[72] GandhiServe India, *Mahatma Gandhi's Life in Colour*, Mumbai: GandhiServe India, 2016.

nonviolence' through the 'means of art and social media'.[73] The organisation was publicly launched on 2 October 2015 with the screening of Attenborough's movie, *Gandhi*. In the years since, they have arranged a Gandhi-centred social media experience and an exhibition of stainless steel sculptures by the Delhi artist Vibhor Sogani, originally commissioned by the Indian government to commemorate the 100th anniversary of Gandhi's return to India from South Africa. On Gandhi Jayanti in 2018, they curated 'Borderless Gandhi Presents Mahatma Gandhi in Colour', consisting of thirty photographs from the GandhiServe archive. The exhibition was held at three locations: the Parliament of Western Australia, Perth airport's International Terminal 1, and at the Pan Pacific Hotel in Perth. A special feature of the exhibition was the competition offering prizes, donated by the organisation's sponsors, for submitted selfies with a photo from the exhibition or with a written quotation from Gandhi. The prizes included two tickets to fly from Perth to India, two nights stay at the hotel hosting the exhibition, and tickets to the Australia–India test cricket match.

The year 1969, the 100th anniversary of Gandhi's birth, was celebrated 'on an international scale' with 'pious eulogies which go with the celebrations'.[74] In Australia, it seems that the Victorian Centenary Committee did the most to rekindle interest in the Mahatma. It commissioned Newman Rosenthal's Gandhi biography, brought Jayaprakash Narayan to Australia, and organised exhibitions, talks, an essay competition, and a film. Where the COVID-19 pandemic restrictions allowed, the 150-year Gandhi birth celebrations in 2019–2020 were the reason for further exhibitions, public lectures, festivals, and articles featuring

[73] See https://www.facebook.com/borderlessgandhi/ (accessed December 2023).

[74] Sibnarayan Ray, 'Introduction', in Sibnarayan Ray (ed.), *Gandhi, India and the World: An International Symposium*, Melbourne: The Hawthorn Press, 1970, pp. 17–18.

Gandhi. Where it did not, lectures and discussions were conducted digitally via Zoom.

When the US President, Donald Trump, visited the Sabarmati Ashram in February 2020, he looked positively uncomfortable and wrote in the visitors' book: 'To my great friend Prime Minister Modi. Thank you for this wonderful visit.' Nothing about inspiration, peace, or Gandhi here. Three years later, in March 2023, it was the turn of the new Australian Prime Minister, Anthony Albanese, who was in Ahmedabad as part of a trade mission to India, to pay his respect to the host country's Father of the Nation. Albanese looked relaxed, even happy, as he toured the grounds and, far more appropriately, wrote in the visitors' book: 'It is a great honour to visit to pay homage to Mahatma Ghandi [sic] whose philosophy and life values continue to inspire the world today. We have a lot to learn from his example.'[75]

Gandhi and the Australian Indian Community

There are Indian organisations in all of Australia's states and most contain umbrella federations of Indian associations. They organise festivals (for example, the Indian Association of South Australia conducts annual Gandhi Jayanti events at the site of the Gandhi bust at the University of Adelaide), edit Indian-language publications, run several Indian-language programmes on radio, and provide opportunities for those wanting to study Indian languages or Indian dance. Many of them work hard to ensure that the younger generation knows something about the Mahatma, and some of them, such as Brisbane's Gandhi Salt March Limited, have an explicitly

---

[75] There is a tendency among Australians who are not from an Indian background, and have little to do with things Indian, to misspell 'Gandhi' as 'Ghandi'.

Gandhian agenda of promoting the teachings of Gandhi and raising awareness of those teachings.

The website of the High Commission of India in Canberra lists Indian associations in Australia. While it is not clear how often the site is updated, in April 2019 the list detailed a surprisingly large number of them: a total of 251 are mentioned, with thirty-two in the ACT, seventy-four in New South Wales, forty-six in Victoria, thirty-one in Queensland, forty-eight in Western Australia, nine in South Australia, one in Tasmania, and ten in the Northern Territory. But, given the diversity of India and the large Indian population (now numbering almost half-a-million overseas-born Indian residents and 619,000 with Indian ancestry) in the country, perhaps it is not that surprising. The list specified organisations representing different language groups (for example, Tamils, Bengalis, Malayalis, and Gujaratis) and geographical regions of India, religious groups, sports and occupational associations, those with an interest in welfare or representing senior citizens, those concerned with the arts or education, and those that group Indian residents from certain areas of the local cities in which they live.

Several of these organisations still regularly hold celebratory functions on significant Indian independence or Gandhi-related dates. If they are held indoors, these generally involve speeches, often by a guest academic or community leader, and catered meals. They are also occasionally accompanied by exhibitions of Gandhi memorabilia (or at least photographs thereof) and framed or projected inspirational quotations attributed to the Mahatma. The outdoor functions are often conducted by one of the country's Gandhi statues. While Indian community leaders are invited to attend university Gandhi-related functions, such as those at the University of New South Wales, the general Indian population tends not to be present in anything but relatively small numbers. Conversely, large numbers of the local Indian population attend the unveiling of Gandhi statues, particularly when an important Indian official performs the celebratory task, and they appear in significant numbers at Gandhi-related functions organised by the consulates or the local Federation of Indian Associations, functions that relatively few non-Indians attend. In other words, the public does attend Gandhi-related functions; it's just that different sections of the public come to different events when they are not together listening to a public talk by a prominent visiting Indian Gandhi spokesperson.

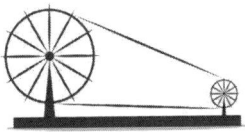

Conclusion

So, what can we make of all this? Are there threads and insights here that make the foregoing more than just a catalogue of every mention of Gandhi by an Australian, however slight or tangential? Was it worthwhile producing this seeming catalogue? Has Gandhi had any meaningful influence in this country?

The obvious places to look for Gandhi's influence in Australia have been in the peace movement, in sympathetic religious denominations, and in social justice and environmental campaigns, as well as in celebrations organised by the Indian community. His impact on local politics and public consciousness can perhaps best be seen in journals that cover such issues, in the discussion his tactics and techniques generated, in government endorsements through the erection of monuments, and to the degree that he made it onto school and university reading lists and courses. Publications about Gandhi, as well as exhibitions and orations featuring him or given in his name are also indications of his influence, as are individuals who professed to be Gandhians or who worked in Gandhian settings.

Although non-Australian books on Gandhi had been published before Holmes' speech and before Rolland's book, these had no discernible impact in Australia. And even Gandhi's own *Autobiography* appears to have had little impact here (unlike in the United States, it was never serialised in the Australian press). Gandhi first seems to have come to the attention of Australians through newspaper reports of the Non-Cooperation movement that he led. Following this, the world saw a spate of publications about Gandhi and some, like Mayo's *Mother India*, were extensively reviewed, but no major Australian publications about the Mahatma appeared in the country until decades later. Given the number of leading American and British personalities who had deep relationships with Gandhi and wrote significant works about him, it is somewhat surprising that in the nineteen hard copy volumes of the *Australian Dictionary of Biography*, covering the lives of 12,500 important representative persons of Australian history, there is only one entry with more than trivial mention of the Mahatma—that of A. B. Piddington.

While it has been demonstrated in the examples given above that there certainly was an Australia/Gandhi connection, it has also been demonstrated that, although our countries are similar, the connection was nowhere near as significant or substantial as the ones in Britain and America. Ramachandra Guha, in the most recent and close to definitive biography of Gandhi, notes that

> British politicians and statesmen wrote of him, and he had an extraordinary impact on ordinary British people too. Gandhi never visited the United States, yet his ideas and movements were discussed in American newspapers, magazines, books and radio shows. They even made their way into popular advertisements.[1]

A race horse aside, such popularisation was not the case in Australia.

Of course, Australia was not Britain, the centre of an empire of which Gandhi was an implacable enemy. Nor was it America with a seemingly insatiable curiosity focussed on the Mahatma. A fair assumption would be that it came somewhere between the two, meaning that coverage in Australia would be significantly less than in either Britain or America. This has proven to be the case, but

[1] Ramachandra, Guha, *Gandhi: The Years that Changed the World 1914–1948*, New Delhi: Penguin, 2018, p. xiv.

Conclusion

the coverage is relatively so small that it begs the question of why this is so. It seems that Australia was never quite certain whether to condemn the traitorous Gandhi or to laud the saintly Mahatma, or whether to simply ignore him. One obvious reason that may go at least part way to explaining this seeming anomaly is simply that the population of Australia was so small compared with that of Britain or America that coverage of Gandhi that matched theirs could not be expected.

While some of us can probably remember the substitution of a laptop for the spinning wheel for different thinking Apple computer users, and while others have attempted to cash in on Gandhi for commercial purposes (to sell furniture, beer, pens, cigarettes, curries, and Visa cards),[2] interestingly (and thankfully in this case), Australia again seems to lag behind the rest of the chiefly English-speaking, or especially the American, world in regard to its interest in the Mahatma. This is further reflected in works such as Cousins' *Profiles of Gandhi*, a collection of American reminiscences of the Mahatma[3] (there being no Australian equivalent), and other books of tributes to Gandhi published in his lifetime, such as Joseph John's compilation, *Gandhi as Others See Him*,[4] and most importantly S. Radhakrishnan's *Mahatma Gandhi*,[5] which, while featuring a diverse range of writers from around the world, contain nothing by an Australian. Gandhi never visited Australia; then again, as already noted, he did not visit the United States either. Population size is surely a major factor, but there are probably other reasons also.

---

[2] See Thomas Weber, '101 Uses for a Dead Mahatma: The Co-option of Gandhi for Non-Gandhian Causes', *Gandhi Marg* 37 (2), 2015, pp. 387–392.

[3] Norman Cousins (ed.), *Profiles of Gandhi: America Remembers a World Leader*, Delhi: Indian Book Company, 1970.

[4] Joseph John (comp.), *Gandhi as Others See Him: A Collection of Articles, Opinions, Speeches, Sermons etc.*, Colombo: Bastion, 1933.

[5] S. Radhadrishnan (ed.), *Mahatma Gandhi: Essays and Reflections on his Life and Work*, Bombay: Jaico, 1956.

Gandhi's Australia/Australia's Gandhi

Australia did not have any well-known Gandhi backer, and only a few internationally known reporters or authors interviewed Gandhi and wrote articles and books reporting on the experience. Australia's knowledge of the Mahatma came mostly from news sources, and those often reflected British interpretations of Gandhi's campaigns. Interestingly, those Australians who did visit Gandhi in India were often surprised by what they found, calling him 'outstanding', 'charming', 'intelligent', 'clean', 'honest', someone with 'tremendous dignity' and 'mental energy', a 'great man' surrounded by an 'aura of peace'. The fact that they were so impressed by him seemed to come as something of a revelation to them, one even commenting that the wrong impression of Gandhi was given by the press in Australia. Why might this have been the case?

By way of explanation, can there be more than a reliance on British sources, a general lack of interest in the politics of a larger world, and disinterest in celebrity and commercialisation? Perhaps the answer is tied up in the question of why it is that some forms of knowing do not come into being in some places when they have done so in others.[6] Were Australians simply more ignorant of Gandhi than their British and American counterparts, or were they deliberately and actively ignoring him more than those others were? Ignorance, after all, is a good way of reinforcing traditional values and maintaining stereotypes. In other words, it may be a valuable, even if unconscious, defence mechanism. The history of Britain and America, being very different from that of Australia, may provide at least a partial explanation. Australia was not a great imperial power under threat and did not have a history that included a war against the British for independence. In short, Australia had less interest in, and coverage of, Gandhi, and what

---

[6] For this issue, see Matthias Gross and Linsey McGoey (eds), *Routledge International Handbook of Ignorance Studies*, London and New York: Routledge, 2015; and Robert N. Proctor and Londa Schiebinger, *Agnotology: The Making and Unmaking of Ignorance*, Stanford, California: Stanford University Press, 2008.

Conclusion

there was tended to reflect the views of the 'Mother Country'. Although there was the occasional voice in the Australian press that praised Gandhi and put forward the case for some measure of autonomy for the Indian colony, generally the press, and presumably therefore the population, where it did show some interest, seems to have privileged the British point of view over the American, and ignorance of possible alternative narratives of the Gandhi story helped to maintain entrenched hierarchies. Chatfield noted that in America, Gandhi was not merely a lens through which India could be viewed, but that Gandhi's image 'was sometimes an instrument of self-examination'.[7] This did not seem to happen in Australia. Possibly this had something to do with the White Australia policy—if Australia had taken Gandhi more seriously, it would have meant an uncomfortable facing up to the issue of institutionalised racism. Was this reflected in the experience of the Scarfes at the ABC?

Since Gandhi's time, Australia has become a far more tolerant and multicultural society. The White Australia policy is now half-a-century in the past and thankfully the racist country he bitterly complained about no longer exists.[8] Of course, this change to Gandhi's Australia had little to do with the Mahatma, but the result is far more in keeping with his view of the tolerant and welcoming society that this country could be. Australia's Gandhi is another story.

Regardless of seemingly little obvious public interest in the Mahatma, in 1969 the Gandhi Birth Centenary was celebrated in

---

[7] Charles Chatfield, 'Introduction', in Charles Chatfield (ed.), *The Americanization of Gandhi: Images of the Mahatma*, New York: Garland, 1976, p. 26.

[8] However, in India it is still well-remembered and possibly colours the Indian views of Australia and contributed to the intensity of India's response to the attacks on Indian students in 2009. See Meg Gurry, *Australia and India: Mapping the Journey 1944–2014*, Melbourne: Melbourne University Press, 2015, pp. 203–204.

Australia, as it was in many places in the rest of the world. This resulted in Ray's and Rosenthal's books about Gandhi, Jayaprakash Narayan's visit to the country, and various exhibitions, talks, and articles in the leading papers. This legacy is now carried on by the Indian community, which celebrates Gandhi's birthday with speeches and communal meals.

A decade ago, John Synott noted that Gandhi was starting to be ignored in Australian universities. As several Gandhi-related courses disappeared or were offered in reduced form, a system of diminishing returns developed. One cannot help noticing the number of personal connections between those with Gandhian interests, which linked academics with their students who become academics in turn, or between academics and activists or Gandhi promoters. With the diminution of courses featuring Gandhi, these connections are also lessened with time. However, more recently there has been something of a revival of university links with Gandhi by way of statues, orations, and public peace celebrations, if not through courses that fostered those connections. It is not so much that the pendulum has swung back to make Gandhi academically 'current' and 'scientific' again; it has probably more to do with the influence of Australia's ever growing Indian population and a desire for more international students.

India and Australia share many links. They were both significant members of the British Empire and both are passionate about cricket (or obsessed, in the case of India). Australia has a large Indian expatriate population of close to half-a-million and, before the advent of the COVID-19 pandemic, hosted many tens of thousands of Indian students every year. Thousands of young Australians visited the subcontinent annually and Indian-inspired yoga and meditation classes abound in Australia. It is therefore somewhat surprising that India does not feature more prominently in dedicated academic History or Politics courses, and that so few students are studying Hindi as a language at the tertiary level. However, given the experience of Britain and the

Conclusion

United States, not merely in terms of curiosity about Gandhi but in terms of social justice rhetoric and the use of his methods in various nonviolence movements, it is perhaps surprising how little he appears to have featured in the Australian psyche or even in local peace and environmental campaigns. But perhaps no story itself is a story. And perhaps, as suggested above, this no story carries deeper resonances than the ones that have seemed most likely to me. Possibly where there is a story, the place to look is not in a desired normative approach to a fairer world, but in the realm of economics and local politics.

It was not just peace campaigns and movements (other than some conscientious objector campaigns) that disregarded a possible boost by employing the name of Gandhi. The literature on Australian environmental movements seems to have fared similarly. While he featured regularly in newspaper reports, the foremost books that chronicle the history of such movements do not mention Gandhi. In other words, Gandhi seemed to be 'more interesting than instructive.'[9]

This may indicate an oversight in the literature; however, Robert Burrowes, the leading personality in the Gandhi-focussed Melbourne Rainforest Action Group, has observed that he had 'never come across one other Australian activist, historically (that is, during or shortly after Gandhi's lifetime) or currently, who has been seriously influenced by Gandhi in any peace, environmental/climate, social justice or union/labour campaign.'[10] It would appear that Burrowes is right in terms of explicit reliance on the nonviolent praxis of the Mahatma, at least in comparison with its employment in Britain and America—we certainly had no one of the stature of Richard Gregg or Martin Luther King Jr. promoting Gandhian nonviolence in the country. Nevertheless, I hope that I have demonstrated that Gandhi has been here all the time if in

---

[9] Chatfield, 'Introduction', p. 25.
[10] Personal communication from Robert Burrowes, 6 May 2018.

more subtle guises, for example as a guiding light for some religious and social justice organisations. And this is given added credibility by the times one hears Gandhi being referred to in traditional media interviews to stress a point, or mentioned in the press and other forms of popular media, spoken of by politicians attending Indian community functions, in the statues of him erected around the country, in his depiction on T-shirts, and even in throwaway lines in general conversation. While knowledge of Gandhi and his philosophy may lack depth, what we do know is generally normative and the use of Gandhian aphorisms (even though most of them are wrongly attributed to him[11]) are so common that, as with the case of Orwell, in Australia there clearly exists an understanding of who Gandhi was and what he stood for.

---

[11] See Thomas Weber, 'If Gandhi Didn't Say It, He Should Have', *Gandhi Marg* 41 (4), 2020, pp. 403–428.

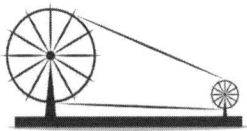

Bibliography

'AAT decision backs TPB finding on grounds of public interest', 10 September 2019. Available at https://www.tpb.gov.au/aat-decision-backs-tpb-finding-grounds-public-interest (accessed December 2023).

Adam-Smith, Patsy, *The ANZACS*, Melbourne: Thomas Nelson, 1978.

Alexander, Fred, 'Mahatma Gandhi: A Saint in Politics', *The West Australian* (Perth), 11 January 1930, p. 4.

Alexander, Horace, *Gandhi through Western Eyes*, Bombay: Asia Publishing House, 1969.

Andrews, C. F., 'Gandhi as I Know Him', *The Australian Christian Commonwealth*, 10 May 1929, p. 6; and 17 May 1929, p. 6.

———, *Mahatma Gandhi's Ideas: Including Selections from his Writings*, London: George Allen and Unwin, 1929.

———, *Mahatma Gandhi: His Own Story*, London: George Allen and Unwin, 1930.

———, *Mahatma Gandhi at Work: His Own Story Continued*, London: George Allen and Unwin, 1931.

Andrews, Dave, *Building a Better World*, Sydney: Albatross, 1996.

———, *Crux: The Place of the Cross in the Process of Transformation*, Melbourne: Mosaic, 2013.

Andriiashina, Anna, 'President Page', *Bhavan Australia*, March–April 2018, p. 3, available at bhavanaustralia.org/upload/Bhavan_Australia_March-April_%202018.pdf (accessed December 2023).

Ansara, Martha, 'Gandhi or Gone with the Monsoon', *Filmnews*, 1 March 1983, p. 15.

Arana-Ward, Marie, 'Rajmohan Gandhi', *The Washington Post*, 15 October 1995.

Bibliography

Arora, Avneet, 'Community says "No" to Gandhi's Statue in Melbourne's Dandenong', SBS Punjabi, 31 July 2018. Available at www.sbs.com.au/yourlanguage/punjabi/en/article/2018/07/31/community-says-no-gandhis-statue-melbournes-dandenong (accessed December 2023).

Ash, David, 'Albert Bathurst Piddington', *NSW Bar Association News*, Summer 2009–2010, pp. 45–58.

Attenborough, Richard, *In Search of Gandhi*, London: The Bodley Head, 1982.

Barcs, Emery, 'He Opposes All Violence: How Gandhi's Fasting Stops Bloodshed', *The Daily Telegraph* (Sydney), 20 January 1948, p. 8.

Barr, Pat, *The Dust in the Balance: British Women in India 1905–1945*, London: Hamish Hamilton, 1989.

Basham, A. L., *The Wonder that Was India*, London: Sidgwick and Jackson, 1954.

———, 'Foreword', in Sibnarayan Ray (ed.), *Gandhi, India and the World: An International Symposium*, Philadelphia: Temple University Press, 1970, pp. 11–13.

———, 'Traditional Influences on the Thought of Mahatma Gandhi', in R. Kumar (ed.), *Essays on Gandhian Politics: The Rowlatt Satyagraha of 1919*, Oxford: Clarendon Press, 1971, pp. 17–42.

Beesey, Allan, 'Gandhi the Film', *Groundswell* 1 (5), 1983, pp. 9–10.

Behn, Mira [Madeleine Slade], *The Spirit's Pilgrimage*, London: Longmans, 1960.

Bennett, Ben, *G. K. Tucker Settlement: An Historical Record 1935–1995*, Melbourne: Brotherhood of St. Laurence, 1995.

Black, Maggie, *A Cause for Our Times: Oxfam: The First 50 Years*, Oxford: Oxford University Press, 1992.

Blackburn, Susan, *Practical Visionaries: A Study of Community Aid Abroad*, Melbourne: Melbourne University Press, 1993.

Blacket, Arthur H., 'Face to Face with Gandhi', *The Advertiser* (Adelaide), 21 December 1929, p. 15.

———, 'Some Notes from India', *The Advertiser* (Adelaide), 21 February 1930, p. 23.

———, 'India in the Melting Pot', *Australian Christian Commonwealth*, 7 November 1930, p. 11.

Bibliography

———, 'Mahatma Gandhi "Patriotism and Self-Renunciation"', *Advertiser and Register* (Adelaide), 22 September 1931, p. 12.

———, 'Gandhi in London: "One of the World's Greatest Characters"', *The Advertiser* (Adelaide), 2 October 1931, p. 22.

———, 'Gandhi's Ideals Christian in Spirit', *The Advertiser* (Adelaide), 9 October 1931, p. 22.

Bloomfield, J. H., 'C. F. Andrews in New Zealand', *The New Zealand Journal of History* 7 (1), 1973, pp. 70–75.

Bolton, Glorney, *The Tragedy of Gandhi*, London: Allen and Unwin, 1934.

Bondurant, Joan V., *Conquest of Violence: The Gandhian Philosophy of Conflict*, Princeton: Princeton University Press, 1958.

Bourke-White, Margaret, *Halfway to Freedom*, New York: Simon and Schuster, 1949.

Brierley, Justin, 'Profile: Jarrod McKenna', *Premier Christianity*, 14 September 2015. Available at www.premierchristianity.com/Past-Issues/2015/October-2015/Profile-Jarrod-McKenna (accessed December 2023).

'Brotherhood Timeline: Through the Decades: 1950: Community Issues'. Available at bsltimeline.pbworks.com/w/page/27549149/Through%20the%20decades%3A%201950 (accessed December 2023).

Brown, Bob, *Optimism: Reflections on a Life of Action*, Melbourne: Hardie Grant, 2014.

Burgmann, Verity, *Power and Protest: Movements for Change in Australian Society*, Sydney: Allen and Unwin, 1993.

Burns, Robin, and Thomas Weber, 'Gandhi and Freire on Campus: Theory and Practice in Tertiary Peace Studies Programs', *Peace Education Miniprint* 76, March 1995, Malmo: School of Education.

Burrowes, Robert J., and Thomas Weber, 'The Strength of Nonviolence', *Arena* 90, 1990, pp. 164–168.

Burrowes, Robert J., 'Nurrungar—A Theoretical Reflection', *Nonviolence Today* 11, October/November 1989, pp. 8–10.

———, 'Monkeywrenching and Nonviolent Action', *Nonviolence Today* 12, December/January 1989/1990, p. 7.

———, 'Nonviolent Struggle for the Rainforests', *Nonviolence Today* 15, June/July 1990, pp. 3–6.

Bibliography

Burrowes, Robert J., 'Rainforest Pickets', *Nonviolence Today* 17, October/November 1990, pp. 10–12.

———, 'The Dimensions of Nonviolent Struggle', *Nonviolence Today* 18, December/January 1990/91, pp. 17–18.

———, 'Rainforest Ship Blockaded and Picketed', *Nonviolence Today* 18, December/January 1990/1991, pp. 9–11.

———, 'Gandhian in Australia', *Nonviolence Today* 18, December/January 1990/1991, pp. 7–8.

———, 'The Gulf War and the Gulf Peace Team', *Social Alternatives* 10 (2), 1991, pp. 35–39.

———, 'Bankrupt Tax Resister Refuses to Cooperate', *Nonviolence Today* 24, January/February 1992, p. 12.

———, 'Defence Statement of Robert J. Burrowes, Tax Resister, before a Federal Court of Australia in Melbourne 27 November, 1991', *Social Alternatives* 11 (2), 1992, pp. 43–48.

———, 'Nonviolence as a Way of Life', *Nonviolence Today* 38, May/June 1994, pp. 4–6.

———, 'Nonviolence and the Inner Voice', *Nonviolence Today* 47, November/December 1995, pp. 8–10.

———, 'The Phases of My Nonviolent Activism', *Nonviolence Today* 48, January/February 1996, pp. 4–5.

———, *The Strategy of Nonviolent Defense: A Gandhian Approach*, Albany: State University of New York Press, 1996.

———, 'The Persian Gulf War and the Gulf Peace Team', in Yeshua Moser-Puangsuwan and Thomas Weber (eds.), *Nonviolent Intervention Across Borders: A Recurrent Vision*, Honolulu: Spark M. Matsunaga Institute for Peace, 2000, pp. 305–316.

———, 'Robert J. Burrowes: If You Live Your Dream, You Have Lived'. Available at robertjburrowes.wordpress.com (accessed December 2023).

———, 'Why Violence?' Available at tinyurl.com/whyviolence (accessed December 2023).

Callcott, Geoff, 'The Greening of the Thin Blue Line', *Police Life*, May 1990, pp. 20–21.

Campbell, Christopher, 'Christopher Campbell Replies to Mr. Bury', *Peacemaker* 29 (4&5), April-May 1967, p. 6.

Bibliography

Carter, I. R., *God and Three Shillings: The Story of the Brotherhood of St. Laurence*, Melbourne: Lansdowne Press, 1967.
Case, Clarence Marsh, *Non-Violent Coercion: A Study in Methods of Social Pressure*, New York: Century, 1923.
Casey, Baron, 'Foreword', in Newman Rosenthal, *The Uncompromising Truth: Mahatma Gandhi 1869–1948*, Melbourne: Nelson, 1969, pp. v–vi.
Casey, Maie, *Tides and Eddies*, London: Michael Joseph, 1966.
Casey, R. G., 'Gandhi—Outstanding Man of India', *The Herald* (Melbourne), 29 April 1946, p. 4.
———, *An Australian in India*, London: Hollis & Carter, 1947.
———, *Personal Experience 1939–1946*, London: Constable, 1962.
Chant, Ngaire, Sue Cochrane, and Robyn Kennedy, 'Foreword', in Sugata Dasgupta, *Towards a Post Development Era: Essays in Poverty, Welfare and Development* (Ngaire Chant, Sue Cochrane, and Robyn Kennedy [comps and eds]), Delhi: Mittal, 1985, p. xi.
Chatfield, Charles (ed.), *The Americanization of Gandhi: Images of the Mahatma*, New York: Garland, 1976.
Chaturvedi, Benarsidas, and Marjorie Sykes, *Charles Freer Andrews*, New Delhi: Publications Division, Ministry of Information and Broadcasting, Government of India, 1971.
Close-Barry, Kirstie, *A Mission Divided: Race, Culture and Colonialism in Fiji's Methodist Mission*, Canberra: Australian National University Press, 2015.
Clymer, Kenton J., *Quest for Freedom: The United States and India's Independence*, New York: Columbia University Press, 1995.
Colebatch, Hal, 'Why Was Gandhi Killed?', *The West Australian* (Perth), 7 February 1948, p. 18.
Collett, Nigel, *The Butcher of Amritsar: General Reginald Dyer*, London and New York: Hambledon Continuum, 2005.
Commonwealth, Parliamentary Debates, House of Representatives, 31 October 1935, Sanctions Bill, second reading, Robert Menzies; 1 November 1935, Sanctions Bill, second reading, Archie Cameron; 9 March 1945, Question, Suggested Medical Plan, Arthur Calwell; 11 November 1954, Question, Mahatma Gandhi, Anthony Luchetti; 11 November 1954, Question, Mahatma Gandhi, Robert Menzies.

Bibliography

Cortright, David, *Gandhi and Beyond: Nonviolence for an Age of Terrorism*, Boulder: Paradigm, 2006.

Cousins, Norman (ed.), *Profiles of Gandhi: America Remembers a World Leader*, Delhi: Indian Book Company, 1970.

Damm, Alex (ed.), *Gandhi in a Canadian Context: Relationships between Mahatma Gandhi and Canada*, Waterloo, Ontario: Wilfrid Laurier University Press, 2017.

Dart, Martha, *Marjorie Sykes: Quaker Gandhian*, York: Sessions Book Trust, 1993.

Das, Durga (ed.), *Gandhi in Cartoons*, Ahmedabad: Navajivan, 1970.

Dasgupta, Sugata, *Towards a Post Development Era: Essays in Poverty, Welfare and Development* (Ngaire Chant, Sue Cochrane, and Robyn Kennedy [comps and eds]), Delhi: Mittal, 1985.

Deane, Bill, *The Earth Has Enough: The Story of Community Aid Abroad*, Melbourne: Community Aid Abroad, 1978.

DeParle, Jason, 'Why Gandhi Drives Neoconservatives Crazy', *Washington Monthly* 19, September 1983, pp. 46–51.

Desai Ashwin, and Goolam Vahed, *The South African Gandhi: Stretcher-Bearer of Empire*, Stanford, California: Stanford University Press, 2016.

Desai, Mahadev, 'How to be Worthy of Our Heritage', *Harijan*, 12 April 1942.

———, 'Two Australian Visitors', *Harijan*, 3 May 1942.

Dhupelia-Mesthrie, Uma, *Gandhi's Prisoner? The Life of Gandhi's Son Manilal*, Cape Town: Kwela, 2005.

DiSalvo, Charles, *The Man Before the Mahatma: M. K. Gandhi, Attorney at Law*, Noida: Random House India, 2012.

Docker, John, and Debjani Ganguly (eds), 'Gandhi, Nonviolence & Modernity', *Borderlands e-journal* 4 (3), 2005. Available at https://webarchive.nla.gov.au/awa/20060820141236/http://www.borderlandsejournal.adelaide.edu.au/issues/vol4no3.html (accessed December 2023).

Doherty, Dennis, 'Nurrungar—Theory in Magnificent Practice', *Nonviolence Today* 15, June/July 1990, pp. 8–11.

Doke, Joseph J., *M. K. Gandhi: An Indian Patriot in South Africa*, London: London Indian Chronicle, 1909.

Bibliography

Douglas, Roger, 'Timber Cutting on Trial: Police, Courts and the Rainforest Action Group', *Interdisciplinary Peace Research* 2 (2), 1990, pp. 74–85.

Draper, Alfred, *Amritsar: The Massacre that Ended the Raj*, London: Cassell, 1981.

Dutt, R. Palme, *India Today*, London: Gollancz, 1940.

Emilsen, W. William, 'Gandhi and Mayo's "Mother India"', *South Asia* 10 (1), 1987, pp. 69–81.

Evans, Selwyn, 'Correspondence', *Peacewards*, 1 September 1931, p. 3.

Farson, Negley, 'Indian Hate Lyric', in Eugene Lyons (ed.), *We Cover the World: By Sixteen Foreign Correspondents*, London: Harrap, 1937, pp. 127–152.

Fischer, Louis, *The Life of Mahatma Gandhi*, New York: Harper and Row, 1950.

Fisher, David James, *Romain Rolland and the Politics of Intellectual Engagement*, Berkeley: University of California Press, 1988.

Fisher, David James, 'Romain Rolland and the Popularization of Gandhi: 1923–1925', *Gandhi Marg* 18 (3), 1974, pp. 145–180.

Fisher, Frederick, 'Gandhi Himself', *Christian Century* 47, 5 November 1930, p. 1345.

———, *That Strange Little Brown Man Gandhi*, New York: Ray Long and Richard B. Smith Inc., 1932.

Forster, E. M., *A Passage to India*, London: Edward Arnold, 1924.

Fox, John, 'Theory and Practice of Non-Violent Action', *The Peacemaker* 30 (4), April 1968, pp. 4–5.

Freudenberg, Graham, *Churchill and Australia*, Sydney: Macmillan, 2008.

Galtung, Johan, 'Violence, Peace and Peace Research', *Journal of Peace Research* 6 (3), 1969, pp. 167–191.

Gandhi, Ela, 'Gandhi: Education Key to Combating Violence', SBS News, 3 September 2013. Available at https://www.sbs.com.au/news/article/gandhi-education-key-to-combating-violence/z7x0r5kmn(accessed December 2023).

Gandhi, M. K., *The Grievances of the British Indians in South Africa: An Appeal to the Indian Public*, Madras: Price Current Press, 1896.

———, *Satyagraha in South Africa*, Madras: Ganesan, 1928.

———, *Hind Swaraj or Indian Home Rule*, Ahmedabad: Navajivan, 1939.

Bibliography

Gandhi, M. K., *An Autobiography or the Story of My Experiments with Truth*, Mahadev Desai (trans.), Ahmedabad: Navajivan, 1940.

———, *Constructive Programme: Its Meaning and Place*, Ahmedabad: Navajivan, 1941.

———, *Ashram Observances in Action*, Ahmedabad: Navajivan 1955.

———, *The Collected Works of Mahatma Gandhi*, Vols 1–100, New Delhi: Publications Division, Government of India, 1958–1991; and revised CD-ROM version, New Delhi: Publications Division, Government of India, 1999.

GandhiServe India, *Mahatma Gandhi's Life in Colour*, Mumbai: GandhiServe India, 2016.

Ganguly, Debjani, and John Docker (eds), *Rethinking Gandhi and Nonviolent Relationality: Global Perspectives*, London: Routledge, 2007; and New Delhi: Orient BlackSwan, 2009.

Ghosh, Sudhir, *Gandhi's Emissary*, London: Cresset, 1967.

Gibson, Ralph, *The People Stand Up*, Melbourne: Red Rooster Press, 1983.

Glamorgan, Adrian, 'Jarrod McKenna, Peace Fellow'. Available at wecan.be/beencouraged/123/ (accessed December 2023).

Glover, Dennis, *Orwell's Australia: From Cold War to Culture Wars*, Melbourne: Scribe, 2003.

Gobbett, Estelle, and Don, 'From Mission Field to Potato Patch', in Bill Metcalf (ed.), *From Utopian Dreaming to Communal Reality: Co-operative Lifestyles in Australia*, Sydney: UNSW Press, 1995, pp. 84–98.

Goldstein, Vida, 'Letters from Miss Goldstein', *Woman Voter*, 3 July 1919, p. 2.

Goodall, Bill, 'The Words of Men of Peace Deserve to Live on After Them', *The Canberra Times*, 8 September 1984, p. 2.

Goodman, T. L., 'The Men Who Count in India's Bid for Independence', *The Sydney Morning Herald*, 9 June 1945, p. 2.

Gordon, Leonard, A., 'Mahatma Gandhi's Dialogues with Americans', *Economic and Political Weekly* 37 (4), 26 January 2002, pp. 337–352.

Graham, Morris, *A. B. Piddington: The Last Radical Liberal*, Sydney: University of New South Wales Press, 1995.

Gregg, Richard B., *The Power of Non-Violence*, Philadelphia: J. B. Lippincott, 1934.

Bibliography

Grenier, Richard, 'The Gandhi Nobody Knows', *Commentary*, March 1983, pp. 59–72.

Groom, Donald G., *With Vinoba*, Varanasi: Sarva Seva Sangh, 1969.

——, 'Gandhi's Challenge', *The Peacemaker* 32 (112), January/February 1970, p. 8.

——, 'Looking Back—Looking Forward', *The Australian Friend*, June 1970, pp. 2–4.

Gross, Matthias, and Linsey McGoey (eds), *Routledge International Handbook of Ignorance Studies*, London and New York: Routledge, 2015.

Guha, Ramachandra 'Introduction to the Indian Edition: Gandhi's Faith and Ours', in J. T. F. Jordens, *Gandhi's Religion: A Homespun Shawl*, New Delhi: Oxford University Press, 2012, pp. xi–xxiii.

——, *Gandhi Before India*, London: Allen Lane, 2013.

——, *Gandhi: The Years that Changed the World 1914–1948*, New Delhi: Penguin, 2018.

Gunther, John, 'The Incredible Mr. Gandhi', *Reader's Digest* 33 (200), December 1938, pp. 111–126.

——, *Inside Asia*, New York: Harper, 1939.

Gurry, Meg, *Australia and India: Mapping the Journey 1944–2014*, Melbourne: Melbourne University Press, 2015.

Hamel-Green, Michael, 'Vietnam: Beyond Pity', *Australian Left Review*, April-May 1970, pp. 53–65.

Handfield, John, *Friends and Brothers: A Life of Gerard Kennedy Tucker, Founder of the Brotherhood of St. Laurence and Community Aid Abroad*, Melbourne: Hyland House, 1980.

Hannon, Mark, 'Gandhi in the New York Times, 1920–1930', in G. Ramachandran and T. K. Mahadevan (eds), *Quest for Gandhi*, New Delhi: Gandhi Peace Foundation, 1970 pp. 164–172.

Hepworth, Margaret, *The Gandhi Experiment: Teaching Our Teenagers How to Become Global Citizens*, New Delhi: Rupa, 2017.

Holmes, John Haynes, *Who is the Greatest Man in the World Today?*, New York: The Community Church, 1921.

——, 'Mahatma Gandhi: The Greatest Man Since Jesus Christ', in Kshitis Roy (ed.), *Gandhi Memorial Peace Number*, Shantiniketan: Visva-Bharati Quarterly, 1949, pp. 239–256.

Bibliography

Howard, Michael S., *Jonathan Cape, Publisher*, London: Jonathan Cape, 1971.

Howse, Janet, 'Nesbitt, Thomas Huggins (1853–1935)', in Geoffrey Serle (ed.), *Australian Dictionary of Biography*, Melbourne: Melbourne University Press, 1988, Vol. 11, p. 2.

Hoyland, John S., *Indian Crisis: The Background*, London: Allen and Unwin, 1943.

Hudson, W. J., *Casey: A Biography*, Melbourne: Oxford University Press, 1986.

———, 'Casey, Richard Gavin Gardiner (1880–1976)', in Geoffrey Serle (ed.), *Australian Dictionary of Biography*, Melbourne: Melbourne University Press, 1993, Vol. 13, pp. 381–385.

Hunt, James D., *Gandhi and the Nonconformists: Encounters in South Africa*, New Delhi: Promilla, 1986.

Husain, Mishal (presented). *Gandhi: The Life and Legacy of India's 'Father of a Nation'*, BBC documentary, 2011.

Hutton, Drew, 'What is Green Politics?', in Drew Hutton (ed.), *Green Politics in Australia*, Sydney: Angus and Robertson, 1987, pp. 1–33.

Huxter, Robert, *Reg and Ethel: Reginald Reynolds: His Life and Work and His Marriage to Ethel Manning*, York: Sessions Book Trust, 1993.

Hyde, Ian A., 'Man of Vision', *The Friend* 116 (52), 26 December 1958, pp. 1664–1665.

'Interview: Gambhir—India's Culture Ambassador in Sydney', *The Indian Sun*, 28 June 2017. Available at theindiansun.com.au/2013/06/28/gambhir-indias-culture-ambassador-in-sydney/ (accessed December 2023).

Isaacs, Harold R., *Scratches on Our Minds: American Views of China and India*, Armonk, New York: M. E. Sharpe, 1980.

Jeffrey, Robin, Lance Brennan, Jim Masselos, Peter Mayer, and Peter Reeves (eds), *India: Rebellion to Republic: Selected Writings 1857–1990*, New Delhi: Stirling, 1990.

Jha, Manoranjan, *Civil Disobedience and After: The American Reaction to Political Developments in India During 1930–1935*, Meerut: Meenakshi, 1973.

John, Joseph (comp.), *Gandhi as Others See Him: A Collection of Articles, Opinions, Speeches, Sermons etc.*, Colombo: Bastion, 1933.

Bibliography

Johns, Anthony H., 'Joseph Jordens (1925–2008)', *Australian Academy of the Humanities, Proceedings* 33, 2008, Canberra, pp. 71–74.

Jones, Barry O., 'India's Father and Mother Figure', *The Age* (Melbourne), 28 January 1978, p. 25.

Jones, Peter, Margaret Pestorius, and Bryan Law, 'The Story of the Australian Nonviolence Network', *Nonviolence Today* 43, March/April 1995, pp. 16–19.

Jordens, J. T. F., *Gandhi: Conscience of Hinduism and Scourge of Orthodoxy*, Canberra: Faculty of Asian Studies, The Australian National University, 1991.

———, *Gandhi's Religion: A Homespun Shawl*, New Delhi: Oxford University Press, 2012.

Juergensmeyer, Mark, 'The Gandhi Revival—A Review Article', *Journal of Asian Studies* XLIII (2), 1984, pp. 293–298.

Kahn, Alec, 'Gandhi …. Hero or Humbug? How "Non-violence" Failed in India', n.p., An International Socialist Pamphlet, 1982.

———, *Gandhi and the Myth of Non-Violent Action*, Sydney: Bookmarks, 1996.

Kapur, Sudarshan, *Raising Up a Prophet: The Afro-American Encounter with Gandhi*, Boston: Beacon Press, 1992.

Kaul, Chandrika, *Reporting the Raj: The British Press and India, c.1880–1922*, Manchester: Manchester University Press, 2003.

Kelly, Anthony, and Peter Westoby, *Participatory Development Practice: Using Traditional and Contemporary Frameworks*, Ruby, Warwickshire: Practical Action Publishing, 2018.

Kendal, Jeni, and Eddie Buivids, *Earth First: The Struggle to Save Australia's Rainforest*, Sydney: Australian Broadcasting Corporation, 1987.

Khanna, Suman, *Gandhi and the Good Life*, Delhi: Gandhi Peace Foundation, 1985.

King, Jr, Martin Luther, *Stride Towards Freedom: The Montgomery Story*, New York: Harper and Row, 1958.

Kirby, Michael, *What Would Gandhi Do?* Melbourne: Penguin, 2013.

Kruegler, Christopher, 'Civilian-Based Defense: The Intellectual Antecedents', *Nonviolence Today* 2, April/May 1988, pp. 13–16.

Kumar, Ravindra, 'Nonviolent Non-Cooperation: An Effective, Noble and Valuable Means for Peaceful Change', *Social Alternatives* 29 (1), 2010, pp. 5–10.

Bibliography

Lack, John, 'Moorehead, Alan McCrae (1910–1983)', in Melanie Nolan (ed.), *Australian Dictionary of Biography*, Melbourne: Melbourne University Press, 2012, Vol. 18, pp. 172–174.

Lanza del Vasto, Joseph Jean, *Return to the Source*, London: Rider, 1971.

———, *Warriors of Peace: Writings on the Technique of Nonviolence*, New York: Knopf, 1974.

Lelyveld, Joseph, *Great Soul: Mahatma Gandhi and His Struggle with India*, New York: Knopf, 2011.

Lester, Muriel, *My Host the Hindu*, London: Williams and Norgate, 1931.

———, *Entertaining Gandhi*, London: Nicholson and Watson, 1932.

———, *It Occurred to Me*, New York: Harper, 1937.

———, *It So Happened*, New York: Harper and Brothers, 1947.

Lian, Jotham, 'AAT knocks back senior CPA's application to stay termination decision'. Available at accountantsdaily.com.au/regulation/13508-aat-knocks-back-senior-cpa-s-application-to-stay-termination-decision (accessed December 2023).

'"Like a Good Garam Masala": PM Hails Multiculturalism at Gandhi Statue Unveiling', SBS News, 23 November 2018. Available at www.sbs.com.au/news/like-a-good-garam-masala (accessed December 2023).

Lim, Ann, 'The Dreadlocked Minister with a Heart for Refugees', *Eternity News*, 19 April 2018. Available at www.eternitynews.com.au/charity/the-dreadlocked-minister-with-a-heart-for-refugees/ (accessed December 2023).

'Loss of a Friend and Dedicated Peace Worker', *Social Alternatives* 4 (3), 1984, p. 61.

MacDonald, Dougal, 'Gandhi has Immense Impact', *The Canberra Times*, 19 March 1983, p. 14.

———, *British India, White Australia: Overseas Indians, Intercolonial Relations and the Empire*, Sydney: University of New South Wales Press, 2020.

Maclean, Kama, 'A Colonial in the Colonies: Governor Casey, Mahatma Gandhi, and the Endgame of Empire', *Journal of Colonialism and Colonial History* 19 (3), 2019. Available at muse.jhu.edu (accessed December 2023).

Bibliography

Mahadevan, T. K., *The Year of the Phoenix: Gandhi's Pivotal Year*, New Delhi: Arnold-Heinemann, 1982.

'Mahatma Gandhi International Prize for Social Responsibility—10 May 2014', International Centre of Nonviolence. Available at www.nonviolence.org.au/10-May-2014/ (accessed December 2023).

Malhotra, S. L., 'A Study of Gandhi's Biographies—Joseph J. Doke and Romain Rolland', *Gandhi Marg* 6 (12), 1985, pp. 845–861.

———, 'A Study of Gandhi's *Autobiography*', *Gandhi Marg* 7 (7), 1985, pp. 424–437.

———, 'Louis Fischer as Gandhi's Biographer', *Gandhi Marg* 8 (5), 1986, pp. 259–270.

———, 'The American Clergy and the Mahatma—Fredrick B. Fisher and John Haynes Holmes', *Gandhi Marg* 9 (10), 1988, pp. 579–596.

Malhotra S. L., 'Vincent Sheean as a Biographer of Mahatma Gandhi', *Gandhi Marg* 10 (6), 1988, pp. 340–349.

Martin, Brian, 'The Pitfalls of Nonviolent Revolution', *Nonviolence Today* 2, April/May 1988, pp. 16–17.

Martin, Brian, and Iain Murray, 'The Parkin Backfire', *Social Alternatives* 24 (3), 2005, pp. 46–49, 70.

Martin, James H., 'Mahatma Gandhi: A Gentlemanly Rebel', *The Sydney Morning Herald*, 4 January 1930, p. 11.

Masselos, Jim, *Nationalism on the Indian Subcontinent: An Introductory History*, Melbourne: Nelson, 1972.

Maynard, John, '"Be the Change You Want to See": The Awakening of Cultural Nationalism—Gandhi, Garvey and the AAPA', *Borderlands e-journal* 4 (3), 2005.

Mayo, Katherine, *Mother India*, London: Jonathan Cape, 1927.

McCamish, Thornton, *Our Man Elsewhere: In Search of Alan Moorehead*, Melbourne: Black Ink, 2017.

McKenna, Jarrod, 'Backyard Missionary Voting for Jesus (Today!)' Available at www.backyardmissionary.com/author/jarrod-mckenna/page/2/ (accessed December 2023).

———, 'Imagination fit for the Larrikin Jesus'. Available at www.backyardmissionary.com/author/jarrod-mckenna/page/2/ (accessed December 2023).

Bibliography

McKenna, Jarrod, 'Jesus bigger than Christianity?' Available at www.backyardmissionary.com/author/jarrod-mckenna/page/2/ (accessed December 2023).

McKie, Ronald, 'Australian Airmen See Gandhi', *The Daily Telegraph* (Sydney), 26 September 1944, p. 3.

———, 'Fasts Aren't a Joke in India', *The Daily Telegraph* (Sydney), 10 September 1947, p. 8.

Mehta, Ved, *Gandhi and His Apostles*, London: Andre Deutsch, 1977.

Miller, Webb, *I Found no Peace: The Journal of a Foreign Correspondent*, New York: The Library Guild, 1936; and Harmondsworth: Penguin, 1940.

Moore, Eleanor, *The Quest for Peace as I have Known it in Australia*, Melbourne: Wilke & Co, 1948.

Moore, R. J., 'Gandhi Criticised', *The Canberra Times*, 17 June 1983, p. 10.

Moore, Tony, 'Indian PM Narendra Modi Unveils Gandhi Statue', *Brisbane Times*, 16 November 2014. Available at www.brisbanetimes.com.au/national/queensland/indian-pm-narendra-modi-unveils-gandhi-statue-20141116-11nwf9.html (accessed December 2023).

Moorehead, Alan, *African Trilogy*, London: Hamish Hamilton, 1944.

———, 'Gandhi: A Last Look', *The Observer*, 1 February 1948, p. 4.

Moorhouse, Frank, 'The Girl from the Family of Man', *Westerly*, July 1970, pp. 25–31.

Moser-Puangsuwan, Yeshua, and Thomas Weber (eds), *Nonviolent Intervention Across Borders: A Recurrent Vision*, Honolulu: Spark M. Matsunaga Institute for Peace, 2000.

Moyal, Ann, *Alan Moorehead: A Rediscovery*, Canberra: National Library of Australia, 2005.

Mulder, William, 'Foreword', in C. Seshachari, *Gandhi and the American Scene: An Intellectual History and Inquiry*, Bombay: Nachiketa, 1969, pp. vii–viii.

Murdoch, Walter, 'Shame or Pride? The Empire', *The Herald* (Melbourne), 16 November 1940, p. 10.

Murphy, Stephen, 'The Different "Gandhis" in Western Biographies', *Gandhi Marg* 12 (3), 1990, pp. 295–316.

———, *Why Gandhi is Relevant in Modern India: A Western Gandhian's Personal Discovery*, New Delhi: Gandhi Peace Foundation, 1990.

Bibliography

———, 'Gandhian Movement of Australia', *Nonviolence Today* 15, June/July 1990, pp. 18–19.

———, 'First Steps of the International Gandhian Movement', *Global Conscience* 2 (1), July–September 1991, p. 7.

———, 'Constructing the Mahatma: The Evolution of Gandhi's Image in His Western Biographies, 1909–1954', Master of Arts dissertation, Department of Politics, School of Social Sciences, La Trobe University, 1992.

———, *The International Gandhian Movement: An Introduction*, Canberra: The International Gandhian Movement, 1998, 3rd ed.

Murray, Nell, 'When Gandhi Goes to London: East End Welfare Worker Will Be His Hostess', *The Herald* (Melbourne), 10 August 1931, p. 6.

Murti, V. V. Ramana, 'Romain Rolland and Gandhi', *Gandhi Marg* 10 (1), 1966, pp. 38–51.

Muzumdar, Haridas T., *Gandhi the Apostle: His Trial and his Message*, Chicago: Universal Publishing Company, 1923.

———, *Gandhi Against the Empire*, New York: Universal Publishing, 1932.

Namboodiripad, E. M. S., *The Mahatma and the Ism*, New Delhi: People's Publishing House, 1959.

Nanda, B. R., *Mahatma Gandhi: A Biography*, Delhi: Oxford University Press, 1958.

———, *Gandhi and his Critics*, Delhi: Oxford University Press, 1984.

———, *In Search of Gandhi: Essays and Reflections*, New Delhi: Oxford University Press, 2002.

Nandan, Satendra, 'The Making of the Mahatma: The Markings of the Outsider-Writer', Charles Sturt University, 3 October 2017. Available at cdn.csu.edu.au/__data/assets/pdf_file/0011/2876339/The-MAKING-of-the-Mahatma-The-MARKINGS-of-the-Outsider-Writer-.pdf (accessed December 2023).

Nette, Andrew, Kate Tempany, and Ian Wilson, 'Nurrungar: Giving Warning', *Arena* 89, 1989, pp. 38–44.

———, 'Rainforest Action', *Arena* 92, 1990, pp. 139–145.

Norman, James, *Bob Brown: A Gentle Revolutionary*, Sydney: Allen and Unwin, 2004.

Ostergaard, Geoffrey, *Nonviolent Revolution in India*, New Delhi: Gandhi Peace Foundation, 1985.

Bibliography

Parel, Anthony J. (ed.), *Hind Swaraj and Other Writings*, Cambridge: Cambridge University Press, 1997.

Patel, Jehangir P., and Marjorie Sykes, *Gandhi: His Gift of the Fight*, Rasulia: Friends Rural Centre, 1987.

Periyathai, C., *Quest for Immortality: Biography of Maharishi Doctor K. Arunachalam*, Madurai: Tamilnadu Sarvodaya Mandal, 1994.

Perkins, Charles, *A Bastard Like Me*, Sydney: Ure Smith, 1975.

Piddington, A. B., *Spanish Sketches*, London: Oxford University Press, 1916.

———, *Worshipful Masters*, Sydney: Angus & Robertson, 1929.

———, *Bapu Gandhi*, London: Williams & Norgate, 1930.

Pittock, Diana, and Barrie, 'Building an Alternative to the War System: Towards Nonviolent Social Change', *Social Alternatives* 3 (2), 1983, pp. 7–12.

Pocock, Tom, *Alan Moorehead*, London: The Bodley Head, 1990.

Polak, H. S. L., H. N. Brailsford, and Lord Pethick-Lawrence, *Mahatma Gandhi*, London: Odhams Press, 1949.

Ponder, H. W., 'Gandhi at Home', *The Telegraph* (Brisbane), 18 November 1940, p. 10.

Ponder, Winifred, *Clara Butt: Her Life Story*, London: Harrap, 1928.

———, 'Rift in the Lute: Miss Slade and Gandhi: Will English Disciple Return to Society?', *The Telegraph* (Brisbane), 29 June 1934, p. 1.

Pooley, A. M., 'Gandhi: He can Wreck the New India Plan', *The Sun* (Sydney), 8 June 1947, p. 8.

'Premier Unveils Sculpture of Mahatma Gandhi', University of Adelaide, News & Events, 19 January 2012. Available at https://www.adelaide.edu.au/news/news50561.html (accessed December 2023).

Proctor, Robert N., and Londa Schiebinger, *Agnotology: The Making and Unmaking of Ignorance*, Stanford, California: Stanford University Press, 2008.

Publications Division, *Romain Rolland and Gandhi Correspondence (Letters, Diary Extracts, Articles, Etc.)*, New Delhi: Publications Division, Ministry of Information and Broadcasting, Government of India, 1976.

Pyarelal, *Mahatma Gandhi, Vol. IX, Book I, The Last Phase, Part I*, Ahmedabad: Navajivan, 1956.

Bibliography

———, *Mahatma Gandhi, Vol. 1, The Early Phase*, Ahmedabad: Navajivan, 1965.

Radhakrishnan, S. (ed.), *Mahatma Gandhi: Essays and Reflections on his Life and Work*, Bombay: Jaico, 1956.

Rasmussen, Carolyn, *The Lesser Evil? Opposition to War and Fascism in Australia, 1920–1941*, Melbourne: The History Department, University of Melbourne, 1992.

Rau, Heimo (ed.), *Mahatma Gandhi as Germans See Him*, Bombay: Shakuntala, 1976.

Ray, Sibnarayan (ed.), *Gandhi, India and the World: An International Symposium*, Melbourne: The Hawthorn Press, 1970.

———, 'Introduction', in Sibnarayan Ray (ed.), *Gandhi, India and the World: An International Symposium*, Melbourne: The Hawthorn Press, 1970, pp. 15–28.

Read, Peter, *Charles Perkins: A Biography*, Melbourne: Penguin, 2001.

Reynolds, Henry, *Unnecessary Wars*, Sydney: NewSouth, 2016.

Reynolds, Reginald, *The White Sahibs in India*, London: Secker and Warburg, 1937.

———, *To Live in Mankind: A Quest for Gandhi*, London: Andre Deutsch, 1951.

———, *My Life and Crimes*, London: Jarrolds, 1956.

Rigney, Victoria, *Peace Comes Walking*, Carindale, Qld: Glass House Books, 2002.

Rivett, Kenneth, *Economic Thought of Mahatma Gandhi*, Bombay: Allied, 1959.

———, 'The Economic Thought of Mahatma Gandhi', *The British Journal of Sociology* 10 (1), 1959, pp. 1–15.

———, 'Gandhi, Tolstoy and Coercion', *South Asia* 11 (2), 1988, pp. 29–56.

Roberts, Andrew, 'Among the Hagiographers', *The Wall Street Journal*, 26 March 2011.

Roe, Michael, *Nine Australian Progressives: Vitalism in Bourgeois Social Thought, 1890–1960*, St. Lucia: University of Queensland Press, 1984.

———, 'Piddington, Albert Bathurst (1862–1945)', in Geoffrey Serle (ed.), *Australian Dictionary of Biography*, Melbourne: Melbourne University Press, 1988, Vol. 11, pp. 224–226.

Bibliography

Rolland, Romain, *Mahatma Gandhi: The Man Who Became One With the Universal Being*, New Delhi: Publications Division, Ministry of Information and Broadcasting, Government of India, 1968.

Rosenthal, Newman, *The Uncompromising Truth: Mahatma Gandhi 1869–1948*, Melbourne: Nelson, 1969.

Ruby, Felicity, and Ian Cohen, 'All the Way with NVA', *Nonviolence Today* 18, December/January 1990/91, pp. 14–17.

Rudolph, Lloyd I., 'Gandhi in the Mind of America', in Lloyd I. Rudolph, and Susanne Hoeber Rudolph, *Postmodern Gandhi and Other Essays: Gandhi in the World and at Home*, New Delhi: Oxford University Press, 2006, pp. 92–139.

Rudolph, Lloyd I., and Susanne Hoeber Rudolph, *The Modernity of Tradition: Political Development in India*, Chicago: University of Chicago Press, 1967.

Sage, H. A., 'If Gandhi "Fasts Unto Death"', *The Sun* (Sydney), 18 September 1932, p. 5.

Salla, Michael Emin, 'Satyagraha in Mahatma Gandhi's Political Philosophy', *Peace Research* 25, 1993, pp. 39–62.

———, 'There is No Nonviolent Future', *Social Alternatives* 15 (3), 1996, pp. 41–43.

Saunders, Malcolm, and Ralph Summy, 'Salient Themes of the Australian Peace Movement', *Social Alternatives* 3 (1), 1982, pp. 23–32.

———, *The Australian Peace Movement: A Short History*, Canberra: Peace Research Centre, Australian National University, 1986.

Scalmer, Sean, 'Globalising Gandhi: Translation, Reinvention, Application, Transformation', in John Docker and Debjani Ganguly (eds), *Rethinking Gandhi and Nonviolent Relationality: Global Perspectives*, London: Routledge, 2007; and New Delhi: Orient BlackSwan, 2009, pp. 177–204.

———, *Gandhi in the West: The Mahatma and the Rise of Radical Protest*, Cambridge: Cambridge University Press, 2011.

Scanlan, Nellie M., 'Gandhi: India's St. Francis of Assisi', *The Brisbane Courier*, 31 December 1927, p. 18.

Scarfe, Allan, and Wendy Scarfe, *J. P.: His Biography*, New Delhi: Orient Longman, 1975; and New Delhi: Orient Longman, 1997, revised edn.

———, *Remembering Jayaprakash*, New Delhi: Siddharth, 1997.

Bibliography

Scarfe, Wendy, and Allan Scarfe, *A Mouthful of Petals: The Story of an Indian Village*, London: Heinemann, 1967.

Scott, David, *He Got Things Done: A Memoir of Gerard Kennedy Tucker, Anglican Priest*, Melbourne: Brotherhood of St. Laurence, 2000.

Scott, David (with Carrie Hutchinson), *Always Say Yes: The Life of David Scott*, Sydney: Pier 9, 2014.

Serle, Geoffrey, *John Monash: A Biography*, Melbourne: Melbourne University Press, 1982.

Seshachari, C., *Gandhi and the American Scene: An Intellectual History and Inquiry*, Bombay: Nachiketa, 1969.

Sharma, Arvind, 'Some Early Anticipations of the Gandhian Interpretation of the Bhagavad-Gita', in Victor C. Hayes (ed.), *Australian Essays in World Religions*, Adelaide: The Australian Association for the Study of Religions, 1977, pp. 66–72.

Sharp, Gene, *Gandhi Wields the Weapon of Moral Power [Three Case Histories]*, Ahmedabad: Navajivan, 1960.

———, *The Politics of Nonviolent Action*, Boston: Porter Sargent, 1973.

Sheean, Vincent, *Lead, Kindly Light*, London: Cassell, 1950.

Shepard, Mark, *Gandhi Today: A Report on Mahatma Gandhi's Successors*, Arcata, CA: Simple Productions, 1987.

———, 'Gandhians After Gandhi', *Groundswell* 29, December/January 1987/1988, pp. 4–5.

———, *The Community of the Ark*, Arcata, CA: Simple Productions, 1990.

Short, Rev. Harold, '"Satyagraha": "Soul Force" is Advocated by Indian Leader, Gandhi', *The Herald* (Melbourne), 21 June 1919, p. 17.

Shridharani, Krishnalal, *War without Violence: A Study of Gandhi's Method and its Accomplishments*, New York: Garland, 1939.

Sibree, Bron, 'Young Pastor at the Forefront of Social Change in Australia', *Sojourners*, 18 May 2012. Available at sojo.net/articles/young-pastor-forefront-social-change-Australia (accessed December 2023).

Snow, Edgar, *Glory and Bondage*, [US title: *People on Our Side*], Sydney: Angus and Robertson, 1946.

Strong, Charles, 'India To-day Gives Cause for Anxiety to the Workers for Peace', *Peacewards* 13 (9), 1930, p. 6.

———, 'Mahatma Gandhi's Ideas', *Peacewards* 13 (11), 1930, p. 2.

Bibliography

Strong, Charles, 'Jesus and Gandhi', *Peacewards* 14 (1), 1930, p. 1.

Strong, Sydney, 'Gandhi in Switzerland', *Peacewards* 15 (5), 1932, pp. 4–5.

Suhrud, Tridip, and Thomas Weber (eds), *Beloved Bapu: The Gandhi-Mirabehn Correspondence*, Hyderabad: Orient BlackSwan, 2014.

Summy, Hilary, 'Ralph Summy: A Journey in Pursuit of Nonviolence', *Social Alternatives* 37 (2), 2018, pp. 41–44.

Summy, Ralph, 'Australia: A History of Nonviolent Action', in Roger S. Powers and William B. Vogele (eds), *Protest, Power, and Change: An Encyclopedia of Nonviolent Action from ACT-UP to Women's Suffrage*, New York and London: Garland Publishing, 1997, pp. 25–32.

———, 'Nonviolence Around the World: The Triumph of Gandhi', *Social Alternatives* 16 (2), 1997, pp. 4–7.

———, 'Nonviolent Politics: From Praxis to Research to Classroom to Praxis to Research to Classroom', *Ahimsa Nonviolence* 1 (4), 2005, pp. 319–326.

———, 'Australia, Peace Movements In', in Nigel J. Young (ed.), *The Oxford International Encyclopedia of Peace*, Oxford: Oxford University Press, 2010, Vol. 1, pp. 155–160.

Swan, Maureen, *Gandhi: The South African Experience*, Johannesburg: Ravan Press, 1985.

Sykes, Frederick, *From Many Angles: An Autobiography*, London: Harrap, 1942.

Synott, John, 'Editor's Introduction', *Social Alternatives* 29 (1), 2010, pp. 3–4.

Tavan, Gwenda, *The Long Slow Death of White Australia*, Melbourne: Scribe, 2005.

Taylor, Cheryl, 'Ronald Cecil McKie (1909–1991)', in Melanie Nolan (ed.), *Australian Dictionary of Biography*, National Centre of Biography, Australian National University, Vol. 19, 2014. Available at adb.anu.edu.au/biography/mckie-ronald-cecil-15568/text26780 (accessed December 2023).

Tennyson, Hallam, 'Preface', in Jehangir P. Patel and Marjorie Sykes, *Gandhi: His Gift of the Fight*, Rasulia: Friends Rural Centre, 1987, pp. vii–ix.

Thomson, Mark, 'Hind Swaraj and the Constructive Work Programme', *South Asia* 9 (2), 1986, pp. 37–54.

Bibliography

——, *Gandhi and His Ashrams*, Bombay: Popular Prakashan, 1993.
Thomson, R. M., 'Gandhi at Sevagram: "India in a Village"', *Gandhi Marg* 2 (8), 1980, pp. 431–452.
Tolstoy, Leo, *The Kingdom of God is Within You: Or, Christianity Not as a Mystical Teaching But as a New Concept of Life*, Leo Wiener (trans.), New York: Noonday, 1961.
Tucker, Gerard, *'Thanks Be': The Autobiography of Gerard Kennedy Tucker*, Melbourne: Brotherhood of St. Laurence, 1954.
Vinoba (Bhave), *Shanti Sena*, Marjorie Sykes (trans.), Varanasi: Sarva Seva Sangh, 1963.
Walker, Charles C., *A World Peace Guard: An Unarmed Agency for Peacekeeping*, Hyderabad: Academy of Gandhian Studies, 1981.
Wallis, Jill, *Mother of World Peace: The Life of Muriel Lester*, Middlesex: Hisarlik Press, 1993.
Ward, John M., 'Stevens, Sir Bertram Sydney (1889–1973)', in Geoffrey Serle (ed.), *Australian Dictionary of Biography*, Melbourne: Melbourne University Press, 1990, Vol. 12, pp. 74–77.
Watts, Gambhir, 'Enduring Legacy', *India Empire Magazine*, January 2013.
——, 'Education on Action in Nonviolence', International Centre of Nonviolence, 27 February 2013. Available at www.nonviolence.org.au/educatioon-on-action-in-nonviolence/ (accessed December 2023).
——, 'President Page: Non-violence', *Non-Violence News* 1 (1), October 2013, pp. 6–7. Available at www.nonviolence.org.au/news-magazine (accessed December 2023).
——, *The White Queen*, published by the author, 2019.
——, *Karmayogi Mahatma Gandhi*, published by the author, 2020.
Weber, Thomas, *Hugging the Trees: The Story of the Chipko Movement*, New Delhi: Viking, 1988.
——, 'Satyagraha', *Nonviolence Today* 10, August/September 1989, pp. 3–4.
——, 'Nonviolence: The Other Reasons', *Nonviolence Today* 13, February/March 1990, pp. 4–6.
——, 'Alinsky and Gandhi on Means and Ends', *Nonviolence Today* 16, August/September 1990, pp. 8–10.

Weber, Thomas, *Conflict Resolution and Gandhian Ethics*, New Delhi: Gandhi Peace Foundation, 1991.

———, 'War Tax Resister Convicted of Contempt', *Nonviolence Today* 27, July/August 1992, pp. 6–8.

———, 'From Maude Royden's Peace Army to the Gulf Peace Team', *Journal of Peace Research* 30 (1), 1993, pp. 45–64.

———, *Gandhi's Peace Army: The Shanti Sena and Unarmed Peacekeeping*, Syracuse: Syracuse University Press, 1996.

———, 'A History of Nonviolent Interposition and Accompaniment', in Yeshua Moser-Puangsuwan and Thomas Weber (eds), *Nonviolent Intervention Across Borders: A Recurrent Vision*, Honolulu: Spark M. Matsunaga Institute for Peace, 2000, pp. 15–41.

———, 'Gandhi's Nonviolence and the Salt March', *Social Alternatives* 21 (2), 2002, pp. 46–51.

———, 'Gandhi and Martin Luther King, Jr: Causal Influence or Backing Support?', *Gandhi Marg* 25 (2), 2003, pp. 191–203.

———, *Gandhi as Disciple and Mentor*, Cambridge: Cambridge University Press, 2004.

———, *Gandhi, Gandhism and the Gandhians: Essays by Thomas Weber*, New Delhi: Roli, 2006.

———, *On the Salt March: The Historiography of Mahatma Gandhi's March to Dandi*, New Delhi: HarperCollins, 1997; and New Delhi: Rupa, 2009.

———, *The Shanti Sena: Philosophy, History and Action*, New Delhi: Orient BlackSwan, 2009.

———, *Going Native: Gandhi's Relationship with Western Women*, New Delhi: Roli, 2011.

———, 'How Outrage Gripped Gandhi's Recalcitrant Nation', *Inside Story*, 27 July 2011. Available at insidestory.org.au/how-outrage-gripped-gandhis-recalcitrant-nation (accessed December 2011).

———, *Gandhi at First Sight*, New Delhi: Roli, 2015.

———, '101 Uses for a Dead Mahatma: The Co-option of Gandhi for Non-Gandhian Causes', *Gandhi Marg* 37 (2), 2015, pp. 387–392.

———, 'The Mahatma and the Fuhrer: "Dear Friend" vs "Shoot Gandhi"', in Thomas Weber, *The Mahatma, His Philosophy and His Legacy*, Hyderabad: Orient BlackSwan, 2018, pp. 195–222.

Bibliography

———, 'Why Gandhi Didn't Go to Finland (or America or China)', in Thomas Weber, *The Mahatma, His Philosophy and His Legacy*, Hyderabad: Orient BlackSwan, 2018, pp. 93–125.

———, *The Mahatma, His Philosophy and His Legacy*, Hyderabad: Orient BlackSwan, 2018.

———, 'Rauwolfia: Gandhi's Favourite Tranquiliser?', *South Asia* 41 (3), 2018, pp. 567–578.

———, 'If Gandhi Didn't Say It, He Should Have', *Gandhi Marg* 41 (4), 2020, pp. 403–428.

Weber, Thomas, and Robert J. Burrowes, 'Nonviolence: An Introduction', Victorian Association for Peace Studies, *Peace Dossier* 27, 1991.

Willis, Constance, 'Non-Violence According to Gandhi', *The Peacemaker* 32 (112), January/February 1970, p. 8.

Zable, Arnold, 'Gandhi', *Cinema Papers* 43, May/June 1983, pp. 159–161.

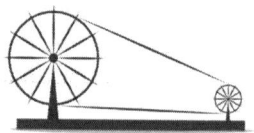

Index

Aam Aadmi Party 252
ABC; *see* Australian Broadcasting Corporation
Aboriginal activists 152
A.B. Piddington: The Last Liberal Radical 57
Adelaide 52, 55–56, 101, 109, 165, 180, 203, 234, 240, 243
  Gandhi statue in 263
Advertiser (Adelaide) 54–55, 62
Advertiser (Bendigo) 83
Afghanistan xxi, 170
African National Congress 254
African Trilogy 271–272
Aga Khan 24, 133, 164
Agarwal, Roshan Lal 163
Age (Melbourne) 70, 86, 98–99, 136
Aggarwal, Niranjan 261
Ahern, Neville 47
Ahmedabad xxiv, 6, 50, 56, 60, 108, 123, 164, 189, 268
Albanese, Anthony 268
Alexander, Horace 23, 25, 43, 157–158, 238
Alinsky, Saul 203, 219
Ambedkar, Bhimrao Ramji 223

American press and Gandhi 1, 16, 24
American reminiscences of Gandhi 273
American War Memorial (Canberra) 260
Americans and Gandhi 10
Amritsar xxi, 6, 21, 23–24, 97–98, 109
Anabaptists 176
Andrews, Charles Freer 12, 24–25, 233–235, 245
  visits Australia 234–235
Andrews, Dave 65, 179–180
Andriiashina, Anna 191
ANU; *see* Australian National University
Arena 172
Arunachalam, K. 233, 251
  background of 250
  visits Australia 249
Ashar, Meera 224
Ashmead-Bartlett, Ellis 112
Asia-Pacific Peace Research Association 220
Asiatic Law Amendment Act 90

Index

Attenborough, Richard 180, 196, 218, 257, 259, 267
Australia
  first mentioned by Gandhi 28
  Indian students in 276
  Japanese visitors to 32–33
  racial prejudice in 36
Australia India Institute 254, 257
Australia-India Society 242
Australian Aboriginal Progressive Association 153
Australian attitudes towards Indians 28–29
Australian Broadcasting Corporation 156, 193, 243, 254–255, 275
Australian Christian Commonwealth 234
Australian Dictionary of Biography 272
Australian Gandhian Movement 166, 180
Australian High Commission (New Delhi) 211
Australian Indian Community Centre 265
Australian Indian Community Charitable Trust 264
Australian Indian Overseas Congress 256
Australian Indians 269–270
Australian National Press Club 257
Australian National University 214, 220, 223, 242, 252, 256

Australian Peace Movement 147, 149–150, 153–154, 199, 202, 270–271
The Australian Peace Movement 147
Australian press and Gandhi 2, 37, 49, 62, 70, 83, 85, 87–88, 94, 96, 100, 102–103, 105, 110, 112, 120, 123, 125, 127–128, 144, 146, 148, 259, 271, 275
Australian Student Christian Movement 234
Australian troops in Bombay 41–42
Australian Women's Weekly 240
Australian Wool Board 79
Australians
  describe Gandhi 53, 66, 83, 97–98, 100
  ignorant of Gandhi 274
  visit Gandhi 49–53, 56–63, 65–72
An Autobiography or the Story of My Experiments with Truth xxii, 8, 12, 27, 102–103, 114, 180, 204, 216, 271

Bahuguna, Sunderlal xxv
Bali, Gandhi ashram in xxvii
Bapu Gandhi 56, 59
Barcs, Emery 143
Barr, Mary xxvii
Basham, A. L. 208, 214, 224
The Battler 217
Bellas, Angie 179
Beloved Bapu: The Gandhi-Mirabehn Correspondence xxvii

Index

Besant, Annie 101
Bhagavad Gita 131, 182, 213, 225
Bharatiya Vidya Bhavan 187–189, 191
Bharat Mitra Samman 212
Bhavan Australia 188, 191, 217
Bhave, Vinoba xxv–xxvi, 160, 241, 250
Bhoodan movement 160, 241, 250
Birla, G. D. 65, 142
Birla House 65, 67, 72, 184, 197
Blackburn, Susan 163
Blacket, Arthur H. 51–56
   background of 52
   visits Gandhi 53
Blacket, John 52
Boer War 6, 86
Bolshevists 99
Bombay 29, 41, 62, 85, 90, 94, 100, 107, 117, 122, 136, 159, 184, 187, 192, 211–212
   Australian troops in 41–42
Bombay Presidency 24, 106
Bondurant, Joan V. 20
'Borderless Gandhi' 266–267
Bose, A. K. xxv
Bose, Nirmal Kumar 208
Boston Tea Party 16, 89
Boulding, Elise xxvi
Bourke-White, Margaret 19, 43
Branagan, Marty 206
Brasted, Howard 206
Brisbane 168, 179–180, 243, 248, 261, 268
   Gandhi statue in 263
Brisbane Courier 86

Brisbane Telegraph 95, 51, 110, 132
British and Indian Empire League of Australia 33
British Friends Service Committee 239
British imperialism 16, 60, 128, 237
British Press and Gandhi 23–25, 110
Brockway, Archibald Fenner 43
Brotherhood of Saint Laurence 161
Brown, Bob 154–155
Building a Better World 179
Burns, Robin 205
Burrowes, Robert J. 166, 195, 212–213, 219, 249, 277
   and GPT 173–174
   and MRAG 170–172
   tax resistance of 168–170
Butt, Clara 49–51

CAA; *see* Community Aid Abroad
Caine, W. S. 31
Calcutta xxi, 15, 29, 58, 60, 62, 78–79, 201, 235
   Gandhi in 7, 74, 141–142
Caliph of Islam 98
Calwell, Arthur 146
Cameron, Archie 146
Campaign for Nuclear Disarmament 149–150
Campbell, Christopher 151
Canada xix, 2, 3, 31–32, 251
Canberra 255, 203, 220, 227, 240, 242–243, 248–249, 252, 257, 260, 269
   Gandhi statue in 146, 261–262

Index

Canberra Catholic Social Justice Group 248
Canberra Times 248
Cariappa, K. M. 260
Case, Clarence Marsh 19–20
Casey, Maie 77
Casey, Richard, G. 73–74, 138, 266
   describes Gandhi 75–76
   meets with Gandhi 76–77
   mentions Gandhi in Australian Parliament 80
   sends Australian wool to Gandhi 78
Centre for Peace and Conflict Studies (Sydney) 226
Ceylon 103
Chaplin, Charlie 24
Chatfield, Charles 2
Chaudhury, Shoma 230
Chennai; *see* Madras
Chicago Daily News 17
Chicago Tribune 17
China 31, 131, 237
Chipko movement xxv, 209
Christian Century 12
Churchill, Winston 3, 118
Cinema 231–232
   Gandhi's view of 70
Civil Disobedience campaign xxi, xxiv, 16, 53, 102, 106, 126, 129, 133, 253
Civil Rights Movement 20, 150, 175
CND; *see* Campaign for Nuclear Disarmament
Collected Works of Mahatma Gandhi xv–xvi, xxviii, 43, 100, 214
Colonial Patriotic Union 86
Commentary 258
Commonwealth Heads of Government Meeting 261
Community Aid Abroad 161–165, 168, 201, 242, 249
Community of the Ark 247
Conflict Resolution and Gandhian Ethics xxiii, 209
Congress, Gandhi retires from 124
Congress Socialist Party 241
Congress Working Committee 67, 69
conscientious objector trials 151, 157
conscription xx, 150–151, 153
constructive programme 8, 201, 207, 248, 250
Constructive Programme 78
Continuum 201
Costello, Tim 231
Courier (Brisbane) 86
Cousins, Norman 18
COVID-19 267
cow protection 37, 250
cow slaughter 37–39
cricket
   Indian team in Australia 144–145
Cripps, Stafford 65, 67, 70
Crux 179
Curtin, John 146
Curtin University 176, 254

Index

CWMG; see Collected Works of Mahatma Gandhi

Daily Express (London) 71, 131
Daily Mail (London) 89, 98, 114
Daily Telegraph (Launceston) 89
Daily Telegraph (London) 112
Daily Telegraph (Sydney) 125
Dalton, Dennis 208
Damm, Alex 2
Dandi Salt March xiv, xxiii–xxvi, 12, 14, 17, 23–24, 43, 53–54, 103, 105, 123, 184, 195, 207, 210, 220, 238
 Boycotted by Muslims 106
Dasgupta, Amit 262–263
Dasgupta, Sugata 163–164, 195, 198, 200–204, 219–220, 232, 247
 at University of Queensland 200, 202
 visits Australia 247–248
Defence Space Communications Station 173
de Jersey, Paul 263
Delhi xxi, xxiv–xv, 7, 64–65, 70–71, 94, 115, 141, 161–162, 164, 183, 198, 209–211, 233, 252, 256–257, 263, 267
 Gandhi in 139, 142, 184
del Vasto, Lanza
 background of 245–246
 visits Australia 247
Dendle, Mike 164
Department of External Affairs 242
Desai, Mahadev 68, 70, 72

Desai, Morarji 241
Desai, Swati 256
Desi Kangaroo TV 255
Dharasana salt works 7, 17, 112
 raids on 7, 17
Dhupelia-Mesthrie, Uma 255
diSalvo, Charles 222
'Dissertation on Shirts' 126–127
Diwakar, R. R. 183
Docker, John 222–223
Dodson, Patrick 227
Doke, Joseph 9
Donald Groom Peace Fellowship 177, 243, 256
Doron, Assa 224
Douglas, Roger 171
Durban University of Technology 186
Dutt, Rajani Palme 217
Dyer, Reginald 21–22

East Bengal 7
Einstein, Albert 261
Emergency (1975–1977) 194, 200–201, 203, 219, 241, 250
Empowering Peacemakers in Your Community 177
environmental campaigns 147–148, 154, 157, 271, 277
Escombe, Harry 90
Evans, Selwyn 116
Evening News (London) 93
Evening News (Sydney) 85, 107, 114

Fabian Society 140
Faine, Jon 255

Index

Farson, Negley 17
Federal Pacifist Council 151
Federation of Indian Associations 270
Federation of Indian Associations in Victoria 264
Fiji 35, 55, 233–234
Fischer, Louis xxii, 13, 19, 20, 43
Fisher, Frederick 12, 19
Flinders University 259
Food for Peace 161–162
Forster, E. M. 22
Fox, John 221
Frankenstein 100
Franklin River campaign 155–156, 168, 172
Freedom from Hunger campaign 165, 180
Freedom from Violence Australia 185
Freedom Rides 152
Freire, Paulo 205
Friedlander, Peter 224
The Friend 240
Friends Peace Committee 160
Friends Rural Centre 159
Fry, Elizabeth 40

Galtung, Johan xxvii, 200
Gandhi (movie) 196, 218, 257, 267
Gandhi (racehorse) 122, 272
Gandhi and His Apostles 196–197
Gandhi and His Ashrams 211
Gandhi and the Good Life 256
Gandhi and the Myth of Non-Violent Action 217
Gandhi, Arun 253
Gandhi as Disciple and Mentor xxvii
Gandhi as Others See Him 273
Gandhi at First Sight xv, xvii
Gandhi Ashram (Bali) xxvii
Gandhi Birth Centenary 74, 193, 207, 266, 275
Gandhi Book House (New Delhi) xxv, xxvii
Gandhi Centenary Celebrations Committee 193, 207, 242, 267
Gandhi, Devdas 251
Gandhi Development Trust 186
Gandhi, Ela 166, 186, 190, 230
background of 253–254
visits Australia 254–255, 266
'The Gandhi Experiment' 198
Gandhi Farm 185
Gandhi, Gandhism and the Gandhians 225
Gandhi, Gopalkrishna 251
Gandhi, Indira 20, 219–200, 241, 250
Gandhi in the West 215–216
Gandhi Jayanti 189, 267–268
Gandhi, Kasturba 135
Gandhi/King/Ikeda Exhibition 188
Gandhi, Leela 222
Gandhi, Maganlal xxvi
Gandhi, Mahatma; see Gandhi, Mohandas Karamchand
Gandhi, Manilal 253, 256
Gandhi Memorial Museum (Madurai) 251

Index

Gandhi, Mohandas Karamchand:
  affinity with Quakers 25, 152, 157–158
  and America 2
  American friends of 19
  in American press 1, 16
  and Americans 10
  American views of 17
  anti-untouchability campaign of 7–8, 102, 123–124, 130, 237
  appearance of 1, 45, 49, 137, 139, 196
  arrests of 6, 7, 17, 44, 88–89, 93, 101–102, 110, 112–114
  assassination of 14, 72, 144–145, 239
  attitude towards Australia 27, 32
  attitude towards smoking 40–41
  Australia first mentioned by 28
  and Australian Indians 269–270
  in Australian peace writing 153–154
  in Australian press 2, 37, 49, 62, 70, 83, 85, 87–88, 94, 96, 100, 102–103, 105, 110, 112, 120, 123, 125, 127–128, 144, 146, 148, 259, 271, 275
  Australians ignorant of 274
  Autobiography of xxii, 8, 12, 27, 102–103, 114, 180, 204, 216, 271
  biographies of 13
  in British press 23–25, 110
  and Canada xix, 2, 31
  as Christian 235
  Civil Disobedience campaign of 7, 16, 53, 102–103, 106, 114, 126–127, 129–130, 133, 135
  comes to world attention 10
  conferences about 196, 222, 225
  constructive programme of 8, 201, 207, 248, 250
  criticised 75
  and Dandi Salt March 23, 43, 53, 103, 123, 184
  debt to Holmes 10
  described by Australians 47, 49, 51, 72–73, 75–76
  describes Australia 67
  desire not to embarrass Britain 128–130
  discussed in Australian Parliament 145–146
  dress of 117, 119
  early life of 4
  exhibitions 266–267
  as fanatic 99, 108, 114, 117, 122, 228
  fasts of 7–8, 100–101, 104, 108, 123, 125, 133–135, 140–144, 205
  first mention in Australian press 83
  and Germany xix, 124
  Harijan campaign of 7–8, 102, 123–124, 130, 237
  Himalayan blunder of 94
  as homosexual 228–229

Index

influence on peace movements 12
inspires pacifists in Britain 27
at Kingsley Hall 44–46
labelled extremist 94, 97, 105, 108, 114
in London 5–7, 24–25, 27, 44, 103, 120–121, 124, 158, 236
loses faith in British rule 22
'Man of the Year' 17, 103
Marxist interpretations of 217
meets Casey 76–77
Mirabehn's letters to xxvii–xxviii
myth of 135, 197
no longer supports nonviolence 111
orations 2, 226–231, 254, 262, 271, 276
and Quakers 157–158
and Quit India campaign 7, 133–134
and racial prejudice in Australia 35–36
retires from Congress 124
at Round Table Conference 7, 24–25, 103, 114, 120–122, 158, 236
and satyagraha 6, 12, 137, 157, 161, 190, 204–206, 209, 219, 224
sent Australian wool by Casey 79
sees Australian treatment of Asians as wicked 34
sexuality of 228–230
silent days of 46
in South Africa xxvi–xxviii, 6
as spiritual seeker 8
statues of 2, 146, 232, 261–265, 269, 276, 278
university courses on 198, 201–202, 205–207
view of Australia 27, 34
view of cinema 70
visited by Australians 49–53, 56–63, 65–72
visits Ceylon 10
visits Rome 122
visits Switzerland 122
and White Australia policy 3. 30, 36, 65–66
women disciples of 209
writings on xxviii, 3, 19–20, 82, 175, 183, 207, 215, 217, 226
Gandhi Museum (Delhi) xxi, 79
Gandhi My Father 259
Gandhi National Museum Trust 249
Gandhi Peace Foundation (Delhi) xxiii, 164, 209, 256
Gandhi, Rajmohan xxv, 253
background of 251–252
Gandhi, Ramchandra 251
Gandhi Salt March Limited 268
Gandhi, Sita 251
Gandhi, Tara 251
Gandhi: The Life and Legacy of India's 'Father of a Nation' 259
Gandhian Forum for Ethical Corporate Governance 256
Gandhian Institute of Studies (Varanasi) 200

Index

Gandhian Movement of Australia 180–181, 249
Gandhian Opinion 182
GandhiServe Foundation 267
Gandhi's Peace Army: The Shanti Sena and Unarmed Peacekeeping xxvi, 209
Gandhi's Religion: A Homespun Shawl 213–214
Ganguly, Debjani 222–224
Ganopathy, Madhusudan 187
Garvey, Marcus 153
Gedong Gandhi Ashram xxvii
Germany 2, 198
Ghana 264
Ghosh, Sudhir 76–77
Gibson, Ralph 216
Global Conscience 182
Global Organisation for People of Indian Origin 227
Glover, Dennis 3
GMA; *see* Gandhian Movement of Australia
Gobbett, Don 165
Going Native: Gandhi's Relationship with Western Women xxvii
Gokhale, Gopal Krishna 28, 101, 208, 233
Goodman, T. L. 138
Green Pamphlet 28, 30
Gregg, Richard B. 20, 218, 222, 277
Grenier, Richard 258
Greste, Peter 227
The Grievances of British Indians in South Africa 28

Groom, Donald 161, 243
background of 158–160
Groundswell 218
Guardian 216
Guevara, Che xxi
Guha, Ramachandra 18, 213, 229, 272
Gujarat Sarvodaya Mandal 256
Gulf Peace Team 173
Gulf War 173
Gunther, John 125

Hamel-Green, Michael 150
Harijan 26–27, 139
Harrison, Agatha 25, 158
Heath, Carl 25, 158
Hepworth, Margaret 197
Herald (Melbourne) 71, 98, 114, 117
High Commission of India (Canberra) 269
Hilmer, Fred 262
Himalayas xxi
Hindi 56, 188–189, 209, 276
Hind Swaraj or Indian Home Rule 10, 265
Hinduism 37, 178, 182, 208
Hindus xxi, 37–39, 45, 95, 98, 100, 102, 109, 123, 142
Hindustan Times 251
Hindustani 61–62, 224
Hirani, Rajkumar 259
Hitler, Adolf 159
Hobart 155, 237, 248
Hodgkin, Erica 159
Holi festival 188, 191

Index

Hollingworth, Peter 261
Holmes, John Haynes 10, 19
House of Lords 97
Houston Post 198
Howard Prison Reform League 134
Hoyland, John S. 25, 158
Hugging the Trees: The Story of the Chipko Movement xxv
Hunt, Frazier 19
Husain, Mishal 259

ICON; *see* International Centre of Nonviolence
IFoR; *see* International Fellowship of Reconciliation
IGM; *see* International Gandhian Movement
Ikeda, Daisaku 188, 190
India League of Australia 64–65
Indian Associations in Australia 269–270
Indian Conciliation Group 158
Indian cows 15
  sent to Australia 36–39, 42
Indian Crisis 25
The Indian Express 252
Indian High Commission 242
Indian National Congress xxiv, 6, 26, 115
Indian Opinion 10, 253
Indian students in Australia 276
Indians, Australian attitudes towards 28–29
Indonesia xxi
Inside Asia 125

Institute for International Affairs 242
International Centre of Nonviolence 166, 186, 254
International Day of Nonviolence 189
International Fellowship of Reconciliation 159–160, 237
International Gandhian Movement 181
International Peace Research Association 202–203, 205
IPRA; *see* International Peace Research Association
Irwin, Lord 7, 115
Islam, Caliph of 98
Islamophobia 230

Jains 149, 208
Jallianwala Bagh 6, 21, 94
Janata government 241
Japan 7, 31–32, 133, 237, 241
Japanese visitors to Australia 33
Java Pageant 48
Jawaharlal Nehru University 257
Jeffrey, Robin xxiii–xiv
Jesus Christ 55, 95, 149, 175–179
Jinarajadasa, C. 94
Jinnah, Muhammad Ali 135–136, 140
Johannesburg 6, 88–89, 92–93, 140
Jordens, J. T. F. (Jos) 195, 208, 213–215
JP; *see* Narayan, Jayaprakash

Kagawa, Toyohiko 148

Index

Kallenbach, Hermann xxvii, 229
karma yoga 182
Kelly, Anthony 164, 195, 198, 203–204, 247–248
Keneally, Tom 227
Khan, Alec 21
Khan, Feroz Abbas 259
Khanna, Suman 255–256
King Jr., Martin Luther: 20, 151, 160, 175, 277
The Kingdom of God is Within You 9
Kingsley Hall 25, 44–46, 236–237
Kipling, Rudyard 21
Kirby, Michael 228–231
Kovind, Ram Nath 265
Krishnamurti, Jiddu 148
Kruegler, Christopher 218
Kumar, Ravindra 221
Kuwait 173

Labor Party (Australian) xxi, 57, 146, 260
Lage Raho Munna Bhai 259
Lambrick, A. 148
La Trobe University 183, 221–222, 242
    Weber at xxii–xxiii, xxvii, 205, 209
Lawson, James 20
Lead, Kindly Light 20
Le Journal (Paris) 119
Lelyveld, Joseph 227
Lenin, V.I. 10
Lennon, John xxii
Lester, Doris 236–237

Lester, Muriel 25, 43, 117, 159, 235–237
The Life of Mahatma Gandhi 20
Linlithgow, Lord 126, 130
London, Gandhi in 24–25, 27, 44, 103, 120–121, 124, 158, 236
London Missionary Society 244
London Peace Society 149
Love Makes a Way 166, 177
Luchetti, Anthony 260

Mabbett, I. W. 208
Macbeth 101
Macdonald, Ramsay 24
Mackay, Hugh 227
Maclean, Kama 224
MacLeod, Jason 207
Madam Tussauds Wax Museum xxi
Madras xxii 58, 62, 244–245
Mahatma Gandhi at Work 234
Mahatma Gandhi Digital Museum 266
Mahatma Gandhi: His Own Story 234
Mahatma Gandhi: The Man Who Became One with the Universal Being 11
Mahatma Gandhi's Ideas 149, 234
The Mahatma, His Philosophy and His Legacy 225
Makwana, Lene and Nilesh 266
Mandela, Nelson 254
Mani Bhavan 164, 184
Mannin, Ethel 239–240
Martin, Brian 226

Index

Marxist interpretations of Gandhi 217
Mashruwala, Shushila 253
Masselos, Jim 208
Maynard, John 153
Mayo, Katherine 15–16, 19, 22–23, 60, 102, 231, 272
Mazgoankar, Michael 256
McKenna Jarrod 166, 175
  background of 175–177
  Gandhi's influence on 178–179
McKie, Ronald Cecil 46
McWha, James 263
Mehta, Ved 196, 231
Melba, Nellie 48
Melbourne 33, 52, 71, 83, 144, 149, 160–161, 164, 175, 190, 194, 203, 214, 222, 234, 248–249, 252, 256–257, 262, 266
  Burrowes in 167–168
  Ela Gandhi in 254–255
  Gandhi statue in 264–265
  Indian students assaulted in 262
  JP in 242–243
  Reynolds in 239–240
  Weber in xx, xxii–xxiii, xxv
Melbourne Cricket Ground 145
Melbourne, Gandhi statue in 264–265
Melbourne Immigration Museum 255
Melbourne Rainforest Action Group 154, 166–167, 170–173, 249, 277
Mennonites 176
Menzies, Robert 146, 260

Meyer, Frederick Brotherton 92
Miller, J. A. 17
Miller, Webb 17, 19, 43
Mirabehn xxvii, 26–27, 45, 105
Mitchell, Natasha 254
M.K.Gandhi: An Indian Patriot in South Africa 9
Modi, Narendra 263, 268
Monash, John 115
Monash University 167, 217
Moore, Eleanor 148
Moore, R. J. 259
Moorehead, Alan 71–73
Moorhouse, Frank 226
Morning Post (London) 22
Morrison, Scott 265
Moslem League 136, 140
Mother India 15–16, 60, 102, 231, 272
Mountbatten, Edwina 140
Mountbatten, Louis 140
A Mouthful of Petals: The Story of an Indian Village 193
Movement for a New Society 152
MRAG; *see* Melbourne Rainforest Action Group
Mumbai 164, 184, 187, 189
Munshi, K. M. 188
Murdoch, Walter 129
Murphy, Stephen 166, 182–185, 209, 249
  background of 180
  launches GMA 180–181
  launches IGM 181
Murray, Nell 117
Muslims: boycott Salt March 106

Index

Mussolini, Benito 127–128
Muzumdar, Haridas 20

Næss, Arne xxvii, 208
Naidu, Sarojini 119
Namboodiripad, E. M. S. 217
Nanda, B. R. 258
Nandan, Satendra 226
Nandy, Ashis 224
Narayan, Jayaprakash xxvi, 192–194, 200, 202, 208, 219, 233, 242–243, 267
  visits Australia 242
Narayan, Prabhavati 193–194, 242
Natal 5, 30–31, 83–87, 89–90, 93
  press in 28–30
Natal Advertiser 30
Natal Legislative Assembly 83
Natal Organisation of Women 254
National Peace Council 160
National Press Club 227
National Service Act 150, 152, 161
Nazism 26, 128
Nehru, Jawaharlal 66, 136, 140, 208, 239
Nehru Memorial Museum xxiv
Nesbitt, Thomas 80–81
New Delhi xxi, xxiv–xxv, 64, 70, 79, 115, 161–162, 210, 211, 252
  Gandhi in 7, 164
  Gandhian sites in xxi, 164, 184
New Guinea 132, 210
New South Wales Parliament House 186
New Statesman 237

New York Times 14, 17
New York World 99
Noakhali xv, 140, 158
Noffs, Ted 152
Non-Cooperation movement 6, 10, 22, 43, 96–97, 208, 271
Nonviolence News 190, 217
Nonviolence Today 172, 218, 249
Nonviolent Revolution in India 218
Northcliffe, Lord 100
Northern Regional Advisory Council 189
Northrop, Justice 170
Nurrangar 173

Oba, Yoshitaka 190
Oka, Ibu Gedong Bagoes xxvii
On the Salt March: The Historiography of Gandhi's March to Dandi xxv
Orwell, George 3–4, 278
Orwell's Australia: From Cold War to Culture Wars 3
Ostergaard, Geoffrey 218
Owen, Hugh 207–208
Oxfam 165

Pakistan xxi, 140, 143, 252
Pal, Gautam 263
Paranjape, Makarand 222
Parathasarathy, Gopalaswami 261
Paris 122, 159, 245
Parkin, Scott 175
Participatory Development Practice 204
A Passage to India 22
Peacemaker 151, 222

Index

Peacewards 116, 149
Pentagon Papers xxi
Perkins, Charles 152–153
Perry, Alexandra 171
Perth 101, 166, 175, 177, 240, 243, 254, 266–267
Phoenix Settlement xxvi, 90, 211, 253–255
Piddington, A. B. 56–63, 65, 272
Pittock, Dianna and Barrie 152
The Point Magazine 255
Polak, Henry xxvii
Police Life 171
The Politics of Nonviolent Action 199, 201
Ponder, Harriet Winifred 48-52
Pooley, A. M. 140
Porbandar 4, 184
Prince of Wales 99–100
Profiles of Gandhi 273
Protest, Power, and Change 148
Puri, Bindu 255, 257

Quakers 147, 160, 162, 176, 232, 240, 244–245
 affinity with Gandhi 25, 152, 157–158
Queensland Council of Social Service 203
A Quest for Peace 148
Quirk, Graham 263
Quit India campaign 7, 133–134

racial prejudice in Australia 36
Radhakrishna, Shobhana 256
Radhakrishnan, S. 273

Rajagopalachari, Chakravarti 251
Rajghat (Delhi) xxi, xxv, 184
Rau, Heimo 2
Ray, Sibnarayan 208, 222, 232
Reader's Digest 18
Red Cross 163
Rees, Stuart 226
Remembering Jayaprakash 192
Rethinking Gandhi and Nonviolent Relationality 223
Return to the Source 246
Returned Soldiers' League 152
Review of Reviews 103
Reynolds, Reginald 24, 158, 232, 237–239, 241
 visits Australia 240
Rivett, Kenneth 224
Rolland, Romain 11–13, 121, 245, 271
Rome 122, 127
Roozendaal, Eric 262
Rosenberg, Samuel 134–135
Rosenthal, Newman 207–208, 267
Round Table Conference 7, 114–116, 149,
 Gandhi at 24–25, 103, 120–121, 158, 236
Rousseau, V. F. A. 47
Rowlatt Act 6, 21, 93
Roy, Anjali 222
Roy, M. N. 208
Royal Life Saving Society Australia 168
Royal Prince Alfred Hospital 191
Royden, Agnes Maude 26
Ruddock, Phillip 175

Index

Rudolph, Lloyd and Susan Hoeber 12, 14
Rühe, Peter 266
Rustin, Bayard 20

Sabarmati Ashram xxvi, 6, 81, 164, 184, 189, 197, 211, 236, 238, 250
   Australian PM at 268
   Trump at 268
   Weber at xxiv, xxvi–xxvii
Sage, H. A. 44, 46
Saint Francis of Assisi 11
Salla, Michael 220, 225
Salt March; see Dandi Salt March
Salt Satyagraha 12–13, 23, 44, 172
Sanger, Margaret 43
Sanskrit 188, 213
Saraswati, Dayananda 213
sarvodaya 182
Sastri, Srinivasa 101
satyagraha 157, 161, 179, 190, 204–206, 208–209, 219, 222, 224, 22
   defined 6, 137
satyagraha brigades 225
Saunders, Malcolm 147, 150
Scalmer, Sean xix, 1, 13, 27, 195, 215–216, 223, 226
Scanlan, Nellie M. 102
Scarfe, Allan and Wendy 166, 192–194, 242
Schumacher, E. F. xxvii
The Scotsman 252
Scott, David 162, 201
Sermon on the Mount 178

Servants of India Society 101
Seshachari, C. 2, 19
Sevagram Ashram xxvi, 76, 138, 164,184, 189, 201, 211, 244–246, 253, 256
Shantidas; see del Vasto, Lanza
Shanti Sena xxv–xxvi, 209
The Shanti Sena: Philosophy, History and Action xxvi, 210
Sharma, Arvind 225
Sharp, Gene xxvii, 20, 199, 201, 206, 222
Sheean, Vincent 20, 43
Shepard, Mark 218
Shepherd, Laura 255
Shirer, William 43
Shivaradruppa, A. L. xxii
Shraddhananda, Swami 213
Shridharani, Krishnalal 20, 218
Simon Commission 62, 113
Sinha, Hari 242
Sino-Japanese War 26
Skaria, Ajay 222
Slade, Madeleine; see Mirabehn
Smith's Weekly 58
Smoking
   Gandhi's attitude towards 40–41
Smuts, Jan 88, 90–93
Snow, Edgar 19
Social Alternatives 199, 219–220, 248
Society of Friends; see Quakers
Sogani, Vibhor 267
Soka Gakkai 190, 254
Sokhodeora Ashram 192
South Africa 235, 264
   Gandhi in xxvi–xxviii, 6

Index

Southern Cross Hotel (Melbourne) 194
Spark M. Matsunaga Institute for Peace 202
Spence, Rebecca 206
Statues of Gandhi 2
   in Australia 146, 232, 261–265, 269, 276, 278
   in Ghana 264
Stevens, Bertram 64–70
The Strategy of Nonviolent Defense 212
Strong, Charles 149
Strong, Sydney 149
Student Christian Movement 44
Suhrud, Tridip xxvii, 222
Sultan of Turkey 98
Summy, Ralph 147, 150, 167, 195, 219–220, 237–248
   background of 198–199
   at University of Queensland 199, 201–202
Sun (Sydney) 123
Sunday Observer (London) 97
Sutar, Ram V. 261, 263, 265
Swarthmore 244
Switzerland 122
Sydney 35, 44, 64–65, 83, 94, 152, 155, 160, 187–190, 234, 240, 243, 252, 254, 256–257, 259
   Gandhi statue in 262, 265
   Indian students assaulted in 262
Sydney Morning Herald 94, 104, 112, 143
Sydney Peace Foundation 226
Sykes, Frederick 24

Sykes, Marjorie 158, 160, 232, 235, 243–245
Synott, John 221

Tagore, Rabindranath 49, 148, 208, 233, 235, 244–2455
Tasmanian Wilderness Society 155
Tax Practitioners Board 192
Tear Australia 180
Telegraph (Brisbane) 51, 70, 95, 110, 132
Tennyson, Hallam 158
Terry, Lindsay 47
Tharunka 151
Theosophical Society 101
Thomas, A. M. 242, 266
Thomson, Mark 195, 210–212
Thoreau, Henry David 20
Thornton, C. V. 44
Tilak, Bal Gangadhar 208
Tilly, Charles 216
Time 17, 23, 103
The Times of India 194
Tolstoy, Leo 9, 90, 179
Transvaal 86–93
Trump, Donald 268
Tucker, Gerard Kennedy 161–162
Turkey, Sultan of 98

United Australia Party 64
United Nations International Non-Violence Day 227
United States of America xix, 1, 4, 13, 19, 173, 250, 252, 272–273, 277

Index

Universal Negro Improvement Association 153
University of Adelaide 180, 363, 268
University of Ghana 264
University of Melbourne xx, xxiii, 71, 208, 214, 216, 224, 242, 254, 257
University of New England 206, 221
University of New South Wales 151, 190, 203, 224, 255, 262
  Gandhi orations at 227, 230–231, 254, 269
University of Queensland 164, 207, 221, 225
  Dasgupta at 195, 200–201, 247
  Summy at 168, 195, 199, 201–202
University of Sydney 57–58, 199, 207, 216, 224–227
University of Wollongong 226
UNSW; see University of New South Wales

Vajpayee, Atal Bihari 261
Victorian Women's Domestic Crisis Service 254
Vietnam War xx–xxi, 150, 155, 199, 243

Waiters' Union 179–180
Walk Against Want 165
Walker, Charles xxv
War Resisters' International 161
Watts, Gambhir 166, 217
  background of 187–188
  launches ICON 186

Wavell, Lord 135, 138
Wayside Chapel 152
Weatherill, Jay 263
Weber, Thomas xx–xxiv, 223
  at La Trobe University xxii–xxiii, xxvii, 205–206, 209
Wells, H. G. 120
West Australian (Perth) 104
Westcity Church (Perth) 177
Westoby, Peter 204
What Would Gandhi Do? 228
White Australia policy 28–30, 65–66, 224
The White Sahibs in India 239
Whitlam, Gough 203
WILPF; see Women's International League for Peace and Freedom
Wilson, Alexander 25
Wolfson, Hugo 242
Women's Christian College Madras 245
Women's International League for Peace and Freedom 25, 148
The Wonder that was India 224
World Pacifist Conference 239
A World Peace Guard xxv
World War I 150
World War II 237
Worshipful Masters 59
Wyllie, Bertram Russell 44

Yerwada Prison 164
Young India 12, 61

Zulu uprising 6